REBOL™ For Dummies®

W9-BAB-731

File Manipulations

Statement	Refinement	Descriptions
read	/binary	Preserves contents exactly.
	/string	Translates all line terminators.
	/direct	Opens the port without buffering.
	/wait	Waits for data.
	/lines	Handles data as lines.
	/part	Reads a specified amount of data.
	/with	Specifies alternate line termination.
	/mode	Block of above refinements.
	/custom	Allows special refinements.
write	/binary	Preserves contents exactly.
	/string	Translates all line terminators.
	/direct	Opens the port without buffering.
	/append	Writes to the end of an existing file.
	/wait	Waits for data.
	/lines	Handles data as lines.
	/part	Reads a specified amount of data.
	/with	Specifies alternate line termination.
	/allow	Specifies the protection attributes when created.
	/mode	Block of above refinements.
	/custom	Allows special refinements.

REBOL Math Operators

Operator	In Statement	Results	Accepted Datatypes
+	x + x2	Returns the sum of x and x2	char, date, money, number, time, tuple
-	x1 - x2	Returns result of subtracting x2 from x1	char, number, money, date, time, tuple
*	x1 * x2	Returns result of multiplying x1 by x2	char, number, money, time, tuple
/	x1 / x2	Returns result of dividing x1 by x2	char, number, money, time, tuple
//	x1 // x2	Returns remainder of dividing x1 by x2	char, number, money, time, tuple

REBOL™ For Dummies®

Cheat Sheet

Comparison Operators

Infix	Prefix	Description
<	lesser?	true if value is less
<=	lesser-or-equal?	true if value is less or equal
<>	not-equal?	true if values are not equal
=	equal?	true if values are equal
==	strict-equal?	true if values are equal and of same datatype
=?	same?	true if values occupy same memory location (for series)
>=	greater-or-equal?	true if value is greater or equal
>	greater?	true if value is greater
	strict-not-equal?	true if values are not equal and not of same datatype
	any	true if any expression returns true
	all	true if all expressions return true
and	and	true if both expressions return true
or	or	true if either expression returns true
xor	xor	true only if one expression returns true

REBOL Special Characters in Strings

Character	Definition
^"	inserts a " (quote)
^}	inserts a } (closing brace)
^^	inserts a ^ (caret)
^/	starts a new line
^(line)	starts a new line
^-	inserts a tab
^(tab)	inserts a tab
^(page)	starts a new page
^(letter)	control-letter (A-Z)
^(back)	erases one character back
^(null)	inserts a null character
^(esc)	inserts an escape character

Logarithmic and Power Operations

Operation	Result
n1 ** n2	returns result of raising $n1$ to $n2$ power.
exp n	Raises E (natural number) to the power n.
log-10 n	returns base-10 logarithm of n.
log-2 n	returns base-2 logarithm of n.
log-e n	returns base-E (natural number) log. of n.
power n1 n2	returns result of raising $n1$ to $n2$ power.
square-root n	returns square root of n.

For Dummies®: Bestselling Book Series for Beginners

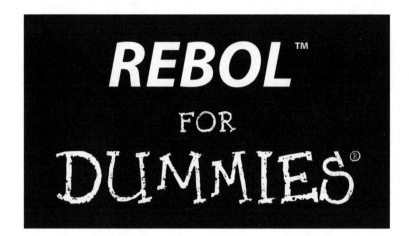

REBOL™ FOR DUMMIES®

by Ralph Roberts

IDG Books Worldwide, Inc.
An International Data Group Company

Foster City, CA ◆ Chicago, IL ◆ Indianapolis, IN ◆ New York, NY

REBOL™ For Dummies®

Published by
IDG Books Worldwide, Inc.
An International Data Group Company
919 E. Hillsdale Blvd.
Suite 400
Foster City, CA 94404
www.idgbooks.com (IDG Books Worldwide Web Site)
www.dummies.com (Dummies Press Web Site)

Library of Congress Control Number: 00-105683

ISBN: 0-7645-0745-1

Printed in the United States of America

10 9 8 7 6 5 4 3 2 1

1O/QZ/RQ/QR/IN

Distributed in the United States by IDG Books Worldwide, Inc.

Distributed by CDG Books Canada Inc. for Canada; by Transworld Publishers Limited in the United Kingdom; by IDG Norge Books for Norway; by IDG Sweden Books for Sweden; by IDG Books Australia Publishing Corporation Pty. Ltd. for Australia and New Zealand; by TransQuest Publishers Pte Ltd. for Singapore, Malaysia, Thailand, Indonesia, and Hong Kong; by Gotop Information Inc. for Taiwan; by ICG Muse, Inc. for Japan; by Norma Comunicaciones S.A. for Colombia; by Intersoft for South Africa; by Eyrolles for France; by International Thomson Publishing for Germany, Austria and Switzerland; by Distribuidora Cuspide for Argentina; by LR International for Brazil; by Galileo Libros for Chile; by Ediciones ZETA S.C.R. Ltda. for Peru; by WS Computer Publishing Corporation, Inc., for the Philippines; by Contemporanea de Ediciones for Venezuela; by Express Computer Distributors for the Caribbean and West Indies; by Micronesia Media Distributor, Inc. for Micronesia; by Grupo Editorial Norma S.A. for Guatemala; by Chips Computadoras S.A. de C.V. for Mexico; by Editorial Norma de Panama S.A. for Panama; by American Bookshops for Finland. Authorized Sales Agent: Anthony Rudkin Associates for the Middle East and North Africa.

For general information on IDG Books Worldwide's books in the U.S., please call our Consumer Customer Service department at 800-762-2974. For reseller information, including discounts and premium sales, please call our Reseller Customer Service department at 800-434-3422.

For information on where to purchase IDG Books Worldwide's books outside the U.S., please contact our International Sales department at 317-572-3993 or fax 317-572-4002.

For consumer information on foreign language translations, please contact our Customer Service department at 1-800-434-3422, fax 317-596-5692, or e-mail rights@idgbooks.com.

For information on licensing foreign or domestic rights, please phone +1-650-655-7098.

For sales inquiries and special prices for bulk quantities, please contact our Order Services department at 800-434-3422 or write to the address above.

For information on using IDG Books Worldwide's books in the classroom or for ordering examination copies, please contact our Educational Sales department at 800-434-2086 or fax 317-572-4005.

For press review copies, author interviews, or other publicity information, please contact our Public Relations department at 650-653-7000 or fax 650-653-7500.

For authorization to photocopy items for corporate, personal, or educational use, please contact Copyright Clearance Center, 222 Rosewood Drive, Danvers, MA 01923, or fax 978-750-4470.

is a registered trademark under exclusive license to IDG Books Worldwide, Inc., from International Data Group, Inc.

About the Author

Ralph Roberts is a long-time computer and general interest writer, with such titles as *Creative Computing, Compute's Computer Viruses, The Official Book of Leisure Suit Larry,* and *Genealogy via the Internet.*

ABOUT IDG BOOKS WORLDWIDE

Welcome to the world of IDG Books Worldwide.

IDG Books Worldwide, Inc., is a subsidiary of International Data Group, the world's largest publisher of computer-related information and the leading global provider of information services on information technology. IDG was founded more than 30 years ago by Patrick J. McGovern and now employs more than 9,000 people worldwide. IDG publishes more than 290 computer publications in over 75 countries. More than 90 million people read one or more IDG publications each month.

Launched in 1990, IDG Books Worldwide is today the #1 publisher of best-selling computer books in the United States. We are proud to have received eight awards from the Computer Press Association in recognition of editorial excellence and three from Computer Currents' First Annual Readers' Choice Awards. Our best-selling ...*For Dummies*® series has more than 50 million copies in print with translations in 31 languages. IDG Books Worldwide, through a joint venture with IDG's Hi-Tech Beijing, became the first U.S. publisher to publish a computer book in the People's Republic of China. In record time, IDG Books Worldwide has become the first choice for millions of readers around the world who want to learn how to better manage their businesses.

Our mission is simple: Every one of our books is designed to bring extra value and skill-building instructions to the reader. Our books are written by experts who understand and care about our readers. The knowledge base of our editorial staff comes from years of experience in publishing, education, and journalism — experience we use to produce books to carry us into the new millennium. In short, we care about books, so we attract the best people. We devote special attention to details such as audience, interior design, use of icons, and illustrations. And because we use an efficient process of authoring, editing, and desktop publishing our books electronically, we can spend more time ensuring superior content and less time on the technicalities of making books.

You can count on our commitment to deliver high-quality books at competitive prices on topics you want to read about. At IDG Books Worldwide, we continue in the IDG tradition of delivering quality for more than 30 years. You'll find no better book on a subject than one from IDG Books Worldwide.

John Kilcullen
Chairman and CEO
IDG Books Worldwide, Inc.

*Eighth Annual
Computer Press
Awards ≥1992*

*Ninth Annual
Computer Press
Awards ≥1993*

*Tenth Annual
Computer Press
Awards ≥1994*

*Eleventh Annual
Computer Press
Awards ≥1995*

IDG is the world's leading IT media, research and exposition company. Founded in 1964, IDG had 1997 revenues of $2.05 billion and has more than 9,000 employees worldwide. IDG offers the widest range of media options that reach IT buyers in 75 countries representing 95% of worldwide IT spending. IDG's diverse product and services portfolio spans six key areas including print publishing, online publishing, expositions and conferences, market research, education and training, and global marketing services. More than 90 million people read one or more of IDG's 290 magazines and newspapers, including IDG's leading global brands — Computerworld, PC World, Network World, Macworld and the Channel World family of publications. IDG Books Worldwide is one of the fastest-growing computer book publishers in the world, with more than 700 titles in 36 languages. The "...For Dummies®" series alone has more than 50 million copies in print. IDG offers online users the largest network of technology-specific Web sites around the world through IDG.net (http://www.idg.net), which comprises more than 225 targeted Web sites in 55 countries worldwide. International Data Corporation (IDC) is the world's largest provider of information technology data, analysis and consulting, with research centers in over 41 countries and more than 400 research analysts worldwide. IDG World Expo is a leading producer of more than 168 globally branded conferences and expositions in 35 countries including E3 (Electronic Entertainment Expo), Macworld Expo, ComNet, Windows World Expo, ICE (Internet Commerce Expo), Agenda, DEMO, and Spotlight. IDG's training subsidiary, ExecuTrain, is the world's largest computer training company, with more than 230 locations worldwide and 785 training courses. IDG Marketing Services helps industry-leading IT companies build international brand recognition by developing global integrated marketing programs via IDG's print, online and exposition products worldwide. Further information about the company can be found at www.idg.com.   1/26/00

Author's Acknowledgments

Thanks to all the folks at REBOL Technologies who make this product what it is.

Publisher's Acknowledgments

We're proud of this book; please register your comments through our IDG Books Worldwide Online Registration Form located at http://my2cents.dummies.com.

Some of the people who helped bring this book to market include the following:

Acquisitions, Editorial, and Media Development

Senior Project Editor: Pat O'Brien

Acquisitions Editor: Judy Brief

Copy Editors: Barry Childs-Helton, Gwenette Gaddis

Proof Editors: Dwight Ramsey, Teresa Artman

Technical Editor: Danny Ramsey

Permissions Editor: Carmen Krikorian

Media Development Editor: Marisa Pearman

Media Development Manager: Laura Carpenter

Editorial Manager: Rev Mengle

Production

Project Coordinator: Amanda Foxworth

Layout and Graphics: Elizabeth Brooks, Jacque Schneider, Gabriele McCann, Jeremey Unger, Erin Zeltner

Proofreaders: Laura Albert, Corey Bowen, Susan Moritz, Marianne Santy, Linda Quigley, York Production Services, Inc.

Indexer: York Production Services, Inc.

General and Administrative

IDG Books Worldwide, Inc.: John Kilcullen, CEO; Bill Barry, President and COO; John Ball, Executive VP, Operations & Administration; John Harris, CFO

IDG Books Technology Publishing Group: Richard Swadley, Senior Vice President and Publisher; Mary Bednarek, Vice President and Publisher; Walter R. Bruce III, Vice President and Publisher; Joseph Wikert, Vice President and Publisher; Mary C. Corder, Editorial Director; Andy Cummings, Publishing Director, General User Group; Barry Pruett, Publishing Director

IDG Books Manufacturing: Ivor Parker, Vice President, Manufacturing

IDG Books Marketing: John Helmus, Assistant Vice President, Director of Marketing

IDG Books Online Management: Brenda McLaughlin, Executive Vice President, Chief Internet Officer; Gary Millrood, Executive Vice President of Business Development, Sales and Marketing

IDG Books Packaging: Marc J. Mikulich, Vice President, Brand Strategy and Research

IDG Books Production for Branded Press: Debbie Stailey, Production Director

IDG Books Sales: Roland Elgey, Senior Vice President, Sales and Marketing; Michael Violano, Vice President, International Sales and Sub Rights

◆

The publisher would like to give special thanks to Patrick J. McGovern, without whom this book would not have been possible.

◆

Contents at a Glance

Cartoons at a Glance

By Rich Tennant

page 349

page 181

page 283

page 47

page 7

page 99

page 407

Fax: 978-546-7747
E-mail: richtennant@the5thwave.com
World Wide Web: www.the5thwave.com

Table of Contents

● ●

Introduction

● ●

Welcome to the wild, wacky, and wonderful possibilities inherent in the Web. In this book, I introduce you to the mysteries of REBOL to build Web pages. The goal is to initiate you into the still-select, but rapidly growing, community of Web authors.

If you've tried to build your own Web pages before but found it too forbidding, now you can relax. If you can chew gum or pull up your socks in the morning, you too can become an author. (No kidding!)

I also include a peachy CD with this book that contains examples from the chapters in usable form — plus a number of versions of REBOL to embellish your own documents and astound your friends. For this edition, I've added discussions of important topics that have come increasingly to the fore (though not yet to the putting green) in the last few years. Finally, the CD also includes the magnificent and bedazzling source materials for the *REBOL For Dummies* Web pages, which you might find to be a source of inspiration and raw material for your own use! And I carry on a time-honored tradition upheld by the computer industry generally and IDG Books Worldwide in particular:

Anything silly you might read herein is a *feature,* not a *bug!*

About This Book

Think of this book as a friendly, approachable guide to tackling terminology and taking up the tools of REBOL to build readable, attractive pages for the Web. Although REBOL isn't hard to learn, it does pack a welter of details. You'll need to wrestle them into shape while you build your Web pages.

Although at first glance it might seem that building Web pages requires years of arduous training, advanced artistic abilities, and intense meditation, take heart: Not true! If you can tell somebody how to find your office, you can certainly build a Web document that does what you want. The purpose of this book isn't to turn you into a particle physicist (or, for that matter, a particle physicist into a Web site); it's to show you all the design and technical elements that you need to build a good-looking, readable Web page, and give you the know-how and confidence to do a great job!

How to Use This Book

This book tells you how to get your page up and running on the Web. I tell you what's involved in designing and building effective Web documents that can bring your ideas and information to the whole online world — if that's what you want to do — and maybe have some high-tech fun communicating them.

All code appears in monofont type like this:

```
<head><title>What's in a Title?</title></head>...
```

Three Presumptuous Assumptions

They say that making assumptions makes a fool out of the person who makes them and the person about whom those assumptions are made (and just who are *They,* anyway? I *assume* I know, but . . . never mind). Even so, practicality demands that I make a few assumptions about you, our gentle reader:

- ✓ You can turn your computer on and off.
- ✓ You know how to use a mouse and a keyboard.
- ✓ You want to build Web pages for fun, for profit, or because it's your job.

In addition, I assume that you already have a working connection to the Internet, and one of the many fine Web browsers available by hook, by crook, by download from that same Internet, or from the attached CD. You don't need to be a master logician or a wizard in the arcane arts of programming, nor do you need a Ph.D. in computer science. You don't even need a detailed sense of what's going on in the innards of your computer to deal with the material in this book.

If you can write a sentence and know the difference between a heading and a paragraph, you're better off than nine out of ten playground bullies — *and* you can build and publish your own documents on the Web. If you have an active imagination and the ability to communicate what's important to you, even better — you've already mastered the key ingredients necessary to build useful, attractive Web pages. The rest is made up of details, and I help you with those!

How This Book Is Organized

This book contains eight major parts (if you count the appendix), arranged in a pleasing order (at least I like it). Any time that you need help or information, pick up the book and start anywhere you like, or use the Table of Contents or Index to locate specific topics.

Here's a breakdown of the parts and what you find in each one.

Part I: Joining the REBOLution

This part sets the stage and includes an overview of and introduction to the terms and techniques that make REBOL do its thing.

Part II: Basic Training

REBOL mixes ordinary text with special strings of characters, called *markup,* used to instruct. In this part of the book, you find out about markup in general, and about the structure of REBOL in particular (including how I structure it in this book).

Part III: Advanced Infantry Training

Part III takes the elements and attributes covered in Part II and explains them in greater detail to help you design and build documents.

Part IV: Live-Fire Exercises

Part IV adds elegance and *savoir-faire* to the basics covered in Part III. By the time you read these chapters, you can build complex Web pages of many different kinds.

Part V: Tactics and Maneuvering (A REBOLer is Born)

In this part, you go a little beyond the built-in capabilities that REBOL delivers to its users. You get to examine some interesting facilities that sometimes show up in Web pages — but not always.

Part VI: REBOL Victories

The most advanced files possible are incorporated in these chapters.

Part VII: The Part of Tens

In the penultimate part of this book, I sum up and distill the very essence of what you now know about the mystic secrets of REBOL.

Appendix

The last part of this book ends with an appendix that lists the details about what's on the *REBOL For Dummies* CD-ROM. By the time you make it through all the materials in the book and on the CD, you should be pretty well equipped to build your own Web documents and perhaps even ready to roll out your own Web site!

Icons Used in This Book

This icon signals technical details that are informative and interesting, but not critical to writing REBOL. Skip these if you want (but please, come back and read them later).

This icon flags useful information that makes REBOL markup, Web page design, or other important stuff even less complicated than you feared it might be.

This icon points out information that you shouldn't pass by — don't overlook these gentle reminders (the life, sanity, or page you save could be your own).

Be cautious when you see this icon. It warns you of things you shouldn't do; the bomb is meant to emphasize that the consequences of ignoring these bits of wisdom can be severe.

Text marked with this icon contains information about something on this book's CD-ROM.

Where to Go from Here

This is the part where you pick a direction and hit the road! *REBOL For Dummies* is a lot like the *1001 Nights:* It almost doesn't matter where you start out; you'll look at lots of different scenes and stories as you prepare yourself to build your own Web pages — and each story has its own distinctive characteristics, but the whole is something to marvel at. Don't worry. You can handle it. Who cares if anybody else thinks you're just goofing around? I know you're getting ready to have the time of your life.

Enjoy!

Part I

Joining the REBOLution

The 5th Wave   By Rich Tennant

"Before the Internet, we were only bustin' chops locally. But now, with our Web site, we're bustin' chops all over the world."

In this part . . .

The beginning is usually the best place to start, or at least where you arrive first. You find out why and how REBOL is a great solution to many e-business problems, learn where to get the latest version *free*, how to unpack and install that version on your computer, and set it up to run. Then you see the basics of running REBOL. Finally, you get a fireman's tour of its powerful-yet-simple features and, so to speak, take it for a run with the siren howling and the red lights flashing. Hang on tight!

Chapter 1

A REBOL Tour

*R*EBOLers (people who program in REBOL) like to call it a *REBOLution.* Just as REBOL itself is revolutionary, so is this book. Let me explain.

Most computer books at this time stress the point that their subject matter covers only Unix, or only Windows 95/98/NT/2000, or only Macintosh. Some of these books even claim that you should program just for systems you know because no one can be an expert in all operating systems.

That premise is correct: Nobody can be an expert in all operating systems, but now — thanks to REBOL — no one *has* to be! So this book has no such limit. I promise you that the explanations and examples that follow will work on many, many systems, and not just the so-called Big Three of Windows, Unix/Linux, and Macintosh. (Don't throw away that Atari just yet!)

Counting the many variants, scores of operating systems exist. The scripts that you write in REBOL on one system run on (as I write this) 37 operating systems, with more on the way.

If I may appropriate the classic Sherwin-Williams paint company ad slogan, REBOL indeed *covers the world,* and this book covers REBOL.

What's REBOL? And How Do You Say It?

REBOL (Relative Expression-Based Object Language) is pronounced REB-el — as in "Rebel Yell" — which is the source for all the word plays that

REBOLutionaries enjoy so much. You see more than a few in this book. Forgive me that little quirk, and I give you an excellent start in learning REBOL in return.

Seriously, REBOL is an entirely new approach to distributed computing. *Distributed computing* simply lets the client computer do some work rather than having the server computer do it all. In short, distributed computing spreads the load, thus making applications smarter, faster, and more universal.

I discovered REBOL while Web-browsing last summer, and it quickly became one of my passions. The advantages are just so immediately obvious. Others join the cause daily. Over 250,000 people have already downloaded the free version of REBOL from `http://rebol.com`.

REBOL is a scripting language similar to Perl. Unlike Perl, however, scripts in REBOL run unchanged on a wider range of systems. REBOL requires much less *syntax* — which is not a *tax* on *sin,* but the structure of commands. That is, code in REBOL is much closer to plain English (or German or Spanish or whatever you speak) than such coding environments as Perl. This means fewer characters, fewer syntax commands, and most definitely a less rigid overall structure. The guiding philosophy in REBOL is to do simple things in simple ways. As a quick example, here's the command for sending some accumulated data to yourself via e-mail:

```
send gwashington@rebolution.com data
```

That's all. No trailing semicolons as in Perl, or anything else that unnecessarily complicates the code. And just as it is easy to "speak" REBOL (that is, write code in it), you can easily communicate with it as well. Using a minimum of code, you can create powerful applications, especially those related to the World Wide Web. REBOL directly handles Internet protocols such as e-mail, Web, FTP, NNTP, and numerous others, without the need for additional libraries or modules.

Yes, it *is* REBOLutionary!

Many platforms, one language

I'm not keen on long tables in books, but Table 1-1 is pretty cool and should pique your interest. It shows (as of this book's writing) just how many platforms (computer operating systems) REBOL runs on. And more are coming!

All the versions of REBOL listed in this table are on the CD-ROM included with this book. Check `http://rebol.com` for the availability of your operating system's version.

Table 1-1   Platforms for Which REBOL Is Available

Group	System-Name	Hardware	Status	Version
Amiga	V2.0-3.1	68020+	Released	2.2.0.1.1
	V2.0-3.1	68000	Released	2.2.0.1.2
Be	Bees R4	PPC	Released	2.2.0.5.1
	Bees R4	iX86	Released	2.2.0.5.2
BSD	Bids	iX86	Released	2.2.0.6.1
	Free BSD	iX86	Released	2.2.0.7.1
	Nets	iX86	Released	2.2.0.8.1
	Nets	PPC	Released	2.2.0.8.2
	Nets	68K	Released	2.2.0.8.3
	Nets	DEC Alpha	Pending	0.0.0.8.4
	Nets	Spark	Released	2.2.0.8.5
	Nets	Ultras arc	Pending	0.0.0.8.6
	Opens	iX86	Released	2.2.0.9.1
	OpenBSD	PPC	Pending	0.0.0.9.2
	OpenBSD	68K	Released	2.2.0.9.3
	OpenBSD	DEC Alpha	Pending	0.0.0.9.4
	OpenBSD	Sparc	Released	2.2.0.9.5
Compaq	Tru64	DEC Alpha	Pending	0.0.0.20
	Open VMS	DEC Alpha	Pending	0.0.0.21
HP	MPE/iX	HP 3000	Pending	0.0.0.26
	HP-UX	HP	Released	2.2.0.12
IBM	AIX	RS6000	Released	2.2.0.17
	OS/2	iX86	Pending	0.0.0.16
	OS/400	AS400	Pending	0.0.0.18

(continued)

Table 1-1 *(continued)*

Group	System-Name	Hardware	Status	Version
Linux	Libc5	iX86	Released	2.2.0.4.1
	Libc6	iX86	Released	2.2.0.4.2
	Linux	DEC Alpha	Released	2.2.0.4.3
	Linux	PPC	Released	2.2.0.4.4
	Linux	68K	Released	2.2.0.4.5
	Linux	Sparc	Released	2.2.0.4.6
	Linux	UltraSparc	Pending	0.0.0.4.7
	Netwinder	Strong ARM	Released	2.2.0.4.8
	Cobalt Qube	MIPS	Released	2.2.0.4.9
Macintosh	Macintosh	PPC	Released	2.2.0.2.1
	Macintosh	68K	Released	2.2.0.2.2
	Macintosh	PPC, 68K	Released	2.2.0.2.3
	OSX	PPC	Released	2.2.0.2.4
Microsoft	95/98/NT	iX86	Released	2.2.0.3.1
	Alpha NT	DEC Alpha	Released	2.2.0.3.2
	Win CE 2.0	SH3/4	Released	2.2.0.15.1
	Win CE 2.0	MIPS	Released	2.2.0.15.2
	Win CE 2.0	PPC	Pending	0.0.0.15.3
	Win CE 2.0	iX86	Released	2.2.0.15.4
	Strong ARM	HP820	Pending	0.0.0.15.5
Novell	Netware 4.0	iX86	Pending	0.0.0.25.1
	Netware 5.0	iX86	Pending	0.0.0.25.2
QNX	RTOS	iX86	Released	2.2.0.22
	Neutrino	iX86	Pending	0.0.0.23.1
	Neutrino	MIPS	Pending	0.0.0.23.2
	Neutrino	PPC	Pending	0.0.0.23.3
Palm	Palm OS	PalmPilot	Pending	0.0.0.14
Psion	Psion	ARM	Pending	0.0.0.13

Group	System-Name	Hardware	Status	Version
SCO	SCO Unix	iX86	Released	2.1.1.19
	Open Server	iX86	Pending	0.0.0.24
SGI	IRIX	SGI	Released	2.2.0.11
Sun	Solaris	Sparc	Released	2.2.0.10.1
	Solaris	iX86	Released	2.2.0.10.2

Messaging the world: Fantastic!

The concept of *messaging* is (aside from a noun mutating into a verb) simply passing messages back and forth. For a computer to run a program, it must be able to converse with the program. And computers — in this day of inter-connectivity — must communicate with other computers. In other words, they must send and receive messages. REBOL's great advantage is that it can send and receive messages in a wide variety of formats, to and from scores of different type systems.

For example, if you have a form on a Web page and want to pass data to a REBOL script for processing, only a single line is required to receive the data into REBOL. Here are the simple steps needed to pass data:

1. Place a standard form in the HTML making up your Web page using the `get` method (which is CGI stuff, not REBOL, but I show you how to do this in Chapter 18). Have the form call your REBOL script using something like `<form method=get action="/cgi-bin/script.r">`.

2. In your REBOL script, the line data `decode-cgisystem/options/cgi/query-string` receives all the data from the form. In Chapter 18, you see how that data is processed. Now, everything filled out on the form is in the word data — having been passed or messaged from the Web page to REBOL.

This example uses the CGI `get` method, which, along with the `post` method, appears in detail in Chapter 18. Both methods, however, are truly trivial to implement in REBOL.

The passing of data between widely different computers and operating systems has long been a headache for programmers. Simply put, computers speak different languages: human, computer, and combinations of both. Getting something intelligible from one machine to another sometimes requires more effort in coding than all the rest of the program put together. REBOL not only offers a solution for this longtime problem of messaging, but also makes such interchange really easy.

Contrary to popular belief, computer system standards are diverging — not converging. More operating systems now run on more types of hardware than ever before. In a few years, 600 million devices will be connected to the Internet — including cell phones, handheld devices, TV set-top boxes, desktop computers, and servers. Besides this usual gang of cybergadgets, imagine an online connection for the hidden computers in microwave ovens, refrigerators, so-called "smart" homes, cars, industry equipment, and business machines. Virtually anything a microprocessor can be crammed into (and microprocessors are getting pretty small) is headed for cyberspace.

Programming all these devices is the Tower of Babel multiplied many times over. But just imagine writing a program that would run on a toaster, a cell phone, a programmable machine tool, a Linux server, or your Windows desktop — even on devices that haven't even been thought of yet — all without modification!

To read a list of the files in the current directory requires a wide range of different commands in varying operating systems — such as dir in DOS, ls in Unix/Linux, and so forth. In REBOL, on all operating systems, the following expression in your script gives this list:

```
read %.
```

Such simplicity means that *you don't even have to know operating system commands*, and that your scripts can do directory listings on operating systems not even invented yet. Who would have thought of such universal power in a scripting language?

Well, Carl Sassenrath and his REBOL development team certainly have! Their vision is to quiet the babble of programming languages and disciplines that currently clutter the universe of smart devices. Their solution is to offer one language — REBOL — that scales to everything: cell phones, PDAs, TVs, desktops, and servers. Carl and his enthusiastic team are showing the potential to pull it off, too; REBOL can run on all 600 million devices currently linked to the Internet. Expect REBOL to run on over 50 platforms — and the list keeps growing.

The heart of their approach is (dare I say it?) to reach for near-universal compatibility. An application written for one type of system can run on 37 others today, *without modification* — no jumping through hoops and loops to port it over from one platform to another. Imagine one program humming along on a PC, a Mac, and a Unix server with no middleman program needed. The sheer elegant wonder of this promise should hook any programmer.

REBOL unites computing, making platforms irrelevant. (Whoa. Talk about radical ideas.) The computer press increasingly agrees that something powerful is happening in Ukiah, California, home to hot tubs and a revolutionary language. For an update, visit the not-so-secret REBOL base on the Web (see Figure 1-1).

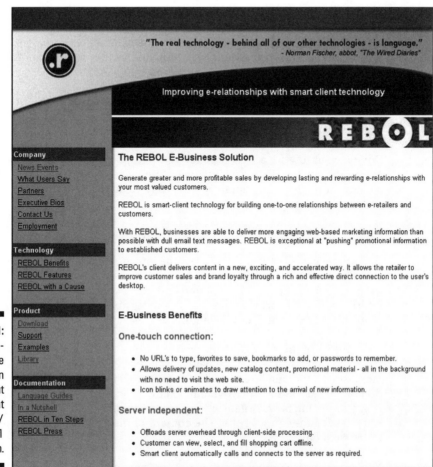

Figure 1-1:
Find up-to-
date
information
about
REBOL at
http://
rebol
.com.

This book, though, is not about what's to come, but rather what is *here* —
REBOL. REBOL is now in version 2.3 release — and free for downloading from
http://rebol.com in versions for many platforms. Every version is on the
CD-ROM included at the back of this book. I run REBOL on my Windows 98
desktop, my company's NT mail server, my BSDI Unix Web server, and my
Linux server powered by Red Hat 6.1. REBOL runs exactly the same on all
those platforms. More importantly, scripts that I write on any platform run
flawlessly on all the others without modification. Even the line endings are
automatically converted, and will eventually run just as well on systems not
even invented yet.

Do you think that's worthwhile? Yep. It sure enough is!

REBOL is a fine tool for both simple and complex applications on your home computer or a business computer on a *LAN* (Local Area Network), such as where you work. But it really shines in messaging (again, simply the exchange and manipulation of information) over a much wider network — the Internet, and its highly extensive subnet, the World Wide Web.

The big dogs on the both the Internet and the Web are *servers,* those computers that "serve" up Web sites and other networked services. REBOL helps you work and run servers in many ways.

Do you want to grab a Web page for your script to *parse* data from (strip off extraneous material) — say, pulling out items you have for sale on eBay and accumulating them in a database? It's easy. Read the Web page that you want to operate on into a *word,* like so:

```
page: read http://rebol.com
```

The primary mechanism that makes the Internet of such value to all of us is called the *World Wide Web.* Clicking a mouse reveals hundreds of millions of brightly colored pages, full of sound and music and pictures that move. Information of all sorts is more quickly accessible and in much greater detail than you find in your hometown library.

Web pages, on their own, are static. They do essentially nothing but show the same thing every time the page is accessed, the same old tired way. Increasingly, the demand today is for Web sites to become more interactive, do more tasks, and feature dynamic content. An example of dynamic content is any of the big news organization's pages, such as `http://cnn.com` or even `http://drudgereport.com`. The content of these sites changes several times each day.

You, or anyone who may hire you to program a Web site or Web application, will want an interactive site with dynamic content. An employer may not say this up front, but that's what is wanted. Trust me.

Dynamic content and interactivity are archived with both server-side (program runs on the server) and client-side (program runs on your computer) techniques. This book shows how REBOL excels at both.

Fitting REBOL in

Many technologies and languages exist for implementing dynamic content and interactivity for Web pages and the other applications that a server on the Internet can do for you — such as e-mail, file transfer, databases, and much more. These include the scripting languages Perl, Python, and the Web-page parsers — as well as PHP, Cold Fusion, ASP, and others of these categories (such as Java, JavaScript, VBscript, and the like). The Web is a big place and a lot of people are doing a lot of things on it.

To all this, now add REBOL. Simplicity is the key. You can write, debug, and publish a short Web application using REBOL in mere minutes. And, that Web application you just ran on your Windows computer runs unchanged on your Unix, NT, Macintosh, or whatever server.

"Not true!" some smart aleck out there cries. (There's one, just one, in every 100,000 readers of this book, eh? Go home, Fred, I see you!) Anyway, as Fred or Alec or whoever continues smugly but mistakenly, "You can't just transfer a script up to a server and expect it to run without converting line endings."

Well, yes, you can. REBOL automatically does that for you. I discuss this in greater detail in Chapter 9.

Simplicity is a word you often see in reference to REBOL.

Sophisticated application developers will love REBOL's ability to manipulate TCP/IP stacks directly without libraries and many other powerful networking and communication features built into this tiny (about 200K) but thunderous script language.

REBOL is Perl without the confusion, I say. This brings me to the biggest and best area of application for REBOL: the many millions of us who want to write quick-but-highly-useful Web applications without the bother of (shudder) Perl's complexities.

As the REBOL Alliance grows, I believe that tons of Perl-aggravated script users will also jump at the much lower learning curve and simplicity (love that concept) of REBOL. But, REBOL should not be viewed as a "Perl killer" (even though it was with me), but as a simple answer to do simple things and to build more sophisticated programming. REBOL, in essence, is the nonprogrammer's best path to quickly becoming a real programmer or (even more important) getting done what *you* want done for your computers.

REBOL itself

The primary version of the REBOL language is called (not too surprisingly) "REBOL" — the one currently available and the topic of this book. Other versions are being developed and tested for various, more specialized applications. Although no firm marketing plans have been announced by REBOL Technologies, certainly some of these will be commercial applications.

REBOL, the core of the language, is now available free of charge from the REBOL Technologies Web site. This is a fully functional product and is totally free from shareware gimmicks, such as time-outs or restricted file access. In addition, the REBOL system distribution will be small enough to download quickly (about as long as it takes to wait for the full display of a major Web site). REBOL is compact and takes less than 30 seconds to download over a 56K modem.

Did I mention simplicity? Yep.

An enhanced version of REBOL now available also includes *dialecting* features that turn it into a multimedia powerhouse. You can even do Web pages without HTML! These are called *reb* pages and the pages linked together are the *Worldwide REB.*

REBOL/Serve

REBOL/Serve, under development now but not yet released in beta, adds to REBOL the ability to truly compete with Perl in applications that require access to other programs on a computer to retrieve data. This includes access to databases and much more. REBOL/Serve will not be free of charge — but REBOL itself, according to all I've seen and heard so far, will remain available without charge.

Other REBOLs

With the power of dialects, we can expect other versions of REBOL. I know that REBOL/Author is discussed on the REBOL mailing list, and no telling what else germinates in Ukiah. Good stuff, we know.

So grab up your musket and follow me, soldier of the REBOLution. It gets even more exciting and satisfying from here on out.

You can often hear talk about a "Linux community" and other online affiliations of enthusiasts for particular operating systems and programming languages. International now, they started small. In a classic case of déjà vu, venturesome REBOL bands are springing up on the Web; Figure 1-2 shows an example.

Figure 1-2:
Another
great
source for
REBOL info
is http://
rebol.
org, an
independent
site for us
REBOLers.

Let the REBOLs Begin (Startup)

At first, you start REBOL and use it mostly from the console as an interpreter. The console is simply the screen that appears after you start REBOL. It has a prompt like most command-line operating systems or programs. A *command-line program* enables you to type in commands, and then it operates on those commands. A *prompt* shows that the program is ready to accept a command and where you should type your command. REBOL's console prompt is two greater-than symbols, like this:

```
>>
```

An *interpreter* is a program that reads in a text file and interprets the lines of commands in the file, acting on them in sequence. Even programs that compile results into an executable standalone program (for example, C++) must first read a series of commands and interpret them. The advantage of an interpretive script language such as REBOL (or Perl or Python, for that matter) is that you can make quick, on-the-fly changes without having to go through a compile process. They are excellent, especially, for Web CGI applications, server maintenance, e-commerce, or any local application where ease of modification is a prime concern.

The disadvantage is that compiled programs run faster. In today's era of cheap, speedy computers, this is not as much of a problem as it was a few years ago. In fact, as you read this book, you may suspect that REBOL has so many advantages that you'll never miss the capability to compile.

Sooner or later, REBOL Technologies or someone will offer a compiler to create executable programs for specific platforms. But the true advantage of REBOL as an interpreter — and I can't emphasize it enough — is that a script you write on your Windows, Amiga, Macintosh, or whatever system runs unchanged on over 37 other platforms. This is no less than awesome!

Starting the console

Back to starting REBOL. On systems with GUIs (Graphic User Interfaces), click the REBOL icon. If you are at the command line in your operating system and are in the same directory as the REBOL executable, just type **rebol** — or maybe **./rebol** on a Unix/Linux system (your mileage may vary slightly from platform to platform). The console appears and some initialization messages appear, and then the console prompt (>>); you are now ready to begin using REBOL. What you see looks remarkably like Figure 1-3:

```
REBOL 2.2.0.3.1
Copyright (C) 1998-1999 REBOL Technologies
REBOL is a Trademark of REBOL Technologies
All rights reserved.

Finger protocol loaded
Whois protocol loaded
Daytime protocol loaded
SMTP protocol loaded
POP protocol loaded
HTTP protocol loaded
FTP protocol loaded
NNTP protocol loaded
Script: "REBOL Extended Definitions" (3-Sep-1999/17:55:08)
Script: "User Preferences" (11-Jan-2000/17:09:11-5:00)
>>
```

Okay, okay (to quote that great philosopher, Joe Pesci), let's do your first program in REBOL. We do the required "Hello World" program most people first attempt on learning a new language. Follow me now. Don't blink or you'll miss it.

At the console command prompt, type

```
print "hello world"
```

This is what you should see:

```
>> print "hello world"
hello world
>>
```

```
R REBOL                                                                    _ | @ | X
File  Edit
REBOL 2.2.0.3.1
Copyright (C) 1998-1999 REBOL Technologies
REBOL is a Trademark of REBOL Technologies
All rights reserved.

Finger protocol loaded
Whois protocol loaded
Daytime protocol loaded
SMTP protocol loaded
POP protocol loaded
HTTP protocol loaded
FTP protocol loaded
NNTP protocol loaded
Script: "REBOL Extended Definitions" (3-Sep-1999/17:55:08)
Script: "My User Preferences " (9-Feb-2000/14:19:41-5:00)
Script: "User Preferences" (13-Apr-2000/14:55:43-4:00)
>>
>> files: read %.
== [%setup.html %nntp.r %notes.html %rebdoc.r %REBOL.exe %rebol.r %feedback.r %user.r %test.html
%weblib.r %webprint.r %webget.r %w...
>> print ["There are " length? files "files in this directory."]
There are  238 files in this directory.
>>
```

Figure 1-3:
Using
REBOL from
the console
looks like
this.

And, after the commotion in Figure 1-3, you are back to the command
prompt. Or you could put it in a variable and print the variable:

```
>> a: "hello world" print a
hello world
>>
```

My point is that coding in REBOL requires nothing more than typing what
you actually want to do — no declaring of variables or other additional steps
often required by other languages, which makes code more complex. This
simplicity carries throughout REBOL, making applications written in REBOL
many lines shorter than in other scripting languages, especially Perl. (I love
the word *simplicity,* I really do. Look it up in the dictionary and you see the
REBOL icon next to it. . . . Okay, okay. Play along with me and just *imagine*
that it's next to the definition. It should be. Remind me to jot a quick note off
to Mr. Webster about that.)

When starting REBOL, you can specify various *command-line options* or
arguments or *switches* that affect how REBOL runs. These options may
be specified also when REBOL is called from a script.

The way that arguments are presented may vary a little from platform to platform, but you can check easily enough by typing the function word usage at the REBOL console prompt like this:

```
>> usage
The command-line usage is:

    REBOL <options> <script> <arguments>

All fields are optional. Supported options are:

    --cgi (-c)       Check for CGI input
    --do expr        Evaluate expression
    --help (-?)      Display this usage information
    --nowindow (-w)  Do not open a window
    --quiet (-q)     Don't print banners
    --script file    Explicitly specify script
    --secure level   Set security level:
                     (none write read throw quit)
    -s               Shortcut: no security
    +s               Shortcut: full security
    --trace (-t)     Enable trace mode

Examples:

    REBOL script.r
    REBOL script.r 10:30 test@domain.dom
    REBOL script.r -do "verbose: true"
    REBOL --cgi -s
    REBOL --cgi -secure throw --script cgi.r "debug: true"
    REBOL --secure none
```

Most of these are discussed elsewhere in this book — but first, one quick comment on the -secure (and its shortcut -s) option. When playing around learning REBOL and evaluating scripts that read and write to files, you may want to start REBOL with the -s option. Otherwise, every time that a file is accessed, REBOL stops and asks you if it should go ahead; this built-in security feature gets old in a hurry when you are just trying to learn.

From a script

Like Unix shell scripts, Perl scripts, and others, a script can be made executable by a call, which starts REBOL interpreting the script and outputting whatever the script requests.

You often use this scheme in writing server and Web CGI applications, and this subject is covered at length in this book. Basically, the technique is easy. (Can I use the word *simple* again? Well, anyway, I think you get the idea.)

To have REBOL execute a script on a Unix/Linux platform, for example, make this the first line in your script:

```
#!/rebol/rebol
```

This command causes the script to call for REBOL in the /rebol directory. If you stashed REBOL somewhere else, you would put in the actual path information of your computer.

Chapter 9 offers information about file permissions. These are not needed on Windows or Macintosh; on a Unix/Linux platform, however, the execute permission must be set on a file before it is allowed to call REBOL for interpretation. Use the Unix command chmod 755 name-of-file, for example, to enable anyone to run this file. Other permissions would restrict running the file to your workgroup, or make it private for you alone.

Again, when starting REBOL from a script, you can still use the options we listed in this chapter. A REBOL script, for instance, that inputs or outputs to a Web page using CGI (Common Gateway Interface) needs to call REBOL using a special switch:

```
#!/rebol/rebol -cgi
```

Much more on this later.

"Hello World" and More

Simple is better, and REBOL excels at simplicity. Take the old hoary standard "Hello World" program that we write first in every language. Here's REBOL's version:

```
print "hello world"
```

Yep, that's it. No trailing semicolon to forget and give you syntax errors as in Perl. Simple. Or here's another neat one, thanks to REBOL's built in powerhouse of standard Internet protocols: Send me an e-mail (try this in one line in Perl<g>):

```
send ralph@abooks.com "Nice book!"
```

Easy! But let's emphasize our opinion by repeating the message ten times (after all, REBOL *is* a messaging language):

```
a: "" loop 10 [a: join a "Nice book! "] send ralph@abooks.com
        a
```

That's it. I'd do the equivalent for you in Perl, but I want to quit writing on time today for a change. Back to REBOL and its simplicity. Let's define a function:

```
sum: func [a b] [a + b]
```

Thereafter (in your program), whenever the function sum is called, you get this:

```
sum 144 87
```

REBOL outputs the answer, which is 231. The function is in clean, human-readable code: In essence, this sentence reads, "The sum of 144 and 87 is 231." I try to show you all this simplicity in easy, useful examples. (One of my pet peeves with programming books is a general lack of useful examples. All I want is for someone to show me how it works and how that benefits me. And how I can use it now. Just a born *Dummies* guy, huh?)

A simple one-line program tells how many days are left — taking leap year into account, 323 days, as of the writing of this paragraph. Running this line:

```
print ["Counting today," 1-Jan-2001 - now "days to the REAL
        Millennium."]
```

outputs this next line:

```
Counting today, 323 days to the REAL Millennium.
```

Which brings up datatypes. Like everything else about REBOL, it's plum danged easy, as my daddy used to say. Note that in the preceding code, I just entered the date and used now for the system time. We don't need to declare no stinking variables; REBOL does that on-the-fly for you.

Another example. Let's manipulate a file:

```
data:  read/lines %file.txt
```

The entire file is read into the variable data line by line. Here's what you can do with it by using actual REBOL code with comments, (and REBOL is kinda like English even without the comments). Remember, in REBOL the semi-colon (;) is used as the comment character. In a REBOL line, following a semi-colon nothing is evaluated. Okay, the following is stuff we can do with the stuff from file.txt that we read into variable data:

```
print first data          ; print the first line
print last data           ; print the last line
print third data          ; print the third line
print pick data 56        ; print the 56th line
print length? data        ; how many lines long?
```

Hey, have you checked your e-mail recently? At the REBOL console, use this:

```
print read pop://username:password@yourdomain.com
```

REBOL checks your e-mail and prints out the messages for you without removing any messages from your mail server.

Okay, that was fun, but the tour moves on as we visit the component parts of REBOL scripting. If you look on your left, you see. . . .

Valuing Things

In any program language, we operate on *things*. We add and subtract things, we poke things into strings, and we loop until *this* thing is now *that* thing. Well, you get the picture. Programming is just one darn thing after another.

Things in REBOL are called values. *Values* are raw data. One of the major advantages of REBOL is its ability to handle values of different types directly without special declaration or other jumping through loops to get a datatype. A *datatype,* by the way, is a certain type of thing — such as a number, a string of characters, a date, time, money, and so forth. When possible, REBOL allows the use of international formats for values such as decimal numbers, money, and dates.

Following is a brief look at the types of values used most often in REBOL. In Chapter 5, you get a more detailed look at values and the spiffy stuff you can do with them. But first things first: What kinds of values do you find, anyway? Well, for openers. . . .

Numbering

Numbers, in REBOL, can be integer, decimal, scientific notation, British, and non-British format. Here are examples:

```
486           ; an integer or "whole" number
15.775        ; a decimal value
1.6E10        ; scientific notation, powers of 10
0,2           ; non-British style, comma instead of decimal
1,3E15        ; non-British style, scientific notation
```

REBOL even enables you to mix the two styles:

```
>> print 1,4 + 3.5
4.9
```

Timing

Now is the time for all good REBOLers to learn about time. Actually, now is the function word used in REBOL to get date and time. Units of time — hours, minutes, and seconds — may be in the following formats:

```
10:19            ; conventional time
23:11            ; 24-hour military style
0:15:31          ; hours, minutes, seconds like a timer
```

Time may be used in script operations, just like any other value in REBOL:

```
>> print 23:14 - 11:01:30
12:12:30
```

You do not have to declare the type of variable, as in some languages. REBOL knows what type it is — time in this case — by the format of the data in the variable. REBOL also knows the exact time and date from your computer's system clock:

```
>> now
== 14-Feb-2000/9:01-5:00
>> now/time
== 9:01:05
>> now/date
== 14-Feb-2000
>> now/zone
== -5:00
```

Happy St. Valentine's Day! Sorry I forgot to get you a card, but the flowers are on the way. Anyhow, the now function word without refinement returns the date, time, and offset from GMT (Greenwich mean time). *Refinements* are the forward slash (/) switches that modify a function word's behavior, such as now/date breaking out the date or now/time presenting only the time. Now/zone gives us our time zone. I am in the eastern standard time zone, for example, which is five hours behind (or minus) GMT in Greenwich, England.

You may also use them as value refinements, such as:

```
>> today: now/date
== 15-Jul-2000
>> time: now/time
== 12:24:58
>> day: now/weekday
== 6
>> month: now/month
== 7
>> gmt-offset: now/zone
== -4:00
```

Dating

Dates are also value variables in REBOL. Here are the formats that may be used:

```
15-Apr-2000              ; U.S. usage
20/Jun/1999              ; U.S. usage
11-12-1945               ; international
2000-2-14                ; international
2000-10-30/8:45          ; date with time
2000-3-15/9:30-5:00      ; date with time and time zone
```

Dates may be operated on (just like any other value):

```
>> 2000-10-30 - 1999-10-30
== 366
>> 2000-10-30 - 30/Oct/1999
== 366
```

Counting money

Money is one of our favorite values — a value with *value!* The money value may have the following kinds of formats:

```
$16.14              ; U.S.
USD$22.79           ; U.S.
CAD$106.15          ; Canadian
DEM$1500,55         ; German Deutsche Mark
```

As they say in Germany, *REBOL ist Perl ohne die Komplikation.* REBOL is Perl without the complication. In the Canadian province of Quebec and in *la belle France* itself, the watch phrase for *le REBOLution* is *REBOL est Perl sans la complication.*

Use money values as you would any other in REBOL:

```
>> $15.86 + $20.34 + $30.20
== $66.40
```

(Tiptoeing through the) tuples

I used to think *tuples* were those cup-shaped flowers that grow in Holland. But, no, those are *tulips.* Tuples are numbers with more than one decimal, such as these:

2.2.0.3.1   my version of REBOL

192.168.0.12   the address of my computer on the LAN

255.255.0   RGB color numbers

In REBOL, you can use tuples to order the computer around, just as you can with any other value. For example, here's a command that prints RGB colors:

```
>> print 255.255.0 - 0.100.0
255.155.0
```

Here's a tuple for you — finding out the IP (Internet address number) of `http://rebol.com`.

```
>> print read dns://rebol.com
207.69.132.8
```

Or in reverse, if we only know the IP number:

```
>> print read dns://207.69.132.8
rebol.com
```

Using strings

A collection of letters and numbers, usually in some readable language, is called a string value in most computer programming languages. Here are some strings in REBOL:

```
"This is a string value."
a: "Come the REBOLution!" ; string into REBOL word
a: http://abooks.com       ; URLs are a type of string
```

Use curly braces ({ }) for longer strings and to maintain line breaks:

```
a: {It was a dark and stormy night when I
sat down to code. Dank, hail-laden wind
crashed my Windows and howled in not-so-
subtle hints of errors to come...}
```

Brrrr. Now *that's* scary. Not particularly good, but scary. This story has a happy ending, however; I now code in REBOL and the errors are fewer.

Tagging

Many years ago, when I was a small boy, I often played the game of tag. Now, grown to adulthood, I find myself still playing with tags, only these are the ones that you find in Hypertext Markup Language (HTML), the stuff of which Web pages are made. REBOL recognizes tags as a value. Here are some:

```
<title>
</body>
<font face="Helvetica" size="2">
```

REBOL includes a function, build-tag, which converts a block value to a tag:

```
>> build-tag [BODY BGCOLOR "#FFFFF0"]
== <BODY BGCOLOR="#FFFFF0">
```

You find tag values and the ways in which REBOL creates and/or manipulates them useful when we get heavily into building Web pages with REBOL in Chapter 16 and CGI Web applications in Chapter 18.

E-mailing with ease

You've got mail! Yep, and REBOL treats e-mail addresses also as values. Such as:

```
ralph@abooks.com          ; my personal address
feedback@rebol.com        ; REBOL technical support
```

Use e-mail addresses with the send function word and you can send just about anything — variables, strings, whatever:

```
send bubba@pineywoods.com "I fixed yer pickup truck."
send nigel@jollyold.com.uk "Tea at 3 p.m., old chap."
Send [a@a.com b@a.com] "Hi guys, how's it going?"
```

The last example sends the same message to a list of recipients.

Locating URLs

A URL (Uniform Resource Locator) is often used for Web addresses, but includes other types of Internet addresses as well:

```
http://rebol.com          ; a Web address
mailto://info@rebol.com   ; an e-mail address
ftp://ftp.a.com/file.txt  ; file transfer protocol address
```

Filing files

The basis on which computers operate extensively involves files. One of the most important aspects of any programming language is the reading and writing of files. Filenames are an important and often-used value in REBOL. Path is the information describing where files are located in your local computer's file system, or over a network. One caveat: A path in REBOL is actually a lot like a word, except it is a path (through a block or object) *to* a word within the block or object. I'll make that clearer in later chapters.

The percent character (%) precedes filenames and tells REBOL what follows is a file value. File values in REBOL include

```
%file.txt
%/rebol/script.r
%/c/windows/temp/some.txt
```

Here's something you can play with right now in learning file values:

```
a: read %. sort a      ; sorted list of current directory
foreach line a [print line]   ; print it out one per line
```

Chapters 9 and 10 cover files and directories in much detail.

Issuing issues

Issue values cover numbers that are issued or assigned to you, such as phone numbers and credit card numbers, or that are issued to a thing, such as model numbers. A leading pound sign (#) informs REBOL that the following is an issue value. Here we have some:

```
#555-512-5555             ; phone number
#0000-9999-0000-9999      ; credit card number
#FRA-467-231-BG           ; model number
```

Biting into binary

A *binary* value is essentially anything except plain text, but important binary values include those that make up executable programs, images, sounds, and so forth. REBOL enables you to work directly with binary representations of data. Binary data may be converted between base2 (binary, the old famous ones and zeros), base16 (hex), and base64 (octet-stream), and manipulated in any of these forms. The default base for binary data in REBOL is base16.

Binary values are represented in REBOL by a pound sign (#) followed by the binary number enclosed with curly braces ({ }). A number in front of the pound sign denotes a base other than 16, such as base2 or base64. Here's how it looks:

```
#{3A18427F 899AEFD8}                        ; default base16
2#{10010110110010101001011011001011}  ; base2
64#{LmNvbSA8yw9CBOaGvXmgUkVCu2Uz934b}  ; base64
```

Here's a start for your playtime with binary values:

```
>> a: 2#{1000100011101001}
== #{88E9}                 ; REBOL returns hex
>> to-integer a
== 35049                   ; REBOL returns base10
```

I put a binary base2 number into variable a. REBOL automatically converts it to the default base16. I hit the variable with the `to-integer` function and, bingo, I have our far more human-understandable base10 value.

Okay, enough for the tour — but not to worry. Much more good stuff is on the way!

Shutting Down for the Day

If you start, you should know how to exit. This is a short section because it's so easy.

At the console, type the word `quit`. If you've had a long day slaving over hot code and even those four letters are too much for you, the letter q is a short-cut, which also shuts down REBOL.

To exit REBOL from within a script, such as you would do in error trapping (getting out quick before the thing explodes), the word `quit` comes into play again. For example, if you want your script to exit when the five o'clock whis-tle blows, use code like so:

```
if now/time > 17:00 [print "Quitting Time!" quit]
```

I use this program to end each day's writing precisely at five. . . .

Yeah, right! I wish. A writer's work is never done. Just ask my editor. He's always asking, "Aren't you done yet?"

Er . . . back to work.

Chapter 2

Interfacing with REBOL

· ·

· ·

*L*ike most scripting languages (and even the old BASIC interpreters that came with computers 20 years ago), REBOL runs in only two ways.

✔ You can start it as a program and run it manually from the console.

✔ You can create a script that calls REBOL and causes its own execution.

By execution, I mean that REBOL interprets the script, evaluates its functions, and acts upon them. Not that the script is truly killed (as in blindfold-and-last-cigarette) — not even if you're bewildered about why it's crashing and you're looking for a large blunt instrument to help you reason with your code. Well, okay, that *does* happen to me occasionally (almost always from errors I've introduced when I was in a hurry). Luckily — having programmed in Perl for some time — I have a goodly supply of blunt instruments. REBOL, in its simplicity, requires fewer of these, so I have some to spare if you're ever in need.

Simple is good. Especially if your daily labor involves writing lines of code by the thousands. Take, for instance, the necessary chore known as debugging.

Finding and correcting errors in any type of computer program is called *debugging*. This term was coined back in the late 1940s, the era of monster "electronic brains." Changing a program was pretty physical; you had to yank out big racks of vacuum tubes and reset hundreds of switches by hand. Errors could be just as physical. Light from the tubes attracted bugs (the six-legged variety); when they fried themselves on the components, they shorted out some logical connections and crashed the machine.

Sounds like an urban legend, doesn't it? But truth is often stranger than folk-lore. A single bug can do immense damage. On the farm where I live, for example, an electric fence keeps large number of cows from wandering off. In summer, as often happens, one bug alighting between hot wires — and bridging an insulator by brushing a metal fence pole — can cause a mile of fence to go off in a spectacular arc. The cows get out, the power grid flinches, and the whole affair doesn't do the bug any good either.

Moral: One small bug in the works can have great consequences, whether for ENIAC or E-I-E-I-O. Fortunately, REBOL code is enough like plain English that mistakes are easy to spot and fix. Even better, the specifics and how-tos of debugging techniques crop up throughout this book.

Meeting the Console

The console provides you direct interaction with REBOL. You can type commands in directly, evaluate snippets of code, load files and data, and do many other useful things here.

Commanding the command prompt

As you've seen, the command-line prompt ($>>$) is how REBOL shows you that it is available for you to input a command. If you don't like the basic prompt, it's easy enough to change by using the REBOL system object — a special variable — or, more accurately, a REBOL word that looks like this:

```
system/console/prompt
```

The folks at REBOL Technologies like to call the special words (like the ones above) *system objects*. Keep this in mind for the moment; I explain more about objects in Chapter 5.

More of these special words crop up, as needed, in the course of this book. For now, typing the following command shows how the prompt works:

```
system/console/prompt: "Type here: "
```

No sooner than you press Enter, your console prompt changes to Type here: instead of the double greater-than symbols ($>>$). Or you could even have a function that REBOL evaluates and uses as the prompt, such as the current time. You do it like this:

```
>> system/console/prompt: [reform [now/time ">> "]]
== [reform [now/time ">> "]]
14:49:26 >>
```

The current time is now your prompt. Hit your Enter key a few times and watch it change.

Don't worry about messing up your prompt. All these changes go away when you quit and restart REBOL. However, should you like the change and want to keep it, that's easy. I cover various methods of both temporarily and permanently customizing the REBOL console throughout this book.

Interrupting a script

Should an error have been introduced, a script can go out into the pasture and just chase horseflies. In effect, it locks up (in an infinite loop) and runs around doing nothing, including paying absolutely no attention to you. Stop such a script by pressing Esc (your Escape key) once. You don't have to pound it through your keyboard's base into the desk. REBOL either stops immediately or, depending on some network operations, as quickly as it can.

Entering command-line input

Command lines are great for stuffing everything you can think of (including the kitchen sink) into one line. Some Unix command-line commands go on for so long that you finally understand the song lyrics "On a clear day you can see forever" because you just passed "forever" and you're still going. And REBOL certainly offers you some powerful one-line programs.

Naturally, there are many times when you want to do loops or other block functions on different lines without having to go through the trouble of editing a text file, then reading it into REBOL. From the console this is possible. REBOL enables you to open a block (one of this language's basic structures) from the command line and keep it open for as many lines as you want before evaluating the block. I discuss blocks extensively in Chapter 5, but the console block input works like this:

```
>> loop 5 [
[    print random 100
[    ]
32
67
30
57
86
>>
```

Try this. First, you type in **loop 5 [**, and the open bracket tells REBOL to wait for additional lines. REBOL responds with a left bracket ([), and you type your second line: **print random 100**. REBOL gives you another left bracket ([). You respond with a right bracket (]), closing the block and telling REBOL to evaluate it. REBOL then gives you five random numbers between 0 and 100 and gives you back the command prompt.

You can stop input at any time by pressing the Escape key.

Viewing history

"Those who ignore history are doomed to repeat it," said someone famous. I believe it was my history teacher in high school.

REBOL has several ways of letting you know what has gone on before, at least during this particular session of REBOL.

First, you can scroll back up through the screen and see all your results. On a GUI (Graphical User Interface) system such as Windows, Macintosh, X-Windows on Unix/Linux, and so forth, do this by using the tab on the scroll bar (which is usually at the far right of your screen). You can also use the page up and page down keys to go up and down and see all that has transpired. Pressing the Enter key at any time returns you to the current console command line.

A second method enables you to see which commands you've entered recently and execute them again, if you like. Use the up and down arrows on your keyboard. The difference in this method is that you are actually changing the command line instead of just looking at past input and output; too, you are only seeing commands, and not output. Simply pressing the Enter key executes whatever is currently on the command line.

A third way enables you to retrieve all history in the current session and even save it as a file for later reference. To save it, use

```
save %history.r system/console/history
```

This makes use of another of those handy words (variables) in the system object that was mentioned earlier. And you can reload it by

```
system/console/history: load %history.r
```

The significance of these two operations is that you could save your current session's history and load it again during your next session. In fact, you could add these two lines to your user.r file and have a history buffer that spans multiple sessions.

 Customizing REBOL's operation is a great idea. However, the user.r file is not the safest place to keep all these marvelous customizations that you spent so long in creating. Each time the set-user function is invoked, the user.r file is overwritten and you lose your changes. I put all my changes in a file called myuser.r, and then just include it with do %myuser.r line. This line can be either in user.r or rebol.r. More on this later.

Busy indicator

The *busy indicator* is a string of characters that show on the console one after the other in a rudimentary form of animation while REBOL is busy with a task. The default string is |/-\ and these give the appearance of a rotating bar. To see the busy indicator at work, read in a Web page or anything else that may keep REBOL occupied for a few moments, such as

```
read http://rebol.com
```

and note the little revolving bar beneath the command line you just typed.

As with most console items in REBOL, you can customize its appearance easily by simply changing a variable in the system object — in this case, system/console/busy. This change, as with saving the prompt, only holds for the current session unless you redefine it by a statement in user.r or rebol.r.

Changing the busy indicator is fun. Try these. The first is courtesy of the REBOL *User's Guide;* the others are just my playing:

```
system/console/busy: "123456789-"
system/console/busy: ".:oOOo:."
system/console/busy: "_ - = ' ' = - _"
```

The busy indicator does not appear if you start REBOL with the quiet option (rebol -q or rebol --quiet).

Pressing special keys

The following table, Table 2-1, presents some special keys useful in REBOL console operations:

Table 2-1	Console Special Keys
Action	*Result*
Delete	Remove current character.
Escape	Halt an operation.
Page Up	Scroll display down one page (GUI versions).
Page Down	Scroll display up one page (GUI versions).
Up arrow	Recall prior command from the history block.
Down arrow	Recall next command from the history block.
Left arrow	Move the cursor left one character.
Right arrow	Move the cursor right one character.
Home	Move the cursor to the head of the line.
End	Move the cursor to the tail of the line.

Using advanced console operations

Most of the advanced console features came about only recently, with the release of REBOL 2.3. REBOL Technologies describes these features as providing "virtual terminal" capability: in effect, operations such as cursor movement, cursor addressing, line editing, screen clearing, control key input, and cursor position querying. These improvements also mean that the console style is more standard in appearance on platforms such as Windows 95/98/NT/2000 and upped the efficiency of operation, making it several times faster.

Cursor control sequences now adhere to the ANSI (American National Standards Institute) standard. This means you have the capability to write terminal programs such as text editors, e-mail clients, Telnet emulators, games, and others that run on an incredibly wide range of computer systems. REBOL Technologies calls this platform-independent; so do I, and so will you. It's all pretty awesome.

These advance console features apply both to input and output. For input, special control keys are converted to multiple-character escape sequences. *Escape sequences* are simply the escape character — represented in REBOL scripts as ^(1B) (a 27 decimal or 1B hex character) — followed by left bracket ([), and then followed by a series of letters and/or numbers that cause the cursor to move in a pre-defined manner. You know, like up or down or sideways. It's nothing complicated but still allows some powerful uses in your scripts.

Table 2-2 shows some of these sequences. Please note that escape sequences are case sensitive; so use them exactly as shown (that is, with uppercase letters).

Table 2-2	Keyboard Escape Sequences
Key	*^(1B[+ letter*
UP	A
DOWN	B
RIGHT	C
LEFT	D
HOME	1~
INSERT	2~
END	4~
PG UP	5~
PG DN	6~

You may specify how many spaces to move in any given direction. This is illustrated in Table 2-3, which shows terminal sequences. You can even move the cursor to a particular point on your screen, such as Row 1, Column 1 — this indicates the uppermost left or left hand corner position.

Table 2-3	Terminal Output Sequences
^(1B) [	*Use This Escape Code Prior to The Following Codes*
D	Moves cursor one space left.
C	Moves cursor one space right.
A	Moves cursor one space up.
B	Moves cursor one space down.

(continued)

Table 2-3 *(continued)*

Using ^(1B) [Prior to	Use This Escape Code Prior to The Following Codes
n D	Moves cursor *n* spaces left.
n C	Moves cursor *n* spaces right.
n	Moves cursor *n* spaces up.
n B	Moves cursor *n* spaces down.
r; c H	Moves cursor to row *r*, column *c*.
H	Moves cursor to top-left corner (home).
P	Deletes one character to the right at current location.
n P	Deletes *n* characters to the right at current location.
@	Inserts one blank space at current location.
n @	Inserts *n* blank spaces at current location.
J	Clears screen and moves cursor to top-left corner (home).
K	Clears from current position to end of current line.
6*n*	Places the current cursor position in the input buffer.
7*n*	Places screen dimensions in the input buffer.

Here are some examples of controlling cursor movements from within a REBOL script:

```
print "^(1B)[20A Hello world!"     ; move 20 down
print "^(1B)[20B Hello world!"     ; move 20 up
print "^(1B)[20C Hello world!"     ; move 20 right
print "^(1B)[10;10H Hello World"   ; position 10,10
```

By the way, a semicolon (;) character serves to add comments to lines of REBOL code, as I've just done.

In the preceding examples, I left a space for readability between the end of the escape sequence and the beginning of the message, "Hello world!" But you don't have to leave this space, and, naturally, leaving the space there causes a space to be printed.

Here's a more sophisticated example of escape sequences? Check on my little dancing lady on the CD-ROM as 4-dancelady.r. I omit the code here because of space limitations, but the following is what you see on REBOL's console screen. She does have some moves.

```
>> do %2-dancelady.r
Script: "The Dance Lady" ("13-Jan-2000")

           Presenting the exotic
              MS. ASCII REBOLI


                .#H#.
              (_#*_*#_
        -----/__\-)----
            _/  /_

           **applause**applause***

           Next Show 10 p.m.
>>
```

And, as an added bonus, an entire escape sequencing chorus line — the REBOL City Music Hall REBOLettes! Check out `2-chorusline.r`. It's also shown in Figure 2-1. Enjoy!

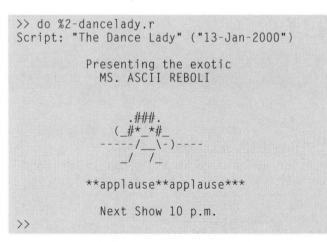

Figure 2-1:
The Dance
Lady and
the REBOL
City Music
Hall
REBOLettes
demonstrate
live escape
sequence
action.

Finding Help

Availability of help for REBOL grows almost daily. In addition to this book, REBOL Technologies provides three types of help you can access with your computer:

- Your own computer
- An extensive Web site
- A mailing list to subscribe to so you can ask questions of those guys and gals out there in the real-world programming trenches

Getting immediate console help

Help is available from within the REBOL console, and it's an immediate kind of online help. If you're not sure what a function does, or perhaps you're a little hazy on its arguments or other syntax, just type the word **help** in front of the function's name, as shown here:

```
>> help loop
Evaluates a block a specified number of times.
Arguments:
    count -- Number of repetitions (integer)
    block -- Block to evaluate (block)
```

This may not look, at first blush, like a tremendous amount of help. But consider: All this help is contained within REBOL and the whole executable file is less than 200K. It's not overly verbose. (Sparse is the word here, eh?) Yet this is more than enough to jog your memory once you are familiar with a function. For example, take loop, which does exactly what the word implies — it circles around a set number of times (Number of repetitions in the code just above), and evaluates a block (Block to evaluate in the code just above) each time, like this:

```
loop 10 [print "test "]
```

Should this type of minimal help still be unclear, you have several choices coming up for more detailed explanations. And, hey, you got this book, right?

You can even create your own functions and document them in the same manner. For instance:

```
test: func ["This prints the word TEST."][print "TEST"]
```

This line of code creates a REBOL function word named `test`. Typing **test** at the console prompt causes the word TEST to be printed. Give it a try. Once it works, type **help test** and you get

```
>> help test
This prints the word TEST.
```

Although this type of help may be sparse, you can get longer blobs of data from the console. For example, type the word **license** and REBOL returns the legal terms under which its use is licensed to you.

Or (less boring and more useful) check out the word `source`. This handy function enables you to actually look at the source code for some of REBOL's built-in functions; this is an excellent learning tool. Here's one of the shorter ones, the `what-dir` function word, which tells you what the current directory is:

```
>> source what-dir
what-dir: func [
    "Prints the active directory path"
][system/script/path
]
```

Hmmm. Exceptionally simple, they are just reading a variable from the system object. But, guess what? Now you know what's variable, and it may just come in handy from time to time.

Accessing extended help

REBOL Technologies provides several help files with REBOL right in the distribution. Two of these, `setup.html` and `notes.html`, you see right off. Just access them with your Web browser to read. To build this documentation, just make sure that your REBOL directory is the current one and type `do %rebdoc.r`:

```
>>do %rebdoc.r
Script: "REBOL Document Generator" (14-Jul-1999/18:38:41)
== { <i>(accepts: char number money time tuple)</i>
    Rebdoc has completed compiling the online documentation.
        View rebdoc.h...
>>
```

REBOL builds `rebdoc.html`, which you can then access with your browser.

The next place for help is the REBOL Technology Web site at `http://rebol.com/docs.html`. Several great resources may be accessed from this page — the *User's Guide,* the *REBOL/Core Dictionary for 2.2.0,* and a *How-To Guide* being the most important.

Subscribing to the mailing list

The online REBOL community is extremely helpful and a tremendously good place to get all the latest news and rumors. It's free, too! Join up right from within REBOL by typing

```
send list@rebol.com "subscribe"
```

If you followed the instructions in the appendix and set up your e-mail address using `set-user`, REBOL sends a message and subscribes you to the list.

Other offline help

Offline help for REBOL — in the form of books and articles — is growing in availability. (A REBOL underground? Why not?) You must have felt the need for such help, or some mystical urging to do battle with evil empires, when you bought this book. Thank you; the REBOLution wants you.

Sending feedback

REBOL Technologies wants to hear from you, and the folks there have made it easy. Typing the `feedback` function word from the console gives you the following choices:

```
>> feedback
Script: "Feedback Submitter" (13-Jan-1999)

FEEDBACK CATEGORY
====================
1 > Bug report
2 > General Question
3 > Enhancement idea
4 > Comment/Praise
5 > Documentation note
6 > Other
7 > Quit

->
```

Type in your choice, and you're guided through sending an e-mail for the chosen topic.

Upgrading

To upgrade your current version of REBOL to the most recent, make sure you are connected to the Internet and type **upgrade** at the REBOL console. That's all you have to do. REBOL determines whether a new version is available for your platform and, if so, downloads it automatically for you.

If you watch the action on-screen, it looks like this:

```
>> upgrade
connecting to: www.rebol.com
Script: "Download Current Version" (15-Nov-
        1999/16:40:23-8:00)
Your copy of Windows 95/98/NT iX86 REBOL 2.3.0.3.1 is
        currently up-to-date.
```

Upgrades for REBOL — like the program itself — are free. (If this be freedom, REBOL in it!)

Part II
Basic Training

The 5th Wave   By Rich Tennant

"I guess you could say this is the hub of our network."

In this part . . .

As boot camps go, this one feels more like a walk in a good old pair of sneakers. The basics of REBOL show up in the company of stalwart friends: the humor that can help save a programmer's hash and a good many practical examples. You can use some of these little gems of code immediately. In writing programming books, I believe you cannot have too many actual working examples of code (as long as they work, that is).

Chapter 3

Starring in Your Own Scripts

· ·

In This Chapter

▶ Creating and editing scripts (adventures in literalism)

▶ Structuring scripts

▶ Stacking blocks to build scripts

▶ Commenting your code for posterity (and sanity)

▶ Using the REBOL style guide

· ·

A movie *script* tells actors what to say, when to say it, and what expression and/or action should accompany the words. A REBOL script is no different in concept; it shows REBOL what to tell your computer to do.

"Okay, REBOL, in this scene your motivation is an anxiety to produce a list of this company's current inventory. So get in there and show me some database record retrieving and sorting. Lights! Camera! Hit *Enter!*. . . ."

Unlike actors, REBOL follows your script exactly and does not ad lib, improvise, throw tantrums over "artistic" interpretation, nor even mispronounce the stirring text you create. Of course, the catch is that computer programs have no imagination; they're literalists. If you make a little mistake, or your flying fingers drop in a wee typo, even these miscues are faithfully executed. We human beings have a name for what happens next: *errors*. From the computer's point of view, it's only doing exactly what it's told. Fortunately, of course, most of us programmers *never* make errors in our work. (Yeah, right.)

Well, okay, just for the sake of thoroughness, I should tell you the word for finding and correcting errors in computer programs — *debugging*. But you never need *that* word again — and yep, Mickey Mouse is a shoe-in for president this next election. Well, that last part may be true; stranger things happen all the time. For instance. . . .

A story comes to mind that emphasizes this point (REBOL doing exactly as you say, not the nuances of Mr. Mouse's politics). Back in 1968, during my army days, I attended OCS (Officers Candidate School) in the snake-infested swamps and mosquito-infected piney woods still known as Fort Benning, Georgia.

One morning, after I'd been kept us up all night (literally!) for tactical training, I was in charge of marching the company off to yet another exercise. With my mind befuddled from lack of sleep, I yelled out, "Column left!" when *right* would have been the correct direction. There was an irregular series of thumps as the front rank of the formation (just as sleep-deprived as I was) hit the side of a barracks.

So, who was in trouble? Perhaps me, for my error that ran several candidates into a wall? After all, the participants — including the wall itself — were the property of the United States Army; I was damaging military property. But was that held against me? Nope. I was in the clear — this was the army, remember? The guys who got in trouble (and who quickly dropped for push-ups) were the ones in the front rank — *because they didn't hit the wall all at the same time.* In the army, you follow orders.

REBOL follows orders, too, doing exactly what it's told, and just as rigidly. Yell "Column left!" and, *whump,* the program crashes.

That's what this chapter is primarily about — how to give REBOL orders (scripting) without running it into a barracks wall. And, speaking of the army, one way to give appropriate orders is to be (ahem) *uniform* in your coding. Fortunately, REBOL Technologies offers suggested styles for scripts that should get you off on the right foot. (Or is that *left?* Right? Left . . . ? Never mind.)

Creating and Editing Scripts

So how about those orders? Exactly what *is* a REBOL script? It's nothing more exotic than a plain old text file (at least at first). As in Perl (and other *interpretive* languages), REBOL reads the file, interprets all those lines of code as instructions, and takes action (appropriate or not) based on what it thinks you told it to do. Even if it hits the wall running.

In REBOL, scripts have a certain *structure* — a set of required items — so that the file can be recognized as containing legitimate (or even illegitimate) commands or data. I show you this structure in a moment, but first, a look at the bedrock under the basics of script files.

Creating text files for REBOL scripts

You need to know a little to make sure that the REBOL script files you create are really text files. Again, you can use any editing software that can read and write standard (ASCII) text files.

Perhaps the biggest (and commonest) mistake made when someone begins programming is writing scripts in a word processing program. Even if the word processing software can save a document as a text file, it may also do weird wrapping (and other mischief to the lines of code) that can induce errors.

Get yourself a good programmer's editing program. Unlike word processing programs, such an editor saves files in various text formats (line endings) that makes them easy to transfer between differing systems such as Windows and Unix. I show you more about line endings later, and the neat way REBOL handles them. For now, realize that different operating systems use different formats to end lines. This means that if you move a file over from one computer to another, it won't read properly.

A programmer's editor helps by saving in the correct format for the target system. It also lets you keep track of your script by automatically indenting, showing line numbers, and using other standard ways of arranging and formatting the text that makes up your code.

My favorite text editor is the one doing a cameo in Figure 3-1. It's available as shareware for only $25 from http://gwdsoft.com. It makes REBOL scripts a breeze to turn out.

Figure 3-1:
It may not look fancy, but a good programmer's editor is the coder's best friend.

```
25  print "</b>A sampling of six random listings from <i><b>The Sanders Price Guide to Autographs
26  print "Order the book today at <b>1-800-472-0438</b> or email <a href='mailto:sales@abooks.c
27  print "<font face='Arial' size='2'><b>sigs</b> = <i>signature</i>,"
28  print "<b>ls/ds</b> = <i>letter or document signed</i>,<br>"
29  print "<b>als</b> = <i>autograph letter signed</i> (i.e. all in the celebrity's hand),"
30  print "<b>sp</b> = <i>signed photograph</i>.<br>"
31
32       print {<tr bgcolor='yellow'><td><font face='Arial' size='2'>NAME</td><td><font face='Ar
33       print {LS/DS</td><td><font face='Arial' size='2'>ALS</td><td><font face='Arial' size=
34
35
36       repeat number 6 [
37
38            print "<tr><td><font face='Arial' size='2'>"
39            line: pick b number
40            c: parse/all line "^-"
41            repeat count (length? c) [
42                   if (pick c count) = "" [insert (pick c count) "-"]
43            ]
44            comment: c/8
45            if comment = none [comment: "-"]
46            sigs: c/4 if sigs <> "-" [sigs: to-money sigs]
47            lsds: c/5 if lsds <> "-" [lsds: to-money lsds]
48            als: c/6 if als <> "-" [als: to-money als]
49            sp: c/7 if sp <> "-" [sp: to-money sp]
50
51            print [c/1 "</td><td><font face='Arial' size='2'>"]
52            print [c/2 "</td><td><font face='Arial' size='2'>" c/3 "</td><td align='right
53            print [sigs "</td><td align='right'>" lsds "</td><td align='right'>"]
54            print [als "</td><td align='right'>" sp "</td><td><font face='Arial' size='2
55
```

Formatting the file that holds the script

At base, a REBOL script is a plain old text file with two qualities that give it big ambitions: its format and its structure. *Format* (a word with many meanings in techie lingo) refers to the type of file that contains a REBOL script. *Structure* refers to the internal arrangement of the text that makes up the script itself.

Okay, technically you can use any word processor (or other text-editing program) to create a REBOL script; just make sure the program can save files in plain text format (with a .TXT extension). For the sake of convenience and efficiency, however, a programming editor is usually a better tool to use.

If you run across several sermonettes on the importance of line endings in text files as you explore this book, it isn't déjà vu; the point bears repeating. Most beginning programmers assume that a text file is a text file is a text file — whether it is on an Amiga, Mac, Windows machine, or Unix/Linux platform. Not so! Different formats of so-called "plain text" files can put the devil into the details in no time. One such detail is how lines of code are terminated.

Amiga, Linux, and Unix operating systems all use line feeds (LF) as line terminators. Macintosh files have carriage returns (CR). And Windows/DOS has both line feeds *and* carriage returns (LF and CR) lurking among its commands.

Ignoring small details — such as line endings appropriate for the system that actually uses the data files you create — can cause big trouble later. REBOL can help you a lot but it can't read your mind.

Fortunately, you don't have to memorize all the different line endings that work for every operating system on the planet. REBOL itself helps you ensure that the text file (REBOL script) you're creating is appropriate for the system destined to run it. The magic command looks like this:

```
write %file read %file
```

If you have to transfer REBOL files to a different system, this same command comes in handy; it helps ensure REBOL creates output files with the correct line endings.

Using the right file suffix

REBOL script files normally have an .r suffix, so that REBOL will know this is a script it should interpret and run. A *suffix* is the letters and/or numbers following the period (dot) in filenames. On systems in which the .r suffix is otherwise in use, .reb may be substituted. These two suffixes are just convenient naming conventions. REBOL actually looks at a file with any suffix and, if it has the proper structure, treats it as a script file. I suggest that you use the .r suffix for your scripts. This enables you and others to readily find a particular REBOL script (or recognize one you've found).

Filenames are one of REBOL's standard values. The percent sign (%) is used in scripts to designate that what immediately follows is a filename. Script names in REBOL look like this:

```
%wherefrom.r
%datamangler.r
%myprogram.r
```

Structuring the Scripts

The body of a REBOL script requires only that lines of code, when evaluated by REBOL, do not cause errors. The REBOL manual calls this "free form." I won't go quite that far myself, but you certainly can pretty much apply your own ideas of indentation and spacing. Use whatever helps you in visually making clear to yourself and others how the script works.

It pays to keep lines under 65 characters wide. Otherwise, they can wrap if you send the script via e-mail to someone. An excessive character count can also cause errors because of literal values, such as quoted strings being broken. Besides, your code is a lot easier for you and others to read without extremely long lines.

Here are some basic rules of REBOL script structure:

- A header must be present.
- Lines should be less than 65 characters wide for ease of reading and exchanging via such medium as e-mail.
- Files should be standard text files.

Although REBOL has few restrictions in the way that you code, REBOL Technologies does promote an overall style of coding. A *style* is simply a list that describes how code should appear in a text file, including how to indent, what should be indented, and so forth. This suggested consistency promotes the exchange of human-readable code. At the conclusion of this chapter, I discuss this guideline that promotes consistency.

Heading up REBOL

In the REBOL documentation, the word *evaluatable* is used to describe a script that REBOL recognizes as one that contains functions and data that it can act upon. *Executable* also refers to such a file, although the latter should not be confused with file permissions, as on Unix/Linux platforms (more about those in Chapter 9). Perhaps even better than those two words is *recognizable.*

In short, REBOL looks in a file, sees a header that tells it this is a REBOL file, and proceeds to run or evaluate the functions and data in the file. The name of the file is immaterial because REBOL doesn't care if it is an .r file or not (that naming convention is just for human convenience); it just looks for a header. Here is the minimum REBOL header:

```
REBOL []
```

This minimal header is simply the word REBOL in all caps and an empty block. This is enough, when at the top of the file, to cause REBOL to evaluate the file as a script. For the interpreter to recognize the header, the block must follow immediately after the word REBOL. Only whitespace (spaces, tabs, and lines) are permitted between these two elements.

A header, then, is just a block of text in a standard format at the start of the file. This block may contain such data as script name, author, date, version, filename, rights, purpose, instructions for running, and anything else that the author considers worthwhile. Here's a header from one of my scripts:

```
REBOL [
    Title:    "ALIEN NAMES Generator"
    Date:     "Oct-31-1999"
    Name:     "Alien Names"
    Version: 2.0.8
    File:     %aliennames.r
    Home:     http://abooks.com/alien
    Author:   "Ralph Roberts"
    e-mail:   "ralph@abooks.com"
    Owner:    "Creativity, Inc."
    Rights:   "Copyright (c)1999, 2000 Creativity, Inc."
    Tabs:     4
    Language: 'English
    Charset: 'ANSI
    Purpose: { ...purpose of script...}
    Comment: { ...text describing development of script... }
]
```

You can put any information you want into a header — simply define it as a regular REBOL variable. Headers do more than just make a text file recognizable as a script to REBOL. An object included automatically with your script's header information offers other scripts a way to generate script directories and cross-references. In addition, the interpreter uses the header for configuration, options, and attributes of the script.

For example, I use the information in the header in my aliennames.r script (as shown in the preceding header example) by accessing the system/script/

`header` system object value that is created when the script is run. Here are some examples:

```
print system/script/header/title
print system/script/header/date
print system/script/header/purpose
print system/script/header/comment
```

Prefacing and embedding scripts

You don't have to place a script's header at the exact top of the file. REBOL scripts may be either *prefaced* (as information preceding the script) or *embedded* (the script is placed in the middle of other information, such as e-mail messages or Web pages). REBOL scans the file for the header and evaluates code from that point on.

REBOL skips any preface material that appears before the header. That means you can put comments, e-mail headers, HTML tags, and so forth in preface material, and REBOL won't mistake that stuff for a value it must use.

Here is how an embedded script may look in an e-mail message:

```
This program kills two stones with one bird, so to speak. It
        shows you how to retrieve information from the
        script header object REBOL creates, and it shows
        an embedded script.

[

REBOL [
        Title: "Get Header Info"
        File: %5-getheaderinfo.r
        Author: "Ralph Roberts"
        Date: 20-Feb-2000
        Purpose: "Example of embedding in REBOL FOR DUMMIES"
        ]

        header: system/script/header

        foreach word next first header [
                print rejoin [word ":" tab tab get in header
                word]
                ]

]

Some more text following the embedded script. Be sure the
        entire REBOL script is enclosed within a block as
        shown,
that is totally within brackets.
```

When running the preceding script, note that it includes some standard items that you did not define; these have the definition of none.

When I discuss the manipulation of objects, you see ways in which you can go back into headers in REBOL and modify them. For example, you may write a script that goes through every REBOL script in a directory and updates copyright information.

Stacking Blocks to Build Scripts

When I was a tiny little boy (as opposed, I suppose, to being a large fat man today), I loved to play with blocks. I remember them well . . . smooth wooden blocks with a large capital letter on each, in mixed colors of green, blue, and red. I could make forts with them, spell out words (mostly by accident in those early days and sometimes, too, in these later days), and do all sorts of fun stuff.

Well, times have not changed that much — I still play with blocks a lot because blocks are fundamental to the way REBOL works. Blocks are used in REBOL for creating databases, directories, tables, sets, sequences, code, functions, and all sorts of series of related values. Once you understand blocks, you write scripts doing pretty much anything you like.

More details about blocks will follow but, in essence, REBOL considers all data as being contained in a block. When a script is loaded and evaluated, the script's data is loaded as elements within a block and evaluated as such. You can nest blocks — put blocks inside blocks inside blocks inside blocks — as deep as you like.

Here are some REBOL blocks:

```
colors: ["red" "blue" "purple" "gold"]
if x = 3 [print "X is equal to three."]
```

And a set of nested blocks:

```
alphabetblocks: [
                wood: ["A" "B"]
                plastic: ["R" "T" "3"]
                style [
            large: ["shiny" "dull"]
            small: ["smooth" "rough"]
                ]
                ]
```

You can save yourself a lot of debugging time and crashing scripts by simply making sure that all blocks have properly paired left and right brackets ([ ]). Otherwise, REBOL errors out because a block is not correctly structured.

Commenting Your Code

Many languages provide a way to embed comments or explanations inside code. In REBOL, there are two ways to do this.

One, you can use a semicolon (;) and everything in a line following the semicolon isn't evaluated. It looks like this:

```
print first a        ; print the first item in a
if x = 2 [print x]   ; if x is equal to 2, print x
load %data.r         ; load data
```

Or, for comments requiring more than one line, do it this way:

```
comment { The use of the REBOL function word 'comment'
          causes the following value to be ignored.}
```

Note that there is no colon after comment, as if you were defining a variable. Once REBOL encounters the function word comment, it just ignores the following block or string of data, but the block does need to be enclosed in brackets ([]), or the string in quotes (" ") or braces ({}).

One great use for the comment word is in temporarily deactivating large sections of code for debugging purposes:

```
comment [ ... several lines of code ... ]
```

This is a great tool for helping you quickly isolate the section of your script that has an error and then correcting it.

Compare the ease of longer comments in REBOL with that of other languages. Take Perl specifically: long, awkward constructions using several lines of text are common, each preceded by a pound sign (#) — which require an often-annoying breaking of lines to keep text readable. This is not required in REBOL.

Using human-readable code (comments)

REBOL code is much like plain English; it skips the extraneous punctuation and other such hieroglyphics that clutter other languages. But don't let its clarity lull you into thinking that it *is* plain English. *Comments* — friendly explanations that the machine ignores but its users might desperately need — are still a fine idea.

I recommend that you make liberal use of comments. Others who try to figure out your wonderful code will bless you. And if you look at your script six months after you write it (having not looked at it in the meantime), you'll bless yourself. For example, a command that looks like this in code (with its comment to the right of the semicolon)

```
print pi * (radius * radius)  ; area of a circle
```

. . . looks like this on-screen:

```
>> print pi
3.14159265358979
```

By the way, REBOL has the mathematical constant pi built in.

Writing documentation

Yes, putting comments in your code may someday save civilization as we know it. Nevertheless, however stingy or liberal their occurrence, comments by themselves are still a far cry from complete documentation. *Documentation* is the writing of separate text — in the form of help files, manuals (gasp!), or other text — explaining in detail how the script works, what sort of input it takes and the output it gives, its theory of operation, and anything else appropriate.

Whether you distribute your scripts to others or just use them yourself, good documentation saves a lot of head-scratching (or head-banging) later.

Using the REBOL Style Guide

REBOL Technologies stresses script style — and it is important. *Style* is the way something is constructed. When I started writing this book, my editor gave me a Word template file and said, "This is our *style*."

What she meant was that the template would show me how to start chapters, do bulleted lists, put in tips and warnings, insert figures, and all the other small items that give this and the other *For Dummies* books their consistency. Styles offer tremendous advantages for book publishing, because all the parts of each book use the same sets of word processing formats for (say) a normal paragraph or a bulleted list. That means an editor working on a book about gardening one day can edit a computer-programming book the next day — and expect to navigate both manuscripts efficiently.

This consistency is even more important in scripting, especially if you are exchanging scripts with others. Instead of looking at something weird, another person can at least recognize the parts of your script (even without reading all the comments that you, having read the earlier part of this chapter, diligently put in).

This is REBOL Technologies' thinking on the subject (with which I agree):

> "Although the formatting of your script does not make any difference in its interpretation, it will make an important difference in its human readability. Because of this, REBOL Technologies suggests a standard scripting style that has been developed over several years."

> "Of course, you don't have to follow any of these suggestions. However, script style is much more important than it first seems. It can make a big difference in the readability and reuse of scripts. Users may judge the quality of your script by the clarity of its style as sloppy scripts often mean sloppy code. Experienced script writers usually find that a clean, consistent style makes their code easier to produce, maintain, and revise."

Sloppy code? Me? Nah. Well, maybe some. But if I (and you) adhere to the REBOL Technologies style guidelines, our code will look much better and be easier to exchange.

Formatting the REBOL way

In REBOL, the standard tab equals four spaces. However — because people use so many different editors and viewers — REBOL Technologies suggests that you use spaces *instead* of tabs, converting files by replacing tabs with spaces before posting or sending them to someone else.

Here's a quick way to do it by using REBOL's detab function, which changes all tab characters to four spaces:

```
write %file.r detab read %file.r
```

The preceding code reads a file, converts every tab to four spaces, and writes the file back to disk. Just that easy, the conversion is complete.

Continuing with format, REBOL Technologies wants the contents of a block indented, but the block's enclosing brackets ([]) are not indented. That's because the brackets belong to the prior level of syntax ; they define the block, but are not contents of the block. Also, as REBOL Technologies points out, it's easier to spot breaks between adjacent blocks when the brackets stand out.

When possible, the opening bracket remains on the line with its associated expression. The closing bracket may be followed by more expressions of that same level. These same rules apply equally to parentheses and braces ({}). Here are the examples that REBOL Technologies provides in the *User's Guide:*

```
if check [do this and that]

if check [
    do this and do that
    do another thing
    do a few more things
]

either check [do something short][
    do something else]

either check [
    when an expression extends
    past the end of a block...
][
    this helps keep things
    straight
]

while [
    do a longer expression
    to see if it's true
][
    the end of the last block
    and start of the new one
    are at the WHILE level
]

adder: func [
    "This is an example function"
    arg1 "this is the first arg"
    arg2 "this is the second arg"
][
    arg1 + arg2
]

An exception is made for some types of expressions that
            normally belong on a single line but may extend to
            the next line:

if (this is a long conditional expression that
    breaks over a line and is indented
)[
    so this looks a bit odd
]
```

This also applies to grouped values that belong together but must be wrapped to fit on the line:

```
[
    "Hitachi Precision Focus" $1000 10-Jul-1999
        "Computers Are Us"

    "Nuform Natural Keyboard" $70 20-Jul-1999
        "The Keyboard Store"
]
```

Creating standardized word names

Words are used in REBOL as the names of both functions and variables. Wherever possible, REBOL Technologies recommends that the words should relate to their English or other common human language equivalent in a simple, direct way.

Here are guidelines for naming words in REBOL.

- ✔ **Use the shortest word that communicates the meaning.**
    - Short, crisp words are best.
    - Examples: size; time; send; wait; make; quit.
- ✔ **Hyphenate multiple-word names to make them more readable.**
    - Examples: group-name; image-file; clear-screen; bake-cake.
- ✔ **Begin function names with a verb.**
    - Examples: make; print; scan; find; find-age; rake-coals.
- ✔ **Data words begin with a noun.**
    - Examples: image sound; file; image-files; start-time.
- ✔ **Use standardized names for similar functions.**
    - Examples: make-newitem; init-newitem; save-newitem.
- ✔ **Use whole words where possible; avoid abbreviations.**

Putting all the right stuff in script headers

I discuss script headers earlier in this chapter and the importance of providing clear, useable information in them. REBOL Technologies emphasizes that as a matter of style, a *minimum header* should include a title, date, filename, and purpose. Other fields can also be provided — such as author, notes, usage, needs, and so forth.

```
REBOL [
    Title: "Store Inventory Lister"
    Date:  11-Dec-2000
    File:  %inventory-lister.r
    Purpose: {
        Print a catalog list of current stock.
    }
]
```

Making informative function headers

Functions let you add a *header* — a description that becomes part of the function — and you should do this for all the functions you write.

```
dir: func [
    "Get a sorted list of the current directory."
][
    files: print sort read %.
]
```

With a description, online help is always available for the function, assuming it is loaded, by typing **help dir**.

Selecting script filenames

Name a file with the idea of finding it easily weeks or months later. Short, clear names are usually the best. Avoid plurals when possible. Names should be as descriptive as possible while remaining short. Consider how they may appear sorted in a directory and take that into consideration. Check out these examples:

```
%store-inventory.r
%store-sales.r
%store-special.r
```

Including files

REBOL Technologies suggests including the names of required files and user-defined functions within the header of a script. Don't assume that people have any of the same functions in their included files (such as user.r).

Embedding examples

Also, when appropriate, provide examples within a script to show how it operates. Nothing is more frustrating, especially when you are first learning a language, than to see a bunch of code with no idea of what it does. Show people your thinking. You could include something like this in your header:

```
...
Output: {This code creates random, pronounceable
         passwords such as these:
         Boppax Peqqix Chushshub Civvef Doththo}
...
```

Debugging embedded code

It is often useful, REBOL Technologies also says, to build in debugging functions as part of the script — especially in the case of networking and file-handling code (when it may not be desirable to send and write files while running in a test mode). Such tests can be enabled with a control variable at the head of the script, like this:

```
verbose: on
check-data: off
```

Minimizing globals

Although most of the scripts you initially write are small, it's not too soon to start thinking big. REBOL Technologies suggests that in large scripts (and anywhere possible), you should avoid global variables that carry internal state from one module or function to another.

If you have a collection of global variables that are closely related, consider using an object to keep track of them, as in this example:

```
user: make object! [
    name:  "Fred Dref"
    age:   94
    phone: #707-555-1234
    e-mail: dref@fred.dom
]
```

And this is how you get information out of the object when it's called for:

```
>> print user/name
Fred Dref
>> print user/age
94
>> print user/phone
707-555-1234
>> print user/email
dref@fred.dom
```

All this simplicity can be habit-forming. That's the idea.

Chapter 4

REBOL's Family Values

A *value* is data.

Everything in REBOL is data.

Data is information communicating something to a computer or to one of us humans.

REBOL Technologies defines this bedrock concept of its language as so:

> *Communication is an exchange of data through a set of values in a form the receiver understands.*

This is the essence of REBOL and why it's called a *messaging,* or communications, language. It doesn't matter whether the communication is between two people, a person and a computer, or two computers. Communication is based on common definitions for specific values. Otherwise the content is lost, and the receiver gets a meaningless jumble of stuff that hardly resembles data.

Let me repeat for the sake of emphasis: Everything in REBOL is data. Variables, function words, and complete REBOL scripts all are just data and handled as such. This chapter is about the different kinds of data REBOL recognizes, so it's really about everything in REBOL.

Putting Values to Work

If you consider a bullet as an individual member of a collective entity called "ammunition," then you can also consider a value as an individual piece of data or information. The term *datatype* refers to the kind of data contained in a value, such as currency amounts, time, date, decimal numbers, integers, and a string of letters and numbers. REBOL recognizes and acts on data in its natural form, such as integers (whole numbers). Some datatypes (for example, date) can work with alternate forms of the same data (say, as July-4-2000 or 4-Jul-2000 or 7-4-2000). REBOL treats such small differences in format transparently. Example? Sure. Coming right up.

Tinkering with datatypes

REBOL works its magic with several types of numerical values — currency, time, date, decimals, integers, strings, and so forth — also called *scalar datatypes.* When you've become an old hand at scalar, you can create your own datatypes. But first things first.

Using scalar datatypes

Well, no, that isn't what you get when you let your pet lizard do your data entry. The word *scalar* means that you can use these datatypes to form more complex data by combining a series of steps (like the rungs of a ladder). Consider the following example:

```
>> print [4-Jul-2000 - now/date "days to fireworks show."]
134 days to fireworks show
```

In this example, a fireworks aficionado used the date scalar datatype to determine how many days remained until the Independence Day celebration. Here's how the command hangs together:

✔ Using the date datatype enabled REBOL to recognize the value 4-Jul-2000 as a date value. Then REBOL could act on the value accordingly (in this case, by subtracting today's date).

✔ The now function word (one of REBOL's built-in functions) returns the current time as kept by the system clock.

✔ The /date refinement tells the now function to return the current date and not to bother with hours and minutes.

Thus the now/date part of the command line tells REBOL, "Plug in the value for today's date and then subtract it from 4-Jul-2000." No problem. Then the game gets interesting.

Creating do-it-yourself datatypes

If you want to change a datatype in REBOL, you can construct your own functions that turn ordinary, mild-mannered datatypes into complex creations called constructed datatypes. These not only define a type of data, but they also include built-in functions that generate data to fit the definition. (What won't they think of next?) Here's an example that adds two numbers and then divides the result by two:

```
>> average: func ["average numbers" a b][divide (a + b) 2]
>> average 25 89
== 57
```

To create the datatype and its built-in function, follow these steps:

1. **At the REBOL console prompt, type in the first line of the example.**

   • This function (average) did not exist until you typed it in and pressed Enter, telling REBOL to evaluate the code.

2. **Type** average **and then type the two numbers that you want to average.**

   • Et voilà — you've created a constructed datatype named average.

Using this technique, you can construct sophisticated and specialized datatypes in REBOL — with almost ridiculous ease. And you can write these datatypes as small scripts that you can load whenever you want to use them. That's almost as good as having your own army of robot butlers, all of them made of data so you don't have to get a bigger garage. In fact, the most important point so far in this chapter is (all together, now): *Everything in REBOL is data.* (Catchy. Didn't know those robots could sing.)

REBOL operates by evaluating data, and if you grab a good handful of data and look closely at it, what you see is the values that make it up. So a script is just a set of values that REBOL evaluates — in the process, picking up its orders to return new values according to your code. Some of these new values may be functions, objects, or complex data structures.

Summing up (for sanity's sake)

If all these possibilities are starting to make the room spin, remember the REBOL mantra: *Everything in REBOL is data.* Repeat until calm. Then consider two delightfully simple facts:

✔ REBOL scripts are just values.

✔ The process of evaluation produces another value (a result) from the values that make up the script.

REBOL Technologies is aware that this concept may seem trivially simple, but hey, sometimes simple is good. In this case, simple is wonderful: REBOL excels at doing simple tasks simply (what a concept). This subversive approach makes REBOL much better for constructing complicated tasks than are many other programming languages. Programming may look like complex conjuration at first glance, but REBOL demonstrates the advantages of taking simple steps as you build your code.

Making datatype models

REBOL can recognize many different datatypes — and has a specific datatype model (format) for each one, which helps ensure proper recognition. This feature packs a bonus: If you find yourself so deep in the wilderness of code that you've lost track of exactly what type of data you're working with, use the type? function and REBOL tells you, like this:

```
>> type? "Now is the time for all good REBOLers to script."
== string!
>> type? 15890
== integer!
>> type? 26.546
== decimal!
>> type? $48.95
== money!
>> type? 11-Dec-2000
== date!
>> type? 9:30
== time!
```

Not only can you find out instantly what kind of creature your data must be, but you can also use make to convert one datatype to another (using the datatype name with an exclamation mark). Behold:

```
>> make money! 25.90
== $25.90
>> make time! [10 4 26]
== 10:04:26
>> make date [6 7 2000]
== 6-Jul-2000
>> make tuple! [198 168 0 1]
== 198.168.0.1
```

Now, that's within shouting distance of magic. The examples so far all require input at the console. You would more normally be acting on variables in scripts, as so:

```
pay: make money! (hours * hourlyrate)
ralph-email: make e-mail! (join "ralph" "@abooks.com")
```

Creating fundamental datatypes

This section is just loaded with brass tacks — the fundamental datatypes of REBOL, the ones with starring roles in the REBOL *User's Guide*. Values can be scalar or, when used to make other functions, constructed values. They may also be divided between scalars and series values. *Series values* hold a sequential collection of elements whether characters (string!, e-mail!, url!, and so forth), integers (tuple!), bits (binary!), or elements (block!, list!, hash!, and more).

Look at these values in these two tables. I take a closer look at them individually with examples later in the chapter. Here they are, scalars (in Table 4-1) and series (Table 4-2):

Table 4-1	Scalar Datatypes	
Datatype	*Description*	*Example*
integer!	Integer number	1234
decimal!	Floating-point number	12.34
time!	Duration or time of day	13:47:02
date!	Day, month, and year	30-June-1957
money!	Currency data (can have two components)	US$12.49
logic!	A value with two possible states	full: true empty: false
char!	Single character	#"A"
none!	Represents the "no value" or null state	none

Table 4-2	Series Datatypes	
Datatype	**Description**	**Example**
string!	Sequence of characters.	"Hello"
binary!	Binary data sequence.	2#{01101101011001 001101000110101001}
email!	Standard form of e-mail address.	info@rebol.com
file!	Filename.	%script.r
url!	URL.	http://www.rebol.com
issue!	Identifying number (as with phone, serial, or model numbers).	#707-467-8000 (phone number); #1234-5678-9012 (credit card number); #0987654321-09876 (serial number)
tuple!	Integers concatenated with decimals.	255.255.0.1 199.4.80.1
tag!	HTML or other markup-language tag.	<IMG SRC="foo.jpg" WIDTH=161 HEIGHT=58>
block!	Type of series with the values contained in square brackets.	[milk bread butter]
hash!	Looks like a block! but much faster to search; works the same as block! [milk bread butter]	to-hash [milk bread butter]
list!	Looks like a block! but its insert/delete operations are faster. CAUTION: Some list! operations differ from block! [milk bread butter]	to-list [milk bread butter]
paren!	Groups values in parentheses.	print (5 + 10) * 2 ;
path!	Refined specification of the root/sub function that identifies a command path.	to-path %/d/rebol

One important datatype is missing from these two tables, the word! datatype. Normally REBOL employs words as the names of specific functions or variables, which can be of many different datatypes. Think of words as a sort of super-datatype.

Using datatype classifications

In addition to the fundamental datatypes, some REBOL datatypes are pseudo-types. No, they're not full of fake data; a *pseudotype* is a definition that identi-fies other datatypes as subsets so that REBOL knows they're legit. For example, the number! pseudotype identifies the integer! and decimal! datatypes as both being logically true, as in these examples:

```
>> num: 14.678
== 14.678
>> type? num
== decimal!
>> number? num
== true
```

```
>> num: 12
== 12
>> type? num
== integer!
>> number? num
== true
```

Pseudotypes are pretty handy to have around. Let's say that you have a func-tion with an argument that can accept a number that's either a decimal or an integer. In such cases, use the number! pseudotype to tell REBOL what's going on. If you don't, you wind up having to specify both numbers, which means longer code and tired fingers. Consider this example, which uses number! to add a number to itself:

```
add2: func [a [number!]] [
    print add a a
    print type? a
]
```

And here are the results (may I have the virtual envelope, please?):

```
>> add2 12.4
24.8
decimal
```

```
>> add2 6
12
integer
```

Neatly handled, yes? Following are all REBOL pseudotypes and the datatypes
they identify. Note that *all* datatypes are identifiable with the `any-type!`
pseudotype. Just for your theoretical knowledge, here is a hierarchical classi-
fication of the current datatypes in REBOL:

```
any-type
    any-function
        function
        native
        action
        op
    any-word
        get-word
        lit-word
        set-word
        word
    char
    date
    logic
    money
    none
    number
        integer
        decimal
    object
        error
        refinement
        set-path
    series
        any-block
            block
            list
            hash
            paren
            path
        any-string
            binary
            e-mail
            file
            issue
            string
            symbol
            tag
            url
        bitset
        port
    time
    tuple
```

And finally, in a bid to cover an even wider range of datatype classifications, REBOL Technologies defines three special datatypes, which appear in Table 4-3.

Table 4-3	Special Types	
Type	_Purpose_	_Comment_
Function:	This datatype is for functions that are neither native datatypes nor operators.	Any function created with REBOL code is given the function! data type.
Native:	A built-in function, implemented in machine code.	Contrast the Native datatype with mezzanine functions (which are built in to the REBOL release and are themselves written in REBOL).
Op:	All infix operators are of this datatype. It permits infix to work.	Contrast this with normal functions prefix in nature; that is, the function name is stated before its arguments. Infix operators take their arguments from both before and after the operator name.

Now, with all the theoretical stuff out of the way, let's look at some practical definitions and uses of datatypes.

Choosing the Right Type of Value

One major advantage of REBOL is that it can handle values of different types directly. You don't have to create special declarations or jump through other hoops, loops, or do calisthenics just to get a datatype. Now that REBOL has made datatypes easier to create, it's worth having a closer look at its building blocks — values — the raw data that REBOL is made of.

Manipulating quantities

The datatypes in this section are all number-friendly; you can use quantities with any of them to determine all those bits of knowledge best expressed in numbers: how much, how long, how expensive, how many, and so on.

Counting on integers

Integers are childhood friends for most of us; they're the numbers everybody first learned to count (and astronauts count backward at launch time). Integers are whole numbers; they can't contain a decimal. (Whoever heard of counting 1, 2, 3.7, 4.859? . . . let's not even go there.) The integer! datatype in REBOL provides 32 bits of room to accommodate positive or negative whole numbers (from –2147483648 to 2147483647), or zero.

In format, integers are easy to recognize: Look for a series of digits, whether positive or negative, with no decimal, but the plus (+) or minus (–) sign must immediately precede the first number without any space. Here are some integers:

```
0  1234  +1234  -1234  00012  -0123
```

Long numbers cannot contain commas, as are sometimes included for the sake of readability. (REBOL seeks universality in its treatment of numbers; some countries use commas in place of decimals, so that's how REBOL reads commas.) You can use an apostrophe to make the number more human-readable, in any order you like, any place after the first number — REBOL still interprets the number (correctly) as an integer.

```
4'899'234'126
```

If REBOL finds a comma or period in an integer, it interprets the number as a decimal.

You can convert other datatypes to integers, using the to-integer function word, like this:

```
>> to-integer "486544"          ; a string value
== 486544
>> to-integer 106.04            ; a decimal value
== 106
```

Note that in this case, the part after the decimal was chopped off (truncated), which means you lose the decimal when you use this method of conversion.

Before you start converting datatypes, use the integer? function to test for integers. Integers that are out of the REBOL range (or those that can't be represented in 32 bits) return an error message when your scripts run.

Doing decimals

Decimal numbers in REBOL are standard, 64-bit floating-point numbers as defined by the good folks at Institute of Electrical and Electronic Engineers (IEEE). The point doing the floating is a decimal point, which is also the only difference between an integer and a decimal number.

Decimal values are a continuous series of numeric digits, followed by a period or comma, followed by more digits. A plus (+) or minus (–) sign may appear immediately before the first digit (no space betweeen) to indicate whether the number is positive or negative. If no sign appears, REBOL assumes that the number is positive; it also ignores any leading zeros that occur before the period or comma. REBOL is a bit of a stickler where decimals are concerned: No extra spaces, commas for formatting (I explain that in a second), or periods allowed. That makes them look a little weird if you're accustomed to decimal numbers in English format (like these):

```
1.23
123.
123.0
0.321
0.123
1234.5678
-36.3
```

REBOL is an international language. Many areas of the world (say, obscure places like Europe) use a comma in place of a period. Here is how that looks:

```
1,23
,04
145,65
-32,3
```

In REBOL (fortunately), decimal numbers with commas work just as well as those with periods (or vice versa, depending on your point of reference). In fact, if you want to confuse everybody but yourself and REBOL, you can mix and match the two formats to your heart's content:

```
>> 115.567 + 2,3
== 117.867
>> ,01 * 2010.5
== 20.105
```

(Aargh. Pass the aspirin.) The multiple formats don't bother REBOL a bit. As with integers, you can use single apostrophes for readability, in any order you like, any place after the first number ,and REBOL still interprets the number correctly. Here's what that looks like:

```
5'124'675'133.56
```

And if you multiply by 2, you still can't faze REBOL:

```
>> 5'124'675'133.56 * 2
== 10249350267.12
```

Well, okay, this result trashes your single apostrophes. But you can write a little routine to put them back in. What? How? (I should have kept my mouth shut; you're making me think now.) Lemme see. Yep. Here, this will do it:

```
REBOL [
...Title:   "Prettify Decimals and Integers"
...File:    %3-prettify.r
...Date:    21-Feb-2000
...Sample:  { outputs number as 1'024'935'026'7.12 }
]

num: 10249350267.12
temp: to-string num

z: 0
y: 0
a: ""
period: 0

foreach char temp [
        z: z + 1
        a: join a char
        if char = #"." [period: period + 1]
        if period = 0 [
                if z = 1 [a: join a "'"]
                if z > 1 [y: y + 1]
                if y = 3 [a: join a "'" y: 0]
                ]
        ]

num: make decimal! a
print a
```

That little hummer is just waiting for you on the CD-ROM; you don't even have to send in a boxtop. But wait, there's more! You can use the to-decimal function word to convert strings and other datatypes to decimal, as in this modest example:

```
>> to-decimal "145.60"
== 145.6
```

Play with the example above, figure out how it works, and make it better.

Dissecting binary

REBOL represents binary values by a *hash mark* (also known as the pound sign, or #), followed by the binary number enclosed with curly braces ({ }). Any number in front of the pound sign denotes a base other than 16, such as base2 or base64. Binary data may span multiple lines. Strings without the correct number of characters are padded on the right. Here's how it looks:

```
#{3A18427F 899AEFD8}                              ; default base16
2#{100101101100101010010110110011011}            ; base2
64#{LmNvbSA8yw9CBOaGvXmgUkVCu2Uz934b}            ; base64
2#{100101101100101010010110110010111
     100101101100101010010110110010111          ; spanning lines
```

Converting other values to binary by putting them through the to-binary function looks like this:

```
>> to-binary "This is some text."
== #{5468697320697320736F6D6520746578742E}
>> to-binary 4806
== #{34383036}
```

Just be glad you don't have to ask, "Where's the hotel?" in binary.

Making time with time

Units of time — hours, minutes, and seconds — may be in the following formats:

```
10:19           ; conventional time
23:11           ; 24-hour military style
0:15:31         ; hours, minutes, seconds like a timer
4:23:11.54      ; hours, minutes, seconds, subseconds
```

In this example, subseconds (fractions of a second) are indicated with a decimal instead of a colon. You can use either a period or a comma as a separator. Note that the hours and minutes fields become optional when the decimal is present. For the obsessively punctual among us, REBOL can display subseconds calculated to the nanosecond (one billionth of a second):

```
0:00:00.000000001
```

REBOL sees time as a set of integers separated by colons (:). Hours, minutes, and seconds can be supplied, but seconds are optional. The time! datatype uses relative rather than absolute time (Einstein would be so proud). For example, 10:30 means 10 hours and 30 minutes of time rather than a specific time of day (10:30 a.m. or p.m.). Within each field, REBOL ignores leading zeros. Both positive and negative values are allowable; even if the minutes and seconds positions hold integers greater than 60 (and they can), REBOL converts the values automatically. They look like this:

```
>> 0:100:90
== 1:41:30
```

Fortunately for human-readability, REBOL accommodates the convenience of specifying a time of day as a.m. or p.m. Simply add **AM** or **PM** and REBOL can convert the values as needed (adding 12 hours to p.m. times):

```
>> 10:15AM
== 10:15
>> 2:15PM
== 14:15
```

Time values have three refinements. They're the ones you might expect:

/hour	Gets the value's hour
/minute	Gets the value's minute
/second	Gets the value's second

Here's how the refinements look in action:

```
>> time: now/time
== 19:43:08
>> print time/hour
19
>> print time/minute
43
>> print time/second
8
```

And here are a couple of ways to use time in your scripts, complete with what they mean:

```
print now/time    ;  What time your system at least thinks it is

wait 0:1:05       ;  A command to pause for one minute, five seconds
```

Finally, a more advanced time script. Hallelujah! Some of the more ancient habits of the computer community are downright scary. For example, many Unix systems use the *epoch date* — the number of seconds since January 1, 1970. Why that date? Don't ask; somebody thought it was a good idea at the time. (Remember Y2K? Programmers *do* things, okay? And we hide it well afterwards. Sometimes.) Anyway, epoch dates are still widely used. Many Internet auctions use them as item numbers because they can be both the item number and the closing date. If you've got an upcoming auction (or want to stun somebody with a really BIG number), generating epoch dates in REBOL is exceptionally easy. Translating epoch dates back into regular date and time is just as easy (ah, progress!). Here's the script that does the magic:

```
REBOL [
    Title:   "Convert Epoch Date to Regular Date/Time"
    Author:  "Ralph Roberts"
    File:    %3-epoch-to-date.r
    Date:    21-Feb-2000
    Purpose: {converts UNIX Epoch time (seconds after 1-1-
             1970) to current date and time }
    Example: {outputs "Epoch date 951142987 is
        21-Feb-2000 14:38:52 GMT or 9:38:52 Local" }
]


            epoch: 951142987        ; input the epoch date

    days:  divide epoch 86400
    days2: make integer! days

    time:     (days - days2) * 24
    hours:    make integer! time
    minutes:  (time - hours) * 60
    minutes2: make integer! minutes
    seconds:  make integer! (minutes - minutes2) * 60
    time2:    make time! ((((hours * 60) + minutes2) *
        60) + seconds)

prin ["Epoch date" epoch "is" 1-Jan-1970 + days2 time2]
print [" GMT or" time2 + now/zone "Local"]
```

Manipulating dates

Dates are also value variables (or is that variable values?) in REBOL. Around the world, dates are written in a variety of formats. Most countries use the day-month-year order. One of the few exceptions is the United States, which commonly uses a month-day-year format. For example, a date written numerically as 2/1/1999 is ambiguous. The month could be interpreted as either February (in the U.S.) or January (nearly everywhere else). Some countries use a dash (-), some use a slash (/), and others use a period (.) as separators. Finally, computer people often prefer dates in the year-month-day (ISO) format so they can be easily sorted. Here are some formats that REBOL accepts:

```
15-Apr-2000               ; U.S. usage
20/Jun/1999               ; U.S. usage
11-12-1945                ; international dd/mm/yyyy
2000-2-14                 ; international
2000-10-30/8:45           ; date with time
2000-3-15/9:30-5:00       ; date with time and time zone
```

Dates may be operated on just like any other value:

```
>> 2000-10-30 - 1999-10-30
== 366
>> 2000-10-30 - 30/0ct/1999
== 366
```

Slowly we learn our lessons in the world of programming. REBOL Technologies says (in a masterful understatement), "It is preferred to write the year in full." Otherwise (ahem) problems occur with date-comparison and sorting operations. (Y2K is dead; let's keep it that way, huh?)

Well, yeah, REBOL does allow you to use shortened year formats (such as 99 for 1999), interpreting them relative to the current year (they're only valid for plus or minus 50 years). Let me say it again: Get used to writing years as four digits. I'm sick of all that survival food, and we all have enough flashlight batteries for the next three millennia.

The now function uses your system clock to give you the date, time, and how much your local time deviates from Greenwich mean time (GMT) (also called Zulu or Universal Coordinated Time). As an old ham radio operator (WA4NUO) who also used the radio a lot in the military, I think of Zulu time as an old friend. Say, how long have I been a ham operator, anyway? I got my license as a teenager; so let's ask REBOL:

```
>> print divide (now - 23-May-1963) 365.25
36.7501711156742
```

Wow, almost 37 years. Time and date manipulations in REBOL are a breeze!

The now function has several refinements which work on the date! value to show time, date, and time zone to make those manipulations even easier, as shown in Table 4-4.

Table 4-4	Refinements for now
Refinement	*Result*
/day	Get the day.
/month	Get the month.
/year	Get the year.
/weekday	Get the weekday (1 through 7, or Monday through Sunday).
/time	Get the time (if present).
/zone	Returns the time zone offset from GMT only.

Using the refinements gives you results like these examples:

```
>> now/year
== 2000
>> now/month
== 2
>> now/day
== 21
>> now/date
== 21-Feb-2000
>> now/time
== 20:35:23
>> now/weekday
== 1
>> now/zone
== -5:00
```

As a final luxury, REBOL can convert a string to a date with the `to-date` function:

```
>> to-date "12 11 1954"
== 12-Nov-1954
```

If I ever get my own time machine, you can bet I'm installing REBOL (right after the bucket seats).

Valuing money

There are only two problems with money — you either don't have enough (and that causes worries), or you have too much (and that causes worries). In the case of REBOL's `money!` datatype, too much is the problem — in particular, the wide variety of symbols for money denominations — deutsche marks, yen, dollars, pounds, francs, and a plethora more. To retain the mantle of universal language, REBOL must handle these varied currencies.

Ever the practical language, REBOL uses a form of monetary representation common to the United States (dollars) as its standard. You can add specific denominations so that it can handle international currencies — rupees, Canadian dollars, guilders, whatever. (I'm not too sure about drachmas.)

Money values in REBOL are represented by an optional currency designator (no more than three letters long, such as *DEM,* for German deutsche marks), followed by a dollar sign ($), followed by the actual currency value. A plus (+) or minus (–) may appear immediately before the first character to indicate whether it is positive or negative. The numeric value should not contain extra spaces, commas, and periods; you can, however, use apostrophes for readability (see the "Doing decimals" section earlier in this chapter). Here's how all this looks in scripts:

```
$16.14              ; U.S.
-$2.00              ; negative value
USD$22.79           ; U.S.
CAD$106.15          ; Canadian
DEM$1500,55         ; German Deutsche Mark
UGX$25.00           ; Uganda Shilling
PHP$445.35          ; Philippine Peso
$1'000'000.00       ; A million bucks should be readable
FUN$1000.00         ; Monopoly(r) money
```

Note that the comma may be used in place of decimals to meet the requirements of a European notation. You can choose the three letters preceding the dollar sign ($) to represent a specific currency, so long as you're consistent in your scripts and don't try to add one type of currency to another without first converting the currencies as needed.

I suggest you use the ISO standard three-letter currency designations published on the Web at `www.id3.org/iso4217.html`. These cover over 180 countries — everything from the Andorran Peseta (ADP) to the Zimbabwe Dollar (ZWD).

The `money!` datatype in REBOL uses standard IEEE floating-point numbers, allowing up to 15 digits of precision (including cents). REBOL limits the length to 64 characters. Values that are out of range (or which cannot be represented in 64 bits) are flagged as an error.

To convert some other value to money, use the `to-money` function word:

```
>> to-money "14.86"
== $14.86
>> to-money 3.16
== $3.16
>> to-money [USD 24 95]
== USD$24.95
```

If you want to investigate whether time really *is* money, now you can.

To convert one type of currency to another when you know the exchange rate, do this:

```
>> rate: 1.2469  ; USD$ to Cayman Islands dollar (KYD)
== 1.2469
>> converted: 87.56 * rate
== 109.17856
>> converted: join "KYD$" converted
== "KYD$109.178564"
>> converted: to-money converted
== KYD$109.18            ; USD$87.56 = KYD$109.18
```

I was able to do the preceding manipulation (decimal! to string! to money!) because the money! datatype is a hybrid variable made up of two parts: a string value (for the three-letter currency designator) and a decimal value (for the amount of money). I do it this way because the to-money function works on raw values, as in this example:

```
>> to-money [KYD 109.18]
== KYD$109.18
```

By the way, to-money rounds off a decimal to the nearest hundredth, even though it was first converted from a string value.

Editing text values

In REBOL, the text datatype describes any file that isn't binary. (Lots of those out there.) The values in this section enable you to manipulate text values.

Lettering character

Characters, I must emphasize, are not strings — they're the individual values that make up strings.

A character (char!) may be: a printable letter, number, or other symbol; an unprintable symbol; or a control character. The alphabet (abcdefghijklmnopqrstuvwxyz — did I get them all?) and the first ten whole numbers (1234567890) are easy to imagine as characters, but punctuation marks, such as periods, commas, colons, and semicolons are also characters, as are the symbols that serve as control characters (escapes, line endings, and so on).

You write a character value in REBOL using a hash, or pound, symbol (#) followed by a string contained in double quotes. The hash distinguishes the character from the string so that REBOL can interpret it correctly:

```
#"R"    ; the single character: R
"R"     ; a string with the character: R
```

Characters may include escape sequences that begin with a caret (^) and are followed by one or more characters of encoding. This encoding may include the characters #" ^A" to #" ^Z" for control A to control Z (upper and lower case are the same). Here's something you can try if you want to see an instant magic trick:

```
print #"^L"
```

Wow, cleared your REBOL console screen, huh? Actually, it only appears to do so, having advanced your screen one full page. Scroll back up (using the scroll bar, if you have a GUI system) and you see the previous information.

Aha, controls! No blinking lights or levers, but REBOL does give you a respectable set of control characters; Table 4-5 provides a quick inventory.

Table 4-5	REBOL Control Characters
Character	*Definition*
#"^(null)" or #"^@"	null (zero)
#"^(line)" or #"^/"	end of line
#"^(page)"	new page (and page eject)
#"^L"	advance page
#"^(esc)"	escape
also #"^["	escape
#"^(back)"	backspace
#"^H"	backspace
#"^(del)"	delete
also #"^~"	delete
#"^^"	caret character
#"^""	quotation mark
#"^(00)" to #"^(FF)"	hex forms of characters

Use the to-char function word to covert string or ASCII numerical values to the character value as so:

```
>> to-char "a"
== #"a"
>> to-char 65
== #"A"
```

By the way, doing a to-integer on a character value will return the ASCII representation of the character:

```
>> to-integer #"A"
== 65
```

Stringing strings

A *string* is a series of characters. Here's how you define a string variable:

```
saying: "REBOL is Perl without the complication."
```

Once created, you can perform any operation on a string that you can on series (which I explore in Chapter 8). For example:

```
>> print find saying "the"
the complication.
>> print length? saying
39
>> copy/part (find saying "Perl")(find saying "the")
== "Perl without "
```

Instead of quotes to enclose strings, as I've shown you so far, you may also use curly brackets or braces. A braced string enables you to have larger sections of text containing several lines, and embedded spaces, tabs, quotes, and linefeeds all as part of the string; the format will be retained. You can even include other braces, so long as they are in even pairs. Like this, it be, matey:

```
{"Once upon a dark and stormy night,"
   the old pirate said, "I set me down
   in front of my computer, yar. And
   programmed a treasure map, I did,
   laddie, and here be the code. Har, har!"
    print { >>>> {Treasure here!} }  }
```

REBOL allows the use of special characters and operations that can be encoded into a string by flagging them with the escape character "^" (caret). This character is used rather than the backslash ("\") because it avoids conflicts with file paths, which on the PC use a backslash. These characters are shown in Table 4-6.

Table 4-6	Special Characters for Within Strings
Characters	*Function*
^ "	inserts a " (quote)
^ }	inserts a } (closing brace)
^ ^	inserts a ^ (caret)
^ /	Starts a new line
^(line)	Starts a new line
^ _	Inserts a tab

(continued)

Table 4-6 *(continued)*

Characters	Function
^(tab)	Inserts a tab
^(page)	Starts a new page
^(letter)	Inserts control-*letter* (A-Z)
^(back)	Erases one character back
^(null)	Inserts a null character
^(esc)	Inserts an escape character
^(*xx*)	Inserts an ASCII character by hexidecimal (*xx*) number

Convert other values to strings using the to-string function:

```
>> to-string 156
== "156"
>> to-string $14.98
== "$14.98"
>> to-string now
== "22-Feb-2000/17:11:38-5:00"
```

Making an issue of it

Issue values cover numbers that are issued or assigned to you, such as phone numbers and credit card numbers, or which are issued to a thing, like model numbers. A leading hash mark or pound sign (#) informs REBOL that what follows is an issue value. Here are some:

```
#555-512-5555            ; phone number
#0000-9999-0000-9999     ; credit card number
#FRA-467-231-BG          ; model number
```

Issue values are a subset of series, and thus may be manipulated as series:

```
>> copy/part find #828-555-1212 "555" 3
== #555
```

Use the to-issue function word for conversion:

```
>> to-issue "212-555-1212"
== #212-555-1212
>> to-issue 25-Feb-2000
== #25-Feb-2000              ; date as model number
```

Do you love REBOL yet? Yeah! It's cool!

Playing tag

Tags are a highly important part of HTML used in programming Web pages, but are useful in many other applications as well. REBOL recognizes tags as a value. Here are some:

```
<title>
</body>
<font face="Helvetica" size="2">
```

REBOL includes a function, build-tag, which converts a block value to a tag with proper attributes for HTML:

```
>> build-tag [BODY BGCOLOR "#FFFFF0"]
== <BODY BGCOLOR="#FFFFF0">
```

You will find tag values and the ways in which REBOL creates and/or manipulates them useful when I explore building Web pages with REBOL in Chapter 16 and CGI Web applications in Chapter 18. Tags are the bedrock of Web pages.

Tags are a subset of series, and thus may be manipulated as such, just like strings, filenames, URLs, and so forth.

The to-tag function handles conversion chores:

```
>> to-tag "HEAD"
== <HEAD>
```

And the build-tag is even more powerful:

```
>> build-tag [img src %mypic.jpg width 150 height 200]
== <img src="mypic.jpg" width="150" height="200">
```

Thinking logic

Logic also has worth, as the following values show.

Creating logic out of chaos

Quick, a pop quiz. What is logic? Answer true or false.

Well, the answer, of course, is either. Logic operations in REBOL, as in other languages, return only a true or a false answer, an on or an off, or that something is there or nothing is there. Here's an example of basic logic:

```
>> apples: 24
== 24
>> apples = 24
== true
>> apples = 23
== false
```

You can base decisions on logic. If 24 apples are present (true), eat an apple.
If 23 apples are there, you've already eaten one. And on physical parameters,
such as the length of a string:

```
>> motto: "REBOL does simple tasks simply."
== "REBOL does simple tasks simply."
>> (length? motto) < 50
== true
```

Logic operations are most often used in conditional functions such as if,
while, until, and so forth:

```
>> x:3
>> if x < 100 [print "test"]
test
```

```
>> while [x < 5] [print [x ". test"] x: x + 1]
1 . test
2 . test
3 . test
4 . test
```

```
>> while [x <> 5] [print [x ". test"] x: x + 1]
1 . test
2 . test
3 . test
4 . test
```

The preceding examples test for true. The complement of true is false,
and you can use the not function to test for that condition:

```
>> there: "North Carolina's Blue Ridge Mountains"
== "North Carolina's Blue Ridge Mountains"
>> if not there [print "Get in car and go."]
== false
```

In my case, the right answer is false because I'm already here (y'all come
visit). And you can also test for on or off, like this:

```
>> print-me: false
== false
>> print either print-me ["turned on"]["turned off"]
turned off
```

```
>> print-me: true
== true
>> print either print-me ["turned on"]["turned off"]
turned on
```

You can always find up-to-date lists of function words and how to use them, including all these logic operators so far mentioned, in the REBOL/Core Dictionary for 2.2.0 at http://rebol.com/dictionary.html.

The to-logic function converts an integer! or none! value to a logic value, like this:

```
>> to-logic 101
== true
>> to-logic none
== false
```

You'll then be able to use these values like I used print-me.

Sometimes none can be a lot

Nothing there, or the concept of no data present, can often be quite useful in your scripts. The none! datatype contains a single value that represents the state of "no value." The value may also be returned from various functions, primarily those involving series (pick, find, and so on).

The none value is not equivalent to zero or false. However, it behaves like false for many functions.

```
>> colors: ["red" "yellow" none "blue"]
== ["red" "yellow" none "blue"]
>> if pick colors 3 = none [print "You forgot a color!"]
You forgot a color!
```

More practically, the none value may be used as a place holder for missing data:

```
62email-database: [
    "Ferdinand" ferd@abooks.com #828-555-1212
    "Mugatroyd" none #212-555-1212
    "Richmond"  luke@rebol.net #408-555-1212
]
```

none may also be used as a logical value. Try the following at the REBOL console for an example:

```
>> secure none
== [net allow file allow]
```

The preceding turns off REBOL's security, allowing unhampered network access and file read/write operations. Add additional security like so:

```
>> secure ask
== [net ask file ask]
```

More about security later in the book. Back to none. The to-none function converts other values to none:

```
>> to-none 45
== none
>> to-none "This is a test string."
== none
```

Saving and retrieving data

Moving information back and forth is a large part of programming. These values let you handle data.

Blocking up data

Blocks are both a fundamental concept and construct of REBOL. Blocks are collections of data. This data may be any type of value or function. Even REBOL scripts themselves are loaded into blocks before evaluation occurs, just as we embedded scripts in blocks earlier in this chapter.

Blocks start with a left bracket ([) and end with a right bracket (]). Other blocks may be nested within:

```
block1 [ block2 [ block 3 [ stuff ] ] ]
```

A block, actually, can contain data of any type of value, like this (showing how data is entered and how you get it out. Try it.):

```
>> data: ["Fred Jones" 27-Apr-2000 $96.37]
== ["Fred Jones" 27-Apr-2000 $96.37]
>> print data/1
Fred Jones
>> print data/2
27-Apr-2000
>> print data/3
$96.37
```

Blocks are used in REBOL for creating databases, directories, tables, sets, sequences, code, functions, and all sorts of series. We meet and play with blocks in various ways again in every chapter of this book. Guaranteed.

The to-block function is quite handy in converting other values to blocks, such as the start of a database on the first U.S. president:

```
>> to-block {"George Washington" 22-Feb-1732 14-Dec-1799}
== ["George Washington" 22-Feb-1732 14-Dec-1799]
```

Or working with Web pages:

```
>> to-block <BODY BGCOLOR="#FFFFF0">
== [BODY BGCOLOR= "#FFFFF0"]
```

Managing files

Filenames are an important and often-used value in REBOL. We look at files in detail in Chapter 9. path (a file path, as opposed to an object path) is the information describing where files are located in your local computer's file system or over a network. The percent character (%) precedes filenames and tells REBOL what follows is a file value. File values in REBOL include:

```
%file.txt
%/rebol/script.r
%/c/windows/temp/some.txt
```

File values are a subset of series just like strings, and thus may be manipulated as a series:

```
>> dir: read %.          ; reads current directory
>> print first dir       ; prints first file name
setup.html
>> print last dir        ; last file name
cal.r
>> print dir/20          ; the 20th file
Websplit.r
>> print length? dir     ; number of files
176
```

Long filenames with spaces in them require special handling, which is covered in Chapter 9.

Data can be converted using the to-file command:

```
>> to-file "test"
== %test
```

Use a block like the following, and you can include path information:

```
>> to-file [d rebol test]
== %d/rebol/test
```

Hiking the right path

The term *path* immediately brings file paths to mind (unless you're a park ranger or a mystic), but in REBOL it means much more. Paths are — as REBOL implements them — a collection of words delineated with forward slashes (†). Words in paths may be defined as blocks, hashes, functions, and objects.

Table 4-7, adapted from the REBOL *User's Guide,* shows the relationship of path forms corresponding with type models, type tests, and conversions:

Table 4-7	Path Forms		
Action	*Type Model*	*Type Test*	*Conversion*
path/word:	set-path!	set-path?	to-set-path
path/word	path!	path?	to-path
'path/word	lit-path!	lit-path?	to-lit-path

Paths are actually a type of series; anything you can do with a series, you can do with path values. Consider this example:

```
>> print second system/console/prompt
>
```

What we got via this series manipulation was the second character of the path's value. This system object stores the characters used for REBOL's console prompt or, in this case, the characters >>. So we can manipulate the value of the path (which can be quite extensive) using all the many series functions in REBOL, but what if we wanted to do something to the path itself? Simple. Just put an apostrophe in front of the path and you've told the series functions to act on the path's name, not on the path's value. It looks like this:

```
=>> print second 'system/console/prompt
console
```

Paths contain a lot of power; they crop up again during the course of this book, especially in Chapter 14.

Building in efficiency

Speed is good in programs (especially if they're running correctly). REBOL offers some values that actually increase efficiency — what a concept.

Hashing data for more speed

The REBOL hash value is a storage method that speeds up the process of finding data in large files. The hash datatype is useful for converting data into a table format (which is readily searchable). hash values operate just like block values. In fact, you can use to-hash to convert blocks to the hash value:

```
>> pies: ["apple" "cherry" "pecan" "peanut butter"]
== ["apple" "cherry" "pecan" "peanut butter"]
>> to-hash pies
== make hash! ["apple" "cherry" "pecan" "peanut butter"]
>> print pick pies 4
peanut butter
```

Listing data quickness

REBOL enables you to use list values to construct linked list data structures that allow fast, efficient modification of values within the list. Here's an example of how a list works:

```
>> frogs: ["bullfrog" "green" "jumpy" "warty"]
== ["bullfrog" "green" "jumpy" "warty"]
>> frogs: to-list frogs
== make list! ["bullfrog" "green" "jumpy" "warty"]
>> type? frogs
== list!                  ; just checking <g>
```

The first order of business here is to create a block of related data. Next, use the to-list function and convert the block to a list (as in the preceding froggy example). Now we can do stuff to the list:

```
>> print third frogs
jumpy
>> replace frogs "green" "yellow"
== make list! ["bullfrog" "yellow" "jumpy" "warty"]
```

Now the joint is jumpin'. Lists are different from blocks in some ways. However, for a look at those, jump over to Chapter 14.

Placing parentheses for fun and profit

Parenthesized expressions and data are actual datatypes in REBOL. Paren values normally hang out in a block, like this:

```
>> blk: [(3 + 3) (3 + 2 - 1) (3 * 3) (6 / 2)]
>> length? blk
4
```

Paren values are a type of series — and that means (all together, now) anything you can do with a series, you can do with paren values. Use the to-paren function to make the conversion:

```
>> to-paren "123 + 26"
== (123 + 26)
```

Surfing Internet values

Then, of course, if you've got to hang ten on the Internet and the dubya-dubya-dubya (World Wide Web), REBOL has you covered. Some great Internet-manipulating values are built right in.

Planting tuples

Tuples are numbers with more than one decimal, such as these:

```
2.2.0.3.1          ; my version of REBOL
192.168.0.12       ; the address of my computer on the LAN
255.255.0          ; RGB color numbers
```

You can tinker with (or tiptoe through) the tuples, just as you can with any other value in REBOL:

```
>> print 255.255.0 - 0.100.0
255.155.0
```

Heads up, sports fans, it's time for Fun with Tuples! My company's Web site, http://abooks.com, has an IP (Internet Protocol) address of 216.122.85.130. Yep, that's a tuple! Well, I've often wondered who my neighbors were (IP-wise, that is). Here's a simple REBOL script to find out the IP addresses on either side of mine (following ten and preceding ten). Here it is:

```
network: 216.122.85.120       ; starting IP
loop 21 [
    print [network " -- " read join dns:// network]
    network: network + 0.0.0.1
]
```

That's it. Not much code for a lot of power, huh? The script's output looks like this:

```
216.122.85.120  --  moneycreek.com
216.122.85.121  --  britsontour.com
216.122.85.122  --  cyberspacedesign.com
216.122.85.123  --  arab-mail.net
216.122.85.124  --  mchill2.com
216.122.85.125  --  compleatWeb2.com
216.122.85.126  --  farpublicidade.com
```

```
216.122.85.127  --   coinfo.com
216.122.85.128  --   century21hughes-carey.com
216.122.85.129  --   style.etrade.com
216.122.85.130  --   abooks.com
216.122.85.131  --   vstorefronts.com
216.122.85.132  --   iproWebs.net
216.122.85.133  --   servcom1.eusrv.com
216.122.85.134  --   Web123.com
216.122.85.135  --   manshow.com
216.122.85.136  --   hypercerulean.com
216.122.85.137  --   xemico.com
216.122.85.138  --   saxmansoftware.com
216.122.85.139  --   Webdesign.Webbeheer.nl
216.122.85.140  --   internetmoneysystem.com
```

Try it yourself. Just be sure you've set up REBOL for networking (see Chapter 13 and Appendix B) and that you are connected to the Internet. But is that all there is to it? No way. Try these hair-raising maneuvers (just kidding):

Use to-tuple as a way to convert other values to, well, tuples. It looks like this:

```
>> to-tuple "120.30.3.1"
== 120.30.3.1
>> to-tuple [144 9 200 3]
== 144.9.200.3
```

Or you could pull a tuple back into a string by using the mold function:

```
>> mold 198.168.0.12
== "198.168.0.12"
```

You can then act on the result (using series functions), convert what you get back into a tuple (using, you guessed it, to-tuple) and no one has to be the wiser.

Sending and receiving e-mail

REBOL even treats e-mail addresses as values. These, for example:

```
ralph@abooks.com        ; my personal address
feedback@rebol.com      ; REBOL technical support
```

Use e-mail addresses with the send function word and you can send just about anything — variables, strings, whatever — like this:

```
send feedback@rebol.com "Great program, folks!"
send billg@microsoft.com read %annualreport.dat
```

REBOL can use a variety of valid e-mail formats. These, for example:

```
info@rebol.com
123@number-mail.org
my-name.here@an.example-domain.com
r@b.to
```

You can also use the /user and /host refinements to pull out separate data from e-mail addresses:

```
>> address: elvis@secret-hideyhole.com
== elvis@secret-hideyhole.com
>> print address/user
elvis
>> print address/host
secret-hideyhole.com
```

Voilà — a conversion from string values to e-mail, using the to-email function:

```
>> to-email "bill.hickok@wildwest.com"
== bill.hickok@wildwest.com
```

Ah, yes, the hand is quicker than the eye and the computer is quicker than both. (Usually.)

Locating URLs

The ubiquitous Uniform Resource Locator (URL) is often used for Web addresses, but it also includes other types of Internet addresses as well:

```
http://rebol.com          ; a Web address
mailto://info@rebol.com   ; an e-mail address
ftp://ftp.a.com/file.txt  ; file transfer protocol address
```

As with filenames and strings, URL values are a subset of — you guessed it — the series! pseudotype. You can operate on them using any series operator, as shown here:

```
>> Web: http://rebol.com/dictionary.html
== http://rebol.com/dictionary.html
>> parse Web "/"
== ["http:" "" "rebol.com" "dictionary.html"]
>> find Web "rebol"
== rebol.com/dictionary.html
```

Chapter 8 gets down to cases with series. You're gonna flat-out love them!

As in so many other areas, REBOL offers immense power via its built-in communications protocols (known in REBOL terminology as *schemes*). This power is certainly true of URLs. Via this value type, REBOL supports the following

schemes: Web pages (HTTP:); file transfer (FTP:); newsgroups (NNTP:);
e-mail (MAILTO:); files (FILE:); finger (FINGER:); whois (WHOIS:); small
network time (DAYTIME:); post office (POP:); transmission control (TCP:);
and domain name service (DNS:).

The first part of a URL value denotes the scheme being used (such as HTTP).
The characters that follow the scheme designator are appropriate to the protocol being used. Here are some examples:

```
http://host.dom/path/file
ftp://host.dom/path/file
nntp://news.some-isp.net/some.news.group
mailto:name@domain
file://host/path/file
finger://user@host.dom
whois://rebol@rs.internic.net
daytime://everest.cclabs.missouri.edu
pop://user:passwd@host.dom/
tcp://host.dom:21
dns://host.dom
```

Some fields are optional. For example, you can follow host with a port
number (if it differs from the default) or you can add a password. Of course,
if you prefer to let the computer do the work, an FTP URL supplies a default
password if one is not specified:

```
ftp://user:password@host.com/path/file
```

If no username or password is included, REBOL attempts to log you in as
anonymous and sends your e-mail address as the password.

Characters in a URL must conform to specified standards. Restricted characters (such as spaces) must be encoded in hexadecimal form. Fortunately,
that's easy to do: You precede them with the escape character (%), and the
result looks like this:

```
http://www.bigemptyWeb.com/empty%20blank%20stuff.html
```

Part III
Advanced Infantry Training

The 5th Wave   By Rich Tennant

RICHTENNANT

"It says, 'Thank you for downloading Gumpton's Compression Utility shareware. Should you decide to purchase this product, send a check to the address shown and your PC will be uncompressed and restored to its original size.'"

In this part . . .

Deep in the swamps of more advanced coding, the intrepid cybertroops unlock even more arcane powers of the REBOLution.

Chapter 5

Values Bravely Advance

● ●

In This Chapter

▶ Using words in REBOL

▶ Building with blocks

▶ Evaluating values

▶ Varying variables

▶ Making functions

▶ Finding paths

▶ Constructing objects

▶ Managing messages

▶ Talking in dialects

● ●

*G*etting friendly with values (as in the very jovial Chapter 4) is a great start — but I'm tellin' ya, Pilgrim, ya gotta *do* somethin' with 'em.

Using Words in REBOL

Now we come to truly one of the major differences between REBOL and most computer languages — *words* — and what a great invention they are. In a computer language, a word can have value (any of the preceding), refer to a function, function as a block of data, and more. Word values can be direct or indirect. (Whoa. What's next? Poetry?)

The powerful usage of words lets REBOL code be *natural language.* This means you can look at a line of code such as:

```
names: ["Richmond" "Ferdinand" "Bentley"] print sort names
```

and pretty quickly figure out the result:

```
Bentley Ferdinand Richmond
```

But REBOL code can be even more natural than that, as these snippets show:

```
read next file
install all files here
on off true false
```

Natural language works awesomely; suitably awesome examples abound in this book. This next one, however, may astound programmers who cut their teeth on *un*-natural languages that forbade the use of certain characters in words. Ready for this one? You can use hyphens (and a few other special characters) as parts of words. To wit:

```
number?
time?
date!
image-files
connection-times
file-size
++
--
==
+
-
*new-line*
left&right
```

Yep. That code listing just fractured most of the major cyber-taboos in several different programming languages. (Feels good, doesn't it?) REBOL defines the end of a word by a space, a new line, or one of the following characters: [ ] ( ) { } " : ; / (wait until my spell checker hits *this* paragraph). Even so, REBOL has a few taboo characters of its own: / @ # $ % ^ , are strictly off limits for any use in word names. At least this taboo has a practical reason: REBOL uses those characters for other purposes (and no, that doesn't include comic-strip-style cussing).

Words, as REBOL sees them, are symbols made up of characters. A REBOL word can have any type of value or function as a definition. This flexible use of words is basic to REBOL — and is a major source of its powerful simplicity. Therefore, you can expect to see words throughout this book (gee, really?), along with the details of how REBOL uses them to take care of business. Table 5-1, courtesy of the REBOL *User's Guide,* shows the relationship of word forms corresponding with type models, type tests, and conversions.

Table 5-1		Word Forms in REBOL	
Action	*Type Model*	*Type Test*	*Conversion*
word:	set-word!	set-word?	to-set-word
:word	get-word	get-word?	to-get-word

Action	Type Model	Type Test	Conversion
word	word!	word?	to-word
'word	lit-word!	lit-word?	to-lit-word

Words are defined or set in this way:

```
age: 42
lunch-time: 12:32
birthday: 20/3/90
town: "Dodge City"
test: %stuff.r
```

Note that the preceding example defined words to be integer!, time!, date!, string!, and file! values. Words can also be defined to be more complex types of values:

```
people: ["Roy" "Gene" "Gabby"]
code: [if age > 32 [print town]]
say: make function! [item] [print item]
```

Convert a value to word! by using to-word:

```
>> to-word "June-Inventory"
== June-Inventory
>> to-word "456"
== 456
```

Also, as shown in the preceding table for "Word Forms," you can convert to the get-word and lit-word (literal word) forms:

```
>> to-get-word "fred"
== :fred
>> to-lit-word "charlie"
== 'charlie
```

REBOL has over *300* words, more than this book can document in detail. There is a fabulously useful dictionary of REBOL words on the Web, the REBOL/Core Dictionary, at the following address:

```
http://rebol.com/dictionary.html
```

Building with Blocks

Another foundation component of REBOL is the concrete block . . . oops, no, I mean the *data block.* Blocks start with a left bracket ([) and end with a right bracket (]). Other blocks may be nested within:

```
block1 [ block2 [ block 3 [ stuff ] ] ]
```

A block, actually, can contain either data of any type value, like this (showing how data is entered and how you get it out — try it):

```
>> data: ["Fred Jones" 27-Apr-2000 $96.37]
== ["Fred Jones" 27-Apr-2000 $96.37]
>> print data/1
Fred Jones
>> print data/2
27-Apr-2000
>> print data/3
$96.37
```

Blocks are used in REBOL for creating databases, directories, tables, sets, sequences, code, functions, and all sorts of series. Here is a simple name and address database (it's on the CD-ROM that accompanies this book, so you won't have to type it in):

```
REBOL [FILE: %5-database.r]

customers: [
        [
        NAME: "Murgathoyd T. Bonkerwumps"
        ADDRESS: "38 East Swamp Ave."
        CITY: "Doflunkle, NY 11111"
        PHONE: #888-123-1234
        ][
        NAME: "Pat T. O'Furniture"
        ADDRESS: "14 Shamrock Lane"
        CITY: "Yellowtail, MT 99999"
        PHONE: #999-321-4321
        ][
        NAME: "Cynthia Camellips"
        ADDRESS: "2345 Dry Pond Rd."
        CITY: "High Top, TN 33333"
        PHONE: #615-555-0000
        ]
]
```

Each customer is in a block of his or her own, and all those blocks are nested inside the larger, customers block. Load this database into REBOL (type **do %1-database.r**), and here is how you can retrieve a list of customers:

```
>> foreach customer customers [print customer]
Murgathoyd T. Bonkerwumps 38 East Swamp Ave. Doflunkle, NY
          11111 888-123-1234
Pat T. O'Furniture 14 Shamrock Lane Yellowtail, MT 99999
          999-321-4321
Cynthia Camellips 2345 Dry Pond Rd. High Top, TN 33333
          615-555-0000
```

And try:

```
sort customers foreach customer customers [print customer]
```

Fun, huh? And potentially most useful. But blocks are not limited to data.
They are also commonly used for code, especially condition statements,
such as:

```
if time > 18:30 [send bobbo@bobbo.com "Supper time!"]
loop 10 [print "Test"]
files: read %. foreach file files [print file]
```

And let's turn that last one into a function using blocks. Type in this code:

```
dir: func [][
   files: read %.
   sort files
   foreach file files [print file]
]
```

Now, just type **dir** and you should get a sorted directory listing.

Evaluating Values

REBOL looks in blocks to see what's there and does anything it recognizes as
being doable. This is called *evaluating*. A block is evaluated from left to right.
Our old friend, the "Hello World" program, is an example (lines typed in at
the console prompt create a block even if the brackets are not there):

```
print "Hello World!"
```

REBOL evaluates the block, applying the print function to it, and

```
Hello World!
```

appears on the screen. Evaluation happens even for just a data block. Take
the data series, for example.

```
a: [one two three four five six seven eight nine ten]
```

Just entering the information into a variable — in this case the a variable — causes evaluation. Thus, you can

```
print first a        ; print the first value
print second a       ; print the second
print last a         ; print the last
print fifth a        ; print the fifth
print a/9            ; print the ninth
```

In the preceding code, the function word fifth is as high as REBOL allows in the first, second, third, fourth, and fifth scheme, but you can use the variable name followed by a forward slash (/) for any number in a series, even out to infinity if you can cram one that large into your machine.

Looping loops

Most of us, from time to time, have gone loopy from too much programming in too short of a time, fueled by too much caffeine. As I was explaining the other day as the rescue squad pried my fingers loose from the chimney and drug me down from the roof of my house, this never happens to me.

But loops are an integral part of programming; we couldn't do without them. Figure 5-1 shows a display that incorporates a loop. Over 20 years ago, when I first met BASIC (right after contending with machine language), the for next loop just awed me with its ease of use. You just did

```
10 for x = 1 to 50          ; BASIC program
20 print "Test"
30 next x
```

Well, hey, it was 1977. I had sideburns and a leisure suit. I was easily impressed. Anyway, here's the equivalent in REBOL:

```
loop 50 [print "Test"]
```

Cool. The block is evaluated 50 times. If you want to keep track of which repetition it is, use this:

```
repeat count 50 [print count]
```

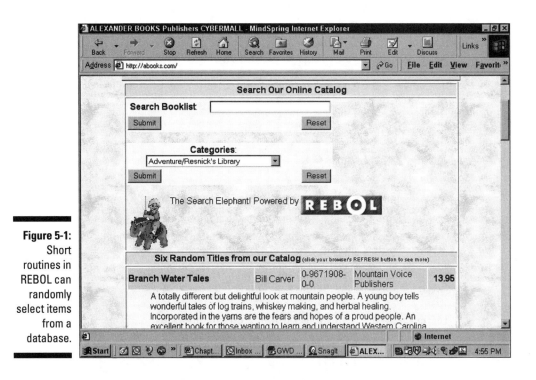

Figure 5-1:
Short
routines in
REBOL can
randomly
select items
from a
database.

Powering with parentheses

As in the preceding example, blocks are evaluated from left to right. For
example, let's add three numbers:

```
print [2 + 3 + 4]
```

REBOL evaluates the block and returns 9 as the answer. But what if we want
to divide the result of the preceding addition by half? This requires evaluating the addition before doing the division. You use parentheses to accomplish evaluation within evaluation in this manner:

```
print [divide (2 + 3 + 4) 2]
```

Actually, the above example gives the same answer with or without parentheses. Be aware that some code gives a different answer, depending on placement of parentheses. I show you the details on this in Chapter 11.

Another example:

```
print [(2 + 4) * (2 + 3)]
```

The answer is 30. So experiment with parentheses in changing the order of evaluation.

Varying Variables

Words can represent functions, but they are also used as variables to hold values. A word followed by a colon sets its value, such as the following:

```
localtime: now          ; function word
name: "Bob"             ; string
coffee-break: 10:15     ; time value
paid_holiday: 4-Jul-2000 ; date value
employees: ["Bob" "Jo" "Bo"]  ; series
```

Using the defined variable without a colon causes evaluation:

```
>> print localtime
14-Feb-2000/14:44:33-5:00
>> print name
Bob
>> print coffee-break
10:15
>> print paid_holiday
4-Jul-2000
>> print employees
Bob Jo Bo
```

A word used as a variable can hold any type of value or function. In fact, this is true of all words in REBOL. It's just that such words such as print, loop, repeat, and all the others in the REBOL Dictionary have already been defined with functions.

You can always find the *REBOL Dictionary* at http://rebol.com/dictionary.html.

Variables are limited to the *context* in which they are defined. There's no way that you can know the many hundreds of words used for the functions making up REBOL, nor do you need to; they are essentially local variables within a particular function. The same word used by you for something entirely different has no effect on the function, and vice versa.

Here's how you can prove this to yourself:

```
>> age: 29
== 29
>> old: func [][use [age][age: 30 print age] print age]
>> old
30
29
```

Define a variable — age — as 29. Then create the function old and employ the use function word to make age a local variable within part of the function only!. Try it. This function uses the same variable with two definitions within itself (picking up your previous definition).

Are we having fun yet? You betcha!

Making Functions

So, speaking of functions, a *function* can be defined as a block, which has local variables given new values each time that the block is evaluated. The local variables are the *arguments* of the function, in effect being just temporary places to store data while the function manipulates it. Look at this simple example:

```
sum: func [a b][a + b]
```

A new function is created that adds the sum of a and b. The local variables a and b are the arguments of the function sum. It works like this, as I show you defining the function and using it:

```
>> sum: func [a b][a + b]
>> sum 14598 206
== 14804
```

Chapter 7 has more on functions.

Finding Paths

The term path, I emphasize, looks like a file path but in REBOL is more. As we apply it here, a *path* is an easy way to add a refinement to a word, showing that more information is needed. As with file paths, the forward slash (/) separates words in the path. Let's hone in on the concept a bit more. Here is a file path:

```
%/c/windows/stone.bmp
```

Paths are used with word variables and quite usefully so. Type this definition at the REBOL console:

```
>> date: now
== 14-Feb-2000/20:37:08-5:00
```

This uses the function word now to put your system's current time and date into the variable date. Using path information, as shown in the following example, it's a snap to pull chunks of data out of the variable, like this:

```
>> print date/day
14
>> print date/month
2
>> print date/year
2000
>> print date/time/second
8
>> print date/zone
-5:00
```

Here is a variable path from a system variable, the one controlling your console prompt:

```
system/console/prompt
```

It's essentially the same thing, just different uses — just like words can contain different types of values. REBOL paths, in addition to being used for files, can also be used for blocks, functions, objects, and strings. Let me show you something neat:

```
>> probe system/console

make object! [
    history: ["probe system/console"]
    keys: none
    prompt: ">> "
    result: "== "
    escape: "(escape)"
    busy: "|/-\"
    tab-size: 4
    break: true
]
```

Okay, I used the preceding probe function, which returned the paths and information in system/console. Now you see some other system variables in there.

There are a good many more. You really want to be careful playing with system variables, but feel free to look at them, and thus gain a better understanding of path values in specific and REBOL in general.

Do not probe just `system` by itself, or `system/words`. So much stuff would be unleashed that your computer would lock down.

Some other system variable paths include `build`, `product`, `words`, `user`, and `script`.

Epoch date

This utility of using system time and date in REBOL is demonstrated by a little script that I wrote for an application in which I needed to find the `epoch date`. The *epoch* is a time measurement used on Unix systems; it's the number of seconds since January 1, 1970. (When you consider that a second is a very long time for a computer, the notion of a mere 30-year "epoch" actually makes some sense.) I have several auctions on the Internet that use the epoch date as item numbers (with a built-in completion date), so getting the correct value is critical in determining when an auction will end.

Here's my code, and it's on the CD-ROM, as well:

```
REBOL[ Title: "Epoch Date"
        File: "%1-epoch.r"
        Purpose: "Number of
seconds since the epoch."
        Date: "14-Feb-2000"
        Author: "Ralph Roberts"
    ]


date: now
```

```
seconds: ((date - 1-1-1970) *
    86400) + (date/time/hour *
    3600) + (date/time/minute *
    60) + date/time/second


zone: now/zone


zone: zone/hour


zone: zone * 3600


seconds: seconds - zone ; minus
    a minus gives plus


print seconds
```

To use it, type *do %1-epoch.r*. Here's the result:

```
Script: "Epoch Date" ("14-Feb-
    2000")
950579758
```

Yes, over 95 million seconds have passed since January 1, 1970. As to getting the epoch date seven days in the future for an auction close, just change the line `date: now` to `date: now + 7`, and REBOL adds seven days for you. Is this easy, or what?

The "System Object Browser," by Bohdan Lechnowsky at `http://www.rebol.org/script/browse-system.r`, is a neat way to browse these system variables or objects in a more organized manner than our manual probing. But, what the hey? Let's probe another one. `options` looks interesting:

```
>> probe system/options

make object! [
    home: %/D/rebol/
    script: none
    args: none
    do-arg: none
    quiet: false
    trace: false
    help: false
    binary-base: 16
    cgi:
    make object! [
        server-software: none
        server-name: none
        gateway-interface: none
        server-protocol: none
        server-port: none
        request-method: none
        path-info: none
        path-translated: none
        script-name: none
        query-string: none
        remote-host: none
        remote-addr: none
        auth-type: none
        remote-user: none
        remote-ident: none
        Content-Type: none
        content-length: none
        other-headers: []
    ]
]
```

Constructing objects

Objects are groups of variables that have a common context. Think of it this way: By putting all the letters from Aunt Maude in one file folder, it's easier to search for references in a particular letter from Aunt Maude. Consider this example:

```
apples: make object! [
    goldendelicious: "yellow and firm"
    grannysmith: "red and sweet"
    macintosh: "good in bits and bytes"]
```

Once the object is entered into REBOL, you can now manipulate it:

```
>> print apples/goldendelicious
yellow and firm
>> print apples/macintosh
good in bits and bytes
```

Note that there are paths into the object, as discussed in the previous sections. Play with this for now, and really get into it in Chapter 14 when I talk about databases in detail.

Managing Messages

REBOL is called a messaging language. A *message* in REBOL is nothing more than a text file sent from one place to another. The message can be sent between computers, processes, or people. The form is always the same and begins with a REBOL header, which can (but does not have to) include the title, date, version, purpose, and so forth. You can add as many as you need or like. Here's a sample header:

```
REBOL [
    Title:   "Example Header"
    Date:    14-Feb-2000
    Author: "George Washington"
    Version: 1.0.0
    Purpose: "Shows an example of a REBOL header"
]
```

After the header comes the content of the message. This can be code, data, or a REBOL script. Messages may be embedded in other forms of content, including Web pages.

Talking in Dialects

Dialects are an important part of the REBOL vision and future, but one that still is much evolving. Here are a few examples of dialects provided on the REBOL Technologies Web site that may be written to solve particular problems.

The possibilities are endless. I cover it in better detail for you in Chapter 19.

Chapter 6

Expressions, Bringing a Smile to Your Face

● ●

In This Chapter

▶ Expressing information

▶ Evaluating expressions

▶ Responding conditionally

▶ Looking inside blocks

● ●

*R*EBOL allows you to express information easily in plain English, or plain German, or plain Portuguese, or plain whatever. *Expressions* can be either functions or data, and you can use them as a standard system, independent means of expressing any kind of information.

Moreover, REBOL — as a computer language — works by evaluating expressions. In other words, REBOL observes each line of code and then computes its value.

That's a pretty important statement and one of the basics to understanding how REBOL works. Let me show you what I mean. Take this simple expression:

```
2 + 2
```

The preceding is an expression in REBOL, just as it was in my first grade class at West Buncombe Elementary School in 1952. The answer — or value — is still the same: 4. The method of evaluation remains similar — two plus two equals four.

Ease and flexibility in expressing information is more than half the battle in any mode of programming. If you can express a problem in simple terms that both you and the computer language understand, then you've pretty much won the battle, and now it's just a matter of mopping up a few last pockets of resistance.

REBOL provides you with a tremendous amount of flexibility in expressing and structuring data. This flexibility boosts both you and your scripts' ability to quickly and easily gain results.

Just as "2 + 2 = 4" is a fundamental of addition learned in grade school, so also is the expression of data in REBOL basic to your understanding and use of the language.

This chapter shows you how expressions work, and one of the various expressions that you create is a smile on your face.

Expressing Information

Your understanding of expressions should not be theoretical, but rather, practical. In the real world, you program for real-world events. Because everyone loves going to the dentist so much, this scenario is the perfect example to illustrate my point.

You call your dentist's office. Again, because you really love going to the dentist, you've put this off for the third time in the past two months. "Okay," the office manager asks with a sigh, "how about March 15 at 10:15?" You reluctantly agree. The office manager types this into the computer:

```
reschedule joe 15-March-2000 10:15
```

This example is an *expression* in REBOL, written in pretty much plain English. Of course, the dentist has this nifty REBOL program that you wrote, so the expression is evaluated and the computer value (the rescheduled date and time) is properly recorded.

Now, I dislike authors who say something like the preceding but don't show you an example of how it's done. So, play with this script:

```
REBOL [
        Title: "Simple expression"
        File: %6-reschedule.r
        Date: 28-Feb-2000
        ]

reschedule: func [patient date time][
    olddate: patient/3
    oldtime: patient/4
    replace patient olddate date
    replace patient oldtime time
    print newline
    print ["RESCHEDULED:" patient/1 patient/3 patient/4]
```

```
     print [newline patient/2 newline]
     ]


Lester: [ "Lester T. Phinklewinkle"
              "Drill big hole in tooth; pour in concrete."
          2-March-2000 10:30]

Marcus: [ "Marcus Tinkledinkle"
              "Scrape his pearly whites hard; find cavity."
          1-March-2000 8:30]

print newline
print "Doctor N.O. Payne, DDS Patient Database Loaded"
print newline
```

Load the patient database by typing **do %6-reschedule.r** at the REBOL console prompt (I'm assuming that you have the script in the current directory). Now you can reschedule the two patients in the database. The update looks like this:

```
>> do %6-reschedule.r
Script: "Simple expression" (28-Feb-2000)

Doctor N.O. Payne, DDS Patient Database Loaded

>> reschedule lester 15-march-2000 9:15

RESCHEDULED: Lester T. Phinklewinkle 15-Mar-2000 9:15

Drill big hole in tooth; pour in concrete.

>> reschedule marcus 15-march-2000 4:15pm

RESCHEDULED: Marcus Tinkledinkle 15-Mar-2000 16:15

Scrape his pearly whites hard; find cavity.

>>
```

Here's how it works. *Reschedule* is a defined function. It accepts the parameters of the patient's name and the rescheduled date and time. By defining functions in this way, you create a type of expression, which can be used like plain English.

The patient names, *Lester* and *Marcus*, are blocks of data containing (among other items) the date and time of their appointments. Now you are set up so that the simple expression

```
reschedule patient date time
```

does exactly what it states — replaces the old date and time in the block of data for the patient with the rescheduled date and time.

Remember what I said earlier about how expressing a problem is half the battle? See how easy it can be? Simple solutions, done simply — the REBOL way.

Just to remind you, an expression represents information. In REBOL, expressions are processed in one of two ways. You can type it at the console prompt and have it interpreted directly. Or, as is more usual, lines of code in a script are defined as being indirectly processed. If you've programmed in other languages, you may need to exert some effort in getting used to seeing code processed as data and data processed as code. The traditional division between data and code often blurs in REBOL, adding powerful flexibility. Essentially, how the expression (information) is processed determines what kind of expression it is.

Here's an example. Try it for yourself. I define the variable *a:*

```
>> a: [loop 5 [print "test"]]
```

If I type **a**

```
>> a
== [loop 5 [print "test"]]
```

all I get are the contents of the variable — it's just data. But, if I use the do function, the expression in the variable is evaluated and it becomes code:

```
>> do a
test
test
test
test
test
>>
```

Getting into blocks

Back to blocks. REBOL code is truly simple — you just combine values (expressions that are data) and functions (expressions that are code) into blocks. In scripts, a block is normally indicated with brackets. A block begins with a left bracket ([) and ends with a right bracket (]). Everything within the brackets is part of the block. The contents of a block can span any number of lines, and it is completely free-format. You can indent it or break it up over lines however you desire, or nest other blocks within it. Here are some data blocks:

```
  ["red" "white" "blue"]
[ food: ["steak" "beans" "pie"]
  beverages: ["coffee" "tea" "corn squeezin's"]
  ]
```

And this is a block used with functions:

```
if smoke-from-still = true [
print "Pappy's making corn squeezin's agin."
]
```

Afore the Revenuers git heah, let me ask you in review: What's the difference between a data block and a function block? Yes, you're right — there is no difference — the distinction lies in how the block is evaluated.

Some blocks do not require brackets; the brackets are implied. The text of a REBOL script is an example of this. Although there are no brackets around the entire script, it is a block. This outer-block of the script is implied. The same is true for expressions typed at the console prompt or REBOL messages sent between computers. Each is an implied block.

Another important observation about blocks is that they provide two pieces of information. They group a set of values in a particular order. This will become more important later when I discuss series in Chapter 8.

Is your expression a smile yet? Good.

Changing values

In Chapter 5, I explain datatypes, namely how specific values — including numbers, money, dates, times, logic, e-mail, strings, files, URLs, blocks, paths, and more — are expressed in REBOL and easily exchanged among so many different platforms. These values are the primary element you use when constructing expressions.

REBOL datatypes are simple; they are expressed in formats that you are used to, such as:

```
10:30                   ; time
12-March-2000           ; date
$14.95                  ; money
ralph@abooks.com        ; email
56.7834                 ; decimal
89                      ; integer
```

Some values — such as money, dates, and decimals — are expressed in alternative international forms; for example, the use of a comma instead of a period as the decimal character:

```
DEM$35,05
1,5
```

All methods are evaluated in the same way when they are used as part of an expression, so pick the method that you like and are most comfortable using.

Such expressions as the preceding ones are called direct values because what you see is what you get. Values are indirect if they require words to express their values, such as the `none`, `true`, and `false` values. Lists, hashes, functions, and objects can also be direct or indirect. These types of values must be constructed with the interpreter by actually running a script. Other values such as lists, hashes, functions, and objects may also be created this way. I show you how shortly.

Choosing the right words

A major difference between REBOL and other modern computer languages is the use of words as expression symbols. Words can and may have meaning to the REBOL interpreter as code in a script, as part of an application interfaced to REBOL, or even just to you.

Other computer languages lack the flexibility that REBOL gives you when using words. The concept is wonderful, albeit not particularly new — the LISP language used it some 40 years ago. REBOL refines it, however.

Because REBOL is intended for more than just jargon-loving, coffee-guzzling programmers (I think I'll brew up another pot), it does not distinguish between uppercase and lowercase spelling of words. For example, blue, Blue, and BLUE all refer to the same word.

See Chapter 5 for the rules governing the naming of words. Here are some more examples of the ways in which words can be used as both variables and functions:

```
blue: ["Prussian" "azure" "turquoise"]; as a data block
gold: func [][print price-of-gold-today] ; as a function
red: 15-May-2000                          ; deadline date
silver: $3.98                             ; money
```

A word may also have more than one meaning, depending on the context. You can prove this to yourself at the REBOL console prompt. Define variable a as 10. Then type (and thereby define a simple function) **sum: func [ ][a b][a+b]**, which you've seen before (it creates a function that adds two numbers). What you are doing is using the variable a for two different meanings. What you see should look like this:

```
>> a: 10
== 10
>> sum: func [a b][a + b]
>> sum 15 36
== 51
>> print a
10
```

You may find that defining and using a in the function sum does not affect the value of a as defined earlier. This is because you have used a in two different contexts; that is, by itself and inside the function.

Evaluating Expressions

REBOL works by evaluating the series of expressions that make up a script. In other computer languages, this evaluation process is termed *execution, running,* or *processing.* This operation (evaluation) is the same whether you type an expression on the REBOL console prompt or evaluate a script from a file.

Using console input

Go back to the example of adding 2 + 2 for a moment. If you type an expression at the console prompt, REBOL evaluates it and then returns its value:

```
>> print 2 + 2
4
```

Typing expressions at the console prompt is very useful for evaluating snippets of code before committing them to a script. This action is also a great way for you to follow along in this book and more fully understand the examples that I provide.

Scanning simple values

Simple values are just that — simple. They evaluate themselves. Take these values, for example:

```
>> 9:15
== 9:15
>> $15.98
== $15.98
>> 12-december-2000
== 12-Dec-2000
```

The preceding values return their value; that's all they are, and REBOL evaluates them as such. Essentially, nothing happens. This is also true for the following:

```
integer    1234
decimal    12.34
string     "REBOL world!"
time       13:47:02
date       30-June-1957
tuple      199.4.80.1
money      $12.49
char       #"A"
binary     #{ab82408b}
email      info@rebol.com
issue      #707-467-8000
tag        <IMG SRC="xray.jpg">
file       %xray.jpg
url        http://www.rebol.com/
block      [milk bread butter]
```

The same principle holds true for the list and hash datatypes as well.

Plugging blocks in as data

Blocks are normally treated as data and are not evaluated, unless you instruct REBOL to do so with a function of some sort. One way to evaluate blocks is to use the do function. In the next example, no evaluation occurs:

```
>> [2 + 2]
== [2 + 2]
>> do [2 + 2]
== 4
```

There's one thing that you need to understand about the preceding example. When using the do function, if the block contains more than one expression, then all expressions are evaluated, but only the value of the last one is returned, as in this example:

```
do [2 + 2
    5 + 4]
== 9
```

The way around using the do function is to use the reduce function, which evaluates all expressions in the block and then returns a block with those results — or, in this case, the sums of 2 + 2 and 5 + 4:

```
reduce [2 + 2
        5 + 4 ]
== [4 9]
```

"Hmm," you say astutely, "but you wrote earlier that entire scripts were just blocks. If that's true, how can a script run if only the value of the last expression is returned?"

Good question. As is often true in REBOL, there's a simple answer. You use a more complex expression — one that includes both a simple value and a function. Check out this example:

```
>> do [print 2 + 2
[      print 5 + 4]
4
9
```

Each line is now evaluated, and the value is returned. Other functions — such as if, loop, repeat, while, for each, and more — also evaluate blocks of data. I discuss these in greater detail in this chapter, but here's an example:

```
>> repeat count 5 [print [count ". Test line."]]
1 . Test line.
2 . Test line.
3 . Test line.
4 . Test line.
5 . Test line.
```

Blocks are considered to be data until they are explicitly evaluated by a function. Only a function causes them to be evaluated.

Following the script

Entire scripts can also be evaluated with the do function:

```
do [print 2 + 2]                    ; at the console
test: [print "testing"] do test     ; as a name value
do %lickety-split.r                 ; as a file
```

In order for REBOL to evaluate a file, it must have a valid REBOL header. The very minimum header is

```
REBOL []
```

or the script does not execute. You should probably get in the habit of including more data than this, however.

Plucking strings

Regular strings may be evaluated with the do function, as well:

```
>> do "2 + 2"
== 4
```

This technique is somewhat slower, however, as REBOL converts the string internally to a block, and then evaluates it.

One cool trick is the creation of your own REBOL console evaluator:

```
>> forever [do ask "next? >> "]
next? >> print "test"
test
next? >> do [print "test"]
test
next? >>
```

By using the forever function, you create a continuous loop that evaluates whatever expressions you type until it errors out, or until you type **quit**. (Typing **quit** exits REBOL, or you can press the Escape key to break the loop. Play with it — you may understand expressions and evaluation a bit better.)

Generally, because it's just as easy to create a block in REBOL as a string, and because blocks evaluate faster, you should use blocks whenever possible in your scripts. Blocks, of course, may contain string values.

Avoiding errors

The errors that you encounter in REBOL when you're first learning to use it are relatively simple to avoid. Dividing a number by zero "errors out" in about every programming language I know:

```
>> divide 100 0
** Math Error: Attempt to divide by zero.
** Where: divide 100 0
```

Using a word that you forgot to define is perhaps the most common error that you see in the beginning:

```
>> print word
** Script Error: word has no value.
** Where: print word
```

Trying blocks

Whenever an error occurs during evaluation, REBOL stops operation. In other words, your program bombs. One way to handle errors more gracefully than having your script grind to a halt is *error trapping*. You can use the `error` function with the `try` function to evaluate a block and find the errors, while letting the rest of the script run. Thus, you eliminate specific sections that are error free. Or, you can just evaluate snippets of code at the console to test suspect areas of a script. This is how it works:

```
>> error? try [divide 100 0]
== true
```

If the word *true* is returned, then you have an error in the block.

Evaluating words

Words are evaluated somewhat differently from simple values because of the many possibilities inherent in them; they can be anything from an integer value, such as 1, up to hundreds of lines or more of code (a function). REBOL must examine them and choose a course of evaluation.

More information on words and functions is detailed in this chapter and in Chapter 7.

Stopping evaluation

You stop evaluation of a script at the console by pressing the Escape key. Inside a program, use the halt or quit functions:

```
if > 17:00 halt
if > 17:00 quit
```

The halt function stops the script and, if the console is active, returns you to the console prompt. The quit function exits REBOL completely.

Responding Conditionally

So far, you've mostly used the do function when evaluating blocks. But perhaps you'd like to evaluate blocks depending on conditions. This action is quite common in all programming languages — although more logically implemented in REBOL. One conditional concept familiar to most of us is if. You know, *if something is true, then do this.* In REBOL, this is how the if function looks:

```
>> a: 5
== 5
>> if a = 5 [print "Variable A is equal to five."]
Variable A is equal to five.
```

Looking inside blocks

The if function is simple in both concept and use. It accepts two arguments — a condition and a block. Take the preceding example. The condition is a = 5. The block is only evaluated when a equals 5 and, thus, returns *true* to REBOL. If a equals any other number than 5, the code in the block is ignored and *false* is returned.

Normally, the if function looks for a true or false expression; a is either equal to 5 or it is *not* equal to 5. For a true expression, the block following the expression is evaluated; for a false expression, the block following the expression is ignored.

In short, the conditions that prevent a block from being evaluated are false and the value none. It is important to understand that these values are not zero. A statement such as:

```
if item = 0 [print "None in stock."]
```

returns `true` and the block gets done. `False` or `none` means that the condition was not met, and the block is not evaluated.

The true condition does not have to be black and white. This comes into play with functions such as `find`, `next`, and `select`, which return values of `none` if an item is absent.

By using the `either` function, a conditional evaluation takes one action for a `true` value and another action for a `false` value. The `either` function accepts a conditional expression followed by two blocks, one which gets evaluated for `true`, the other for `false`:

```
>> either now/time > 17:00 [print "Quit!"][print "Work!"]
Work!
```

The blocks for the `either` function may contain functions themselves. You can define a couple of quick functions and do the preceding example in this manner:

```
>> work: func[][print "Get back to work!"]
>> home: func[][print "Okay, okay... so go home."]
>> either now/time [work][home]
Get back to work!
```

Brackets are very important in REBOL. One of the most common mistakes that beginning coders make is forgetting the second block on the `either` function or adding a second block to the `if` function. Such errors are hard to find while debugging a balky script, so keep them in mind if the function is not doing what you expect.

REBOL supports a wide range of logical comparisons that you can use in making up `if` and `either` expressions. I examine these in detail in Chapter 11.

Doing any and all functions

The `any` and `all` conditional functions, when combined with other conditionals such as `if`, are cool because they give you a lot of programming power. See the following example, in which I define three variables — a, b, and c. You can then ask, "Are any of these true?" and then evaluate a block if one is true.

```
>> a: 5 b: 10 c: 20
>> if any [a = 4 b = 9 c = 19][print "Something is true."]
== none
>> if any [a = 4 b = 10 c = 19][print "Something is true."]
Something is true.
```

In the preceding example, when none are equal, REBOL returns a false value. The second try, when b meets the criteria, REBOL evaluates the block and prints your message. This works equally well for hundreds of items where one or more return true.

Be aware that the any function stops checking after finding the first true condition. If you need to check every value, you use a loop, as shown in the following section.

The any function returns the value of the first expression in the block that doesn't evaluate to none or false. In a block, all will return the value of the entire block if nothing evaluates to none or false.

The all function requires that every condition listed in the condition block (the first block) be true. As so:

```
>> if all [a = 5 b = 10 c = 20][print "All are true."]
All are true.
```

Coding conditional loops

Two conditional functions — until and while — evaluate a block over and over again, waiting for a certain condition to be met. In this example, that condition is the *tail,* or last item:

```
>> flavors: [salty sweet sour tart tangy hot cool]
>> until [print first flavors
     tail? flavors: next flavors]
salty
sweet
sour
tart
tangy
hot
cool
```

The while function operates similarly, except that it evaluates the expression that precedes the block to be evaluated:

```
>> while [not tail? flavors] [print first flavors
                   tail? flavors: next flavors]
salty
sweet
sour
tart
tangy
hot
cool
```

The distinction between these two methods of conditional looping is more significant than may first appear. In real world programming, if your program logic is a tad off, this could mean the difference between a quickly running script or one that hangs up on you. So, never enter into a condition loop unless you know the way back out.

Speaking of breaking out of a loop, the break function is useful. You can add a break to code like below, the break function itself being a conditional expression:

```
>> x: 1
>> while [x < 101][print x
    x: x + 1
    if x = 5 [break]]
1
2
3
4
```

Without the break, the preceding conditional loop goes to 101. With the break line in place, the conditional loop exits when x is 5 and before the value can be printed.

You can also use the /return refinement with break in a loop as in this example:

```
>> repeat count 10 [
    if count = 5 [break/return "Gave up at five."]
    ]
== "Gave up at five."
```

Ducking common mistakes

Conditionals are only false for values of false and none. Everything else is true. All of these examples return true — even the zero and empty block values:

```
if true [print "yep"]
yep
if 1 [print "yep"]
yep
if 0 [print "yep"]
yep
if [] [print "yep"]
yep
```

These return false:

```
if false [print "yep"]
if none [print "yep"]
```

It is an error to enclose your conditional in a block instead of using parentheses. You always get a true result:

```
if (false) [print "yep"]
if [false] [print "yep"]
yep
```

Another source of errors is if you intend to write

```
either some-condition
    [code-if-true]
    [code-if-false]
```

but instead write

```
if some-condition
    [code-if-true]
    [code-if-false]
```

This may not be an error, but your second block won't get evaluated.

The opposite is also true; if you write

```
either some-condition
    [code-if-true]
```

without a second block, then the `either` function does not evaluate the correct code and may produce an erroneous result.

Chapter 7

Expressions, Your Smile Widens

● ●

In This Chapter

▶ Repeating evaluation

▶ Selecting what to evaluate

▶ Evaluating words

▶ Furnishing functions

▶ Evaluating objects

● ●

Chapter 6 is fun, and this chapter will keep you smiling. Expressions are so . . . well . . . expressive, huh? In this chapter you learn how to loop, select what to evaluate, and dive into functions and objects. The "in plain English" aspect of coding in REBOL is just one of the several things I show you in this chapter that will keep that smile on your face.

Repeating Evaluation

Okay, not to get repetitive, but I like loops. Loops are one of the most useful constructs in all of computer programming, and REBOL has some powerful ones. For example, and with my apologies to the Kellogg's folks in Battle Creek, Michigan, here is my version of fruit loops:

```
>> fruits: [apple pear orange banana grapefruit]
>> foreach fruit fruits [print fruit]
apple
pear
orange
banana
grapefruit
```

Perhaps I should lay off the coffee before I become a cereal killer, eh?

Looping

The loop function is simple yet powerful:

```
>> loop 40 [prin "="]
========================================
```

This example, using prin instead of print so that no new line is added, prints 40 repetitions of the equals character (=).

You can also use the loop function to return the result of the last evaluation of a loop:

```
>> x: 0
>> loop 25 [x: x + 10]
== 250
```

Repeating

The repeat function loops by taking an argument (count in the following example) and reiterating it the number of times specified.

```
>> repeat count 5 [print [count ". Test"]]
1 . Test
2 . Test
3 . Test
4 . Test
5 . Test
```

count in the preceding example, or whatever argument name you choose, is a *local variable,* meaning it only has value inside the loop itself, although you can give it a starting value. The value is not limited to numbers. The following example features a timing loop that waits one second before printing the first time, two seconds the second time, and so on. The word timer used in this repeat function is independent of any global setting. Here's the code:

```
>> timer: 00:00:05
>> repeat timer 5 [wait timer print ["waited" timer
            "seconds"]]
waited 1 seconds
waited 2 seconds
waited 3 seconds
waited 4 seconds
waited 5 seconds
```

The `repeat` function also returns the last value:

```
>> y: repeat count 5 [x: x + 10]
>> print y
50
```

Using the for function

The `for` function extends the `repeat` function by allowing a starting, ending, and increment value to be specified. Any of the values can be positive or negative:

```
>> for count 0 100 20 [print count]
0
20
40
60
80
100
```

You can also use a negative value to get a descending loop:

```
>> for count 100 0 -20 [print count]
100
80
60
40
20
0
```

The `for` function also works for decimal numbers, money, times, dates, series, and characters. Be sure that both the starting and ending values are of the same datatype:

```
>> for loan-balance $10'000 $0 -$2'000 [print loan-balance]
$10000.00
$8000.00
$6000.00
$4000.00
$2000.00
$0.00
```

The `for` function also works on string values:

```
>> str: "abcdef"
>> end: find str "d"
>> for s str end 1 [print s]
abcdef
bcdef
cdef
def
```

Benefiting from the foreach function

A `foreach` loop, using the function word of the same name, handles each value in a series one at a time. A most excellent example of using a `foreach` loop is loading the filenames in the current directory into a REBOL word (I use `files` in the following example), sorting the list, and printing the directory one file per line, as shown in Figure 7-1:

```
files: read %.
sort files
foreach file files [print file]
```

I've written a short REBOL script using a `foreach` loop to give me a Web page of all my company's eBay pics. These (after the book has sold) can take up a lot of room on the server. My handy little REBOL application makes keeping space on the server a snap. I show you how to do this and a lot more in Chapters 17 and 18.

Figure 7-1 shows that I have plenty of files in this directory. But what if you just want the REBOL scripts (the `.r` extension files) listed in the directory? Okay, now that you know what they are, just add in a conditional expression:

```
foreach file files [if find file ".r" [print file]]
```

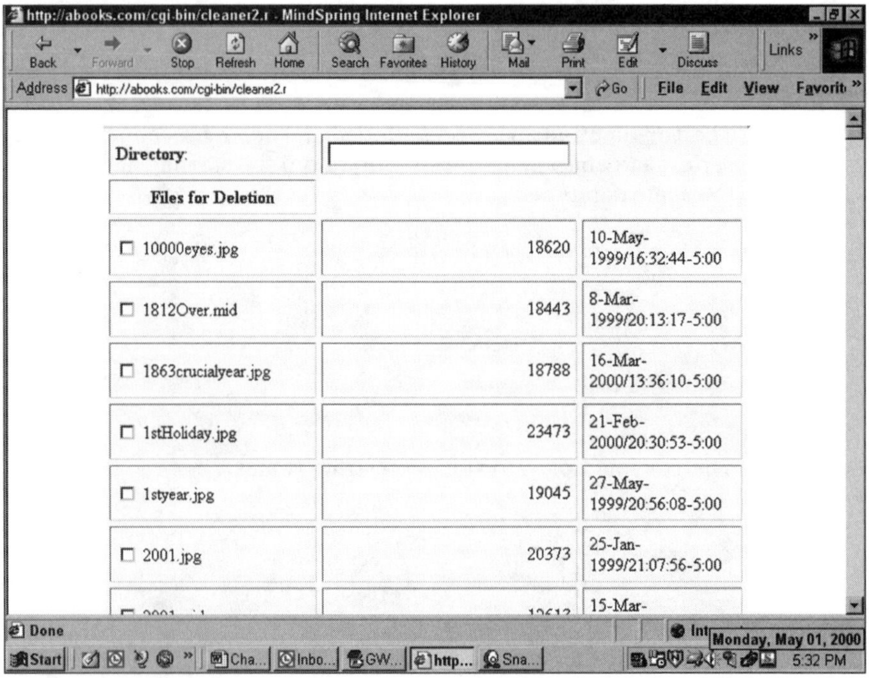

Figure 7-1:
The Web page that results from running my eBay pictures monitoring script.

A lot of power can go on one line of REBOL code!

The foreach function is also adept at stepping through more than one value per line. In the following example, I list the values of some signed celebrity photographs. As co-author and publisher of *The Sanders Price Guide to Autographs,* I usually have a few lying around. First, I set up a block with some autograph info:

```
autographs: [
      "Fred Astaire" "Entertainment" $268
      "John Glenn" "Astronaut" $120
      "Marilyn Monroe" "Entertainment" $5167]
```

Now I add the foreach loop with a little formatting stuff to make the output neat:

```
prin-tab: func [s] [prin s loop 20 - length? s [prin " "]]
foreach [name category value-signed-photo] autographs [
   prin-tab name prin-tab category print value-signed-photo
]
```

And this is the result:

```
Fred Astaire          Entertainment       $268.00
John Glenn            Astronaut           $120.00
Marilyn Monroe       Entertainment       $5167.00
```

The foreach function is a mighty tool, and I visit it again several times.

Making forall and forskip friends

Like the foreach function, the forall function steps through the series one at a time. The important difference is that the forall function changes the index position (more on this in Chapter 8) as it steps through the series.

```
>> colors: [red green blue yellow]
== [red green blue yellow]
>> forall colors [print first colors]
red
green
blue
yellow
```

If you try the print first colors command now, you get an error because the index is now at the tail of the series. You can reset it (and restore your series) by typing

```
colors: head colors
```

The utility of the forall function is that it allows you to exit somewhere in the middle of a series — when a certain condition is met — and you can begin your next operation here because the index position is set. I show you how to do this in Chapter 8, where I discuss series.

The forskip function performs the same as the forall function, except that you can make the steps incremental instead of linear. Here's an example that shows both the incremental method and what moving the index position can do:

```
>> a: [1 2 3 4 5 6 7 8 9 10]
== [1 2 3 4 5 6 7 8 9 10]
>> forskip a 2 [print a]
1 2 3 4 5 6 7 8 9 10
3 4 5 6 7 8 9 10
5 6 7 8 9 10
7 8 9 10
9 10
```

As with the forall function, you can reset the series by typing

```
a: head a
```

Keep going forever

On a clear day, you can loop forever, and that's exactly what the forever function does. It just keeps looping until something breaks the loop. One useful application is waiting for a file to appear, such as this example:

```
forever [
    if exists? %datafile [
        data: load %datafile
        delete %datafile
        break
    ]
    wait 10:00     ; ten minutes
]
```

This snippet of code checks for the existence of a file every 10 minutes. When the file appears, it is downloaded into the data variable, and the file is deleted.

Breaking evaluation

You can stop the repeated evaluation of a block with the break function. This function is useful if you encounter an unusual condition and the loop should be stopped. The break function works with all loops. Here's an example:

```
repeat count 10 [
    print [count ". test"]
    if count = 5 [break]
]
```

Which gives the result (breaking at 5):

```
1. test
2. test
3. test
4. test
5. test
```

Selecting What to Evaluate

REBOL provides several ways for you to selectively evaluate expressions based on a key value. The select function is the first way I show you.

Selecting

Using the select function, you can easily find and act on a specific case. An important case to those of us in the working class is our break times. So in this example, I construct a quick little database and stuff it into a variable:

```
breaktimes: [
    9:00 [print "Take off coat break."]
    10:00 [print "Coffee break"]
    11:00 [print "Restroom, previous break."]
    12:00 [print "Lunch"]
    1:00 [print "Restroom, for coffee with lunch."]
    2:00 [print "Afternoon nap in back of stockroom."]
    3:00 [print "Afternoon coffee break."]
    4:00 [print "Restroom break."]
    5:00 [print "Quitting time."]
]
```

Like those breaks? Okay, now I can use select to find and evaluate a block based on a case (the time of day):

```
>> do select break times 10:00
Coffee break
>> do select break times 2:00
Afternoon nap in back of stockroom.
>> do select break times 3:00
Afternoon coffee break.
```

The select function returns data unevaluated; it just selects it.

Switching

You may find that the select function is an often-used function. It is so handy that a special version of it called the switch function was added to REBOL. The difference between select and switch is that switch includes an evaluation of the selected block. This added option makes it easier to perform inline selective evaluation. For example, if you want to switch on a simple numeric case, define x as 7 and then use the switch function with x as an argument:

```
>> x: 7
>> switch x [
       1 [print "1"]
       5 [print "5"]
       7 [print "7"]
   ]

7
```

The switch function also works with cases of any valid datatype, including numbers, strings, words, dates, times, URLs, files, and so forth:

```
>> x: "red"
>> switch x [
       "blue" [print "hello"]
       "red" [print "goodbye"]
   ]

goodbye
```

You can also call files with the switch function. Perhaps you want to write an inventory program for an auto parts store and you want to load in a database for a specific class of parts:

```
item: "axle"
switch item [
    brakes [do %breaks.r]
    cylinders [do %cylinders.r]
    axles [do %axles.r]
    hubcaps [do %hubcaps.r]
]
```

You can also specify a default case — a good one to use if none of the specified cases match:

```
time: 11:00
switch/default time [
    9:00 [print "Meeting, conference room"]
    10:30 [print "Mr. Brown to discuss account"]
    12:00 [print "Lunch with boss"]
```

```
       17:00 [print "Quitting time!"]
  ] [print "no appointment"]
  no appointment
```

Spend a little time playing with `switch` and its refinement `/default` (for default case). Knowing these functions will pay off for you when writing future code.

Evaluating Words

Words are used in every aspect of REBOL; they can represent symbols or they can contain data including functions. Here's the difference:

```
>> size: [big small medium]
>> print second size
small
```

The variable `size` has meaning; it holds a block of sizes. The sizes — `big`, `small`, and `medium` — are just symbols holding no value. You can print them out as shown, but you cannot evaluate them without causing an error because they are "empty."

Reading word names

The names of words may be made up of letters and numbers, and any of the following characters:

```
? ! . ' + - * & | = _ ~
```

So these are all valid words:

```
word! test? this-one that.word ++
```

Some restrictions may apply to words that can also be numbers. For example, `-1` and `+1` are numbers, not words.

Spaces normally end a word but other characters (called *delimiters*) can also end words. These delimiter characters are

```
[ ] ( ) { } " : ;
```

The brackets ([]) surround a block and are not part of the word:

```
[some words]
```

REBOL does not distinguish between uppercase and lowercase spelling of words. (REBOL is intended for users, not just technicians.) The words

```
GREEN green Green gREen
```

all refer to the same word.

Words can be of any length, but they cannot extend past the end of a line.

```
Here-we-have-a-pretty-darn-long-word-used-as-an-example
```

The current version of REBOL supports the standard 256 extended-character set. International 16-bit character sets will be supported in later releases.

Determining usage

As you've already seen, words can be symbols or they can contain data; in the latter case, the words are either functions or information. In other words, a word defined as data may have executable code in it, or the word may just be used as a storage variable.

Look again at this example:

```
size: [big small medium]
```

size is a REBOL word containing a block of data, but big, small, and medium are just symbols, having no value in them. Any unused word you can concoct becomes a word or container for data simply by *setting* it, as in these examples:

```
reds: ["sunset hues" "Marx & Lenin" "Cincinnati baseball"]
time: now/time
iou: $3.00
fast-food: "greasy hamburger"
sum: func [a b c][a + b + c]
```

The following example is a function (containing code to be evaluated while the preceding words simply contain data). After a function is defined, you can use it like this:

```
>> print sum 14 33 119
166
```

More about functions comes up later in this chapter, but first, here are the four different ways in which you can write words and control how they are evaluated:

Table 7-1	Evaluating Words	
Method	*Result*	*Comment*
word	Evaluate the word.	This is the most natural and common way to write words. If the word holds a function, it is evaluated. Otherwise the value of the word is returned.
word:	Define or set the word.	Give it a new value, which can be anything, including a function.
:word	Retrieve the word's value.	Does not evaluate it. This is useful for referring to functions and other types of data without evaluating them.
'word	Refer to the word as a symbol.	Does not evaluate it. The word is treated as the value itself.

Setting words

You can *set* words in several ways (give them a value). The one you use most is the word followed by a colon (:), as in these examples:

```
focus: "sharp"
golfers: [Arnold, Jack, Tiger]
age: 39
dir: func ["Current directory"][ print sort read %.]

email: support@rebol.com
url: http://abooks.com
```

The preceding examples include string, block, integer, function, e-mail, and URL values. And, of course, words may be defined in REBOL according to any of the many other values discussed in Chapter 6.

Several words may be *cascaded,* or defined at once:

```
time: log-time: start_time: runtime: now/time
```

Hmmm. That looked interesting. Now I show you what I got by printing all four:

```
>> print [time tab log-time tab start_time tab runtime]
14:42:46    14:42:46    14:42:46    14:42:46
```

Yep, all four got the same value.

You may also use the `set` function for defining words. But if you do, add an apostrophe in front of the word so that it becomes a literal value. Otherwise, REBOL tries to evaluate it before you get the definition in, and an error results:

```
>> set 'time 11:45
>> print time
11:45
```

The `set` function evaluates several words at once also (and no apostrophe is needed because the words are inside a block):

```
>> set [log-time start_time runtime] 8:32
>> print [log-time tab start_time tab runtime]
8:32      8:32      8:32
```

Or you can use two blocks and set the values individually:

```
>> set [four five six][4 5 6]
>> print [four five six]
4 5 6
```

Getting words

You can *get* a word's value and assign it to another word by placing a colon (:) in front of the word, and thereby preventing evaluation. I make the print statement work in French as an example:

```
>> imprime: :print
>> imprime "test"
test
```

Good, it works. You can also do several languages at once:

```
set [imprime druck stampa impressão impresión] :print
```

That's French, German, Italian, Portuguese, and Spanish. Did it work?

```
>> imprime "oui"
oui
>> druck "ja"
ja
>> stampa "si"
si
>> impressão "si"
si
>> impresión "si"
si
>> print "and print itself still works"
and print itself still works
```

Most excellent. You can now code the function `print` in six languages.

Other functions in REBOL operate on a word's reference rather than its value. These are `native?`, `function?`, and `op?`. Functions built into REBOL are called *native functions*. The `function?` function checks function words to see if they are functions (try saying that 100 times real fast). The `action?` function checks action datatypes like `trim`, `tail?`, and so forth (type `help action!` to get a list of these). And the `op?` function refers to operators like addition (+), greater than (>), and so forth. Use them like this (remember the colon in front):

```
>> native? :print
== true
>> function? :sum
== true           ; assuming you defined it earlier
>> op? :=
== true
```

Using literal words

Here's an example of using *literal words,* or words that have no value. In this case, I use them as fieldnames in a database record:

```
books: [
    title "REBOL FOR DUMMIES"
    author "Ralph Roberts"
    length "pretty long"
]
```

Remember, to use a literal word (words without evaluation) you include an apostrophe in front of it. Like this example:

```
>> print select books 'length
pretty long
```

The literal quote symbol is often referred to as a *tick.* My old hound dog presents another definition for that word but . . . anyway . . . English and REBOL are both purely malleable, huh?

A shortcut for the `select` function is to use path notation, and then you can get rid of the tick (see that old dog's tail wag?):

```
>> print books/length
pretty long
```

Handling unset words

A word can be undefined with the unset function:

```
>> unset 'sum
```

Using unset requires the apostrophe or tick in front of the word to make it literal and to prevent evaluation.

You can also use the value? function to see if a word is unset (that is, is it available for use?) like this:

```
>> value? 'x
== false
>> x: 12
>> value? 'x
== true
```

A false is returned for an unset word — because it has no value. Or you can test with the unset? function:

```
>> unset? x
== false
```

The false shows that the word does contain a value, or is set. A return of true means that the word has no value and is available for new usage. Obviously, unset? works directly opposite of value?, being respectively true if empty and false if set.

Protecting words

To keep a word from accidentally being redefined later in a script, use the protect function:

```
>> protect 'time
```

Now any attempt to redefine time produces an error.

Here's something that's mighty important when you are first starting to learn REBOL: All currently set words can be protected by using the protect-system function. This protects words in system/words from redefinition.

If protect-system is set in the user.r file, then all words set within REBOL are protected from modification because this file is called by REBOL just after initializing itself. To do this, just open user.r and add the function on a line like this:

```
REBOL [
    Title: "User Preferences"
    Date:  12-Feb-2000/11:16:27-5:00
]

set-net [
    ralph@abooks.com mindspring.com none none none none
]
protect-system
```

Understanding word datatypes

The different written forms of words correspond to the internal datatypes set-word, get-word, word, and lit-word, with appropriate type models and type tests as shown in Table 7-2:

Table 7-2		Word Datatypes	
Action	*Type Model*	*Type Test*	*Conversion*
word	word!	word?	to-word
word:	set-word!	set-word?	to-set-word
:word	get-word!	get-word?	to-get-word
'word	lit-word!	lit-word?	to-lit-word

Furnishing Functions

Two types of functions exist in REBOL: built-in (native, op, and action) and user-defined, or mezzanine (function). The *built-in* functions come with the language; all the rest you can make yourself or download from a growing number of sources on the Internet, such as http://rebol.org.

Native functions, of course, are the built-in functions upon which all other functions are based. The functions foreach, select, do, print, and many others are native to the system.

User-defined functions, again, are those functions that you or some other fearless coder creates with REBOL code. You can construct functions to do any special operations that you need.

Functions are somewhat similar to subroutines in other languages. If you have an often-used routine that requires 10 lines of code, write it once as a function instead of repeating it perhaps dozens of times. Also, after you've built a library of custom and/or acquired functions, your REBOL code goes even faster.

Providing arguments

A *function* is a defined word that does some action. Usually that action requires some input data to act on; this data is the function's *argument* (or arguments, as the case may be). In this example, I use the summing function again:

```
sum: func [a b][a + b]
```

That's how a very basic function is defined. The variables a and b in the first block define the function's arguments. So if you actually use this function in REBOL, it looks like this:

```
>> sum 12 487
== 499
```

See? The number 12 is the a argument and 487 is the b argument. In the second block of the function REBOL evaluates the instructions — a + b or add a to b — and returns the value which, in this case, is 499.

You can have fewer or more arguments, depending on the function. Here's a function that's a bit more complex:

```
average: func [a b c d e][divide (a + b + c + d + e) 5]
```

This function accepts five numbers and gives you the average of those numbers by dividing by five. You can use it, for example, to get grade averages for a series of five tests, entering the grades for each student like this:

```
>> average 78 88 75 50 90
== 76.2
>> average 100 90 88 77 100
== 91
```

Getting help for functions

What if you don't know how many arguments or which arguments a function requires? The answers are simple enough to find; just type **help** and the name of the function at the REBOL console:

```
>> help print
Outputs a value and starts a new line.
Arguments:
    value -- The value to print
```

The preceding is for the print function, one of the native REBOL functions. The help given for all these functions is minimal, in keeping with maintaining such a small footprint for the entire language (less than 300K currently). Yet, it should be all you need. REBOL tells you what it does ("outputs a value and starts a new line") and what its argument — just one for this function — is ("value to print"). So, you now know how to use print:

```
print {To find help, type 'help name-of-function'}
```

This works for all types of functions, not only native ones, but also user-defined functions — assuming the user has done a proper job of adding a little help.

To view a list of all functions available in REBOL, type **what** at the console prompt (you get a *long* list) or browse the REBOL dictionary (http://rebol.com/dictionary).

In REBOL/Core 2.3 (coming out just as this book is going to press, and included for you on the CD), the *help* function can be used on part of a word. If that word does not match a function or word, a listing of all words and functions that match the pattern is listed along with the type of value defined to the word, like this:

```
>> help fo
Found these words:
    for           (function)
    forall        (function)
    foreach       (native)
    forever       (function)
    form          (native)
    forskip       (function)
    found?        (function)
    fourth        (action)
    info?         (function)
    reform        (function)
```

Or you may also use a string, such as this one:

```
>> help "for"
Found these words:
    for           (function)
    forall        (function)
    foreach       (native)
    forever       (function)
    form          (native)
    forskip       (function)
    reform        (function)
```

Implementing user-defined functions

You can create your own functions by using the `func` function. Back to the `sum` example of a function, which is a user-defined function. So far, I've defined it each time as something like this:

```
sum: func [a b][a + b]
```

You may not readily know how to use this function, so I add a help feature in this example:

```
>> sum: func ["Adds a + b like 3 + 2" a b][a + b]
```

The format for the first block argument of `func` is your help message (keep it short but pithy) inside quotes or braces, and then the argument (or arguments). The second block, of course, is the function itself — the code that does the work. But I try help for the `sum` function in this example:

```
>> help sum
Adds a + b like 3 + 2
Arguments:
   a --
   b --
```

You can save your tasty homemade functions in the handy container of a REBOL script, like this:

```
REBOL []
sum: func ["Adds a + b like 3 + 2" a b][a + b]
```

Include a REBOL header, preferably with a few more details than the preceding minimal one. Of course, you can add a number of your functions in the same script and then just call in your small but powerful library by inserting

```
do %my-functions.r
```

near the top of any script from which you want to have access to your functions. This saves lots of work and time.

Okay, you've seen how you can define your own user functions by structuring them with the required arguments in the first block and then placing the code that acts on those arguments in the second block. It's good programming practice, however, to restrict the type of data going into an argument, and REBOL lets you do this easily. You certainly don't want to divide apples by oranges, so to speak.

Just like you can include the function's description by placing a string inside the argument block before the arguments, you can also show explanations for each argument.

An argument's descriptions are indicated by a string placed after each declared argument. Accepted arguments are restricted by a block placed after the argument in which the accepted types are listed.

Back, yet again, to my old pal sum. In the next example, I elaborate on this function a bit more by including argument descriptions and restricting those arguments to accepting values only of the number! datatype (integers and/or decimals). It looks like this:

```
sum: func [
    "Adds a + b like 3 + 2"
    a [number!] "first number"
    b [number!] "second number"
][
    a + b
]
```

Good. Now when you type **help sum** at the console, you get this:

```
>> help sum
Adds a + b like 3 + 2
Arguments:
    a -- first number (number)
    b -- second number (number)
```

And if you add a decimal and an integer, your sum function works fine:

```
>> sum 12.5 6
== 18.5
```

But if you try mixing in a datatype that you have not authorized, like money!, then you get (as you should) an error:

```
>> sum $10 + 2
** Script Error: sum expected a argument of type: number.
** Where: sum $10.00 + 2
```

If you want sum to work for money values also, just change your arguments to look like this:

```
    a [number! money!] "first number"
    b [number! money!] "second number"
```

I touch on this in Chapter 6, but it bears repeating for emphasis — all the words used as names for arguments are local to the function. This includes refinements and their arguments (see "Making refinements" later in this chapter), and this also means that the value is only affected within the function. If the word exists outside the function, it is not modified.

Additional local words can be specified by using the local refinement. Why is this important? Well, the words you use are for arguments — in the case of the sum function, a and b are words — only they are automatically made local values. If you use other words in the second block (the code for the function), you most likely want some of those to be local also. REBOL does not know this unless you tell it. And you do so in the argument block:

```
random-color: func ["Generates a random color."
    /local colors
    ][
        colors: [red green pink gold brown lavender yellow
                purple rose turquoise silver gray black
                orange tan sand crimson ivory beige rust]
        print pick colors random 20
    ]
```

In the preceding example, I define colors as a local variable and use it to store data. You can use the name colors elsewhere in your script and this data is not affected. Here's proof:

```
>> colors: "This is a test."
== "This is a test."
>> random-color
gray
>> print colors
This is a test.
```

See, I defined colors, called the function using my other instance of colors, and then I printed the original colors, finding it still unchanged. Cool, indeed. Try it.

Controlling arguments

You can control how a function evaluates arguments, making your code both flexible and powerful. To make a function's arguments optional, use the any-type! datatype identifier in the block for arguments, like this example:

```
print-val: func [val [any-type!]] [
    print either value? 'val [val]["No value given"]
]
```

When you try it for yourself, do these two things:

```
>> print-val $12
$12.00
>> print-val
No value given
```

In the first console line, an argument is given with the function and that argument is printed. In the second console line, no argument is given but the function, instead of bombing with an error, graciously informs you that no value was provided. This is the way programming should be.

Making refinements

Refinements are switches or modifications that you can add to REBOL functions to modify their behavior. For example, if you use the read function to copy the http://rebol.com index page into the variable a, and then print a using the first function, you get only the first character, which is a less than symbol (<):

```
>> a: read http://rebol.com
>> print first a
<
```

But if you use the /lines refinement, which causes read to pull in data by line instead of by character, you get the entire first line:

```
>> a: read/lines http://rebol.com
>> print first a
<!DOCTYPE HTML PUBLIC "-//W3C//DTD HTML 3.2//EN">
```

You can easily find all of a function's refinements by using help. Like those of read:

```
>> help read
Reads from a file, url, or port-spec (block or object).
Arguments:
    source -- (file url object block)
Refinements:
    /binary -- Preserves contents exactly.
    /string -- Translates all line terminators.
    /direct -- Opens the port without buffering.
    /wait -- Waits for data.
    /lines -- Handles data as lines.
    /part -- Reads a specified amount of data.
        size -- (number)
    /with -- Specifies alternate line termination.
        end-of-line -- (char string)
    /mode -- Block of above refinements.
        args -- (block)
    /custom -- Allows special refinements.
        params -- (block)
```

But, what about your own functions? Glad you asked. Back again to the sum function, which you should know quite well by now. Modify it to add an /average refinement that causes sum to average the two arguments instead of adding them:

```
sum: func [
    "Adds a + b like 3 + 2"
    a [number!] "first number"
    b [number!] "second number"
/average "Average instead of add."
    ][
either average [a + b / 2][a + b]
]
```

And here's how it works now, using first your default and then the refinement:

```
>> sum 12 34
== 46
>> sum/average 12 34
== 23
```

And, if you type **help sum**:

```
>> help sum
Adds a + b like 3 + 2
Arguments:
    a -- first number (number)
    b -- second number (number)
Refinements:
    /average -- Average instead of add.
```

You can add refinements to your functions anyway you like, but certain conventions are suggested. Table 7-3 details these conventions.

Table 7-3	Refinement Conventions
Refinement	**Action**
/all	remove all whitespace, parse all characters including spaces
/allow	specify protection attributes
/any	enable * and ? wildcards, allow wildcards, allow any type of value, and zero or more repetitions
/append	add data at end
/args	set argument string from this value
/auto	auto-indent lines relative to first line

Refinement	Action
/base	conversion base
/binary	preserve contents exactly (they're binary)
/case	become case-sensitive
/compare	use this comparison function
/custom	allows special refinements
/day	day info
/date	date info
/deep	propagate operation throughout nested data
/default	what to do when nothing else matches
/direct	open without buffering
/dup	duplicate the operation N times
/head	operate at head
/header	obtain/use/write with header
/hide	mask input with '*' (as with passwords)
/initial	initial value
/lines	handle data as lines and replace line breaks with space
/match	return TAIL of match (find THROUGH it)
/mode	multiple refinements presented as a block
/month	month info
/name	name identifying something otherwise unnamed
/new	create
/off	disable
/on	enable
/only	treat series value as single block value; send only one message to multiple addresses
/part	a specified amount of data
/radians	use radians instead of degrees
/read	read only (disable writing)

(continued)

Table 7-3 *(continued)*

Refinement	Action
/return	force to return a value
/size	spaces per tab
/skip	fixed size to skip over each time
/some	one or more repetitions
/string	translate all line terminators
/tail	return end of series; operate at end
/tcp	Internet-related
/time	time info
/wait	wait for data
/weekday	day-of-week info
/with	specified characters: alternate wildcards for * and ?, remove specified characters, alternate line termination, and specify alternate acceptable responses
/word	return datatype as a word
/write	write only (disable reading)
/year	year info
/zone	time zone info (offset from GMT)

I discuss additional features of functions in Chapter 8.

Evaluating Objects

Objects are actually pretty simple. They provide a way to group a collection of values together so that the group can be acted on as a single whole. A good example is a record in a name-and-address database. Each record may contain an individual's name, street address, city, state, ZIP code, telephone number, occupation, birthday, and so forth. Turning collections of fields such as these into objects makes collections easy to handle (and to perform operations upon, if you're the mad-scientist type).

Making objects

New objects in REBOL are created with the make function and may be *unique* (created from scratch) or *derived* from other objects. To create a unique object, such as a name and address database in the preceding example, do this:

```
Finklewumper: make object! [
    first-name: "Marley"
    last-name: "Finklewumper"
    address: "8411 Thumper Lane"
    town: "Rabbitsrun"
    state: "NC"
    zip: "28700"
]
```

The new object is created by the make function and can be handled as any other value. Each of the words defined within the block becomes an accessible word within the object. These words are often called *instance variables* in object terminology. Yep, finklewumper is now an instance variable.

Accessing

Okay, carrying on with finklewumper, how do you access the data grouped within this object? One method is to use paths, like this example:

```
>> print finklewumper/address
8411 Thumper Lane
>> print finklewumper/first-name
Marley
```

You can just as easily modify data in an object as you can access it using paths. Take Mr. Finklewumper's first name — it's *Narley,* not Marley. How did you ever make such a silly mistake? No problem, here's how you change it:

```
>> finklewumper/first-name: "Narley"
== "Narley"
>> print finklewumper/first-name
Narley
```

Yes, just redefine it by using the full pathname, as you would for any other variable — in this case, a string value.

Using derived objects

If you *derive* an object, you are simply using another object as a template for a new one, like this:

```
>> new-finklewumper: make finklewumper []
>> probe new-finklewumper
make object! [
    first-name: "Narley"
    last-name: "Finklewumper"
    address: "8411 Thumper Lane"
    town: "Rabbitsrun"
    state: "NC"
    zip: 28700
]
```

Determining self values

Every object in REBOL automatically contains the word self as the first word in its word. This refers back to the object itself. This word can be used from within the object to pass the object to other functions or return it as a result of a function.

Chapter 8

The World Series

A *series* of values is just that, a group of values in a row. A series may be either strings or blocks of associated values; and the values may differ within the series. For example, blocks containing the names of baseball players, their batting averages, and the amount of their multimillion-dollar playing contracts would contain string, decimal, and dollar (high-dollar!) values, respectively.

In this chapter I show you ways of creating, moving through (traversing), extracting data from, modifying, copying, and sorting data for basic series.

In other words, it's time to see all the neat things you can do *to* and *with* series in REBOL.

Meeting Series

REBOL offers many ways of evaluating various series of values and returning a value from a specific position in that series. A *series of values* can be just about anything — strings, lists, directories of files, e-mail messages, URLs, or just about any other group of values I mention in previous chapters. The definition of a *series,* then, is a set of values organized in a specific order. The following are all series:

```
towns: [Asheville Alexander Weaverville Leicester]
text:  "This string is a series."
debts: [$10.00 $12.95 $67.48]
url:   http://rebol.com
```

Mastering the concept of series and the methods of extracting data from them or adding information to them puts you in a position to write powerful REBOL scripts that do useful real-world tasks. Series, in my opinion, are also one of the most fun items to play with in all of REBOL. So, batter up! Let's toss a few series around.

The following list gives you a good indication of the sheer inclusiveness of series:

- Set of values
- String of characters
- Directory of files
- Mailbox of messages
- Group of tasks
- Database of records (as in a checkbook)
- Sequence of images (as in a movie)
- Sequence of sounds
- Array of pixels (as in an image)
- Array of samples (as in a sound)
- And more. . . .

How do you manipulate a series in REBOL? Easily. Define the a word as a series — in this case a string containing a sentence.

```
>> a: "Now is the time to write victorious code."
```

REBOL gives some basic functions to perform operations on this string:

```
>> print first a      ; print the first character
N
>> print second a     ; print the second character
o
>> print last a       ; print the last character
.
```

But what if you want to use full words instead of characters? First, *parse* the sentence into words. Parsing is the powerful dialect included in REBOL for recognizing and acting on sequences of characters. Yes, it is similar to but more sophisticated than the series manipulations covered in this chapter, and I look at parsing in the detail it deserves in Chapter 12. Meanwhile, you can use parse to slice and dice the sample sentence into words:

```
>> b: parse a " "
== ["Now" "is" "the" "time" "to" "write" "victorious"
        "code."]
```

All you did was tell REBOL to slice the string in the REBOL word a apart between words (that is, wherever it found a space) and put the results into word b.

Now try first and the other series functions again:

```
>> print first b        ; print the first word
Now
>> print second b       ; print the second word
is
>> print last b         ; print the last word
code.
```

Good. Now you're acting on words instead of characters. Not REBOL words, mind you, but a series of strings in a block. REBOL gives you only first, second, third, fourth, and fifth function words, but you can use the following two techniques for numbers in series greater than five:

```
>> print b/7            ; print the seventh word.
victorious
>> print pick b 7       ; same using 'pick'
victorious
```

The preceding is the most basic but yet powerful and easy series manipulation. REBOL gives you the tools to use. Something comes first, then there's a second, a third, a fourth, a fifth; then you can use pick with the word followed by a forward slash (/) and the number of the desired position. Something else comes next. There is a head and a tail. You can skip forward or backward in the series. You can count its elements and refer to them by their location. And more:

```
>> print skip b 5       ; skip first five words
write victorious code.
>> print at b 5         ; go to fifth word
to write victorious code.
>> print length? b      ; number of words (or characters)
8
>> b: tail b            ; set b to its tail (end)
>> print skip b -3      ; print last three words
```

```
write victorious code.
>> b: head b              ; set the series back to start
>> b: skip b 5            ; set the position to sixth word
>> print first b          ; 'first' now prints sixth word
write
```

I look in more detail at the preceding operations and the other series related functions in this chapter.

Creating Series

You may create a series using the make function or by just defining a variable that fits within one of the series! datatypes (string, block, URL, tuple, path, and so forth). There is also the copy function, which lets you use an existing series as a template.

```
>> new-string: make string! 100
== ""
>> new-block: make block! 100
== []
>> even-newer-string: copy new-string
== ""
>> even-newer-block: copy new-block
== []
```

Making series is truly trivial in REBOL and using them is not much more complicated.

Traversing

To *traverse* is to move back and forth. In this case, you move back and forth through series of values, jump to specific positions within series, and loop through series.

Moving back and forth

The act of traversing a series may be likened to crossing a creek, something I know a lot about here in the Carolina hills. You start by hopping to the first of a series of stones (the *head*); then hop from one stone to the next until you reach the other side of the creek (the *tail*). During the process of moving across the creek, your current position is marked by where you are standing. If you encounter an error, it means you fell into the creek.

Sorry, I couldn't resist that last paragraph, but the creek crossing analogy is good. Let's look at a creek full of rocks . . . I mean, a series:

```
creek: ["granite" "flint" "slick" "mossy" "marble"]
```

Yep, watch that `slick` rock! Okay, more series seriously, `creek` is a word referring to a block of data, which is a series. You can traverse the series (cross the `creek`) by hopping from rock to rock. Use your old friend, the `foreach` loop, to do it:

```
>> foreach stone creek [print creek creek: next creek]
granite flint slick mossy marble
flint slick mossy marble
slick mossy marble
mossy marble
marble
== []
```

Now the play by play. The granite rock is at the head of the series, and you hop on it first. All the other rocks — `flint`, `slick`, `mossy`, and `marble` — remain, the rapid current swirling water around them. Because you are at the head of the series, all the names of the rocks are printed out (see the preceding example).

You jump to the `flint` rock, easily landing on its flat surface. Your position has changed and this is recorded by the bit of code

```
creek: next creek
```

which changes the current position in the series (called the *current index*), so only the rock you are standing on and the remaining rocks in the series are printed, `granite` now being history in the old "been there, done jumped on that" tradition:

```
flint slick mossy marble
```

Next jump to the `slick` rock. Oops! Your feet slide, your arms windmill! You finally get stabilized (well, I told you it was slick). Anyway, your current index is now:

```
slick mossy marble
```

This means that all operations take place referenced from the position of `slick`. If you type **first creek**, `slick` will be returned, and so forth. But continue on by hopping to `mossy`, and then to `marble`, and then jump to the far bank. Congratulations, you've just survived your first traverse of a block and you are now at the `tail` of the series.

Referring back to the `foreach` loop, you see that the last line indicates an empty block ([]) because the current index is now completely past the series (one position past the end of the series, to be precise). Type **print creek** and you get nothing. Have you lost all your rocks? Nah. Do this to reset to the head of the series:

```
>> creek: head creek
== ["granite" "flint" "slick" "mossy" "marble"]
```

Changing positions

You can obtain the value from a specific position in a series by using the `pick` function or any of its shorthand functions (`first`, `second`, `third`, `fourth`, and `fifth`):

```
>> print pick creek 3
slick
>> print pick creek 4
mossy
```

This creek is a freezing cold mountain stream, so you may not want to chance skipping across the rocks; however, it's possible to skip *around* in a series using the `skip` or `at` functions:

```
>> print skip creek 3
mossy marble
>> print at creek 3
slick mossy marble
```

The two preceding examples also show the difference between `skip` and `at` — which is `skip` jumps three rocks to print the fourth, where `at` prints starting with the third rock, or at it. The `at` word is an action function that returns the value of the series from the current index point.

You can also use `skip` and `at` to print back from the end of the series if you first set its tail to `series`, or set the current index beyond where you want to print:

```
>> creek: tail creek
>> print skip creek -1
marble
>> print at creek -2
mossy marble
```

The tail of a series is one position past its last element, so no elements exist there. The tail is used for many things that include appending elements to the end of series. To do that, first make sure you are at the tail, and then use the `insert` function (see also Figure 8-1):

```
>> creek: tail creek
>> insert creek "muddy"
>> creek: head creek
>> print creek
granite flint slick mossy marble muddy
```

Yes, you picked up a big old muddy rock and tossed it into the creek. Be careful stepping on that one, too.

If you are not sure you are at the head or tail of a series, use the `head?` and `tail?` functions — they return `true` or `false`.

The creek analogy here may be a little cutesy, but believe me, falling into a creek from a slick rock is harder (which, take my word for it, is not hard at *all*) than traversing series. And, as you traverse, you can do things, such as when we added the muddy rock above.

Here's one more practical example — put a rock in front of the slick rock (currently the `third` rock in the series):

```
print insert at creek 3 "flat"
>> print creek
granite flint flat slick mossy marble muddy
```

Good. Step on the flat rock and over the slick rock, and then jump the muddy rock to the bank. Say — since you're manipulating series, why don't you just take that slick rock out of the creek so you don't bust your . . . er . . . rearward components by slipping on it (in other words, remove `slick` from the series):

```
>> remove at creek 4 "slick"
== "slick"
>> print creek
granite flint flat mossy marble muddy
```

Now let me introduce the concept of multiple references to a series. Take our chilly, rock-filled creek above. Joe can stand on one stone while Jane is standing on another, and they are both referencing the same series. It looks like this:

```
>> creek: ["granite" "flint" "slick" "mossy" "marble"]
== ["granite" "flint" "slick" "mossy" "marble"]
>> joe: next creek
== ["flint" "slick" "mossy" "marble"]
>> jane: head creek
== ["granite" "flint" "slick" "mossy" "marble"]
```

Jane is on the `first` rock, the granite one; Joe is on the next rock from the head of the series, the flint rock. You can see which point in the series a word references by using the `index?` function as follows:

```
>> rock: index? joe print pick creek rock
flint
>> rock: index? jane print pick creek rock
granite
```

Now, what would happen if Jane moves over to the next rock, the one Joe is standing on?

```
>> jane: next creek
== ["flint" "slick" "mossy" "marble"]
```

Nice jump, Jane . . . but, say, wasn't Joe on that rock? We can use the `same?` function to see if two words reference the same point in a series:

```
>> same? joe jane
== true
```

Hmmm. While that is true in REBOL, in the real world Joe is flat on his back in the frigid creek and not at all happy with Jane. Quit laughing, Jane! Now, let me show you loops. Keep an eye on those rocks, though. You're not finished with that series yet.

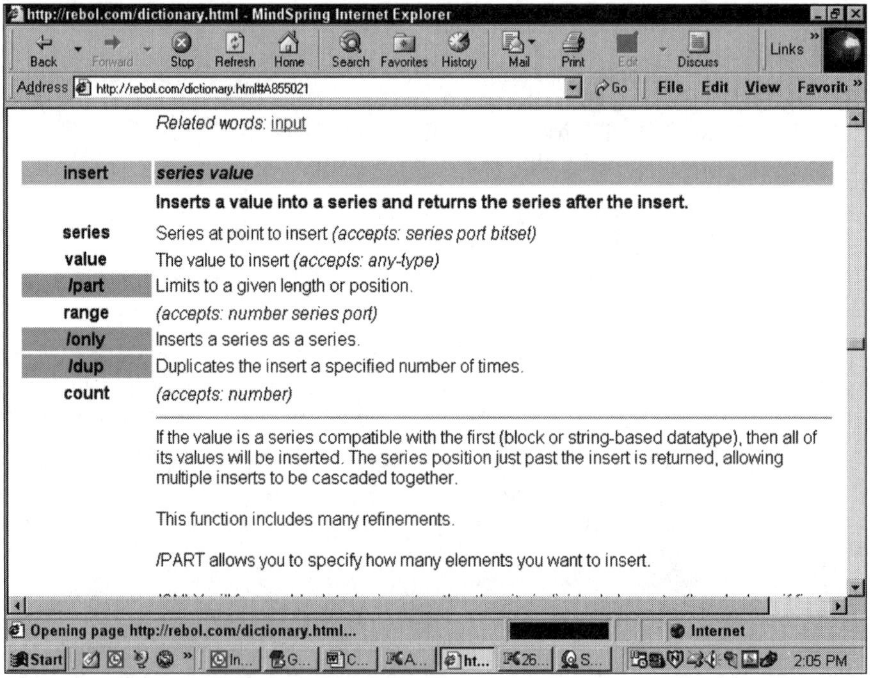

Figure 8-1:
The REBOL
Dictionary
at
rebol.com/
dictionary.
html is a
handy
online
reference
for specific
commands.
Here you
see the
insert
function
word.

Looping

A *loop* is when you go in a circle. Looking at a series, you go from head to tail in sequence, touching each element, like hopping over rocks in a stream:

```
>> forall creek [print first creek]
granite
flint
flat
mossy
marble
muddy
```

As REBOL goes through the series, the current position is changed. The current index or position of the creek series in the preceding forall operation is left at the tail of the series. You need to reset it to the head before doing another action referenced from the head of the series (creek: head creek).

If you are really brave — and that's not me — you could skip across those rocks, starting at the first, two at a time (remember to reset to the head before trying this):

```
>> forskip creek 2 [print first creek]
granite
flat
marble
```

This function also leaves the series at its tail, so reset before trying something else.

Finally in loops, the foreach function also lets you touch on each element, but with a little more power than forall. One of these powerful additions is that foreach does not change the current index. Here's an example:

```
>> foreach [stone1 stone2] creek [print [stone1 stone2]]
granite flint
flat mossy
marble muddy                     ; prints groups of two
```

You can use the power of foreach to process your series data:

```
>> foreach [stone1 stone2] creek [
    stone1: join "big " stone1
    stone2: join "-- small " stone2
    print [stone1 stone2]
    ]
```

```
big granite -- small flint
big flat -- small mossy
big marble -- small muddy
```

```
>> print creek
granite flint flat mossy marble muddy
```

Nice, and note that by using the `stone1` and `stone2` local variables, you did not change your basic data.

By the way, the `forall` and `forskip` functions are called "traversal functions" because they move the current index along the series as it "traverses" the series.

The `foreach` loop does not change a series' current index as do other loops.

Using Common Series

A series is just some values in a row — rocks in a creek, words, numbers. A lot of items can be a series, and in fact, a series itself is a kind of value in REBOL.

Pseudotyping to your advantage

As I mention earlier in this book, a series is a *pseudotype* — a collection of values that can be operated on in the same manner. In the case of the series pseudotype, here's REBOL's internal definition:

```
series
        any-block
            block
            list
            hash
            paren
            path
        any-string
            binary
            email
            file
            issue
            string

            tag
            url
```

So a series is a pseudotype for strings, files, URLs, e-mails, and blocks. Also, because the list and hash types are a type of block, they fall under the series pseudotype.

Look at a few examples of series:

```
string: "George Washington traversed the Delaware."
URL: http://abooks.com/rebol    ; my personal REBOL site
file: %file.txt
email: ralph@abooks.com
block: [one two three four]
hash-table: to-hash [1 2 3 4 5]
list: to-list [1 2 3 4 5]
path: 'a/path/that/leads/to/no-where
```

An apostrophe in front of a path makes it literal so that you can perform series operation on the path itself instead what it contains.

If you're not sure a word is a series, test it like this:

```
>> series? creek
== true
```

Checking length

The length? function returns the length of a series from the current index position to the end of the series:

```
>> balls: [baseball football basketball golfball]
== [baseball football basketball golfball]
>> print length? balls
4
```

```
>> print length? skip balls 1      ; current index 2
3
```

Jumping to head or tail

When the current index is at the tail of a series, the series appears to be empty:

```
>> balls: tail balls
== []
>> print balls                  ; we get nothing
```

But appearances are often deceiving. Even when you do

```
>> print empty? balls
true
```

the `true` result does not mean the series is empty but only that no elements are between the current index and the tail of the series, and

```
>> print empty? head balls
false
```

shows us elements are between the head of the series and its tail, as you can see by:

```
>> head balls
== [baseball football basketball golfball]
```

Finding out if you are at the head or tail of a series and doing something based on those conditions is easy:

```
>> balls: head balls
== [baseball football basketball golfball]
>> if head? balls [print "Play ball!"]
Play ball!
```

```
>> balls: tail balls
>> if tail? balls [print "game over!"]
game over!
```

Dealing with none

The `none` value is also a very useful test. In the balls series, you have four balls. If you pick the third in the series, `basketball`, and place it into a defined REBOL word, you have a value. If you pick the tenth value in a series of four, you also get a value — none, because the series only goes to four. Here's how you code REBOL to check for `none` and to do something if the value is nothing:

```
>> b: pick balls 3
>> either none? b [print "You lost the ball!"] [print b]
basketball
>> b: pick balls 10
>> either none? b [print "You lost the ball!"] [print b]
You lost the ball!
```

Extracting Data

A series is often used to hold data but, of course, you need to pull that data out and use it. Here's a series to play with:

```
elephants: ["African" "Indian" "gray" "dusty" "Jumbo"]
```

This chapter looks at ways of retrieving data from a series. But first I show you another useful series manipulation:

```
>> print sort elephants
African dusty gray Indian Jumbo
```

Ah, that's better. Now the series is alphabetized.

Employing the simple method

I review the four simple ways of extracting data from a series:

```
>> print pick elephants 3        ; use function pick
gray
>> print second elephants        ; use shorthand functions
dusty
>> print elephants/1             ; use path notation
African
>> select elephants "gray"       ; select returns next value in
                                   series
== "dusty"
```

The shorthand functions, again, are first, second, third, fourth, fifth, and last.

You can use loop functions to extract all items:

```
>> foreach elephant elephants [print elephant]
African
dusty
gray
Indian
Jumbo
```

Comparing the values

You can also compare two series and perform operations to print out the differences, where the series intersect, and where the series join.

You can start with the differences.

The difference function uses two arguments, both of which are series to compare. This function returns all elements within the two series not existing in both:

```
>> difference [red white blue] [red yellow gold]
== [white blue yellow gold]
```

The differences are returned, but red is not shown because it is common to both series. Now, here's the difference between two strings:

```
>> string1: "CBAD"     ; A B C D scrambled
>> string2: "EDCF"     ; C D E F scrambled
>> print sort difference string1 string2
ABEF
```

The intersect function returns all elements found in both series:

```
>> intersect [red white blue] [red yellow gold]
== [red]
```

Only red, of course, exists in both series. And the same with the scrambled strings above; only the elements common to both strings are returned:

```
>> print sort intersect string1 string2
CD
```

Finally, the union function allows you to join the unique elements of two blocks (that is, duplicates are removed):

```
>> colors: sort union [red white blue] [red yellow gold]
== [blue gold red white yellow]
```

And, the two scrambled strings:

```
>> print sort union string1 string2
ABCDEF
```

Also, doing a union on two arguments of the same series returns a series with the duplicates removed:

```
>> string: "ABACBDCEDFEG"
== "ABACBDCEDFEG"
>> print sort union string string
ABCDEFG
```

Searching a Series

Searching a series is as easy as all the other series manipulations in this chapter. First, you need a series to search and make it a little longer this time:

```
>> states: ["North Carolina" "Maine" "California" "Texas"
            "Arizona" "Tennessee" "Missouri" "Nevada" "New
            York" "New Mexico" "Michigan" "Florida" "Georgia"
            "Idaho"]
```

Finding

Before you can do anything to an item in a series, you must first find it. The find function uses two arguments, the first is the series to search; the second, the value to search for.

```
>> states: ["Florida" "Georgia" "Idaho" "Michigan" "Missouri"
            "Nevada" "New Mexico" "New York"]
>> find states "Missouri"
>> if find states "Missouri" [print "found the 'Show Me'
            state!"]
found the 'Show Me' state!
```

What happens is that find returns the series with the current index set to Missouri, so Missouri and all the states after it are returned. If you want just the search criteria returned, you can do it like this:

```
>> print first (find states "Missouri")
Missouri
```

Refinements to the find function can be specified to allow you to control the direction (backward or forward) as well as the pattern matching (like case sensitivity and wildcards):

```
>> help find
Finds a value in a series and returns the series at the start
        of it.
Arguments:
    series -- (series port bitset)
    value -- (any-type)
Refinements:
    /part -- Limits the search to a given length or position.
        range -- (number series port)
    /only -- Treats a series value as a single value.
    /case -- Characters are case-sensitive.
    /any -- Enables the * and ? wildcards.
    /with -- Allows custom wildcards.
        wild -- Specifies alternates for * and ? (string)
    /match -- Performs comparison and returns the tail of the
        match.
    /tail -- Returns the end of the string.
    /last -- Backwards from end of string.
    /reverse -- Backwards from the current position.
```

As shown in Figure 8-2, online help for coding in REBOL is always available at the REBOL Web site.

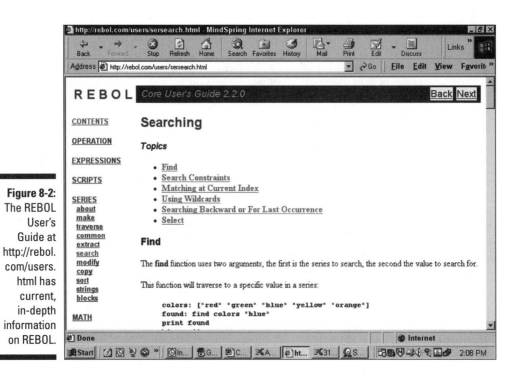

Figure 8-2:
The REBOL
User's
Guide at
http://rebol.
com/users.
html has
current,
in-depth
information
on REBOL.

Applying constraints

You can restrict searching to particular areas of a series. Take the two examples that follow — Georgia is not in the first because only the leading four states in the series are looked at, but in the second, the 13th state is looked at and Georgia is the 13th state in the series:

```
>> find/part states "Georgia" 4
== none
>> find/part states "Georgia" 13
== ["Georgia" "Idaho"]
```

In an actual script using find/part, you would want to isolate the result and put it into a variable, perhaps, for additional use:

```
>> state: first find/part states "Georgia" 13
== "Georgia"
```

Matching

REBOL uses the /match refinement to obtain matches at the current index returning the series with the current index set just after the matched series. If no match is made, none is returned. /match is especially useful with the /any refinement, discussed next:

```
str: "abcde"
print (either (a: find/match str "abc") [a]["unmatched"])
de
```

In the preceding, the find/match function finds a match and prints all of the series after the match. In the following, no match is found because the current index is now set after the string to be matched, so an unmatched message is given.

```
print (either (a: find/match str "bcd") [a]["unmatched"])
unmatched
```

Using wildcards

The /any refinement sets aside the asterisk (*) and question mark (?) characters as wildcards where they would otherwise be used literally. When this refinement is used, ? will match any single character while * matches any number of characters:

```
a: "Roses are red, violets are blue, REBOL is nice, and that
         must suffice."
```

```
>> find/any a "n*e"
== "nice, and that must suffice."
>> find/any a "m?st"
== "must suffice."
```

The current index is moved to where the match is made in the returned series.

Going backward

The /last refinement searches for the last occurrence of the search value:

```
>> str: "abc1abc2abc3"
>> print find/last str "abc"
abc3
```

The /reverse refinement searches in reverse. Use this feature to search backward for values when the current index is advanced into a series:

```
>> str: tail "abc1abc2abc3"
>> print str: find/reverse str "abc"
abc3
```

Modifying

REBOL gives you simple, but powerful, functions for modifying series data. This section discusses these functions, how they work, and their refinements.

Powering modification functions

Here are the basic functions for changing elements in a series:

- ✔ change — change elements
- ✔ insert — add elements
- ✔ remove — remove elements
- ✔ clear — clear to end
- ✔ reverse — reverse the order of elements in a series
- ✔ poke — change element by index position
- ✔ append — append elements to end
- ✔ replace — replace one or all occurrences of element

Here's another series to play with:

```
>> lunch: ["hot dog" "potato chips" "Coke(r)" "cupcake"]
```

Not much of a lunch, but I'm trying to get this chapter finished. Hey, wait, I'm on a diet. Maybe I should modify that menu by using REBOL's change function. Hmmm.

```
>> change lunch "tofu"
>> print mold lunch
["tofu" "potato chips" "Coke(r)" "cupcake"]
```

The change function worked. This function takes two arguments — the name of the series and the new element. The change occurs at the current index, (here, the head of the series). The existing element is replaced by the new one. You can also have refinements of change/part (restrict to a range), change/only (changes a series as a series), and change/dup (duplicates the change a specified number of times).

Type **help change** at the console prompt to see the options of this function and **help name of function** any time you're not sure what refinements a particular function has:

```
>> help change
Changes a value in a series and returns the series after the
        change.
Arguments:
    series -- Series at point to change (series port)
    value -- The new value
Refinements:
    /part -- Limits the amount to change to a given length or
        position.
        range -- (number series port)
    /only -- Changes a series as a series.
    /dup -- Duplicates the change a specified number of
        times.
        count -- (number)
```

The insert function lets you insert elements at the current index position:

```
>> insert next lunch "alfalfa sprouts "
>> print mold lunch
```

And remove takes elements out. There is only one argument for remove, the name of the series, so you have to be a little careful. If you type **remove third lunch** (potato chips being the third element), only the first letter of the element is removed. Not good enough, so use the find function to help define what you want removed:

```
>> remove (find lunch "potato chips")
>> print mold lunch
["tofu" "alfalfa sprouts" "Coke(r)" "cupcake"]
```

Okay, onward in making my lunch healthy. The clear function removes elements from the current index to the end of the series, but leaves the current element:

```
>> clear at lunch 3
>> print mold lunch
["tofu" "alfalfa sprouts"]
```

Ah, a nice healthy lunch is shaping up. You can look at this two ways, using the reverse function to reverse the order:

```
>> reverse lunch
>> print mold lunch
["alfalfa sprouts" "tofu"]
```

The poke function is useful for replacing an element at a certain position:

```
>> poke lunch 2 "wheat grass"
>> print mold lunch
["alfalfa sprouts" "wheat grass"]
```

Yum, indeed. But not yet a complete meal. Use the append function to add something:

```
>> append lunch "black turtle beans"
>> print mold lunch
["alfalfa sprouts" "wheat grass" "black turtle beans"]
```

Okay, the wheat grass has to go. What about lentils? Use the replace function:

```
>> replace lunch "wheat grass" "lentils"
>> print mold lunch
["alfalfa sprouts" "lentils" "black turtle beans"]
```

Effecting changes

Changing series can have effects you need to watch out for. Here's an example using two words referencing the same series:

```
>> skies: ["cloudy" "gray" "blue" "sunny"]
>> skies-2: skip skies 2
>> print skies
cloudy gray blue sunny
>> print skies-2
blue sunny
```

The first defined word, skies, shows the entire series because, by default, the initial current index position is at the head of the series. The second word, skies-2, shows the series beginning at the third element, because you told it to skip the first two. That's fine for your script, of course, unless you throw in something like:

```
>> insert skies "stormy"
>> print skies
stormy cloudy gray blue sunny
>> print skies-2
gray blue sunny
```

The series now referenced by skies now has an additional element, stormy. This also changes the value of the series referenced by skies-2. Because it is based on skipping the first two elements of skies, it changes in value by getting the extra element.

Copying and Adding a New Reference

Copying a series — duplicating in total or in part — is also a snap using REBOL.

✔ A series may be referred to by many different names, but remains just one series (referencing). Any change made to any of these names affects all names the same.

✔ If a copy is made, two independent series exist and changes do not affect the other.

Adding a new reference to a series

To reference a series to another series:

```
>> ranks: ["lieutenant" "captain" "major" "colonel"]
>> officers: ranks      ; the new reference
>> print officers
lieutenant captain major colonel
```

You can easily check to see if two words reference the same series:

```
>> print same? ranks officers
true
```

Of course, if the current index positions are different in the two series, same? would not give you the right answer, but you can get around that by:

```
>> print same? (head ranks) (head officers)
true
```

The preceding technique shows two words referencing a series at the same location.

Copying a series

To make an independent copy, you use the copy function and then test for sameness like so:

```
>> paygrades: copy ranks
== ["lieutenant" "captain" "major" "colonel"]
>> same? ranks paygrades
== false
```

REBOL knows they are now different series, even with the same content.

Copying part of a series

Copying just part of a series is simple by using the copy/part function/ refinement:

```
>> print copy/part (find ranks "captain")(find ranks
          "colonel")
captain major
```

In this example, copy/part uses the find function and copies from captain (including the element) to the element colonel (but does not include it).

Copying an embedded series

What about copying something in an embedded series — that is, a series having one or more elements, which are also series. Like this:

```
>> ranks: [lieutenant ["first" "second"] "captain" "major"
          "colonel"]
```

Use copy/deep function/refinement for an embedded series and employ path notation:

```
>> louies-copy: copy/deep ranks
>> print mold louies
[lieutenant ["first" "second"] "captain" "major" "colonel"]
>> print same? ranks/lieutenant louies/lieutenant
false
```

Initializing a series

copy can initialize a series, making sure that it starts out with no value. Using copy assures a new series reference is defined to the word every time the initialization takes place. In this example, a is assigned the uncopied series each time the function is called:

```
print-foo: func [/local a] [
    a: ""
    insert a "foo"
    print a
]

>> print-foo
foo
```

```
>> print-foo
foofoo
>> print-foo
foofoofoo
```

This is the sort of small bug in a script that can drive you bonkers. Insert the preceding function into the REBOL console and play with it. Then redefine it with:

```
a: copy ""
```

Try it again and you now get the correct result every time.

Sorting

REBOL excels at sorting, as it does in the other methods to manipulate series.

Sorting quickly

Basic sorting is accomplished with the sort function:

```
>> letters: ["z" "f" "p" "c" "q" "m" "A" "a" "B" "h"]
>> sort letters
A a B c f h m p q z
```

Default sorts are case insensitive:

```
print sort "gCcAHfiEGeBIdbFaDh"
AabBcCdDeEFfgGHhiI
```

Numbers may be sorted:

```
print sort [321.3 78 321 42 321.8 12 98]
12 42 78 98 321 321.3 321.8
```

Sort alphanumerically:

```
print sort "g4c28f9i15ed3ba076h"
0123456789abcdefghi
```

Other datatypes may also be sorted using the preceding technique.

Refining your sorts

The sort function can use refinements for powerful sorting operations.

Available refinements are

- ✔ /case — case-sensitive sorting
- ✔ /skip — sectional sorting
- ✔ /compare — use custom sort algorithm

The sort/case function/refinement makes sorting case sensitive:

```
>> print sort/case letters
A B a c f h m p q z
```

And sort/skip restricts sorting to a particular area in the series:

```
>> golfscores: [
    "Sam Sneed" 72
    "Arnold Palmer" 71
    "Tiger Woods" 70
    ]
```

Sort the preceding by first names:

```
>> print sort/skip golfscores 2
Arnold Palmer 71 Sam Snead 72 Tiger Woods 70
```

Sorting by scores? Easy enough if you reverse the information:

```
>> reverse golfscores
>> print sort/skip golfscores 2
70 Tiger Woods 71 Arnold Palmer 72 Sam Snead
```

Finally, the /compare refinement takes a function's defining components as its argument. This function is a user-defined algorithm that sort uses to perform custom sort operations. The function passed to sort/compare must strictly contain two arguments in its argument block and will be evaluated true or false. The function arguments represent elements of the series being sorted. When the first argument evaluates to less than the second, sorting is ascended; when it evaluates to greater, sorting is descended. The function returns true or false as a comparison operation.

Part IV

Live-Fire Exercises

The 5th Wave

By Rich Tennant

In this part . . .

Time now to start putting the basics to work with techniques useful in real-world coding. This part shows how REBOL works with online resources to build and compile fast, flexible online documents.

Chapter 9

Files: Teaching Them Reading and Writing

• •

In This Chapter

▶ Naming files

▶ Reading files

▶ Writing files

▶ Handling complete lines

▶ Converting line endings

▶ Obtaining information about files

▶ Utilizing File Permissions

• •

A computer *file* is an electronically recorded collection of letters, numbers, and/or other symbols of a specific length, with a specific name, in a specific place. You can't get more basic. Web pages, databases, REBOL scripts, the pieces that make up the operating system running your computer, Lara Croft's latest tomb-raiding adventure, a word processing program, this very manuscript I write; they are all files.

That computer sitting patiently on your desktop, or crouching beneath the table hoping you won't spill your coffee or cola down its venting slots, works by reading files into its working memory, manipulating those files, and writing them back out. Computers store (record) files on such media as hard drives, floppy disks, other computers like local network or Internet servers, and so forth. Reading files is also called *accessing* files. All the churning, grinding, and hard-drive light-blinking your machine does? It's reading and writing files.

The very basis on which computers operate extensively involves files. By easy and logical progression, you'll agree one of the most important aspects of any programming language is the reading and writing of files. As I show you in this chapter, file manipulation follows the powerful REBOL simplicity shown in previous chapters.

Here's a quick comparative example. A while back, I added a highly simplistic hit counter in Perl to one of my Web pages. Perl is currently the most widely used scripting language for Internet and CGI (Web) applications (at least until the REBOLution comes!). Designed several years ago, and for various reasons I don't have space to go into, Perl's syntax is more convoluted than REBOL's. (Now *there's* what I call irony in the writing game.)

My following Perl routine, included in a longer Perl script, just opens a file, reads the previous number of hits, adds one, and writes the new number of visitors. The Perl code for the hit counter is

```
$hits_file = "hits.txt";          #Perl code
open(THEFILE,"<$hits_file");
($hits) = <THEFILE>;
close THEFILE;
$hits = $hits + 1;
open(THEFILE,">$hits_file");
print THEFILE $hits;
close THEFILE;
```

Not bad, but here's the same thing in REBOL:

```
hits: load %hits.txt save %hits.txt hits + 1
```

Oh, my, that's much shorter, isn't it? Not to mention understandable. And semicolons at the end of lines? REBOL don't need no stinkin' semicolons — to paraphrase those banditos in the 1941 Humphrey Bogart flick *High Sierra*.

The philosophy of REBOL's creators is to do "simple things in simple ways." In the preceding comparison, all I am doing is loading a single number, adding one to it, and replacing the number saved on disk with the new number. Perl has me opening the file for reading, reading the file, closing the file, incrementing the hits variable, and then opening the file for writing, and finally closing the file. That's a lot to remember and type in correctly. Plus the code is not what I would call immediately obvious as to purpose.

The one-line REBOL equivalent makes typing the code a whole lot easier — and it is considerably more human-readable. "Define the word *hits* as the loaded value of the file `hits.txt` and save it back to disk with one added to whatever number was in the file originally." (Wow. Even the English version is clumsier.)

Do you hear the drums and fifes of the REBOLution yet? Do you see the banners waving? And do you think you can program a lot easier in REBOL? Yeah, programming is suddenly fun again!

Now on to reading and writing files — and other neat and useful things.

Naming

What's in a name? Well, a file's name is important and should provide a convenient, logical handle (something easy to remember) so you can find the file again. REBOL's file naming convention lets you write code that generally works — without change — on over 35 platforms (at the time of this writing). Occasionally, minor convolutions handle special cases — such as long filenames with spaces in them (as Windows95/98, Windows NT, and Windows 2000 allow). I show you how to use these special names in this chapter.

A REBOL script file normally has an .r suffix, so REBOL knows this is a script it should interpret and run. On systems where this suffix is otherwise in use, .reb may be substituted.

As I explain in Chapter 4, a filename is one of REBOL's standard *values*. The percent sign (%) is used in scripts to designate that what immediately follows is a filename. Like this:

```
%wherefrom.r
%readme.txt
%prettypicture.jpg
```

The preceding are, in sequence, a REBOL script file, a text file, and a binary file. Two basic types of files exist: text and binary. REBOL scripts — like Perl scripts, HTML Web pages, and other programs in other scripting languages — store themselves as simple text files. If you open the script or the readme.txt file, you'll find they contain human-readable lines of letters and numbers.

The prettypicture.jpg file is a binary file, which is computer-readable instead of making sense to you and me. It is a jumble of letters, numbers, and lots of weird symbols. The computer converts this weirdness and displays a pleasant vista of mountains, green trees, and azure blue, cloud-studded skies on your screen.

Binary files can be images, executable programs, or even fancy word processing files like the .doc files that Word 2000 (the word processor that I am using to write this book manuscript) creates.

To make this even simpler, a binary file is anything that isn't a text file — that is, human-readable. REBOL reads and writes text and binary files the same way, but the way you and your script handle the data is different.

Putting spaces in filenames

Filenames with spaces in them are called *long filenames* on a Windows or NT system. The name of the file in which I am saving this chapter is REBOL 9 Files, Teaching Them Reading and Writing.doc. Because this file has spaces in its name, you have two choices when you access it in a REBOL script. You can enclose the name in quotes, or you can substitute the *hex escape* (%20) for the space character. URLs (Uniform Resource Locators or Web addresses) are handled in this same manner because Web addresses can't have spaces in their names. If there are spaces, they have to be "escaped out" by using the %20 symbol (space).

Here are examples of these two methods:

```
%"A Test File.txt"
%A%20Test%20File.txt
```

The first allows spaces because the name is enclosed in quotes. The second needs no quotes as the spaces are escaped (filled in) by the %20 space symbol. Of these two methods, the second looks weirdest but is preferable because it's more universal and your code will work on more systems. This is especially true when you're constructing URLs.

Don't confuse the percent character (%) that precedes — and is actually part of — the filename in REBOL with the percent sign in the hex escape sequence (%20). The first is a REBOL convention for filenames; the second comes from outside REBOL and has nothing to do with filenames, other than representing a space in long filenames.

Both methods certainly work well, but it's always good programming practice to be as universal as possible. This is especially true because REBOL runs on such a wide variety of platforms. In creating new files, use an all lowercase name without spaces. These days, length does not restrict you like the old eight number/letter, three number/letter extensions on those ancient eight-bit machines that ran Microsoft DOS.

If you do want separations in the filename, use the underscore (_) character or the hyphen (-). Here are some universal filenames:

```
%report26.txt
%12march2001
%inventory-june
%use_this_data_first.aa1
```

Why not use upper/lowercase? Again, it's not universal. If you write a program file named

```
%Hitcounter.r
```

on your Windows computer and upload it to a Unix or Linux server, the file on the server will have a slightly different name. Probably something like this:

```
%HITCOUNTER.r
```

That messes up every reference to your file within a script, because Unix and Linux systems are case sensitive. I got bit by this myself when I wrote my first REBOL CGI Web applications for my server. Scripts working grandly on my Windows machine bombed on the Unix server. I made my filenames all lowercase to solve that aggravation.

 Using all lowercase letters and/or numbers in filenames with no spaces is the best policy. You can mix in underscores (_) and hyphens (-) to keep the filenames readable if you like.

Using a URL scheme

REBOL is nothing if not flexible. Filenames may also include a URL scheme, just like a Web page address (http://) or FTP site (ftp://), and others covered elsewhere. A scheme like http:// is really a prefix for the rest of the URL and tells REBOL what kind of connection it's looking to achieve. Some filenames in this format are

```
file://manual.txt
file://working%20draft.txt
```

Please note that when you use the URL scheme for file naming, you can't use quote marks. So replace the space with a hex escape (%20). Remember, don't confuse the percent symbol in the escape sequence with the one used in REBOL filenames.

In essence, the percent character (%) preceding a filename is a shortcut, which replaces the URL scheme. In practically all REBOL scripts, the percent character is the preferred method of indicating the following name is that of a file. I highly recommend you get in the habit of using it. But at least you know that, as usual in REBOL, there's a second way of doing things.

Attaching paths

If the file you want to read or write to is not in the current directory, the filenames also include *path* information. (See Figure 9-1.) The path information shows which directory contains the file. An old but still effective analogy compares files to those manila folders that real papers are stored in, the directory to the drawer of a file cabinet, and your hard drive to the file cabinet. And you may have several cabinets in your office, as well as the potential to access hundreds or thousands of "cabinets" across local and wide area networks, not to mention the Internet itself. Finding a file requires that its exact location be known out of the thousands upon thousands of places it can be.

```
R REBOL                                                                    _ ☐ ✕
File  Edit
>> list-dir
11-alphanum.r        9-myuser.r          ac.r                aliennames-back.r
aliennames.bak       aliennames.r        amazon.bak          amazon.r
amazon.txt           ANAMES.R            appointments.bak    appointments.r
ARRSOFT.R            auc.bak             auc.r               auction-scan.r
auto.db              auto.r              autoclose.r         autographs.bak
autographs.r         autos.txt           b.r                 banner.bak
banner.r             beer.r              BIO.R               biography.txt
booklist.txt         books.bak           books.r             breaktimes.bak
breaktimes.r         browse-system.r     build-lib.r         build-site.r
build-website.r      bulklister.r        cal.r               cat.r
catdefs.bak          catdefs.r           cgi-input.r         cgicomment.r
chorusline.bak       chorusline.r        christmas.r         civil.bak
civil.txt            civilwar.txt        cleaner.bak         cleaner.r
cleaner2.bak         cleaner2.r          cleanhttp.r         Cls_r.htm
colors.bak           colors.r            config.r            convert-csv.r
countweb.r           cw.txt              dancelady.bak       dancelady.r
Definitions.r        delete.bak          delete.r            detach.r
dir-sizer.r          dir-tree.r          dir.bak             dir.r
dispcat.bak          dispcat.r           displist.r          dns.bak
dns.r                easter.r            ebay-2.bak          ebay-2.r
ebay.bak             ebay.r              epoch-to-date.bak   epoch-to-date.r
epoch.bak            epoch.r             examples.r          experts.html
factorial.r          feedback.r          file list.txt       filelist.r
findagent.r          formletter.r        ftpdownbin.r        ftpread.r
ftpwrite.r           gedcom.bak          gedcom.r            hc.r
headfull.r           helloworld.txt      horror.r            http-post.r
iho-tools.r          incdec.r            include.r           index.html
inhide.r             inhtml.r            jobbot.r            judaica.txt
lister.txt           loglooker.r         mailautoreply.r     mailboxsave.r
mailcc.r             maildespam.r        mailfile.r          mailfiles.r
mailfilescomp.r      mailfriends.r       mailheader.r        mailpage.r
mailping.r           mailsave.r          mailsend.r          mailsendgroup.r
mailserver.r         mailsniff.r         mailview.r          messenger.r
mike.html            monitorsize.r       mystuff.bak         mystuff.r
Start  ☐ ☺ ♨ ☻ »  ☐L. ☐G. ☐C. ☐A. ☐h. ☐S. ☐C. ☐R.      ☐☐☐☐☐☐☐☐  3:23 PM
```

Figure 9-1: From the REBOL console, type the REBOL function word list-dir for a sorted, multicolumn listing of the current directory.

The collection of hard drives, floppies, CD-ROMs, and so forth that are physically part of your computer are its *file system*. REBOL can access this file system via pathnames. If the computer is attached to other computers and/or the Internet, you can also access other computer's file systems. I examine this connectivity briefly in this chapter and at greater length in Chapter 13.

Pathnames are important because they're the roadmaps that your computer uses in reading and writing files at the direction of your REBOL scripts. Naturally, sending data to the wrong destination confuses things. Giving proper directions saves much aggravation, both for yourself and your computer.

Two methods exist for expressing paths — relative and absolute. Relative paths usually work only on the same drive but offer convenience and simplicity in filenames. If the file happens to be on another drive or somewhere on a network, REBOL requires an absolute path.

Relative paths

The *relative* path depends on the current directory. A file located in the current directory doesn't need any path information because REBOL can easily find it. So you reference that filename directly. A file one subdirectory down may be read or written to by giving simple relative path instructions. Say the subdirectory of our current directory is named secrets and you want to read a file named rebolution.txt. The filename with relative path information is

```
%secrets/rebolution.txt
```

Often, in your scripts, you'll find it easier (and certainly more elegant) to change directories, making the current directory the one you are reading and writing files within and giving you all the advantages of relative paths. As a matter of fact, this is the preferred method.

Avoiding absolute paths whenever possible insures that your scripts are more likely to work unmodified on many different platforms.

In general, any path information that does not include a leading forward slash (/) may be considered a relative path. A double dot (..) indicates a move up the directory tree and a single dot (.) with nothing behind the dot refers to all files and subdirectories in the current directory. Here are some more file-names with relative paths:

```
%rebolution/agenda.doc
%rebolution/secrets/agents/codenames.txt
%"declarations of independence/rebol programmers"
%../password-generator.r
%../../rebolution/schedule.r
%.
```

You can create a variable and read into it all the filenames in the current directory plus the names of any subdirectories. And, oh yes, the output is a sorted list. From the console or within a script, type

```
files: read %. sort files
```

REBOL returns the following, giving you just enough data to show it completed your command:

```
== [%ac.r %aliennames-back.r %aliennames.r %amazon.r
        %amazon.txt %anames.r %arrauction.r %arrsoft.r
        %atest.r %auction-scan.r %autoc...
```

Absolute paths

An *absolute path* contains complete information to the location of a file, as opposed to the partial paths of relative paths. Assume your current directory is named `rebolution` and is a subdirectory of your computer's root direc-tory on the current hard drive. On most machines, running whatever plat-form, REBOL sees the root directory as simply a forward slash mark (/). This is true even on Windows systems; universal, remember? So if you are in a subdirectory anywhere on the same hard drive, the absolute path to your file is this:

```
%/rebolution/secrets/strategy.txt
```

Here are some other filenames with absolute paths:

```
%/www/rebol
%/D/rebolution/secrets/victories.txt
%"/d/rebol for dummies/book outline.doc"
file:/C/rebol/demo/filelist.r
```

Some systems, especially in the Unix/Linux world, occasionally require paths that include device names. These look like this:

```
%/cd1/webapps/auction.r
```

Reading

REBOL can read all files of the two general types — text and binary. These files may either be on your system, or any network up to and including the Internet itself.

As with all other functions in REBOL, methods of accessing files are quite simple when compared to other scripting languages.

Getting text

A *text file* is just a human-readable series of letters and numbers, such as words, figures, or anything else of that order. REBOL presents you with an incredibly rich array of ways to search and manipulate text files, many of which you see in this book. But to just see what's in a text file, use the following method, which works either from the console or as an expression in a REBOL (.r suffix) script:

```
print read %file.txt
```

This reads the file on the disk as one big string and sends the entire file to your screen.

And I guess I should remind you how to stop output if you happen to stumble into a 200K file with a zillion lines of text scrolling rapidly down the screen. Just press your Esc (Escape) key. That terminates REBOL programs.

In the actual REBOL scripts you write, dumping a bunch of text to the screen is not all that useful. You'll want REBOL not just to read a file but also to do things with it.

```
A very basic way of having a file at your mercy is reading it
         into a REBOL word. Here's how: file: read %file.txt
```

Understanding REBOL code is pretty easy, huh? The preceding reads the contents of `file.txt` into the word `file`.

You use a semicolon (;) to comment code in REBOL. When REBOL encounters a semicolon in a line, it ignores everything from the semicolon to the line's end. Unlike Perl, which requires the semicolon in almost all cases to use the pound character (#) for comments, the semicolon is completely optional in REBOL (as in, "We don't need no stinkin' semicolons").

Now that you've read the text file into the word, I'll show you a few quick things you can do to that REBOL word, with comments.

```
length? file    ; number of total characters?
first file      ; what is the first character?
file/1          ; same as above
last file       ; what is the last character?
file/25         ; what is the 25th character?
pick file 25    ; 25th another way
```

And, for a change, more than one character:

```
first25: copy/part file 25    ; the first 25!
```

"Reading is fundamental," say the ads of a recent literacy advocation program. They could have been talking about REBOL as well. Master these simple techniques and all I've shown you will be just a start of the many ways to manipulate files, text, data, and more in REBOL. I share more advanced examples with you later in this book.

Handling binary files

Binary files are all files that are not text files. Binary files are a jumbled mess of letters, numbers, and symbols, and certainly not human-readable. Binary files include executable programs, image files, sounds, and proprietary format files like those written by word processing programs, databases, spreadsheets, and the like.

Making changes to a binary file is somewhat harder than editing a text file. If you change the file (edit it), this may cause corruption that would confuse the program that normally uses it. But many useful tasks are still possible. For example, if you want to check the length of an image file, you can use the length function like this:

```
print length? read/binary %rebol-hq.jpg
```

If REBOL gives you an access error, it means that you supplied an incorrect filename.

You tell REBOL you are reading a binary file with the /binary refinement to the read function, just as you can use /lines to read a file line by line, as you see shortly. You can get all the refinements for read (or any other function) by typing

```
help read
```

at the prompt on the REBOL console or by checking the REBOL dictionary at rebol.com/dictionary.html for a more detailed explanation.

If you want to check the total size of every file in the current directory, here's how:

```
REBOL [File: %9-size.r]

total: 0          ; zero the variable

foreach file read %. [total: total + size? file]
print ["The size of this directory is" total "bytes."]
```

If you don't zero your integer or digital variables, running code like the preceding twice or more from the REBOL console gives you an assumptive total (what the script assumes is correct) because REBOL remembers the previous total. And running the code remotely, such as a Web CGI program, gives you an error message because REBOL wants to know the starting value. Otherwise the foreach loop in the above example will error out if a starting value is not defined for the word total regardless of whether it is run remotely, locally, or from the console.

An example of a useful real-world task for the reading of binary sizes is my eBay image directory on my Web server. Although I have 300 megabytes of Web space, with all the junk I've hung off the server, space is at a premium. So I monitor various directories, especially ones that have transient content such as photographs of auction items that are just space wasters after the items sell. REBOL keeps me alert as the space is being used, telling me when it needs to be cleaned.

In fact, if you have your own Internet server or even just a Web site, you'll find yourself using REBOL for these types of little maintenance utilities all the time. Most involve reading and writing files in some manner. And as I show you later in this book, REBOL is indeed the best thing since sliced bread for live-on-the-net CGI applications such as forms, dynamic content Web pages, various other spiffy Web apps, and other stuff.

Now back to learning the basics of reading and writing files.

Reading over networks

REBOL can also read files on other computers over a network. You accomplish this by using one of the several communications protocols built into REBOL.

One of these protocols is FTP (File Transfer Protocol), a long-time method of moving data back and forth in the Unix world and on the Internet. Here's an example from the user's manual, which uses a public access file on the REBOL Technologies server:

```
print read ftp://ftp.rebol.com/test.txt
```

Run it from the REBOL console and (assuming you set up REBOL for networking and are connected to the Internet) you get a nice little welcome message from those kind folks in Ukiah, California. Try it and see what they say.

Retrieving a Web page is another way of reading files over a network. To get the rebol.com index page, type

```
print read http://rebol.com
```

Whoa, Nellie! That's a lot of lines. And because you did it outside of a Web browser, it's just a bunch of HTML tags and text with no images or colors. You can play with HTML later. But I wonder how many lines that Web page is?

```
print length? read/lines http://rebol.com
```

The page was 190 lines long when I ran this, but it gets updated with news pretty often, so the length will change.

Other methods of reading files over a network include email, whois, dns, finger, and others — I talk more about them in Chapter 12.

Selecting parts

Times exist when reading only part of a file is appropriate — especially if the file is very large, like an access log file tens of megabytes in size on a Web server. Very large files also exceed your working memory, and REBOL can't read them in total. Finding out how to hack out a digestible chunk worked for our primordial ancestors when they hunted the mighty mastodon, and it works in REBOL.

You can see this in action — reading part of a file that is, not mastodon hunting. My wife and I collect small elephants; they take offense to mastodon hunting, or the hunting of anything else vaguely pachyderm-like.

Okay, here's one method. You can find the first instance of a word and copy everything from that word to the end of the file. You have already read a text file into the variable file.

```
a: copy/part (find file "secret") (tail file)
```

The part of the file from where the word secret first appears to the end will be read into the a variable. Or, you can reverse it and read from the start of the file to the first appearance of secret like this:

```
a: copy/part (head file) (find file "secret")
```

Later in the book, I give you other ways of reading parts of a file, including by position and a specific byte size.

Writing

"Garbage in, garbage out," chant those old programmers who rode the big iron, the mighty mainframe. In your case, it's important and highly sensitive data in, important and highly sensitive data out. And don't forget to use four digits for a year date. (Yeah, 20 years ago I was one of those programmers saving a couple of lousy bytes per date<g>.)

Like reading files, REBOL simplifies writing files all rather dramatically.

Saving text

At the beginning of this chapter, I discuss simple visitor counting, which goes something like this: A very small file containing just the number of previous visitors is on the server. When someone loads a Web page, a simple REBOL script is called, as in this example:

```
#!/rebol/rebol -cs
REBOL []
hits: load %hits.txt write %hits.txt hits + 1
```

The first line tells the server where REBOL is, so that it can be called to interpret the script. This line has a -cs switch telling REBOL it has permission to read and write files for this script. The second line is the minimal header (my actual script has more info in it, like purpose, copyright, and so on). The third line reads the file hits.txt and writes it back to the disk after adding one more visitor to my total.

In the file writing part, I use the function word `write` without any modifiers (refinements). This function replaces the file totally. The basic methods for writing text that creates or replaces an existing file includes

```
write %file.txt "Text stuff to a file."
a: "Some stuff in a variable." write %file.txt a
write %file.txt now/time        ; the current time
write %file.txt now/date        ; the current date
write %new.txt read %old.txt    ; one file into another
```

Using the function word `write` without any modifiers, or refinements as REBOLers refer to them, overwrites any existing file of the same name.

Writing binary files

Like `read`, `write` has several modifiers, one of which is `/binary` for writing binary data to files. Binary files can be images, executable programs, sounds like `wav` files, and so forth.

You can see all the refinements for `write` (or any other function) by typing

```
help write
```

at the prompt on the REBOL console or by checking the REBOL dictionary at `rebol.com/dictionary.html` for a more detailed explanation.

When you write a binary file, you must be careful not to reformat it in any way, such as adding line endings and so forth. Otherwise, the application using that binary file finds it corrupt and barfs it back onto your keyboard, which you just got the coffee out of anyway. This is the purpose of using the `/binary` modifier — making sure the binary file remains binary. An example: `write/binary %new-carl.gif read/binary carl.gif`

A new photograph of Carl replaces an older one for the Web site. The existing file is erased and the new file is written without an error message.

You can also use REBOL in creating new binary data. This data saves to a file like this:

```
Write/binary %rebolution.bin data
```

Writing over networks

Just like reading files across a network, you may also write them. The basic technique is

```
write ftp://ftp.somewhere.com "some text"
write ftp://ftp.somewhere.com read %inventory.txt
```

The first sends some text. This could be a command, login information, or whatever. The second copies a file from your system to the remote host.

In Chapter 13, I get more into FTP and other methods of writing files over networks.

Appending

Often times, the plan you have for your script calls for adding data to an existing file while leaving intact any existing information in that file. Accumulating data over a period of time in a file is one of the more common applications any programming language must handle. The modifier /append fills this bill nicely for REBOL. Some examples:

```
write/append %file.txt reduce ["^/" now/date]
write/append %file.txt read %new.txt
write/append %file.txt "That's All Folks!"
```

In Chapter 4, I explain that the special symbol for a line ending is ^/. I use this symbol in the first preceding example so that today's date will be added to the file on a new line after the current end of file.txt. In the second example, a new file's contents are added. Finally, a bit of text indicating the end.

Handling Complete Lines

As previously shown, you can modify how a file is read. If you want to read the file into a variable by lines instead of as one big glop, do it like this:

```
a: read/lines %file.txt
```

Then you can do line-related things like:

```
length? a           ; how many lines in the file?
print first a       ; print the first line
```

A little more sophisticated example? Okay, take the file read into the variable a and print it out with each line numbered. The following simple loop counts until the last line of the file, and then prints the count, adds a period and a space after the count to "prettify" the listing, and prints the line.

```
REBOL [File: %9-count.r]     ; abbreviated header

a: read/lines %file.txt
count: 0                     ; zero the count

foreach line a [
        count: count + 1
        print [count ". " line]
        ]
```

When you run a script with REBOL, it looks for the header information. Including all the header information you can is good programming practice, but in the interest of brevity, I give you just enough here so that the script actually runs. And when you do run it, have a file in the same directory named file.txt, or change the name in the script, which is a good exercise anyway.

Take this script as a start and play with it, adding features, reading files with paths in the filenames, and so on. I've always found playing makes learning both faster and more enjoyable. Plus you pick up all sorts of neat little tricks that come in handy for serious programming.

Here's a way of writing lines:

```
REBOL [File: %9-count-write.r]

a: read/lines %file.txt

count: 0                 ; zero the count

write %newfile.txt ""    ; make sure file is empty

foreach line a [
        count: count + 1
        write/append %newfile.txt join count ". "
        write/append %newfile.txt join line  "^/"
        ]
```

The function of the first line of the preceding foreach loop is pretty obvious, it just increments the word's value by one each time through the loop. The loop, by the way, ends automatically at the end of the a series; no need for counting lines and telling the loop how many times it should go around as in other languages.

The next line write/appends the count plus a period and a space for formatting purposes. The `write/append` word normally accepts only one argument. By using the `join` function, which joins two arguments together, I can condense four lines into two lines of code — two on each line.

The last line of the loop joins the line with a *newline* character, making sure the next line will begin at the beginning of the next line in the file. Otherwise, all the lines would jumble together with no breaks at their ends.

Converting Line Endings

A universal language should handle the basic formats of text files from system to system, and REBOL does. In fact, wonderfully so.

One of the pitfalls new CGI Web application programmers fall into — especially, as I've often witnessed, in the Perl world — are line endings. Most newbies assume a text file is a text file is a text file, whether it's on Amiga, Windows, or Unix/Linux. Not so. There are different formats of "text" files and the difference lies in how lines are terminated.

Editing a Perl script, for example, with an editor on a windows system, and then uploading it to a Unix/Linux server will most generally return only a server error instead of running properly. The line endings must be converted. This is a manual process for Perl (so use a good programmer's editor that handles line endings between systems). REBOL helps you out a lot more.

You don't have to really understand the difference between the way lines end in text files from system to system, just that there is a difference and how to ensure REBOL handles it for you.

Amiga, Linux, and Unix operating systems all use line feeds (LF) as line terminators. Macintosh files have carriage returns (CR). And Windows/DOS has both line feeds and carriage returns (LF/CR).

REBOL makes the text files it generates universal by converting line endings all to the newline character first shown in detail in Chapter 4. Files read in from various systems are automatically converted from LF, CR, or CR/LF to the equivalent number of newlines.

If you copy a file from another type of system and then read it into a variable via

```
a: read %file.txt
```

the line endings are automatically changed so that your system can now use the text without problem.

When writing the data back to disk, REBOL records the line endings to match that of your system. In other words, it uses LFs for Unix/Linux, CRs for Mac, and CR/LFs for PCs. This is necessary so that other programs on your computer can properly read and use these files.

You can use REBOL to retrieve files from remote systems and convert the line endings in one step, as so:

```
write %test.txt read ftp://ftp.rebol.com/test.txt
```

Try this (it actually works), using the preceding test file, which is on REBOL Technology's Internet site. Then read the text file in from your system and see what you got. Neat, huh?

If you don't want line ending conversions to take place, just use `read/binary` and `write/binary` refinements and line endings will remain the same as those of the remote system.

Obtaining Information about Files

REBOL has a rich collection of function words, which let you find out information about things in general and, in specific here, about files. What do you or one of your scripts during operation need to know about a file? Lots of stuff. Is the file even there, or at least where you think it is?

```
probe exists? %file.txt
```

The preceding REBOL `probe` word is quite a handy one. It lets you look at a value without any evaluation occurring. If you have a script that is not returning the values you expect, use `probe` as a debugging aid by inserting it anywhere you want to see the values that are being passed on to the next step. As to the preceding code, it returns `true` if the file is there, or `false` if not.

The early beta version of the REBOL manual I have suggests using the `probe` word in retrieving file information, but I've found the various words which return information on a file work just as well — both from the console and in scripts — without the `probe` word even being present.

As you may have already noted, I am defining function words only as they are used in examples. REBOL is a fast-growing language with many word functions yet to be added. For a list of the multitude of already defined words and to find new ones just being introduced, I highly recommend checking the REBOL Technologies Web site, and especially `rebol.com/dictionary.html`, the online dictionary.

If a file exists, you can use the following information in a script to specify whether an operation should occur:

```
if exists? %file.txt [a: read %file.txt]
if not exists? %file.txt [print "File not found."]
```

You can also use this technique just to make sure you are not overwriting a file already there and destroying its data:

```
if not exists? %file.txt [write %file.txt data]
```

But in running a REBOL script, you may want to control where this information response goes for later reference (like into a variable), or how it's displayed so that the results are usable. Here's an example:

```
a: if exists? %file.txt
```

The word `true` is placed into the a word if the file is in the current directory, or `false` if not. Later in your script, you can base a decision on this information, such as:

```
if a [write %newfile.txt data]
if a [write %file.txt]
```

In Core 2.3 (the latest version out just as this book goes to press), `if` returns `none` instead of `false` for false conditions. This is the new behavior and solves a lot of legacy problems.

The value of a is a logical value, so don't use quote marks. These two lines, which can appear many lines later in your script, tell REBOL what to do. Should there be an existing file, write the data to a new file. But if there is no file, it's okay to use this filename and create one.

Having confirmed the file exists, you may want to know its size:

```
size? %file.txt
```

This line returns the file's size in bytes. Next, check the last date it was modified:

```
modified? %file.txt
```

The date and time the file was last written, or written to (via a `write/append` operation) is returned in this format: `4-Feb-2000/20:06:46-5:00`. This is the date, the time, and lastly (the `-5:00` part) the offset from GMT or Greenwich Mean Time or (as it was called for a few years) Universal Coordinated Time.

Greenwich mean time (GMT)

As you know, there are 24 hours in a day (I could use more in writing this book). The earth, therefore, has 24 time zones. Somewhere had to be picked as the zero point, and England won, designating Greenwich the site of a royal observatory researching time and space for the last three centuries. Many computer systems, especially large Internet servers, reference GMT.

To write universal scripts, REBOL can track where you are from the GMT zero time point by using your computer's system time. In my case, living in the Eastern time zone, I am minus five hours from GMT.

Something else may be in the current directory besides files — other directories! If you attempt to read a filename in a directory that is really the name of a subdirectory, you get more than you bargained for — in other words, a block of files in the subdirectory. You probably want to avoid this condition by working in only one directory at a time. Getting the information for whether a specific name is a file or a directory is simple in REBOL. Just type

```
dir? %secrethandshakes
```

Well, doesn't every REBOLution have secret handshakes so its agents can tell who's on their side? That's a little hard to do over the Internet, but I'm sure the REBOLers out in California will have it in beta soon.

Oh, back to our information gathering about files. If this is a directory, `true` is returned or `false` if not. As the preceding example shows, you can then have the script base decisions on this data.

Yet another way exists of getting information about a file, using the `info?` function word. This one returns the size, modification/creation date, and whether the name is a file or a directory as an object. Because the result is an object, use `probe` so you can see the result at the console when you try it. The line works like so:

```
probe info? %file.txt
```

REBOL returns the following code:

```
make object! [
    size: 22
    date: 4-Feb-2000/20:06:46-5:00
    type: file
]
```

The preceding object shows three types of information — size, date, and type of file. Here's how you use this file information object. First, put it in a variable by typing

```
fileinfo: info? %file.txt
```

To retrieve the information in the object, type this:

```
print fileinfo/size        ; size of file
print fileinfo/date        ; date of file
print fileinfo/type        ; file or directory
```

But what if you want just two of these or a piece of data that the function info? does not include? Well, as Chapter 5 shows, creating your own function is a breeze. What else is nice to know about the file? Well, you can do a quick function that uses the file information in this section. It's a standalone script.

Call your new function fileinfo? and have it find size, modified date, content of the file, first line, last line, and the number of lines. All return to an object so these snippets of file information can be reused in the script. Did I forget type of file? No, use the code

```
if not dir? file
```

as a safety valve. If the filename called is a directory, the function exits instead of bombing back an error message.

You can include this function in your scripts by calling it with a do function, do %9-fileinfo.r (which adds the function into the current REBOL session) or by just cutting and pasting it at the top of any script you want to use the function in. Here is the code for your new function:

```
REBOL [File: %9-fileinfo.r
       Purpose: {A file information function}]

  fileinfo?: func [
       file
       ][
       if not dir? file [    ; make sure it's a file
.........make object! [
              ...current-time: now
.........size: size? file
              date: modified? file
              content: read/lines file
              firstline: first content
              lastline: last content
              numberlines: length? content]
       ]
       ]
```

Here's what's returned with `probe` after loading and running your new function.

```
probe fileinfo? %file.txt
```

```
make object! [
    time: 5-Feb-2000/15:34:13-5:00
    size: 22
    date: 4-Feb-2000/20:06:46-5:00
    type: false
    content: ["test" "test" "test" "test"]
    firstline: "test"
    lastline: "test"
    numberlines: 4
]
```

Run it from the console like this (placing the file information object in word `a`):

```
a: fileinfo? %file.txt
```

Gee, it works just like an official REBOL function word, huh? What hath you wrought, great programmer? Something useful, I say. Retrieve information out of the object like so:

```
print a/lastline
print a/current-time
print a/date
print a/numberlines
```

And so forth and so forth. Is this fun, or what? Yes, it's simple — but REBOLutionary — stuff. You can use your new function in a simple directory lister:

```
REBOL [File: %9-listing.r
       Purpose: {Directory Listing}]

do %9-fileinfo.r   ; just to make sure
                   ; fileinfo? is loaded
```

Play with that and see if you can improve the formatting, add more information, and generally make it better. Note that I use the `prin` word to print some things on the same line without a line return (newline) being generated.

File Permissions

File permissions are extremely important on Unix/Linux systems where there are world, group, and owner read, write, and execute permissions for files. These permissions are a security feature and control access for other reasons, such as privacy.

Using default permissions

Any time REBOL creates a file, it automatically sets the default access permissions for the type of system on which it's currently running. For Windows and Macintosh systems, the default is full access privileges. On Unix/Linux, the default permissions are those of the current umask setting (consult your Unix/Linux system's manual for more about this).

Setting new permissions

The REBOL open or write function words with an /allow refinement sets permissions. This option only sets permissions for operating systems that use them and is most useful on Unix/Linux systems.

REBOL can set read, write, and execute permissions on Unix or Linux files, but only for the user. World and group permissions are removed. Keep this in mind. Often you may have to use the chmod command on Unix/Linux systems to manually set the permissions correctly, especially for CGI applications.

Set permissions on files like this:

```
write/allow %file.txt [read]
write/allow %file.txt [write]
open/allow %file.txt [read execute]
write/allow %file.txt [read write execute]
open/allow %file.txt []
```

In sequence, these are: read only; write only; read and execute; read, write, and execute; and lastly, no privileges.

Bonus script

As a final exercise in reading and writing files, do something using the techniques of this book — a sorted directory lister function.

Yes, REBOL comes with list-dir that gives you a sorted, multicolumn listing of files from the console. But no information appears other than the file's name. The directory lister that follows gives a sorted list of files along with their lengths, points out subdirectories, counts the number of files in the directory, and gives us the total size and the total number of subdirectories.

The following code is a *function*. To use it, start REBOL and from the console, type this command:

```
do %9-dirlist.r
```

Then type

```
help dir
```

to see how to use it. As Chapter 3 explains, simple documentation can be (and should be) easily included in the functions you write. Compare what is returned when you do the preceding commands with the following script — and note how I've documented the function's required parameter with examples. Here's the code:

```
REBOL [
Title: "Directory Lister"
File:  "%9-dirlist.r"
]

dir: func [{Simple directory lister. Examples: dir %.  dir
            %/c/rebol/demo.} path
][
a: ""
        z: 0
        count: 0
        dsize: 0
        dirs:  0

    a: read path sort a
    if path = %. [path: ""]

    foreach line a [
            prin line
            z: length? line
            loop 50 - z [prin " "]
            if path <> "" [line: join path line]
            make file! Line
            if not dir? line [print size? line
            dsize: dsize + size? line]
            if dir? line [print "DIRECTORY"
            dirs: dirs + 1]
            count: count + 1
        ]

print [newline "Directory" path "has" count "files totaling"
        dsize "bytes."]
print ["There are" dirs "subdirectories."]
]
```

Figure 9-2 shows the script in operation.

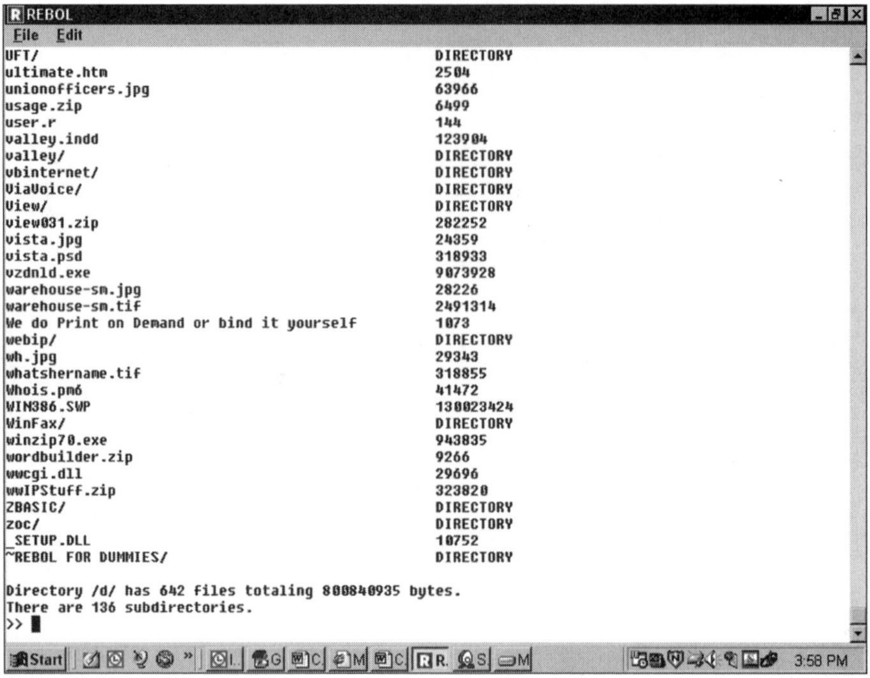

Figure 9-2:
Using this
function
with an
argument of
%/d/ (the D
drive on my
writing
computer).

The theory of operation is simple. You get the list of files in a directory and read them into a variable. REBOL gets the names as file values, which makes sorting easy. (Sorting the same variable if it were a string value would jumble all the letters for all the names together, like *aaaaaaaabbbb,* and so on.)

The sorted list of filenames may now be used to get information about each file using a foreach loop and using line as the filename. The following error-trapping line lets REBOL know not to try putting a pathname in front of files in the current directory:

```
if path = %. [path: ""]
```

To make the listing more readable, I use the following code:

```
z: length? line
loop 50 - z [prin " "]
```

This takes the length of the filename and subtracts it from 50, and then prints the number of spaces required for the next column of information to begin always at the same position. It gives a nice readable format. (I use 50 because I have a lot of long filenames; change it to whatever looks good for you.) Play with this script, elaborate it, find out its ins and outs, and then polish it to meet your needs and wants for a quick directory lister. Enjoy!

Chapter 10

Directories and Ports

*T*he old sailor's cliché goes, "any port in a storm." *Ports* in REBOL are places you can specify where data flows back and forth between REBOL and other devices or things such as files and directories. You'll find ports mighty handy, but you first need to know a bit about directories themselves.

In this chapter, I show you how to navigate directories, make ports as often and surely as the U.S. Navy, control access to files, and handle very large files. You're now ready to up anchor and start your funtime, suntime cruise.

Traversing Directories

In Chapter 9, I introduce the old analogies that files are like file folders, hard drives or file systems are like file cabinets, and directories are like drawers. In real file cabinets, drawers have tabbed dividers like A, B, C; or perhaps category labels such as Invoices, Bills, REBOLution Member Files, or whatever.

On a computer, the directories are more like an upside-down tree. The top or *root* file branches out into subdirectories, which in turn can have subdirectories, and so on. REBOL provides powerful (but simple) functions that can help you manage directories. And if you need more unique directory management help, you can create custom functions to do the job. Refer to Chapter 7 to see just how easy creating custom functions can be.

Directory management tasks that you want your REBOL scripts to accomplish include the following:

- Reading directories
- Managing subdirectories
- Opening directories (path information is always necessary for precise location of files and data in objects)
- Making new directories
- Getting, changing, and listing the current directory
- Renaming files
- Deleting files

Getting the current directory

First, it always helps to know where you are in the file system. Use the command

```
>> what-dir
== %/D/rebol/
```

to return the name of the current directory. REBOL returns the directory name on your console screen. You can also find the same information in system/script/path:

```
>> print system/script/path
/D/rebol/
```

When you need to ensure that the script is accessing the right directory, you can type

```
>> if system/script/path = %/d/rebol/ [print "This is the
        REBOL directory."]
This is the REBOL directory.
```

Changing the current directory

Here's an example of how changing directories can help you do your work. On my Windows system, my REBOL directory is on the D: drive. I want to change directories from the current directory (C: drive) to the REBOL directory on D: so that I can use relative (short) file/pathnames in calling various programs to test their operation (that is, just type %test.r instead of a longer absolute path like %/d/rebol/test.r). See Chapter 9 for a discussion of relative versus absolute pathnames. In the REBOL console at the >> prompt, I ask REBOL to kindly change directories by typing (here, I have to use an absolute pathname):

```
change-dir %/d/rebol
```

REBOL returns the following information, also at the console prompt:

```
== %/d/rebol
```

This response shows me that my REBOL directory is now the current one — precisely what I asked for. Note that forward slashes (/) are used, not the backward slash (\) that you normally see on Windows and DOS systems. REBOL, being a universal system, uses the more common forward slash. Therefore, your filenames work unchanged on many platforms.

You can find all REBOL special function words, like change-dir from the preceding example, in the REBOL dictionary at http://rebol.com/dictionary.html for handy online reference. Methods of using REBOL functions are detailed in the excellent online user's guide at http://rebol.com/users.html.

Listing files in the current directory

The way you get a list of files in the current directory from the command console is by typing the following:

```
list-dir
```

The results of this function look like this:

```
countWeb.r       cw.txt           definitions.r
dir-sizer.r      dir-tree.r       displist.r
ebay.r           epoch.r          examples.r
factorial.r      feedback.r       file list.txt
findagent.r      formletter.r     ftpdownbin.r
ftpwrite.r       hc.r             headfull.r
http-post.r      iho-tools.r      incdec.r
```

Right, just a list of filenames. You can't use list-dir in a script to pull a list of filenames into a variable and do stuff with them. But you can accomplish this in other ways. The next section covers how you can manage directories by using REBOL scripts.

Manipulating Directories

I just bought a new computer; it has 120 gigabytes (GB) of storage space. I say this not to brag (okay, some) but simply as an indication of how cheap vast amounts of storage space are these days. A personal computer with 20GB of hard drive space is becoming quite common; the trend in Internet servers is to have more and more space. The only — and let me emphasize obvious — way of maintaining any sort of logical control over the thousands upon thousands of files these huge new drives can hold is by putting them in directories, and subdirectories, and subdirectories of subdirectories.

Think of the biggest tree you've seen recently — a stately old oak or a towering redwood. They have thousands of branches that sway gently in the breeze or really whip around in a thunderstorm. Next imagine that you're a bird, and you want to make a landing on one of those moving branches — not just any branch, but a particular branch. Sometimes it's a moving target, sometimes not.

That, my friend, should give you an idea of the complexity of directory manipulation and why it's so darned important.

Two pieces of good news — you are not a bird and REBOL makes directory manipulation easy.

In the following sections, I show you how to find out what's in directories, how to manage directory systems, the ways of finding and accessing files in a particular directory, and the other basics your scripts need in all of the vast file systems growing on today's computers.

Reading what's in your directories

To easily read a directory and get a listing of all its contents, type the following command:

```
read %.          ; read current directory
```

REBOL returns the directory contents — the subdirectories and filenames — as a block of names. Any names that are subdirectories instead of files have a trailing forward slash (/).

You can use a variation of the `read` command to easily read the current directory into a REBOL word with the names sorted alphabetically. Here's an example:

```
a: read %. sort a
```

In this case, the word is called a. You define and use words in REBOL scripts to hold values (like directory contents) that you can then manipulate in other ways. For example, you can print out the sorted list with just one name per line, as follows:

```
foreach line a [print line]
```

Bingo! You have a sorted list of files.

Would you like to see me do that in Perl? Sorry, I'm on deadline here. I'll stick to the simple REBOL way. You want it even simpler? Okay, no problem. (And they laughed when I first sat down to play the computer; thanks, REBOL!) How about the following situation? I can read my root directory from any sub-directory (doesn't matter where) and print out a sorted list of file and directory names by using just one line of code. And here it is:

```
a: read %// sort a foreach line a [print line]
```

Ah, what fun.

Managing directory systems

Managing directory systems involves knowing the hierarchy of directories, subdirectories, and files. One important item to know, then, is where the sub-directories live. REBOL gives you a simple method of filtering out filenames and listing only the subdirectories of the current directory, as follows:

```
foreach file read %. [if dir? file [print file]]
```

This command lists only one level of subdirectories: those in the current directory. To get a list of all subdirectories, including subdirectories of subdi-rectories, you use a *recursive* (back and forth) technique that I show you in Chapter 17.

Opening and closing directories

All the directory manipulations that I've introduced in this section so far involve simply reading the directory name or listing the names of files and subdirectories therein. You get a block of names that you can do all sorts of stuff with in REBOL. Even so, you're working with just directory names and filenames, and nothing changes on the disk. In order to edit filenames and directory names, delete selected files in a directory, or do other such modifi-cations, you can use the open and close functions. After you open a direc-tory or file, you can do all sorts of funky stuff to it.

Here's how simple the open function is

```
dir: open %.
```

By using this function, you create a port to the current directory, and the directory is at your utter mercy. You can use commands like the following to find the names of files or directories at specific locations (first and last, in the examples) or to see how many files and subdirectories comprise the current directory:

```
print dir first          ; first file or subdirectory
print dir last           ; the last
print length? dir        ; how many in this directory?
```

After you open a port to a directory, you can delete or rename files and sub-directories. Doing so, however, requires care. Deleting or renaming directory elements can raise problems such as causing other scripts and programs to bomb because you've removed the directory names they are looking for. This is especially true for multiuser systems like Internet servers.

Create a temporary trash directory and put some temporary files in it before playing around with the functions that remove and rename stuff. (And make sure that you're actually in your temporary trash directory when you do.)

You can also, as previously noted, make changes to the contents of an open directory! The following examples show functions that help you do just that:

```
remove dir                  ; deletes the first file
remove dir last             ; delete the last file
remove skip dir 2           ; delete the third file
change skip dir 1 %newfile  ; rename the second file
```

Notice in the renaming example that you don't have to use the percent sign (%) in front of the filename. The percent sign denotes to REBOL that the name following it is a file value, but this is unnecessary for the renaming example because the directory is open (that is, in memory) and the change is not written directly to the disk. REBOL actually writes the change to the disk after you (or your script) tell it to do so.

After you or your script finishes modifying an open directory, you close it by typing

```
close dir
```

Creating new directories

When you create a new directory, both relative and absolute paths work. Following are examples of both. In the first example, the path is relative, as shown by there being only the directory name with no path. And in the second example, the path is specified, making it absolute.

```
make-dir %demos/          ;adds to current directory
make-dir %/d/rebol/projects/reports     ; absolute
```

Before you or your scripts go making new directories, use a good programming practice by checking to make sure that you are not overwriting an existing directory. Here's one way:

```
if not exists? %newdir [make-dir %newdir/]
```

In the latest version of REBOL (2.3 as this book goes to press), the /deep refinement is added to make-dir. This refinement enables entire file paths to be created in one fell swoop:

```
>> exists? %/d/one
== false
>> make-dir/deep
          %/d/one/two/three/four/five/six/seven/eight/nine
          /etc
== %/d/one/two/three/four/five/six/seven/eight/nine/etc/
>> exists? %/d/one/two/three/four/five/six/seven/eight/nine
          /etc/
== true
```

Renaming files

The preceding sections show you how to open a directory, remove or rename files, and close the directory again. If that three-step process looks a little complicated (well, not really), you'll be happy to note that, as usual, REBOL provides an easier way. That easier way is the rename function, which you use as follows:

```
rename %file.txt %newfile.txt
```

You may use either absolute or relative pathnames for this function. And you may want to find out whether a file is where you think it is (and that it has the name you expect) before trying to rename it. If you don't do this check, REBOL generates an error if your path or filename is wrong. Try the following code to check before renaming:

```
if exists? %file.txt [rename %file.txt %newfile.txt]
```

Deleting files

One of the givens concerning recording files is that eventually they must be deleted, or the file system fills up and no more room is left. When a file is no longer necessary, you need to get rid of it. REBOL gives you the tools needed for file deletion.

The delete function removes filenames from a directory's contents list:

```
delete %file.txt
```

As with all direct file operations, both absolute and relative pathnames work. And you are not limited to deleting just one file at a time. REBOL lets you delete blocks of files, as follows:

```
delete [%file1.txt %file2.txt %file3.txt]
```

You can also feel free to use wildcards — like an asterisk (*) to stand for several letters and a question mark (?) to stand for a single letter — to wipe out a bunch of files at once. Use the delete/any refinement as follows:

```
delete/any %file*
```

This code gets rid of all filenames beginning with the letters *f-i-l-e* and residing in the current directory.

To delete directories using relative or absolute naming conventions, you simply need to add a trailing forward slash (/):

```
delete %dir/
delete %../rebolution/old-troop-rosters/
```

Opening Ports

Ports are places where data flows back and forth between REBOL and other devices or things like files. Serial and parallel ports, network protocols like TCP/IP, and even files can be ports. A port is really nothing more than an input/output *buffer* facilitating the exchange of information between two different entities. (Whoa, *X-Files*-like talk there; I mean devices.) A buffer is an interface created in memory that facilitates communication between devices or files.

When you open a port to a file, REBOL knows to use the *file scheme* for exchanging information with the file. Other schemes exist for transferring data to and from other types of ports. (Mulder to Scully: Find out what entities he's buffering with.)

Using simple techniques to open and close ports

Actually, the read and write functions use open to create a port to a file for their operations; it's just transparent to you. Under the hood, so to speak, all the cylinders swap in a consistent manner with a minimum of clanging. Opening a file is like opening a directory, as outlined in "Opening and closing directories," earlier in this chapter:

```
text: open %file.txt
```

The word file now refers to the actual file on disk, file.txt. After you open a file, you can use various series functions (refer to Chapter 8 for series manipulations) on the file port. You can type

```
copy/part (find text "password")(find a newline)
copy/part (find text "Fred")(find text "Marvin)
```

These two lines of code work as follows:

- ✔ **First code line:** Copies everything from the first instance of the word password to the end of the line it's on.

- ✔ **Second code line:** Copies everything from the first instance of Fred to the first instance of Marvin, no matter how many lines it takes.

After a file port is open, you can also modify its contents with code like this:

```
remove/part (find text "password")(find a newline)
```

The preceding code removes everything from the word password to the end of the line it is on. When you are finished with any changes, closing the file port saves your modifications. You type

```
close text
```

While a file is open, you can keep it open but save your changes with the update function, as shown here:

```
update text
```

Opening new files

Just as the `write` function creates a new file on disk if one does not exist, the `open` function does, too. The following code examples show some ways that you can open new and existing files:

```
text: open %file.txt
image: open/binary %rebolflag.gif
refdata: open/read %data.txt          ; read only
formletter: open/lines %letter.txt    ; in lines
```

The first example above opens a file named `file.txt` in the current directory. If a file by that name isn't found, REBOL creates it. The second line opens a GIF image using binary data (that is, no line endings or anything else in the file is converted, the format is retained exactly). The third example opens a file in the *read-only* mode; no changes are allowed. The last example opens `letter.txt` in line mode, where you can make changes to each line without affecting the others. Using `read/lines` actually creates a block with each line being a separate element in that block.

Overwriting files

Opening an existing file and overwriting all the data in it (initializing it for new data) is done by typing

```
datastuff: open/new %file.txt
```

An example of why you'd want to do this may be a weekly report. On Monday, REBOL overwrites last week's file and starts accumulating this week's data.

Using line access

Using `line access` to a file port is similar to `read/lines` and `write/lines` in regular file read and write operations. With line access, you can look at and change individual lines without affecting the rest of the file. The difference here is that you are operating on a file port instead of directly to the file itself. To open a file with line access, type

```
text: open/lines %file.txt
```

You can then do line-related things like

```
length? text          ; how many lines in the file?
print first text       ; print the first line
```

After you open the file port in lines mode, you can use functions like `change` and `replace` to modify the text. The following code is an example:

```
change text "Now is the time for all REBOLers"
```

Use the `update` or `close` functions to save any modifications that you've made to an open file port.

Controlling access to files

The ideas behind controlling access to an open file relate to ensuring data integrity and smoothing I/O operations. REBOL allows for two primary forms of controlled file access:

- ✓ **Read-only** is a pretty obvious concept: It lets you open a file port (buffer) and see the data from a file. You can make changes to the data in the buffer, but it will not be written back to the file even if you — or more likely your script — update or close the file. With read-only access, you can protect data that simply needs to be read and not changed. REBOL helps you open a file for read-only access like this:

```
text: open/read %file.txt
```

- ✓ **Write-only** is a different concept. Here you open the file but don't read the data into the buffer. A caution here: This operation is not similar to `write/append`, because it overwrites the existing file instead of appending data to it. Open a file for write-only access like this:

```
Logfile: open/write %file.txt
```

Handling files larger than memory

The technique for reading, modifying, and otherwise handling files larger than available memory involves looking at the file one chunk at a time. This process is easy, and I show you how to construct a function that does it nicely when I discuss server logs in Chapter 17.

Each time someone accesses a Web page, an entry with certain information about the hit is placed in the server's logs. Server logs grow notoriously fast and quickly can reach tens of megabytes in size, even for Web sites with relatively low traffic. Keeping control of these files and getting useable statistics from them is a job made for REBOL. Figure 10-1 shows the REBOL log stats script that I wrote for my own server. And the following code gives you a start on the basics of handling large files. Open the file with the `/direct` refinement, which opens an unbuffered port to the file.

```
logstats: open/direct %access_log
```

The only trick after that is controlling which chunk of the file you are looking at, and I show you how in Chapter 17.

Passing references

A file port's reference, or point of operation, is easily changed to another point in the file. You want to change a file's reference point to find specific data, to add data to the end of the file, and for other types of file manipulation. When you first open a file — as in the following code — the point of reference is at the head, or beginning, of the file.

```
text: open %file.txt
```

To change the point of reference, use the find function as follows:

```
text: find text "REBOL"
```

And, assuming that the file contained the word REBOL in the first place, its point of reference is now the beginning of the word.

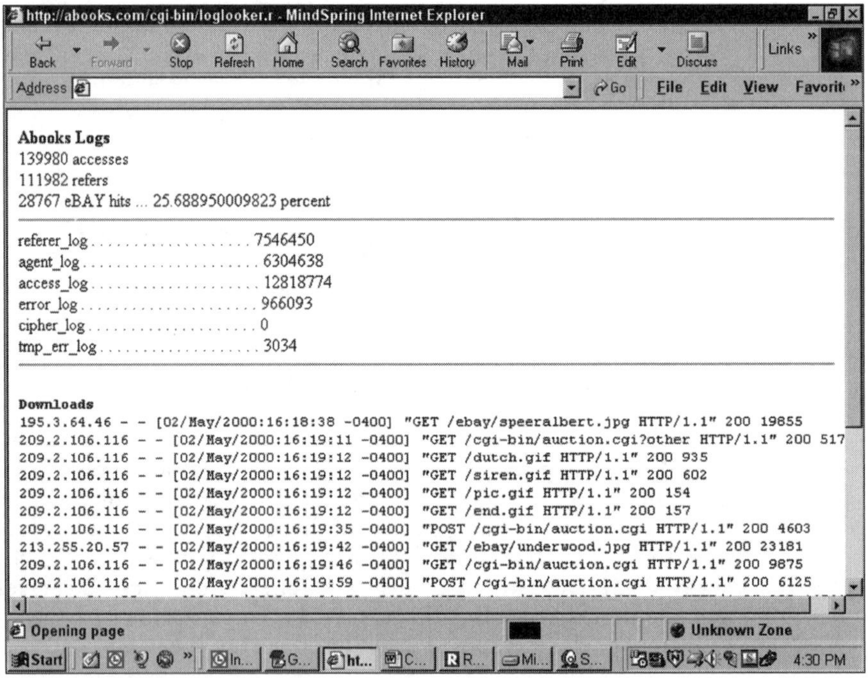

Figure 10-1:
My own
server's
REBOL log
stats script
in operation.

Chapter 11

Math: Minus the Complexity but Plus the Usefulness

*R*EBOL provides powerful ways of manipulating numbers and doing trigonometric operations. In this chapter, I introduce you to basic arithmetic and give you examples of helpful functions using more advanced math. I also show you just how logical logic can be.

Two terms used throughout this chapter that you should be familiar with are *operator* and *argument*. An operator does something to something — in REBOL, the function word `divide`, for example, is an operator as are `add` and `subtract`. An *argument* is data given to an operator to act upon. In the following code, `add` is the operator and the two twos are arguments:

```
>> add 2 2
== 4
```

The following works equally as well in REBOL:

```
>> 2 + 2
== 4
```

Operators and arguments — it all adds up to a great implementation of often used math techniques in the REBOL tradition of doing simple things simply.

Constructing Your Mathematical Statements

When you construct statements with any kind of mathematical, logic, or comparison operators, you need to keep a couple of basic rules in mind:

- ✔ **Separate your operators from your arguments:** REBOL needs a space as a delimiting character (a separator) so that it can distinguish words. Make sure that you always include a space between and around logic and comparison operators to separate the operator from what it operates on. See the following code as an example:

```
i > 3           ; <-- correct form
i>3             ; <-- wrong, appears to be a word
```

- ✔ **Place your operators correctly:** Infix operators appear between the arguments, like the plus sign (+) in the calculation 2 + 2. Prefix operators appear before the arguments, like the add function used in the REBOL statement add 2 2.

- ✔ **Specify the evaluation order for your mathematical operations:** By default, REBOL evaluates a series of mathematical operations from left to right. You achieve accurate results for your calculations by placing calculations in the default order or by using parentheses to change the default order. See the section "Controlling precedence with parentheses" for examples.

Adding the Basics

The REBOL language includes numerous mathematical operators and various datatypes. You can use many combinations of operators and datatypes to perform math tasks. This section shows you the more basic ones.

Here are some ways of using operators on datatypes:

```
>> $12.96 * 3                    ; multiply a money! datatype
== $38.88
>> divide 15.68 2                ; divide a decimal! datatype
== 7.84
>> 207.195.3.2 + 6               ; add to a tuple! datatype
== 213.201.9.8
>> 3 + 3                         ; add two integer! datatypes
== 6
```

```
>> now/time - 1:00              ; subtract an hour from
                                  current time
== 10:06:08
>> now/date + 5                 ; add five days to current
                                  date
== 26-Jul-2000
```

Using scalar datatypes in math operations

Many of the math operators in REBOL can handle multiple datatypes, including integer, decimal, money, tuple, time, date, logic, and char datatypes. Some of these datatypes may even be *mixed*. By that I mean you can multiply, for instance, a money! datatype by an integer! datatype or a decimal! datatype, and so forth. Here are some of the so forths:

```
>> $15.39 * 1.5                 ; money! multiplied by decimal
== $23.09
>> 1.1.1.1 * 6                  ; tuple! divided by integer!
== 6.6.6.6
>> divide now/day 1.5           ; divide day of month (date!) by
                                  decimal!
== 14
```

For more on the many datatypes (values) available in REBOL and the rules for using them, please refer to Chapters 4 and 5 in this book.

In REBOL, these fundamental datatypes are also called *scalar datatypes.* The word *scalar,* in this context, means expanding, or growing bigger, and refers to the way REBOL programs are constructed. That is, a series of datatypes combine to form more complex data. For example, if I sell five books in my company's bookstore (Publisher's Overstock Outlet, Alexander, North Carolina — y'all come visit) and I want an average price per book, I can combine scalar datatypes to answer my question in this manner:

```
>> print (($4.95 + $9.95 + $24.95 + $14.99 + $8.95) / 5)
$12.76
```

In effect, I add several money! datatypes and divide by an integer datatype! for an average price. That's scalar datatypes in a nutshell.

Following are some examples of basic mathematical statements using the integer and decimal datatypes. The lines beginning with >> show what you type at the REBOL console. The lines beginning with = = show the value that you see returned. (You can try them for yourself at the REBOL console.)

```
>> 2 + 2
== 4

>> 2 * 2
== 4

>> multiply 2 2
== 4

>> divide 2 2
== 1

>> (2 + 2) + 3
== 7

>> divide (2 + 2) 5
== 0.8

>> print divide (multiply 2000 0.195) 12
32.5
```

Basic math operations are just as easy with other datatypes:

```
>> current-time: now/time
== 14:25:02

>> print current-time + 4:10:00
22:10:52                           ; time

>> current-date: now/date
== 21-Jul-2000

>> print current-date + 12
24-Mar-2000                        ; date

>> print divide $156.02 2
$78.01                             ; money

>> print 192.168.0.1 + 0.0.0.1     ; tuple
192.168.0.2
```

When you attempt mathematical operations by using incompatible data-types, REBOL responds with an error, letting you know which datatype is incompatible with what operator. In the following example, REBOL tells you that you can't add the number 3 to the letter b that has been assigned the value test.

```
>> b: "test"
== "test"
>> print b + 3
** Script Error: Cannot use add on string! value.
** Where: print b + 3
```

Operating on numbers, REBOL provides you with several handy tables detailing basic mathematical operators. In Tables 11-1 and 11-2, v stands for value, an input that can be one of several datatypes. The term *number* is used to describe either the integer or decimal datatype. Values (*x*) are shown in situations where datatypes other than integer or decimal are allowed.

All math operators are classified as either infix or prefix based on the operators' placement within mathematical statements. That is, *infix* operators appear between their arguments, and *prefix* operators appear before their arguments.

Here's an example of a statement containing infix operators:

```
>> print 2 + 25 + 50
77
```

The addition signs (+) in the preceding statement are infix operators. You can also use a prefix operator, the add function, to perform this same addition:

```
>> print add 2 2
4
```

Table 11-1	Infix Math Operators		
Operator	*In Statement*	*Results*	*Accepted Datatypes*
+	x + y2	Returns the sum of x and y.	char, date, money, number, time, tuple
-	x1 - x2	Returns result of subtracting x2 from x1.	char, number, money, date, time, tuple
*	x1 * x2	Returns result of multiplying x1 by x2.	char, number, money, time, tuple
/	x1 / x2	Returns result of dividing x1 by x2.	char, number, money, time, tuple
//	x1 // x2	Returns remainder of dividing x1 by x2.	char, number, money, time, tuple

Table 11-2		Prefix Math Operators	
Operator	*In Statement*	*Results*	*Accepted Datatypes*
-	- x	Negates the sign of x.	bitset, money, number, time
abs	abs x	Returns the absolute value of x.	number, money, time
absolute	absolute x	Returns the absolute value of x.	number, money, time
add	add x1 x2	Returns result of adding x1 to x2.	char, number, money, date, time, tuple
divide	divide x1 x2	Returns result of dividing x1 by x2.	char, number, money, time, tuple
multiply	multiply x1 x2	Returns result of multiplying x1 by x2.	char, number, money, time, tuple
negate	negate x	Negates the sign of the "number" x.	number, money, time, bitset
remainder	remainder x1 x2	Returns remainder of dividing x1 by x2.	char, number, money, time, tuple
subtract	subtract x1 x2	Returns result of subtracting x2 from x1.	char, number, money, date, time, tuple

The above tables give you a wealth of information about the math operators in REBOL — play with them until they become familiar. You'll find these operators to be useful friends in many fine scripts to come.

Controlling precedence with parentheses

All math operations in REBOL, by default, evaluate from left to right, as in the following example:

```
>> print 34 + 1452 + 10 - 29
1467
```

The default evaluation order works fine for getting solutions in a nice linear manner (as in the preceding example). But what happens if you mix operations? Perhaps you need to add some numbers and divide them by another.

REBOL still evaluates from left to right, but you can use *parentheses* to control the *precedence* — that is, to specify which parts of your mathematical statement to solve first.

```
>> print divide (94 + 54 + 28 + 47) 5
```

The divide function is a prefix operator. The statement in the preceding example evaluates in this manner: REBOL sees the addition segment inside the parentheses, totals it, and then divides by 5 to return the final value.

Unless you correctly use parentheses, you may get a different result than expected. Take these two operations:

```
>> print .07 * 94 + 54 + 28 + 47
135.58
>> print .07 * (94 + 54 + 28 + 47)
15.61
```

In the top example above, .07 is multiplied by 94, and that number is added to the other three numbers. In the bottom example, the four sums are first added and then multiplied by .07, giving a very different answer. Make sure that you control the precedence with parentheses for the correct result.

You may also *nest* (have parentheses inside parentheses) mathematical operations for more complex statements:

```
>> print multiply (divide (25 + 5) 2) 4
60
```

Actually, the example above gives the same answer without the parentheses. Here's one that does not:

```
>> print multiply .5 25 + divide 5 2 * 6 * .01
33.3333333333333
>> print multiply .5 25 + (divide 5 2 * 6) * .01
0.127083333333333
```

Watch those parentheses!

You can even force right to left evaluation by clever nesting of parentheses:

```
>> print (2 + (2 * (2 + (4 / 8))))
7
```

REBOL sees this last example as follows:

1. Evaluate the right-most nested parentheses, dividing 4 by 8 to get .5.

2. Add the result, .5, to 2 (the next number to the left) to get 2.5.

3. Multiply the result, 2.5, by 2 to get 5.

4. Add the result, 5, to the left-most 2 for the final value, 7.

Generating random values

The random function returns a random value of the same datatype that you provide as its argument (char, integer, decimal, money, date, time, logic). You may find this function useful, for example, when generating passwords for users of an application. And you can control the range of the value returned by supplying a maximum value:

```
>> print random 10        ; random number from 1 to 10
5
>> print random $5        ; random money
$2.00
>> print random #"Z"      ; random character
!
>> print random 10:00     ; random period of time
0:06:20
```

Printing a random series of numbers:

```
>> loop 5 [print random 100]
96
67
32
53
12
```

Or with a little thought, you can specify a range of values. In this case, random numbers between 400 and 600:

```
>> loop 5 [print 400 + random 200]
410
559
561
486
549
```

The /seed refinement restarts, or randomizes, the random value generator. If you want true random value generation, try seeding random before using it. Also, avoid the use of static seeds like an integer, but rather use a dynamic seed such as the current time. The following is an example of why not to use an integer:

```
>> random/seed 456
>> loop 5 [print random 100]
56
68
44
60
83
>> random/seed 456
>> loop 5 [print random 100]
56
68
44
60
83
```

If you run this random generation twice, you receive the same results! Now try doing the same thing using a dynamic random seed like the time:

```
>> random/seed now/time
>> loop 5 [print random 100]
28
97
37
35
47
>> random/seed now/time
>> loop 5 [print random 100]
27
19
68
56
98
```

REBOL returns two different sets of random values.

Handling math errors

Mathematical calculations must adhere to a strict set of rules. Because of this, having improper operations or values creep into your mathematical statements is common. But never fear, REBOL double-checks all your calculations and reports math errors for two main reasons:

✔ For an attempted illegal operation, such as division by zero:

```
>> print divide 1 0
** Math Error: Attempt to divide by zero.
** Where: print divide 1 0
```

✔ For a number that is too large to process:

```
>> print 11111111111111 *
          11111111111111111111111111111111111111111111111111111
          1111111111111111
** Syntax Error: Invalid integer --
          11111111111111111111111111111111111111111111111111111111
          11111111111111111.
** Where: (line 1) print 11111111111111 *
          11111111111111111111111111111111111111111111111111111111
          1111111111111111
```

Converting datatypes

You'll find many occasions to perform mathematical operations that combine datatypes. For example, multiply a price (money! datatype) by two (integer! datatype):

```
>> $1.98 * 2
== $3.96
```

When you perform mathematical operations between datatypes, normally the noninteger, or decimal, datatype is returned — just like the example above, if you multiply a money! datatype by an integer or decimal number, the result is a money! datatype. When you use integers and decimals in the same calculations, REBOL returns a decimal datatype.

The following example makes this even clearer. If you add a decimal like 2.5 to an integer like 3, REBOL returns the resulting value as a decimal datatype:

```
>> print 2.5 + 3
5.5
```

This may seem simple and logical to you, but wait until you have a script — with a bunch of different datatypes — that's not acting as you expected. The datatype that REBOL returns from your math operations can become exceptionally important for resolving bugs.

The rule of thumb for the datatypes returned by math operations is simple. Whenever you add, multiply, divide, or subtract any datatype by or with an integer or decimal, the datatype remains unchanged. `Money!` plus a decimal is still `money!`, `time!` minus an `integer` is still `time!`, and so forth.

The REBOL online documentation provides tables covering all these datatype conversions.

Using Advanced Mathematics

I recently attended my 35th high school reunion (Class of '64). There I saw my high school trigonometry teacher, Mrs. Inez Brown, still looking fine after all these years. I hastened to tell her I'd have that homework assignment finished any day now. She laughed, thinking that I was kidding. Well, REBOL helps with your trig and other higher-level math operations. By taking advantage of REBOL, I may even get that homework done — finally!

In addition to trigonometric operations, REBOL helps you out with log, powers of number, and roots. In this section, I review some uses of these advanced techniques.

Nitish Verma wrote a nice script, called `primes.r`, that calculates prime numbers. Figure 11-1 shows a sample output from Nitish's script that lists all the prime numbers up to 5000. You may find this script useful if you need to generate a series of prime numbers. The script is available at `http://rebol.org`.

Logging logarithmic and power operations

The following code shows examples of REBOL mathematical operations involving powers and logs:

```
>> print square-root 144      ; square root
12
>> power 10 10                ; raise 10 to the 10th
== 10000000000
>> log-10 200                 ; log 10 of 200
== 2.30102999566398
```

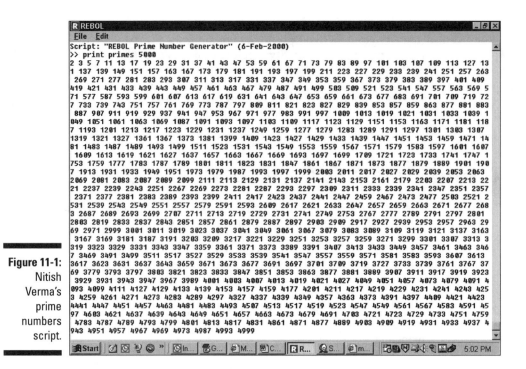

Figure 11-1:
Nitish
Verma's
prime
numbers
script.

REBOL doesn't need logs to add and subtract, but your scripts can do neat, under-the-hood type stuff with higher-level math manipulations. I recommend that you brush up on these techniques to help with writing programs, because math-related functions are part and parcel of just about any real-world application. I've been brushing up so that I can better handle the accounting tasks in writing e-commerce scripts.

Here are some examples of log and power operators:

```
>> 10 ** 100            ; raise 10 to the 100th power
== 1E+100
>> log-10 10            ; base-10 logarithm of 10
== 1
>> log-2 10
== 3.3219280948873     ; base-2 logarithm of 10
>> square-root 2        ; square root of 2
== 1.4142135623731
```

Angling trigonometry operations

REBOL's trigonometric functions by default deal with values in degrees. But you can use the /radians refinement to have your results returned in radians. (No, I didn't have to call Mrs. Brown and ask her what a radian is; I remember that much!) A *radian* is a unit of angular measurement that relies not on the standard 360 degrees of a circle, but on the measure of the radius of the circle.

Using trig functions in REBOL is simple. Here are some examples:

```
>> print sine 45                    ; sine 45 degrees
0.707106781186547

>> print cosine 45                  ; cosine 45 degrees
0.707106781186548

>> print tangent 45                 ; tan 45 degrees
1

>> print tangent/radians 45         ; tan in radians
1.61977519054387
```

Coding with Logic

Logic is an important concept in math specifically and in programming in general. Logic operators such as and are exceptionally useful. The following is an example of and logic used in a block of REBOL code:

```
>> phasors-armed: true
>> klingon-in-range: true
>> if phasors-armed and klingon-in-range [print "Fire
            phasors!"]
Fire phasors!
```

The first two lines in the preceding code show the defined REBOL words (phasors-armed and klingon-in-range) that are assigned true logic values. The third line demonstrates the use of and in a conditional statement that prints its message when both values are true. Although this example is a valid use of logic operators, this section gives more examples of how to use logic with advanced math procedures. For example, the use of logic allows your scripts to respond intelligently to varying conditions and inputs. The REBOL logic operators covered in this section include and, or, xor, not, and related functions.

Using REBOL logic

The logic operators in REBOL act on two levels — on the value of the datatype (such as an integer number) and, at an even more powerful lower level, on the binary ones and zeros that make up the datatype's value. On this second level, the operators work directly on the bits that make up the integer, char, logic, tuple, or bitset datatype values.

You can manipulate the bits that make up your data via the operations shown in the following examples. Please note that and, or, and xor are *polymorphic* functions. That is, they have different behavior for operations on logic values versus integer values. They perform *boolean* and/or logic operations on *logic* values and *bitwise* one/zero operations on integer values.

This concept may be a bit (pun, as ever, intended) confusing at first. The best way to explain these operations is with a few simple examples. The smart folks who designed REBOL recognized this and created a print-binary function that prints the binary value of an integer or char. I use this function in some of the following examples to help you understand bit logic.

For your convenience, I include the print-binary function on the CD-ROM that comes with this book as function 11-binary.r. You may want to load it and follow the examples. See Appendix D for instructions on loading functions from the CD.

```
REBOL [
      file: "%11-binary.r"
            ]
print-binary: func [a [integer! char!]][
    bin: enbase/base (load rejoin [
        "#{" to-hex either char? a [to-integer a][a]
    "}"]) 2    print find/last/any bin "????????" ; last 8
            bits
]
```

After you load this function, using it to convert an integer to its binary value is simple. Just type

```
>> print-binary 1
00000001
>> print-binary 100
01100100
```

Applying logic operators

The and operator compares two logic values and returns true if both values are true. If both or either value is false, the comparison returns false:

```
>> print  (1 < 2) and (2 < 3)
true
>> print (1 < 2) and (4 < 3)
false
```

When you use the and operator with integers, it returns the *bitwise-and* of two numeric arguments. That is, and compares the arguments bit for bit and returns 1 if both bits are 1, otherwise it returns 0. What does that really mean? Simply that REBOL looks at the binary value of two numbers bit by bit. The following example shows the results of using the and operator with the integers 3 and 5.

```
>> print 3 and 5
1
```

The value returned, 1, means there was one instance when the bit positions of both integers were 1. Otherwise, the corresponding positions were 1 and 0, or 0 and 0, and thus did not meet the test condition of both being true (that is, both 1). You can use the binary-print function to prove this, as follows:

```
>> print-binary 3
00000011

>> print-binary 5
00000101

>> print-binary 3 and 5
00000001
```

By comparing the two binary numbers visually, you see that only the right-most position in both match up. Computers see numbers and other values in this way — as series of 1s and 0s. Being able to write programs that manipulate data at this level gives you faster and more powerful applications — so spend a little time and master these logic operations. You can refer to Table 11-3 for the returned values from the and, or, and xor operators.

Table 11-3		AND, OR, and XOR Results		
Arg1 Bit	*Arg2 Bit*	*AND Result*	*OR Result*	*XOR Result*
0	0	0	0	0
0	1	0	1	1
1	0	0	1	1
1	1	1	1	0

The or operator compares two logic values and returns true if either of them is true. If both values are false, the comparison returns false:

```
>> print (1 < 2) or (2 < 3)
true

>> print (1 < 2) or (4 < 3)
true

>> print (3 < 2) or (4 < 3)
false
```

When used with integers, or returns the *bitwise-or* of two numeric arguments. That is, or compares the arguments bit for bit bits and returns 1 if either bit is 1, otherwise it returns 0. Here's the print-binary proof, or you can try it for yourself:

```
>> print 3 or 5
7

>> print-binary 3
00000011

>> print-binary 5
00000101

>> print-binary 3 or 5
00000111
```

The xor operator compares two logic values and returns true only if one is true and the other false. If both are true or both are false, it returns false:

```
>> print (1 < 2) xor (2 < 3)
false

>> print (1 < 2) xor (4 < 3)
true

>> print (3 < 2) xor (4 < 3)
false
```

When used with integers, xor returns the *bitwise-xor* of two numeric arguments. That is, xor compares arguments bit for bit and returns 1 only if one bit is 1 and the other is 0. Otherwise, it returns 0:

```
>> print 3 xor 5
6

>> print-binary 3
00000011

>> print-binary 5
00000101

>> print-binary 3 xor 5
00000110
```

The final logic operator, not, takes a single logic value and returns true if the value is false, and false if the value is true. It is used to invert logic and works only on logic values.

Note that the not operator doesn't do bitwise operation (the complement function described next does this), so avoid using it on bitwise values:

```
>> print not (1 < 2)
false

>> print not (2 < 1)
true
```

REBOL's complement function returns the *bitwise complement* of a value. That is, it examines the argument bit by bit, returning a 1 for every 0 and a 0 for every 1. It is useful for bitmasking of integer numbers and inverting bit-sets, which you will want to do in code requiring such logic checking. The following lines show the results of using the complement function:

```
>> print complement 3
-4

>> print-binary 3
00000011

>> print-binary complement 3
11111100
```

Comparing Numbers

REBOL has a rich collection of *comparison* operators. Comparison operators compare values and return true or false. You commonly use these operators to effect switches between different logic states. In an e-commerce program, for example, you would want a shipping routine that picked the best one based on the customer's location.

Using comparison operators

Any datatype may be compared with another. Comparisons take values such as numbers, money, and dates, and return a logic result (true or false) appropriate to the comparison. Here are some comparisons:

```
>> print 6 < 10          ; less than
true

>> print 6 = 10          ; equal to
false

>> print 6 > 3           ; greater than
true

>> print 6 >= 6          ; greater than or equal to
true
```

The usual comparison operators are infix (like all those in the preceding examples), which means that they appear between the arguments. REBOL also provides a set of prefix comparison operators, most of which act as a complement to an infix counterpart. Prefix operators appear before any of their arguments:

```
>> print lesser? 4 9
true

>> print equal? $10.00 $5.00
false
```

REBOL also has two comparison operators available to handle powerful operations such as finding out whether two values with matching datatypes are the same (==) and whether two words (or variables?) are referencing the same series (=?):

```
>> print $3.98 == 3.98
false

>> print $3.98 == $3.98
true

>> dogs: [stray mangy]
>> mutts: dogs
>> print dogs =? mutts
true
```

Chapter 12

Parsing, or Watching Stuff Fall to Pieces, Fun!

*P*arsing, in most languages that have the feature, is a way of letting your program recognize characters or values appearing in a certain order.

I prefer a somewhat sharper definition: Parsing is the slicer and dicer of REBOL. You've seen those advertisements on TV where a simple innocent potato — eyes wide with fright — is slammed unmercifully into a gleaming vegetable mangler, its body parts reappearing as crinkled fries, chips, or various other shapes in curls and twirls and whirls, only to be thrown into hot oil and . . .

I'm sorry, I digest, er, digress. Some of my best friends are potatoes, and I'm always buttering them up.

But imposing the same fate on strings and blocks in REBOL is often useful; that is, slicing and dicing them, pawing through the pieces for usable bits of information, matching this shape and that shape, and cooking up notorious and useful portions of code for your own scripts. Even finding and modifying substrings (or just indexing them) is useful.

I show you all that and more in this chapter and how watching stuff fall to pieces can be both fun and profitable. Not to mention delicious.

About Parsing

Tearing strings apart lets you look for specific sequences of characters or values in some specific order. Examining pieces of strings is a very rudimentary type of regular-expression pattern matching. Plus, REBOL's powerful parsing dialect lets you further modify the way in which strings are split and patterns are matched for specific purposes in your own custom REBOL dialect.

A *dialect* in REBOL is a subset of the language, just like y'all might say Southern American is purely a dialect of the English language. We Southerners have specific words to fit specific tasks. Regional meanings exist in other areas of this country and around the world. I examine the whole concept of dialects in general come Chapter 19. You find out how to create your own custom dialects, but the parse dialect that I discuss here is already built into REBOL and ready for your use.

You've already met very simple methods of parsing or pattern matching, such as the find function:

```
>> a: "Roses are red / violets are blue"
>> find a "violets"
== "violets are blue"
```

The above searches for and finds the word violets and returns the remainder of the string from there to the end of the line. Although such functions are useful, at times you'll want to move beyond the limitations of a simple single pattern match. REBOL's parse dialect allows you to do so with as much sophistication and power as you may need.

The parse dialect has the general form of:

```
parse string rule
parse block rule
```

The function word parse is REBOL's defined built-in parse dialect. This function takes the arguments of a string or a block to be parsed and a rule by which the parsing is controlled. If the input argument is a string, a character parses it. A block parses by value (returning true or false).

The rules by which parsing occurs can vary from a simple string (one character or more) to extensive blocks of rules for elaborate multicase conventions of awesome power and flexibility.

Get out your old slicer and dicer. Here you go!

Splitting

Here's a simple example of parsing, using only the space character as a rule to split a string into its component words (if you're following along on the REBOL console, as I hope you are, you should still have onscreen the poetic REBOL definition of the word a that's mentioned earlier):

```
>> b: parse a " "
== ["Roses" "are" "red" "/" "violets" "are" "blue"]
```

What this very simple parsing did is split the string apart at every space and create a block of the results in variable b. And now that all the words are sep-arate, stir-frying the sliced and diced results (such as sorting them) is easy:

```
>> sort b
== ["/" "are" "are" "blue" "red" "Roses" "violets"]
```

I can get a word count by typing

```
>> print length? b
7
```

But that's awfully simple. I can also just let REBOL write some poetry of its own based on the parsed results:

```
>> loop 5 [
        loop 7 [prin [pick b random 7 " "]
]
        prin "^/"
        ]
/ violets  are  are  violets  red  are
/ red  /  are  violets  violets  are
violets  are  red  blue  are  are  are
red  blue  are  red  red  are  violets
Roses  are  Roses  violets  Roses  are  are
```

I bet you're going to get you a set of bongos and hit the next poetry slam, huh? Simple splitting is not limited to spaces; you can use any single charac-ter. Try it on phone numbers:

```
>> phone: #212-555-1212
== #212-555-1212
>> parse phone "-"
== ["212" "555" "1212"]
```

Try it on a space on a snippet of HTML code:

```
>> b: parse <IMG SRC="test.gif" WIDTH="123"> " "
== ["IMG" {SRC="test.gif"} {WIDTH="123"}]
>> print b/2
SRC="test.gif"
>> print b/3
WIDTH="123"
```

The parse function has two refinements. The /all refinement causes the function to include all characters including spaces in the parsing (otherwise, spaces affect splitting). An example follows, without /all and with:

```
>> address: "Bob Borkworkle, 304 E. Fink, Murk NJ 12121"
== "Bob Borkworkle, 304 E. Fink, Murk NJ 12121"
>> parse address ","
== ["Bob" "Borkworkle" "304" "E." "Fink" "Murk" "NJ" "12121"]
>> b: parse/all address ","
== ["Bob Borkworkle" " 304 E. Fink" " Murk NJ 12121"]
```

Note that parse by itself uses both the default space character and the comma to split the string. Not a useful result. But parse/all uses only the comma and gives you something you can use, the component parts of ole Bob's address.

By the way, because parse/all leaves some extra spaces, you need to get rid of these spaces in actual usage. An easy way to do so is by using the trim function:

```
>> foreach s b [trim s]
== "Murk NJ 12121"
>> probe b
["Bob Borkworkle" "304 E. Finkle" "Murk NJ 12121"]
```

The trim function gets rid of both leading and trailing spaces.

The second refinement for parse, which is /case, gives you case-sensitive parsing; that is, it recognizes the difference between upper- and lowercase letters:

```
>> b: parse/case "AAABBBaaaBBBAAAaaa" "A"
== ["" "" "" "BBBaaaBBB" "" "" "aaa"]
>> print b
BBBaaaBBB    aaa
```

You just parsed out all the uppercase A's while leaving all the lowercase a's.

You can also use more than one character in the rules string (with or without refinements):

```
>> b: parse/case "AAABBBaaaBBBAAAaaa" "AAA"
== ["" "" "" "BBBaaaBBB" "" "" "aaa"]
>> print b
BBBaaaBBB    aaa
```

You may even use both `parse` refinements together.

```
>> a: "Aaaaa Aaaaa Aaaaaaa Aaaaa"
>> b: parse/all/case a "A"
>> print b
aaaa   aaaa   aaaaaa   aaaa
```

Characters in simple string parsing rules may include end of lines (^/) and special control characters, such as those that sometimes separate records in databases like tabs and nulls. Tabs may be represented as ^(tab) or ^- and nulls as ^(null) or ^@. Using special characters looks like this in actual parsing:

```
>> a: "Billy Jo Jones^(tab)Bobo Baggins^(tab)Bozo T. Clown"
== "Billy Jo Jones^-Bobo Baggins^-Bozo T. Clown"
>> parse/all a "^(tab)"
== ["Billy Jo Jones" "Bobo Baggins" "Bozo T. Clown"]
```

By the way, you can't wrap these types of strings. If your result will be wrapped (broken into more than one line), change the string to be contained in braces.

Creating Grammar Rules

More complex parsing rules than the simple character strings above are called *grammar*. Inside the `parse` rule, the normal command syntax and vocabulary of REBOL is altered to make it similar in structure to the well-known BNF (Backus Naur Form), which is commonly used to specify language grammars, network protocols, header formats, and so forth.

In fact, those of you who have been around computers for a few years — especially the Unix world and the early PC computer games — will note the similarity of parsing to what happened in such classic games as *Adventure* or *Nethack* when you typed in a sentence. You may even notice the similarities in the early escapes of *Leisure Suit Larry*, about whom I've written four books.

You can go even earlier (like back in the late seventies) to some of the first experiments in artificial intelligence, such as *Eliza*, the cybernetic pop psychologist program.

Parsing in general is nothing new; it's been around for decades. What is new is the power with which REBOL lets you approach parsing tasks.

In addition to the simple string rules in the preceding section, you may also use a *block* of rules for more complex parsing. This follows the form:

```
parse string ["a rule"]
```

Here's an actual parse rule using some of the special words included in the parse grammar or dialect (more about those shortly):

```
>> a: "Some people have cats as pets."
>> parse a [to "cats" to end]
== true
```

We found cats in that string and the value true was returned. The parse function approaches the parsing of a string by traversing a string. Each character in the string is checked to see if it is the beginning of the pattern cats, as seen in the example above. So, in a sense, parse is in fact parsing character by character as it traverses the string series one character at a time to see if the current character is the beginning of a matched pattern. It is. If it wasn't, as in

```
>> parse a [to "frogs" to end]
== false
```

a value of false is returned. If you want some part of the string returned rather than true or false, that's easy to do as well, following my slice-and-dice philosophy of programming:

```
>> parse a [to "people" copy b thru "cats"] print b
people have cats
```

How about a real world application? My company (Alexander Books) publishes *The Sanders Price Guide to Autographs*. I wanted to (and did) put our extensive database of autograph prices online. The problem I faced was that everything was in a tab-delimited text file. Parsing in REBOL provided a simple answer to how I could extract this data and use it. I did it like this:

```
c: parse/all line "^-"
```

Was that hard? Nah. The Name, Category, Prices, and Comment, as shown in Figure 12-1, are now in the block, c. So I simply use print c/1 for the Name, print C/2 for Category, and so forth. There's a bit of HTML formatting involved, but you play with those in Chapters 17 and 18.

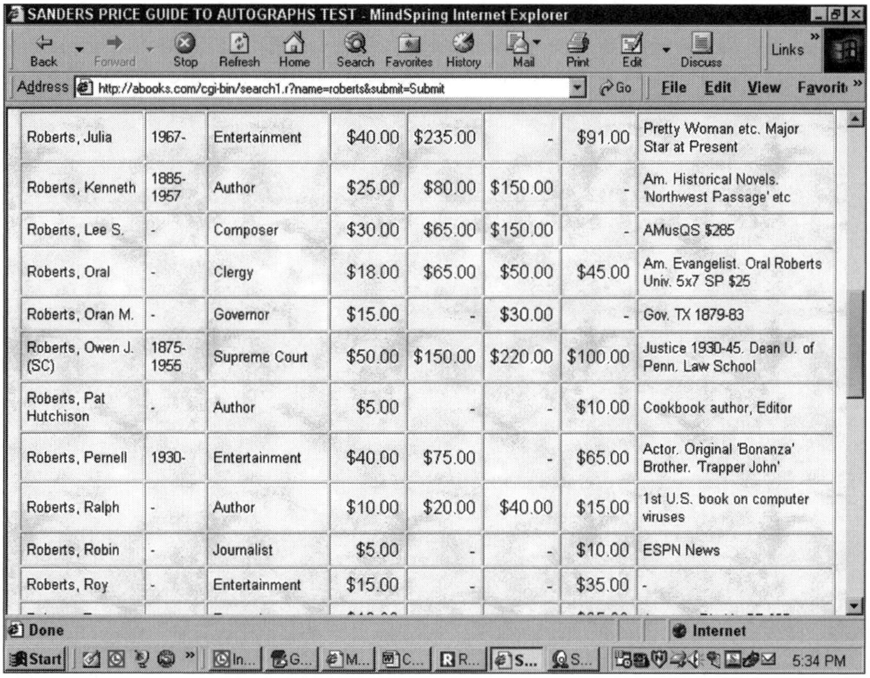

Roberts, Julia	1967-	Entertainment	$40.00	$235.00	-	$91.00	Pretty Woman etc. Major Star at Present
Roberts, Kenneth	1885-1957	Author	$25.00	$80.00	$150.00	-	Am. Historical Novels. 'Northwest Passage' etc
Roberts, Lee S.	-	Composer	$30.00	$65.00	$150.00	-	AMusQS $285
Roberts, Oral	-	Clergy	$18.00	$65.00	$50.00	$45.00	Am. Evangelist. Oral Roberts Univ. 5x7 SP $25
Roberts, Oran M.	-	Governor	$15.00	-	$30.00	-	Gov. TX 1879-83
Roberts, Owen J. (SC)	1875-1955	Supreme Court	$50.00	$150.00	$220.00	$100.00	Justice 1930-45. Dean U. of Penn. Law School
Roberts, Pat Hutchison	-	Author	$5.00	-	-	$10.00	Cookbook author, Editor
Roberts, Pernell	1930-	Entertainment	$40.00	$75.00	-	$65.00	Actor. Original 'Bonanza' Brother. 'Trapper John'
Roberts, Ralph	-	Author	$10.00	$20.00	$40.00	$15.00	1st U.S. book on computer viruses
Roberts, Robin	-	Journalist	$5.00	-	-	$10.00	ESPN News
Roberts, Roy	-	Entertainment	$15.00	-	-	$35.00	-

Figure 12-1: This entire table of values from the online *The Sanders Price Guide to Autographs* is produced by a simple one-line parse statement in a REBOL script.

What about some other powers of grammar parsing? If you put each word in quotation marks, you can have any amount of space or no space at all between the words:

```
>> a: "the         test"
>> parse a ["the" "test"]
== true
```

Using a bar (|), the REBOL `parse` dialect allows more than one rule to be applied to a parsing operation, such as:

```
>> a: "the lawnmower"
>> b: "a goat"
>> parse a ["a" "goat" | "the" "lawnmower"]
== true
>> parse b ["a" "goat" | "the" "lawnmower"]
== true
```

What you now have (and this more than hints at the power of parsing) is a rule that can recognize two pretty diverse cases, `a goat` and `the lawnmower`. The presence of either case causes the return of `true` in the preceding examples. By using this technique of grammar rules for parsing, you can have an infinite number of cases in which this simple snip of parsing code can return `true`, triggering whatever else you want to happen. Imagine, for example, a small REBOL script (and it would be small) that can check news groups every day for scores of topics you're interested in monitoring, pulling out a synopsis and a reference to where you can find the full article. The possibilities are endless!

You can also have subrules by nesting blocks, and you can assign those rules to variables for ease of use, like so:

```
lawn: [ [to "a" | to "an" | to "the"] [to "grass" | to "goat"
        | to "lawnmower"] to end]
```

The construction of the rules is pretty simple. The subfunction `to` (available only in the `parse` dialect) causes parsing up to the first instance of the rule, and then you move `to end`. The latter code is necessary to tell `parse` to continue to the end of the input stream. Otherwise, you get `false` even though the rules were matched in the string. The `parse` function only returns `true` if it has traversed a string completely to its end. This set of rules, `lawn`, finds the first instance of the following in a string:

```
a grass
the grass
a goat
the goat
a lawnmower
the lawnmower
```

The `end` subfunction of `parse` will specify that nothing follows in the input stream. This subfunction is optional depending on whether the `parse` function's return value is to be checked. For example, if you're just looking for patterns and copying them out to words, you may not care whether a `true` or `false` is returned for the entire string. But if you're testing for the `parse` function's return, the `end` subfunction is required.

Yeah, it's Spring here in the mountains now and my lawn is growing faster than Grant took Richmond, but back to parsing. Use the `lawn` rule like this:

```
>> a: {As the light of dawn brightened toward day, I suddenly
        saw that a goat was cropping the grass next to
        where I had parked the lawnmower.}
>> parse a lawn
== true
```

A minor change in your rule set shows what you found:

```
>> lawn: [ [to "a" | to "an" | to "the"] [to "goat" copy g to
        " " | to "grass" copy gr to " " | to "lawnmower"
        copy l to "."] to end]
>> parse a lawn
== true
```

What I added was the copy subfunction (this is the copy that is part of the parse dialect) to pull the result into a word, namely gr for grass, g for goat, and l for lawnmower. You check your result by printing those three words:

```
>> foreach val [g gr l] [
   print [
     :val "-" either value? val [get :val]["no value"]
   ]
]

          g - goat
          gr - no value
          l - no value
```

Okay, it found goat and then quit. How do you get it to parse out more than just the first item matched? You want slice and dice chop chop chop, not just slice. The any subfunction fits this bill neatly (I go over all the parse sub-functions with you later in the chapter):

```
>> lawn: [ any [to "goat" copy g to " " | to "grass" copy gr
            to " " | to "lawnmower" copy l to "."] to end]
>> parse a lawn
== true
>> print [g gr l]
goat grass lawnmower
```

Now it finds all three. You astute programmers will realize that this example only works in the sequence goat grass lawnmower — in real-world applications, you need to do a bit more coding to cover all cases, but for the time being, you're off to parsing grammar rules.

In addition to matching a single instance of a string, you can provide a count or a range to be specified that repeats the match. For instance,

```
[3 "a" 2 "b"]
```

will match

```
aaabb
```

You can also specify a range:

```
[1 3 "a" "b"]
```

that will match

```
ab aab aaab
```

The starting point can also be zero, meaning that it's optional.

```
[0 3 "a" "b"]
```

will match

```
b ab aab aaab
```

More likely, however, you won't know specific numbers in patterns you want to match. The `some` and `any` subfunctions (you've already seen the latter in use) fill that need, like this:

```
>> text: "ab aaab aaaab"
>> parse text [some ["a" | "b"] to end]
== true
>> text: "b ab aab aaab aaaab"
>> parse text [any ["a" | "b"] to end]
== true
```

You can also make good use of the `none` value, or the fact that you find no matches in a string. By putting `none` into your rules, parsing will return `true`, even if the search pattern(s) are not present. Here's how you do that:

```
>> a: "This is a great big tasty test."
>> parse a [to "crabapple" | none (b: none) to end]
== true
>> print b
none
```

Crabapples, of course, are not tasty so `crabapple` isn't found here. But by having the `none` value in the rule, you can make the variable b equal to `none`, and you have a switch that's useful later in the program, such as `if none? b then do this`. This technique also works in handling errors and optional cases, such as what to do when an expected pattern isn't found.

Skipping Forward

The `skip`, `to`, and `thru` parse subfunctions allow you to skip input.

Here are examples:

```
>> text: "abc"
>> parse text ["a" skip "c"]
== true
```

This subfunction matches abc, adc, azc, aFc, and so on, and skips or ignores one character in the matching pattern. You may also tell it to skip more than one character:

```
>> text: "a12345c"
>> parse text ["a" 5 skip "c"]
== true
```

The to subfunction lets you skip everything until the start of the matching pattern is reached:

```
>> text: "Fast flew the nimble fingers."
>> parse text [ [to "nimble" copy a to " "] to end]
== true
>> print a
nimble
```

The thru subfunction skips everything up to and including the end of the matching pattern:

```
>> text: "a9876c"
>> parse text ["a" thru "c"]
== true
```

Matching Types

You can perform parsing operations by using the following datatypes:

- ✔ "abc": Matches an entire string
- ✔ #"c": Matches a single character
- ✔ <tag>: Matches a tag
- ✔ end: Matches the end of the input
- ✔ bitset: Matches any specified character in the set

If you need to parse datatypes other than these — such as URLs, dates, time, and so on — simply convert them into a string, complete the operation, and convert the result back to the appropriate datatype. The following is an example that I've elaborated some from the user's manual that employs all the datatypes shown here except bitset:

```
>> htmlstuff: {
    <B>excellent!</B>
    <B>incredible!</B>
    }
>> parse htmlstuff [any [to <B> [to "excellent" | to
        "incredible"]] to #"!" to </B> to end]
== true
```

A very useful application for the `parse` dialect in REBOL is the retrieval of
Web pages with the ability to strip worthwhile information from amid all
those HTML, PHP, and other tags that otherwise clutter the native text and
send it into unreadability.

The one datatype in the bulleted list that I haven't examined yet is `bitset`. A
`bitset` specifies a collection of characters in an efficient manner — that is,
as binary. Because this is frequently done, the `charset` function is provided
to simplify its use. The function allows specifying individual characters or
ranges of characters, like this:

```
>> digit: charset "0123456789"
== make bitset! #{
000000000000FF03000000000000000000000000000000000000000000000000
        000
}
```

Now that the character set is defined, you can use it in parsing rules, such as
matching phone numbers:

```
>> phone: #828-555-1212
>> parse phone [any [3 digit "-" 3 digit "-" 4 digit] to end]
== true
```

To accept any number of digits, write your rule in the form:

```
digits: [some digits]
```

You can also specify ranges of characters. For instance, the digit set can be
written

```
digit: charset [#"0" - #"9"]
```

Or, specific characters and ranges of characters can be written as:

```
the-set: charset ["+-." #"0" - #"9"]
```

To expand on this, the entire alphanumeric set of ASCII characters can be
written

```
alphanum: charset [#"0" - #"9" #"A" - #"Z" #"a" - #"z"]
```

Here's how you can use these:

```
>> alphanum: charset [#"0" - #"9" #"A" - #"Z" #"a" - #"z"]
>> a: "a"
>> parse a [alphanum]        ; yes, it is an alphanumeric
== true
>> a: "^/"
>> parse a [alphanum]
== false                     ; no, a new line is not
```

Recursing Rules

This section provides suggestions on how to write grammars that make use of recursion (a term that refers to itself). The following is an example of a set of rules that will parse mathematical expressions and give a *precedence* (priority) to the math operators:

```
expr:    [term ["+" | "-"] expr | term]
term:    [factor ["*" | "/"] term | factor]
factor:  [primary "**" factor | primary]
primary: [some digit | "(" expr ")"]
digit:   charset "0123456789"
```

Enter the preceding rules into your REBOL console so that the examples that follow will work correctly when you try them. Both of the following two lines of code return `true`, with and without spaces:

```
>> parse "1 + 2 * ( 3 - 2 ) / 4" expr
== true
>> parse "4/5+3**2-(5*6+1)" expr
== true
```

Notice that some of the rules refer to themselves. For instance, the `expr` rule includes `expr`. This technique is useful for defining repeating sequences and combinations. It is recursive — it refers to itself.

When using recursive rules, care is required to prevent endless recursion. For instance,

```
expr: [expr ["+" | "-"] term]
```

creates an infinite loop, because the first thing `expr` does is use `expr` again.

Evaluating Code

The whole idea of parsing or slicing and dicing a string or block is to obtain some result. The result may include pulling out substrings from various parts of the string, or creating blocks of related values, or computing a value.

An example of pulling out substrings is shown in the following block value:

```
colors: ["a red sunset" "a pink carnation" "a gold coin"]
```

Here's how you can pull out any strings that contain pink:

```
foreach example colors [
    if parse example [to "pink" to end] [print example]
    ]
a pink carnation
```

Returning value

To return a value (true or false), parse must traverse completely through the string. Even if your grammar gives parse matching rules of a hundred patterns and it finds all hundred, traversing stops after the last pattern is found. This is okay if you're pulling substrings out and, again, don't care about the result. But to get the result, be sure to use the end subfunction. Here's another example so that you can prove this for yourself:

```
>> waves: [any ["red" | "white" | "blue"] to end]
>> a: "Over the fort, flew the red, white, and blue."
>> parse a waves
== true
```

If you leave out the to end code, false is returned:

```
>> waves: [any ["red" | "white" | "blue"]]
== [any ["red" | "white" | "blue"]]
>> parse a waves
== false
```

Pulling apart expressions

Expressions are regular REBOL statements, such as:

```
print "Hello World!"
```

Without special provision, expressions don't work inside a parse rule. Remember, parse is a dialect of REBOL, not a subroutine. Different rules may and quite often do apply in dialects, whether built into REBOL or your (or someone else's) creation. But a provision has been made to include regular REBOL expressions (or this section wouldn't be here). Just put the expression inside parentheses.

Okay, time to have some fun. A wonderful poem by Robert W. Service is titled *The Cremation of Sam McGee*. Long since in public domain, I include it on the CD that comes with this book as 12-sam.txt. The poem begins

```
There are strange things done in the midnight sun
By the men who moil for gold;
The Arctic trails have their secret tales
That would make your blood run cold;
The Northern Lights have seen queer sights,
But the queerest they ever did see
Was that night on the marge of Lake Lebarge
I cremated Sam McGee.
```

If you're following along on the REBOL console, read it as:

```
>> sam: read/lines %12-sam.txt    ; read by lines
```

Now here's an example that includes REBOL expressions inside a parse grammar. Print the lines of the poem that have McGee in them:

```
>> foreach line sam [
     parse line [to "McGee" (print line) to end]
     ]
THE CREMATION OF SAM McGEE
I cremated Sam McGee
Now Sam McGee was from Tennessee,
     to whimper was Sam McGee.
     that was left of Sam McGee.
     and I stuffed in Sam McGee.
I cremated Sam McGee.
```

You can also get a count of how many times the last name McGee appears:

```
>> count: 0 foreach line sam [
   parse line [any [to "McGee" (count: count + 1) to end]]
   ]
>> print count
7
```

Copying input

I discuss the `copy` subfunction of `parse`, which lets you pull out substrings, earlier in this chapter. Now you can find the first instance of `strange` and copy from there to the first instance of `sun`, which works as follows:

```
>> sam: read %11-sam.txt      ; read in as one large string
>> parse sam [to "strange" copy strange thru "sun"]
== false
>> print strange
strange things done in the midnight sun
```

Note that you got a return of `false` because I didn't care whether the evaluation was complete. The sliced and diced substring was copied into the word `strange`.

Marking input

Maybe you don't want to copy substrings, but you want to know where they are in a string. Parsing may be used to index a string (or a block or a file). For instance, take the word `McGee` in this poem. You now know there are seven occurrences, but where precisely do they live within the string? Here's how to index by using `parse`:

```
>> mcgee: make block! 20      ; a place to put the index
>> parse sam [any ["McGee" mark: (append mcgee index? mark) |
          skip] ]
== true
>> print mcgee
22 347 362 957 1900 3481 4726  ; characters into the string
```

Modifying input

Rewriting *The Cremation of Sam McGee* in any way would truly be a crime. I guess I'm willing to take that chance. You can also use the `parse` function's dialect to modify (slice out potatoes and dice in some carrots). Here's one way to do so:

```
>> parse sam [to "strange" begin: thru "sun" ending:
      (change/part begin "some less than normal things done in
            the half past eleven at night sun" ending)
      ]
== false
```

Although I got a `false` because I didn't tell `parse` to go all through the string, the change did take place. Print `sam` and `strange things done in the midnight sun` is now `some less than normal things done in the half past eleven at night sun`. **Now you can see why I write computer books rather than poetry.**

Parsing objects

For `parse` grammar rules that you use a lot, you can avoid possible confusion with other uses of the same words by putting them into an object as follows:

```
>> my-grammar: make object! [
    waves: [any ["red" | "white" | "blue"] to end]
    digit: charset "0123456789"
    alphanum: charset [#"0" - #"9" #"A" - #"Z" #"a" - #"z"]
]
```

Use rules from your grammar object, such as:

```
>> a: "Over the fort, flew the red, white, and blue."
>> parse a my-grammar/waves
== true
```

Debugging

A simple way to debug your parsing grammar (to find out where it breaks down when the results aren't what you expect) is to add a `print` statement after each rule. By using this method, you can see which rules are not being triggered. Here's an example:

```
>> a: "Over the fort, flew the red, white, and blue."
>> waves: [any [[to "red" (print 1)][to "white" (print 2)][to
            "blue" (print 3)]] to end]
>> parse a waves
1
2
3
== true
```

Handling Spaces

The parse function ignores intervening white space between the patterns it examines. For instance, the rule

```
["a" "b" "c"]
```

will match

```
abc
a bc
ab c
a b c
a  b   c
```

and other similarly spaced combinations.

To enforce a specific spacing convention, use parse with the /all refinement. In this example, this refinement causes the spacing to only match the first case (abc).

When you use the /all refinement, every character in the input stream must be dealt with, including spaces and so on. Use a charset to specify the valid space characters:

```
spacer: charset reduce [tab newline " "]
```

Now write

```
["a" spacer "b" spacer "c"]
```

to require a single space between each letter. To allow multiple spaces, define

```
spaces: [some spacer]
["a" spaces "b" spaces "c"]
```

Using the parse Dialect

The following tables summarize operations and words for REBOL's parse dialect:

Table 12-1 lists the general forms that parse rules may take.

Table 12-1	**General Forms**
|	alternate rule
[block]	subrule
(paren)	evaluate a REBOL expression

Table 12-2 shows how you specify quantities in parse operations.

Table 12-2	**Specifying Quantity**
none	match nothing
opt	zero or one time
some	one or more times
any	zero or more times
12	repeat pattern 12 times
1 12	repeat pattern 1 to 12 times
0 12	repeat pattern 0 to 12 times

Use the skip rules in Table 12-3 if you're parsing in REBOL.

Table 12-3	**Skipping Values**
skip	skip a value (or multiple if repeat given) to advance input to a value or datatype
thru	advance input thru a value or datatype

Table 12-4 shows how you retrieve values from parsed data.

Table 12-4	**Getting Values**
set	set the next value to a word
copy	copy the next match sequence to a word

Finally, Table 12-5 shows the way word values are used with parsing.

Table 12-5	Using Words
word	look-up value of a word
word:	mark the current input series position
:word	set the current input series position
'word	matches the word literally (parse block)

Chapter 13

Networking and Other Ways of Reaching Out

· ·

· ·

*M*y computer chats with your computer; your computer rattles on with others in your home or office; those computers interface with a thousand others on the Web. They trade files; they read Web pages; they send and receive e-mail; they do bunches of additional interactive stuff. It's called *networking* — this network of computers, whose most basic subset is your machine on your desktop, can extend to your local area network or to the Internet, and thus connect to virtually any other computer in the world instantaneously.

The several ways in which computers exchange information (networking) are collectively called *protocols*. These protocols include FTP (File Transfer Protocol), HTTP (HyperText Transfer Protocol, which makes Web pages possible), e-mail protocols, such as POP for receiving messages and SMTP for sending them, NNTP (Network News Transfer Protocol), and more.

To use these protocols in other programming languages requires messy or at least tedious interfacing with shared libraries and other coding convolutions. In REBOL, your most commonly used networking aids are built in, ready to use from scratch! When you start the REBOL console, you see the following after the copyright/trademark notice:

```
Finger protocol loaded
Whois protocol loaded
Daytime protocol loaded
SMTP protocol loaded
POP protocol loaded
HTTP protocol loaded
FTP protocol loaded
NNTP protocol loaded
```

You're going to jump right in and try out a few protocols just to see how easy it is. First, make sure that you're connected to the Internet and start the REBOL console. Add a little dash of parsing for flavor and then type the following:

```
>> parse read http://rebol.com [thru <title> copy title to
        </title> to end]
connecting to: rebol.com
== true
>> print title
REBOL Technologies
```

Okay, that's a neat little technique to retrieve titles of Web pages; you do a more sophisticated version of that later in this chapter. You can also just grab the whole Web page easily enough and stuff it into a word, like so:

```
>> a: read http://rebol.com
```

Try that and then play with FTP:

```
>> a: read ftp://rebol.com/test.txt
>> print a
Hello
there
new
user!
```

For one more example, you can check your e-mail:

```
>> a: read pop://your_username:your_password@your.dom
connecting to: your.dom
```

Now all your pending incoming e-mails are in word a. How many are there? Type the following to find out:

```
>> print length? a
```

I show you how to read, send, and otherwise manipulate e-mail in the following pages and in much more detail in Chapter 15. First you need to make sure that you're ready for networking. You find the basics in this chapter, and Chapters 15, 16, 17, and 18 expand on these ever-so-handy features of REBOL and coding techniques.

Setting Up Networking

You find the network settings for REBOL in the `system/` object. You have the following six main network settings to be concerned about:

- **E-mail address:** `system/user/e-mail`
- **SMTP Server (outgoing mail):** `system/schemes/default/host`
- **POP server name or address (incoming mail) (optional):** `system/schemes/pop/host`
- **Proxy server name or address (optional):** `system/schemes/default/proxy/host`
- **Proxy server port number (optional):** `system/schemes/default/proxy/port-id`
- **Proxy protocol (optional):** `system/schemes/default/proxy/type`

These settings are contained in your `user.r` file in a block called `set-net` and in the same order as these six are listed: e-mail address, outgoing mail, incoming mail, proxy server (if needed), proxy port number, and proxy protocol. Here's my default setup:

```
set-net [ ralph@abooks.com abooks.com 198.168.0.1 mickey 1080
          socks ]
```

The `198.168.0.1` IP address is my company's mail and Web server, whose name is `mickey` (named not after the famous mouse but after one of our company mascots, Mickey T. Elephant — in fact, most of our company computers are named after elephants, but that's another book). The easy way to change your user settings is with the `set-user` function word:

```
>> set-user

Some network functions, such as sending e-mail or
using anonymous FTP, require you to provide an e-mail
address. (Or, you just press ENTER to skip it.)

E-mail address?
```

Configuring REBOL with your own network settings. Just realize that you can have your scripts change any of these settings by redefining the `system/` object on the fly. For example, I can code in a line, such as:

```
system/user/e-mail: sales@abooks.com
```

if I had a script that sent out automatic e-mails, and I didn't want my personal e-mail address on it (that is, let one of my employees handle the replies). I'd need to change it back later in the script. Each time REBOL is invoked, your settings return to those in the `user.r` file which, you write via the `set-user` function word.

Using URLs

As you may have already noticed, REBOL uses URLs (Uniform Resource Locators) to communicate with its various built-in network protocols. A URL consists of a `protocol`, `site`, and `port`, in the following form:

```
network_protocol://site:port/
```

Here's a breakdown of the aspects of a URL:

- `protocol`: The network protocol being used (HTTP, SMTP, POP, and so on)
- `site`: The site (server name) being accessed (such as `www.rebol.com`)
- `port`: The remote port being accessed (optional) (23, 21, 8080, and so on)

Some protocols support the added contents `login` and `password` within URLs in the following form:

```
network_protocol://login:password@site:port/
network_protocol://login@site:port/
```

Next are some simple examples of what URLs look like when used in expressions:

```
print read finger://user@somesite.dom/
dir-list: read ftp://ftp.somesite.dom/
my-ftp-dir: read ftp://user:password@ftp.somesite.dom/
Web-page: read http://www.somesite.dom/
write ftp://user:password@www.site.dom/index ; read Web-page
```

URLs are used to read from and write to computers that your own computer may be networked with, such as those on the Internet. The read and write functions (see Chapter 9) are used with REBOL's supported network protocols. Some functions have an implicit read or write associated with them. Functions such as size? and modified? have an implicit read while save has an implicit write. You can use these functions with URLs as well:

```
read http://www.rebol.com/              ; read a Web page
write ftp://ftp.somesite.dom/ data       ; write to a ftp
          site
size? ftp://ftp.asite.dom/pub/file.txt     ; find size
modified? ftp://ftp.asite.dom/pub/file.txt  ; date changed
```

Now you get to see some of these protocols in action.

Working the Web with HTTP

Two more acronyms to know, if you don't already — HTTP and HTML. These basic technologies enable the Worldwide Web, and you probably use them every day. HTTP, the Hyper Text Transfer Protocol, controls how Web servers and Web browsers (HTTP clients) communicate with each other. HTML, or HyperText Markup Language, controls how a Web browser displays a Web page. To retrieve a Web page, the Web browser communicates with a Web server by using the HTTP networking protocol (as you recall, one of the many ways to network) and, having received the Web page requested, interprets the HTML code it contains and displays the page.

REBOL has the HTTP protocol built into it and provides for communicating with a Web server that's based on HTTP. REBOL's support for HTTP allows REBOL to act as an HTTP client. You can use read to access any Web page on the Internet. If you supply read with the Web page's URL, REBOL contacts the Web server and downloads the Web page.

Great, but why do you want to do that when your computer has a perfectly good Web browser? The ready answer is *to pull out and manipulate information.* Here's an example, using my company's main Web page. I'm going to pull out the e-mail addresses on that page. Here's how easy it is (two lines!):

```
>> a: read http://abooks.com          ; get the Web page
>> b: make block! 10
>> parse a [any [to {<a href="mailto} copy e-mail thru </a>
   (append b e-mail)] to end]        ; parse out e-mails
```

Now all the e-mail addresses on that page are in variable b.

```
>> print length? b                         ; how many addresses?
7
>> foreach line b [print line]          ; print them out
<a href="mailto:sales@abooks.com">sales@abooks.com</a>
<a href="mailto:ralph@abooks.com">Ralph Roberts</a>
<a href="mailto:pat@abooks.com">Pat Roberts</a>
<a href="mailto:gayle@abooks.com">Gayle Graham</a>
<a href="mailto:pam@abooks.com">Pam Davis</a>
<a href="mailto:vanessa@abooks.com">Vanessa Razzano</a>
```

These e-mail addresses are still in HTML link format. I can drop them into a Web page, and they will work perfectly. Or I can further parse them to only the address for adding to a mail list:

```
>> foreach line b [
    parse line [thru "mailto:"
copy adr to {"} (print adr)]
    ]
sales@abooks.com
ralph@abooks.com
pat@abooks.com
gayle@abooks.com
pam@abooks.com
vanessa@abooks.com
```

Network protocols, parsing, and all the rest of REBOL provide you with some real power. Don't misuse it for something like spamming.

After you retrieve a Web page, you can process it like any other REBOL string. Print it on the screen by using print (you see HTML source, not images) or save it to a file using save. You can even combine steps into one line of code, such as getting and printing a page:

```
>> print read http://rebol.com
connecting to: rebol.com
<!DOCTYPE HTML PUBLIC "-//W3C//DTD HTML 3.2//EN">
<HTML>
<HEAD>
    <META HTTP-EQUIV="Content-Type"
CONTENT="text/html;CHARSET=iso-8859-1">
    <META NAME="KEYWORDS" CONTENT="programming, scripting,
            distributed, dialect, distributed computing,
            platform independent, internet messaging, rebel,
            language, smart content, smart client"> ; etc,
            etc.
```

You can also send a Web page to someone; for instance, I'm sending myself a copy of my company's main Web page here:

```
>> send ralph@abooks.com read http://abooks.com
connecting to: abooks.com          ; getting the page
connecting to: 198.168.0.1         ; sending to mail server
```

You can even check the modification date of at least some Web pages:

```
>> print modified? http://rebol.com
connecting to: rebol.com
19-Apr-2000/0:20:16
```

The preceding technique doesn't work on dynamically generated pages or others for various reasons, but you may find it very useful for monitoring your own pages.

If the page you check for changes doesn't return a modification date, you can use the checksum method:

```
>> print checksum http://abooks.com
14706823
```

Keep track of the checksum; when it changes, the page has changed.

If you need to make changes in how REBOL communicates using the HTTP protocol, all its settings are stored in the system/schemes/http object. Just make darned sure you know what you're doing before you make any changes.

I revisit HTTP in Chapter 16 and take a more advanced look at manipulating Web pages in lots of ways by using REBOL.

Fingering Information

The finger command is long familiar to those of us who've traveled in the brightly lit realms of Unix for, lo, these many years. In Unix operating systems, or compatible systems like Linux, finger retrieves user-specific information that's stored in the user's configuration file: /etc/passwd. The finger command has since been ported to other operating systems. Using finger retrieves user information based on the e-mail address of the user. Some finger servers return a listing of all known users, if the username is omitted from the request.

Many servermeisters consider finger to be a security breach, and their servers refuse this protocol. Rebol.com appears to be one of these. Try a finger request to finger://rebol.com, and you get an error:

```
>> print read finger://carl@rebol.com
connecting to: rebol.com
** Access Error: Cannot connect to rebol.com.
** Where: print read finger://carl@rebol.com
```

But try the `finger` protocol on someone whose server allows it — such as the excellent system at the Mountain Area Information Net, managed by my friend Wally Bowen — and you get an answer:

```
>> print read finger://wallyb@main.nc.us
connecting to: main.nc.us
Login: wallyb                    Name: Wally Bowen
Directory: /home/wallyb          Shell: /bin/bash
On since Fri May  5 08:58 (EDT) on ttyp0 from mo4
   11 minutes 40 seconds idle
     (messages off)
No mail.
No Plan.
```

I see Wally is online, but he hasn't typed anything for the past eleven minutes. Okay, so I try `finger` again without a specified user and get all users who are currently logged in:

```
>> print read finger://main.nc.us
connecting to: main.nc.us
Login     Name              Tty  Idle  Login Time     Office
robinson  Robbie Robinson   *p1   20   May  5 12:55  (mo2)
robinson  Robbie Robinson   *p2   45   May  5 13:25  (mo2)
robinson  Robbie Robinson    p3    6   May  5 13:32  (mo2)
tracey    Michael Tracey     p5   11   May  5 14:43  (mo5)
wallyb    Wally Bowen       *p0        May  5 08:58  (mo4)
```

Robbie must be working on the system to have three terminals going. Now I check the Buncombe County server:

```
>> print read finger://buncombe.main.nc.us
connecting to: buncombe.main.nc.us
No one logged on.
```

No one on now—but just wait until this evening. A whole lot of surfing goes on then.

Fingering can be useful if the system you need to check allows it. The REBOL `finger` protocol settings are stored in `system/schemes/finger`.

Transferring Files with FTP

The preferred method for transferring files to a remote host on the Internet — such as Web pages for a Web site or archived and compressed binary files for an online file archive — is FTP or File Transfer Protocol. FTP has been around for a long time, dating back to the beginnings of Unix in the late 70s. But FTP is still just as useful and important today as when it was first implemented.

If you deal with the creation or modification of Web sites, or you just like to grab the occasional freeware or shareware program off the Internet, FTP is for you. You may already have a favorite FTP program on your computer (I do). REBOL doesn't replace that software, but it does give you the ability to add powerful FTP protocol functions into your scripts. And you don't need any libraries or anything else that's not already part of REBOL/Core.

Traditionally, dedicated FTP client software is used to communicate with FTP servers. Interacting with FTP sites involves four steps:

1. **Connection**
2. **Authentication**
3. **Directory tree traversal**
4. **Getting (downloading) and putting (uploading) files**

I think I'll whip up some REBOL scripts, automating the above four steps.

Retrieving files

Authentication requires a username and a password. Many sites support an *anonymous* login, which allows you to login with the username anonymous and your e-mail address as the password. This method has long allowed the interchange of files by people who don't have an account on a specific server.

I suppose anonymous is the first "big" word we old-time Unix-heads learned to spell, just so we could get access to all those el neato programs out there. Remember Jack Nicholson as the Joker in the first Batman movie? Batman has just done some neat stuff with things from his marvelous utility belt and the Joker asks, "Where does he get all those wonderful toys?" Anonymous FTP, that's where. It's great stuff and even in today's Web-driven Internet, there's still a golden universe out there full of FTP resources.

REBOL supports access to remote sites by FTP utilizing the same words that are used to manipulate local files, such as read, write, load, save, do, exists?, size?, and others. REBOL distinguishes between local files and files accessible by FTP through the use of an FTP URL for FTP access.

If you don't specify a username and password, REBOL automatically puts in anonymous for username and your e-mail address as the password. For the anonymous password to work correctly, you must include your e-mail address in your network setup by using the set-user function (see "Setting Up Networking" earlier in this chapter). If the target server allows anonymous FTP access (many don't these days for security reasons), you'll be connected. Here's an example where I retrieve a directory listing:

```
>> a: read ftp://rebol.com
connecting to: rebol.com
== [%incoming/ %os2sdk/ %pub/ %test.txt]
```

I now have the top FTP-accessible directory of ftp://rebolcom in the a word. In the top directory, trailing forward slashes (/) indicate directories, whereas names without the slash are files, such as the preceding test.txt. The subdirectory pub/ normally indicates a "public" directory, in which anyone logging in under anonymous FTP has access and can download the goodies contained there, or in further subdirectories. To see what's in the REBOL /pub directory, now that you know it's there, type the following (always include a trailing forward slash in directory requests, as shown here):

```
>> a: read ftp://rebol.com/pub/
== [%corebeta/ %downloads/]
```

Ah-ha! Downloads! Now type

```
>> a: read ftp://rebol.com/pub/downloads/
== [%rebol011.lha %rebol012.lha %rebol021.sit.hqx
        %rebol022.sit.hqx %rebol023.sit.hqx
        %rebol024.tar.gz %rebol031.zip %rebol032.zip ...
```

Looks like all the versions of REBOL are available. REBOL Technologies makes it easy for you by listing all these versions on its Web site and making FTP downloads more transparent to the end user. But everything in this downloads subdirectory is now in word a, so you can see how many items are there by typing

```
>> print length? a
37
```

Okay, no new versions of REBOL/Core yet, but I'll keep monitoring that as I write this book. To get a complete listing of the files present in this directory, type the following:

```
foreach line a [print line]
```

You find out more about directories later in this section.

Reading text files

Reading text files on a remote, networked server that allows FTP access is simple in REBOL. You see one example at the beginning of this chapter; here's another:

```
>> print read ftp://ftp.abooks.com/pub/rebol/testfile.txt
This is a test file created for and used as an example
in REBOL FOR DUMMIES by Ralph Roberts.
```

If you want to retrieve a text file via FTP and save it to your system, the following method works nicely:

```
>> write %testfile.txt
   read ftp://ftp.abooks.com/pub/rebol/
```

Note that the technique is exactly the same as `read` and `write` files, which I cover at length in Chapter 9. Just be sure to get things in the correct order; that is, tell REBOL what to do (write a file) and then where to get the information to write (the `read ftp://` command).

FTP was designed to use the same set of functions as local files. This includes not only `read` and `write`, but also `load`, `save`, `do`, `exists?`, `size?`, and so on (see Chapter 9).

As a further example, here's a program on my FTP server that you are welcome to run using the `do` function via FTP:

```
>> do ftp://ftp.abooks.com/pub/rebol/secret.r
Script: "A Secret Message" (6-May-2000)

At  6-May-2000 21:11:09 Agent X-48 sends you the following
          secret message:

fuaqech      ciikech      huoney       riobah
raoboh       theoshich    zeathag      koabom
qooyoq       fouzuv       yiotog       coochol
siehan       jaochuy      ziicith      qaucac

Please decode and reply immediately
```

This script, `secret.r`, resides on my Alexander Books server but executes on your computer when called by the FTP technique above. If you want to see the code for `secret.r`, you can get it by typing

```
print read ftp://ftp.abooks.com/pub/rebol/secret.r
```

Reading binary files

If all the regular file-manipulating function words work with FTP, you already know how to read a binary file (such as an image or executable program). The only difference from downloading a text file is that you use the /binary refinement to read. You want to download a binary file by typing

```
file: ftp://ftp.abooks.com/pub/rebol/abarn.jpg
write/binary %abarn.jpg read/binary file
```

Try that. It's a 32K jpeg file that is truly a picture of my barn — well, two of them actually. Enjoy.

Sending files

If using the ftp:// protocol in REBOL to read text and binary files over a network is as easy as reading the same types of files on your own system, you'd naturally think it's just as easy to send files? Right? Well . . . yes it is.

Sending text files

All REBOL scripts are text files. Suppose that I just finished modifying a script and want to upload it to the cgi-bin directory on my company's server. Here's an example of how you write a text file over a network by using FTP:

```
write ftp://abooks.com/cgi-bin/search.r read %search.r
```

This specific line of code won't work for you if you try it, because I cunningly left out my username and password (I show you how authentication works shortly).

Another very useful method of writing a text file — whether to your local computer or via a network protocol like FTP — is the save word function. Using save rather than write preserves REBOL datatypes so that the data may be loaded into other REBOL scripts and used. I look at this in detail in Chapter 14 (up next!) as I play with databases. But here's an example so that you can prove this for yourself:

```
>> rebol-dirlist: read %.          ; get directory
>> save %dirlist.txt rebol-dirlist ; save as a text file
>> a: read %dirlist.txt            ; read file to word
>> a: to-block a                   ; change to block
>> type? a/1                       ; check type
== file!                           ; yes! same datatype!
```

The FTP version of the preceding save operation is the following:

```
save ftp://abooks.com/dirlist.txt rebol-dirlist
```

Hey, wanna try the actual file that I used? Go ahead. Be sure you're connected to the Internet and then type the following on your REBOL console:

```
>> a: read ftp://ftp.abooks.com/pub/rebol/dirlist.txt
>> a: to-block a
>> foreach file a [print file]
```

You get the listing of my REBOL directory, saved as the a block of file values, and brought into your own REBOL as a file datatype. This works just as well with the many other REBOL datatypes, including time, money, decimal, integer, tuple, and so on.

Sending binary files

Sending a binary file is the same as sending a text file except, like writing a binary file on your own computer, you use the /binary refinement:

```
write/binary ftp://abooks.com/pic.gif read/binary %search.gif
```

Manipulating items on the server

This section expands your REBOL FTP knowledge to manipulating more than just a single file on a remote server.

Accessing user accounts

As I talk about earlier, networking must be configured to connect to remote sites. If the remote site accepts anonymous login and your e-mail address has been configured by using set-user, then the basic code

```
>> print read ftp://main.nc.us/
connecting to: main.nc.us
bin/ etc/ lib/ misc/ pub/
```

returns a directory listing. But the majority of servers on the Internet today do not allow anonymous FTP access; you must have a valid account with a proper username and password.

To include your login information in an ftp:// request (or any other protocol requiring login data), use this format:

```
read ftp://user_name:password@abooks.com
```

Just put in your username, a colon (:), your password and the at sign (@), and then the rest of the FTP URL as you normally would.

Appending to files on FTP sites

As the `write/append` function appends text to a regular file on your computer, the same command in front of an FTP URL appends text to a file on a remote server, as follows:

```
write/append ftp://ftp.abooks.com/pub/rebol/testfile.txt
            {^/^/This line was appended using the write/append
            function.}
```

On servers on which you have an account, it's quick, slick, and exceptionally useful.

Reading a directory

Here's an extensive anonymous FTP site, the directory of which you can readily read:

```
>> print read ftp://ftp.uu.net
.forward/ .hushlogin .kermrc .notar .tmppriv/ .vol/ admin/
archive bin/ by-name.gz by-time.gz compress.tar dev/ doc/
etc/ faces government/ graphics/ gzip.tar help home/ index/
inet/ info/ kernel-bsdi/ languages/ library/ lost+found/
ls-1R.Z ls-1R.gz ls-1tR.Z ls-1tR.gz mm.status networking/
packages/ private/ pub/ published/ sco-archive systems/
tmp/ unix-today unix-world usenet/ usr/
uumap uumap.tar.Z uunet-info vendor/
```

If you see something interesting, such as the `languages/` subdirectory, continue exploring on down the tree:

```
>> print read ftp://ftp.uu.net/languages/
abc awk eli emacs-lisp eulisp icon lisp ls-1R.Z ml perl
            python sather sr tcl tools txl
```

What! Nothing about REBOL? Well, fellow REBOLians, come the REBOLution, all that will change.

If you want the remote directory in a REBOL word in which you can manipulate the list, use techniques such as:

```
>> dir-list: read ftp://ftp.uu.net/
>> foreach file (sort dir-list) [print file]
```

Go ahead and try that; I'll wait for you.

Getting information

Obtaining information about a file on a remote server via FTP works precisely the same way it works for a local file on your computer. By the way, REBOL returns file sizes in bytes. Here are three examples (which you can try):

```
>> size? ftp://ftp.abooks.com/pub/rebol/abarn.jpg
== 32622
>> modified? ftp://ftp.abooks.com/pub/rebol/abarn.jpg
== 6-May-2000/21:16
>> exists? ftp://ftp.abooks.com/pub/rebol/testfile.txt
== true
>> checksum ftp://ftp.abooks.com/pub/rebol/abarn.jpg
== 835545
```

Or you can get several items of information on a file (local or remote) with the info? function:

```
>> probe info? ftp://ftp.abooks.com/pub/rebol/testfile.txt

make object! [
    size: 150
    date: 6-May-2000/22:37
    type: file
]
```

Making a directory

Creating a new directory on a remote server via FTP is done much the same way you would create a directory on your local machine:

```
make-dir ftp://ftp.abooks.com/pub/rebol/new-directory
```

Deleting files via FTP

You remove files on a remote server via FTP (assuming you have the proper permissions) as you would delete a file locally:

```
delete ftp://ftp.abooks.com/pub/rebol/oldfile.txt
```

Using wildcards

For very long directory listings — yes, locally or over a network — you may want to use a wildcard method to filter out just the files you desire. Here's an example using FTP in which you look only for the .txt files.

```
>> dir: read ftp://ftp.abooks.com/pub/rebol/
>> foreach file dir [
    if find file ".txt" [print file]
    ]
dirlist.txt
testfile.txt
```

The find and parse functions in REBOL give you zillions of ways to filter any kind of list.

Protecting your password

For greater security, consider: When you're writing lines of code in the form

```
read ftp://username:your_password@your.com
```

your username and password are easily readable in the script. Do not place such scripts out in the open where someone else can read them and scarf up your login information!

REBOL scripts are simple text files. Any password information can be easily read by anyone with access to the script. To protect this type of information, don't put these scripts in any publicly accessible place, either on the Internet or in a nonpassword-protected directory that others can peruse on your local area network.

You've Got Mail!

In this section, I take a very brief look at e-mail, because it does involve networking. For an in-depth discussion of e-mail, scurry on up to Chapter 15.

Grabbing mail with POP

You get mail from the Internet or a local mail server by using the Post Office Protocol (POP). REBOL has POP built in, and this is how you use it to get your messages:

```
>> messages: read pop://username:password@abooks.com
connecting to: abooks.com
>> length? messages
== 14
```

I show you neat ways of reading these messages (and otherwise manipulating them) in Chapter 15.

Sending mail by using SMTP

SMTP (Simple Mail Transport Protocol) controls the transfer of e-mail messages on the Internet and is usually what your system uses to send mail. SMTP defines the interchange between Internet servers who engage in transporting e-mail from a sender to its destination.

REBOL provides the `send` function for sending a message to a receiver based on SMTP. It expects your network configuration to be set up in the `user .r` file. You send mail this way:

```
>> send ralph@abooks.com {Hey, nice book, Ralph. Thanks.}
```

I show you how to construct headers and other stuff in Chapter 15.

Finding Domains

You navigate the Internet thanks to two things: DNS (Domain Name Service) and IP (Internet Protocol) addresses.

Domains are the dot(.) coms and other Web addresses almost everyone now recognizes, such as: `abcnews.com` for ABC's news site, `abooks.com` for my company's Web domicile, or `rebol.com` for the cybernetic abode of REBOL Technologies and REBOL itself.

IP addresses are the underlying numerical addresses that tell your browser or other network-aware programs where to find a connection for specific domains. IP addresses are `tuple` numbers in the format 0.0.0.0. And, yes, you remember correctly that `tuple` is one of REBOL's many native datatypes — which means that handling IP information is a snap.

Requests for either IP addresses or domain names (DNS) use the `dns://` networking URL. Connect to the Internet and start your REBOL console. Here's how it works:

```
>> read dns://abooks.com
== 216.122.85.130
>> read dns://rebol.com
== 207.69.132.8
```

Or, if you know the IP address instead of the domain name, just use that `tuple` number rather than the domain name:

```
>> read dns://216.122.85.130
== "abooks.com"
>> read dns://207.69.132.8
== "rebol.com"
```

Looking up DNS names and IP numbers

Both methods — domain names and IP addresses — should be part of your arsenal of REBOL coding tricks. If, as happens frequently on the Net, a Web hoster offers a better deal, a domain may be switched to a different server. In such cases, the underlying IP address, which is really the address of a particular server, will change. So knowing the domain name lets you find the server or, in reverse, a given IP address returns the domain name assigned to it.

Using read dns:// without a domain name or IP address returns your computer's domain, like this:

```
>> print read dns://
richmond
```

There is no dot-com or other domain-name extension because this computer is on my company's LAN (Local Area Network) and connected to the Internet through a firewall or proxy server. Knowing the name, you can now find the local IP address:

```
>> print read dns://richmond
198.168.0.12
```

Converting to domain names

Finding the IP addresses for blocks of domain names is also easy. Just define a block of domain names you want addresses for and then type the second and third lines below. Try it:

```
>> domains: [cnn.com drudgereport.com abcnews.com]
>> foreach domain domains [
print [domain " -- " read join dns:// domain]]
cnn.com  --  207.25.71.5
drudgereport.com  --  216.55.4.252
abcnews.com  --  204.202.136.30
```

Next I do a little more-sophisticated lookup. I've written the simple script that follows to see who's using some of the neighboring IP addresses to my company's Internet server and for what those addresses are being used. Purely nosey but fun. You can change the dns variable for a different starting address if you like:

```
REBOL [
   TITLE: "DNS Examiner"
       PURPOSE: "Sample script for REBOL FOR DUMMIES"
       DATE: 7-May-2000
       FILE: %13-dns.r
       AUTHOR: "Ralph Roberts"
   ]

 dns: 216.122.85.130

 number: 7          ; number IP addresses to examine

 loop number [
       site: join dns://.dns
       Website: either a: read site [a]["No Domain"]
       either error? try [Webpage: read join http:// dns] [
       title: "no website"
   ] [
       parse Webpage [
thru <title> copy title to </title>]
   ]

       prin Website
       z: length? Website loop 30 - z [prin " "]
       print title

       dns: dns + 0.0.0.1
       ]
```

Run the script as follows:

```
>> do %13-dns.r
Script: "DNS Examiner" (7-May-2000)
connecting to: 216.122.85.130
abooks.com          ALEXANDER BOOKS Publishers CYBERMALL
connecting to: 216.122.85.131
vstorefronts.com              vstorefronts.com Web Site
connecting to: 216.122.85.132
iproWebs.net              iproWebs.net Web Site
connecting to: 216.122.85.133
servcom1.eusrv.com        Page d'accueil provisoire
connecting to: 216.122.85.134
Web123.com                Web123.com Web Design
connecting to: 216.122.85.135
manshow.com               Man Show Home Page
connecting to: 216.122.85.136
hypercerulean.com         Hypercerulean, Inc.
```

Finding who's who with who is

The whois protocol is a handy way to find out who owns a particular domain name, who its technical contact is, how he or she may be reached, and more. All this is public information. You can even run searches that return all listings that match a search string. For a long time InterNIC was the main domain name registrar here in the U.S., but many others now exist and provide whois service.

By the way, do not use www in whois queries. The names are registered without it.

Next I want to retrieve a listing of all servers that contain the word REBOL in their registration from the whois server provided by InterNIC. To do so, I use the following query:

```
>> print read whois://rebol@internic.net
```

The answer comes back:

```
REBOL.ORG
REBOL.NET
REBOL.COM
```

To find data on one specific domain name, use only that name:

```
>> print read whois://rebol.com@internic.net
```

You can also use an asterisk (*) as a wildcard to find even more names at once. For example,

```
>> print read whois://abook*@internic.net
```

returns 78 domain names with the string abook in them. Considering the millions of domain names out there, I guess my abooks.com is pretty nearly unique after all.

Looking up names in domain databases

Other whois lookup services give more information. I use Network Solutions to register all my domains, and I like their server. Go ahead and look up my domain name (public info, after all). You do so by typing

```
>> print read whois://abooks.com@networksolutions.com
```

Monitoring for domain-name availability

The new real estate boom exists in cyberspace — the buying and selling of domain names. Almost all the really, really good names are taken, especially the dot-com names. That's the bad news. The good news is that a domain name is typically registered for only a year or two, at the most. If the name is not renewed, it becomes available again.

Here's a simple REBOL script allowing you to monitor domain-name availability:

```
REBOL [
    TITLE: "Domain Name Available!"
        PURPOSE: "Sample script for REBOL FOR DUMMIES"
        DATE: 7-May-2000
        FILE: %13-domain-avail.r
        AUTHOR: "Ralph Roberts"
    ]

domains: [                          ; list of domains you'd like
    blue.com
        red.com
        green.com
        yellow-roses-dripping-dew.com
        purple.com
        ]

foreach domain domains [
        domain: join domain "@internic.net"
        a: read join whois:// domain
        if find a "no match" [
                b: parse domain "@"
                c: join b/1 " is available!!!!"
                send you@your.com c
                ]
                ]
```

Of those names, http://yellow-roses-dripping-dew.com is (not surprisingly) the only unregistered name, and the script sent me e-mail to that effect. But, hey, I don't want it, so feel free.

If you have access to a Unix or Linux server with cron, you can set a script like the preceding one to periodically check for names you want. I certainly have one running. Domain names these days can be gold. Thanks to REBOL, such tasks are now easy.

Timing Yourself with daytime

daytime retrieves the current day and time of day by using SNTP (Simple Network Time Protocol). Many servers support the daytime protocol. To connect to an SNTP server type:

```
>> print read daytime://everest.cclabs.missouri.edu
connecting to: everest.cclabs.missouri.edu
Mon May  8 10:54:45 2000
```

If the server does not support `daytime`, REBOL returns an error.

Accessing News with NNTP

The Network News Transfer Protocol (NNTP) is one. NNTP is the basis for tens of thousands of newsgroups that provide a public forum for millions of Internet users. REBOL includes two levels of support for NNTP.

- ✔ The built-in support for NNTP is based on a slim package of functionality, the `nntp` scheme.
- ✔ An extended level of functionality is provided by the news scheme that is implemented in a file distributed as `nntp .r`.

This section is about the built-in `nntp` scheme that exists in REBOL when you start it (not to be confused with the contents of the file `nntp.r`, which I cover in Chapter 19, the chapter about dialects). The news scheme implemented by `nntp.r` is much more powerful, but you'll be mighty pleased by REBOL's built-in `nntp://`, so here you go.

Get some good news-reader software to enjoy reading news. (For good freeware or shareware readers, look at `filedudes.com` or `davecentral.com`.)

First of all, there are a lot of newsgroups. The technique that follows downloads all active groups on your news server. The address shown is for my ISP, Interpath, in North Carolina. It won't work for you unless you are an Interpath subscriber. Find out from your own ISP what your news path is, but here's how to get all the groups — there are a lot, so leave a bit of time for downloading:

```
>> newsgroups: read nntp://news.interpath.net
>> print length? newsgroups
36122
```

As you see, I have access to 36,122 newsgroups. That's more than I have time to read right now. But I can narrow it down. One way is to look for newsgroups about books:

```
>> b: []                        ; make a block for results
>> foreach group newsgroups [
     if find group "book" [append b group]
   ]
>> print length? b              ; how many book newsgroups?
176
```

I'm reading a book at the moment by the South African writer, Wilbur Smith.
Smith is a highly popular, bestselling author these days, but I've read him for
20 years or more. I wonder if there's a newsgroup about him? To find out, I
type the following:

```
>> foreach group newsgroups [
    if find group "wilbur" [print group]
    ]
alt.fan.usandwilbur
alt.books.wilbur-smith
```

I don't know what `alt.fan.usandwilbur` is about; many weird newsgroups
exist out there, but I see the one I want to explore. To do so, I type

```
>> smith: read nntp://news.interpath.net/alt.books.wilbur-
        smith
connecting to: news.interpath.net
>> print length? smith
7
```

Seven messages. Okay, I want to read their subjects. As I find interoperability
in all of REBOL, I can use the same techniques as I can on e-mail. Using the
dandy `import-email` function (which turns both news and e-mail messages
into objects, which are easier to work with), I type

```
>> foreach msg smith [
    b: import-email msg
    print b/subject
    ]
O.T.-Hi !
Re: O.T.-Hi !
Re: 59648
Re: Italiano
What are the best Wilbur Smith books?
Re: What are the best Wilbur Smith books?
Any books set in Okavango Delta or Victoria Falls?
```

Okay, I agree with Allan. Lots of good titles from Smith. Check him out.

Some newsgroups run to thousands of messages at any one time. You need to
handle those differently, rather than jamming up your computer's memory
with everything at once. In REBOL, you use a port to the newsgroup (or any
other source larger than available memory) by typing

```
>> writing: open nntp://news.interpath.net/misc.writing
```

With the port open, you can now retrieve messages, such as

```
>> a: writing/986              ; get message 986
>> msg: import-e-mail a/1      ; import it into object
>> print msg/subject          ; read the subject
Re: Warning for ILOVEYOU - the virus. Do NOT open it if you
             get it!!!!!
```

The code `print msg/from` tells you who the message is from; `print msg/content` gives you the body of the message.

Always close a port when you're finished with it to release networking resources.

Again, I'm not suggesting you actually read news in REBOL, or at least not until you use the techniques I show you to build a nice, user-friendly reader. But a tremendous lot of manipulation is possible in these simple commands.

Networking with Ports

In addition to REBOL's direct support for protocols, such as HTTP, FTP, POP, and SMTP, REBOL also provides support for low-level port access. Ports can be used to access files, the console, and for networks. You see examples of that versatility in the preceding section and in Chapter 9 for opening files larger than memory.

Ports are the key to implementing REBOL Internet servers, such as Web servers or chat servers. Schemes control how ports act. Networking is typically based on the `tcp` scheme.

Here's an easy example of opening ports using the same machine. First I open a listening or server port. I'm using port number 8000. Port numbers may have a value of up to 65,635. The port numbers up to 1024 are reserved for commonly used Internet applications. For instance, FTP uses ports 20 and 21, Telnet uses port 23, HTTP servers use port number 80 by default, NNTP uses port number 119. Port number 8000 is commonly used for experimental, or special purpose Web servers. Okay, open the server, says me:

```
>> server: open tcp://:8000
```

Now I need a sending port, which is called a `client`:

```
>> client: open tcp://richmond:8000
```

I used the same port number and the name of my local machine, which I know is Richmond (named after Richmond T. Elephant, another long story). Now I can use the client and server ports like so:

```
>> insert client "Hi, there."
>> close client
>> port: first server
>> print copy port
Hi, there.
```

My goodness, I've just communicated by using ports. Not hard at all in REBOL, and a start for your more complex projects.

You can open the two tcp ports in a single or in two separate REBOL shells. Please note that the sender port must be closed before the listening port will collect the message and make it available to the print function.

The open function is exceptionally useful and supports several refinements. Use open/string to automatically convert platform-specific line terminators between sending and receiving ports. The open/lines refinement converts a string consisting of several lines to a block of lines. The line terminators are removed.

As the REBOL user's manual tells you, it's rarely useful to monitor the client to determine when it closes the connection and then to manually initiate the readout of the data received. Normally, a server process runs in an endless loop and is expected to collect data as it arrives. Some indicator — perhaps a reserved control-character — may be used to signal the server that it's time to quit. Here's an example:

1. Open REBOL and enter this code:

```
>> server: open tcp://:8000

>> forever [
      port: first wait server
      print copy port
      ]
```

The little busy indicator shows that the port is now listening.

2. Leave the script running, minimize REBOL, open another instance of the console, and then type this code:

```
>> client: open tcp://richmond:8000
>> repeat count 10 [
      insert client
      (escape)
>> repeat count 10 [
      insert client count
      ]
>> close client
>> repeat count 10 [
      insert client count
      ]
>> close client
```

3. **Switch back to the first copy of REBOL running.**

   You should see

   ```
   12345678910
   ```

   with the busy indicator still merrily twirling, which indicates that the port is still listening.

4. **Press the Esc (Escape) key to stop the server.**

   Always remember to close the server after you're finished with it by using the command `close server`.

The REBOL user's manual includes a good introduction to the more sophisticated uses of network ports at `rebol.com/users/netports.html`.

Part V
Tactics and Maneuvering (A REBOLer is Born)

The 5th Wave   By Rich Tennant

"We're here to clean the code."

In this part . . .

This part is even more powerful. You see even more practical, actual applications in each area covered, including some short, *useful* scripts.

Chapter 14

Rounding the Databases

● ●

In This Chapter

▶ Using blocks of values

▶ Building simple databases

▶ Structuring datbases

▶ Saving and loading databases

● ●

*T*his chapter is about creating relatively simple databases, but you'll find that these simple databases afford you immense power that's useful in real-world applications. REBOL/Core — the version of REBOL that this book covers — doesn't feature external program access, OBDC (Open Database Connectivity), nor any other kind of SQL (Structured Query Language) database access. The forthcoming REBOL/Command provides this connectivity, but it's likely to be a commercial product. REBOL/Core is, and will continue to be, free.

The databases that I show you here are more like *flat-file* databases, which are essentially just structured text files. I like to call them "quick and dirty" databases because you can implement a full-blown application with them in minutes. REBOL handles these files, even those containing many thousands of records, quickly and with elegantly sparse but powerful code. For example, I'm running the online version of *The Sanders Price Guide to Autographs* with REBOL/Core, and it now has over 130,000 prices. Searches are fast! REBOL was an excellent solution for my group because development time was practically nil.

REBOL has two overwhelming advantages over other scripting languages like Perl for the fast development of small database applications. First, the code is much less complicated to gain similar results and, perhaps most importantly, REBOL's parsing ability makes turning both structured or even unstructured text files into databases really easy.

In this chapter, I don't spend a lot of time explaining every little nuance of the code I use (refer to earlier chapters for the basics). Instead, I give you a broad overview of using simple databases by using REBOL examples. I hope you enjoy it!

Getting Comfy with REBOL Databases

REBOL handles lots of datatype values easily and directly — `decimals`, `integers`, `money`, `time`, `tuples`, `strings`, `dates`, `tags`, `issues`, and more. Manipulating all these values requires minimal plain English code. This facility and power is all ideal for smaller database applications. I can mention mailing lists, membership rosters, address books, and financial data, but this is merely scratching the surface. The potential is limitless.

I already use REBOL databases on my company's Web servers to maintain lists of users in our auctions, items being auctioned, autograph prices, the complete offerings of books sold by our company (a searchable file with hundreds of titles), listings of files on the server in various categories (thousands), and much more. Before REBOL came along, I did most of this type stuff with Perl, and that was a major pain. REBOL uncomplicated my Webmaster duties considerably, especially in handling bunches of data.

Types of databases

Three major types of databases exist, each with advantages and disadvantages. These are

- **Flat-file:** Simple text files with data stored exactly as originally organized. These files are "quick and dirty" in that scripting languages like REBOL can easily access and manipulate them. The main disadvantages: You can not change one part without having to rewrite the entire file and using very large flat-files is slow.

- **Electronic:** Such programs as Excel and Lotus 123 store date in a single (sometimes rather large) table or datasheet. Using the program, you can sort data and perform queries. But due to the way data is stored, this can be tedious. Formats are proprietary and hard to use unless you have the creating software.

- **Relational:** I include both relational databases and object databases as one category. These are the top of the heap, so to speak. Data is stored in multiple interactive tables which allow you to easily sort data, extract and filter data, perform advanced queries, and customize output. Examples include software like Microsoft Access, Visual FoxPro, MySQL, Oracle, and so forth. This software can cost hundreds or even many thousands of dollars. You need special interfacing software to access these databases.

I'm here to testify (Can I get an amen?)!

Why am I writing a programming book? For the money? Nah. After 20 years of writing computer books, I've found better and easier ways of making a living. I'm sacrificing time and income here for one reason — I truly believe in REBOL and its ability to let you, me, or anyone who uses it develop quick, powerful Web applications.

I learn things quite often by writing books about them — by immersing myself in a subject until I become truly proficient at it. The discipline of

doing a *For Dummies* book keeps your toes toasted and your nose ground to a nub (just ask my editor<g>). This is good. It's working! I'm now able to visualize and churn out REBOL scripts for our Web sites by the bucketfull. Just as fast and easy as I had hoped.

This is what I'm sharing with you in this book. REBOL is worth the effort. It will benefit you in lots of ways. End of testimonial.

Creating (and goofing around with) a simple flat-file database

REBOL can speedily manipulate flat-file databases with thousands of records. REBOL/Core is free, text files are easy to create and edit; thus for the expenditure of no money and little time, you can easily code database projects either for your local use or as live Web applications. After you reach tens of thousands of records, you may want to look at a relational database, but you can continue to use flat-files for simple applications. Why make it hard on yourself?

The following shows the syntax for entering a simple, three-record, flat-file database (named the ducks database) in REBOL.

```
>> ducks: [
    "yellow rubber" "yellow plastic" "blue rubber"]
```

The ducks database now contains three records.

If your name is Ernie and you have a particular preference for rubber ducks, you can perform a simple search on your database, pulling from it the ducks made of rubber. You type

```
>> foreach duck ducks [if find duck "rubber" [print duck]]
```

The output looks like the following:

```
yellow rubber
blue rubber
```

To search for blue ducks (maybe you're Captain Call from *Lonesome Dove*), you type the following:

```
>> foreach duck ducks [if find duck "blue" [print duck]]
```

The output looks like the following:

```
blue rubber
```

Now for an example of some razzle-dazzle, replacing a found record with a new record:

```
>> foreach duck ducks [
    if find duck "yellow plastic" [replace duck "yellow
        plastic" "green rubber"]
    if find duck "rubber" [print duck]
    ]
yellow rubber
green rubber
blue rubber
```

You can perform much more sophisticated operations with the same ease of coding.

Using Blocks of Values

Everything in the REBOL language — from databases to code — is stored as blocks (set off by a leading left bracket ([) and a trailing right bracket (])). This simple fact makes REBOL's data manipulation power possible because it, in effect, already separates and presorts data. This makes it easier for you to find and use pertinent parts. Some examples of blocks are provided in Table 14-1.

Table 14-1	Using Blocks in REBOL Databases		
Block type	**Example**	**Output**	**What It Does**
Executable code	`>> print ["Today is" now/date] ;`	`Today is 12-May-2000`	This code evaluates Executable code and is pretty straightforward. You run it, REBOL evaluates it, and you get a result.

Block type	Example	Output	What It Does
Lines in a file	`>> a: read/lines %14-dbgen2.r >> print type? a`	The CD file `14-dbgen2.r` as a block of lines.	Compare this to `>> a: read %14-dbgen2.r ; >> print type? a`, which prints the file as a string. The ability to parse a text file into a block of lines allows you to treat any text file as a database for searching, printing, and so on. Reading blocks is a powerful tool.
Integers	`>> b: [1 15 10 148] >> print divide (b/1 + b/2 + b/3 + b/4) length? b`	43.5	This code finds the average of all the numbers in block *b* by adding them together and dividing by the length of *b* (the number of numbers). The answer is 43.5.
Decimal numbers	`c: [3.14 58.457 9.3 20.391] >> print ["Highest value is" last sort c]`	`Highest value is 58.457`	This code sorts the numbers in the c database and prints the last value (which is also the highest).
Mixed values	`>>e: ["apples" 78 $14.34] >> print [e/2 e/1 "sold for" e/3]`	`78 apples sold for $14.34`	This code simply outputs the different types of values in the desired order. This code snippet could be useful for storing the daily sales in a produce market.

(continued)

Table 14-1 *(continued)*

Block type	Example	Output	What It Does

Nested blocks	`>> f: [ [12 25 4]`
	`[5 2 "pie"]] >>`
	`print (pick second`
	`f 2) + (pick first`
	`f 3)`
		6	This code adds the value of the second value of the second block to the third value of the first block, or 2 + 4.

The `read/lines` example is especially important because it affects the way you would handle an unstructured database; that is, reading a plain old text file in and treating it as a database. For example, you can open the `14-dbgen2.r` file on the *REBOL For Dummies* CD as a text file and as a database of lines. For example, if you use the `read` statement (without the `lines` refinement) using the following syntax:

```
>> a: read %14-dbgen2.r
>> print type? a
```

Then the output is a string. A big blob of text is hard to manipulate in a meaningful, pattern-oriented way, as you want to do with databases.

But, if the `/lines` refinement is added, as follows:

```
>> a: read/lines %14-dbgen2.r
>> print type? a
```

Then bingo! The result is a block of lines. You can now easily do manipulations like printing out only the lines containing the `write` statement, which you can accomplish as follows:

```
>> foreach line a [if find line "write" [print line]]
```

The output of this statement is

```
        write/append %pepperpicker.db picker
        write/append %pepperpicker.db " picked "
        write/append %pepperpicker.db random 1000
```

Using a Script to Build a Database

Essentially, two types of simple databases exist — those your scripts create from data they generate and those created from an existing file such as a report from some other program saved as a text file. This section looks at building a database by using a script.

Looking at a database-building script

Okay, now actually build us a database of your very own. I've already done most of the measuring of boards and sawing for you. So it's your turn to start nailing stuff up.

Be sure to have REBOL set to the same directory these example programs are in before running them.

To see how a script can create a database, take a look at the script 14-dbgen1.r, which generates a database by using data from REBOL's current directory.

To work with this script, type the following:

```
>> do %14-dbgen1.r
```

What this script does is pull all the filenames, the sizes of the files, and the dates that the files were last modified into the word filedb. This resulting database of file information is then queried to the total number of files in the directory and total size, as well as the largest, smallest, newest, and oldest files.

The script generates the following output:

```
Script: "Database Generator 1" (12-May-2000)
There are  256  files occupying  6034306  bytes of space.
Largest...:  auto.r 1138620 19-Apr-2000/15:12:16-4:00
Smallest..:  helloworld.txt 0 13-Feb-2000/19:41:48-5:00
Newest....:  dbgen1.r 1460 13-May-2000/16:45:02-4:00
Oldest....:  nntp.r 21363 21-May-1999/17:10:40-4:00
```

To see the raw data, type the following:

```
>> foreach block filedb [print block]
```

The output appears as follows:

```
setup.html 29570 29-Oct-1999/17:58:50-4:00
nntp.r 21363 21-May-1999/17:10:40-4:00
notes.html 45613 29-Oct-1999/17:58:50-4:00
rebdoc.r 4363 14-Jul-1999/11:38:40-4:00 .......... (more)
```

To see the structure of `filedb`, type the following:

```
>> probe filedb
```

The following output appears:

```
[[%setup.html 29570 29-Oct-1999/17:58:50-4:00] [%nntp.r
21363 21-May-1999/17:10:40-4:00] [%notes.html 45613 29-Oct-
1999/17:58:50-4:00] [%rebdoc.r 4363 14-Jul-1999/11:38:40
-4:00] [%REBOL.exe 177152 29-Oct-1999/17:56:50-4:00]
.......... (more)
```

To save, retrieve, and reuse the database, type

```
>> save %filedb filedb
>> filedb: load %filedb
```

You can use the `load` function when reading data from a file that you want translated into REBOL values.

Understanding database scripts

Suppose that you have a list of people that you call regularly and have been accumulating for some time in a text file. You may have several hundred names and numbers, especially if you are on one of those cheap long distance plans. (Okay, in reality, you probably have a contact manager but bear with me here — chances are good that you can export the list into a text file.)

As it happens, even if you don't have a text file on your hard drive, you can use the `phonelist.txt` file that appears on the CD.

Now suppose that the time comes when you want to be able to access your phone database via your Web site for the sake of convenience (suppose that your laptop breaks while you're out on the road, for example).

Your first step is to read your text file into a variable. To do so, type the following:

```
>> phonelist: read %14-phonelist.txt
```

Doing so stores the phonelist.txt file into the phonelist variable. You can print it out by typing the following:

```
>> print phonelist
```

The following output appears:

```
Bob J. Finklewumpus, 828-555-1212
Molly Mangletangle, 612-555-1212
Fergus Dumplelump, 212-555-1212
Billy Bob Bosluple, 202-555-1212
Lil Lazyboneapoop, 812-555-1212
Sam Rablepaver, 907-555-1212
Tellie Talkermalk, 303-555-1212
Murvin Monkerhonk, 404-555-1212
Don Doodleslump, 714-555-1212
Susie Ablebakerbop, 623-555-1212
```

But the phonelist variable is still just a big glob of text, which is hard to manipulate. By manipulate, I mean do things like quickly find Aunt Lil's phone number, or change Don Doodleslump's old number to his new one.

To make the information more malleable, you can convert the text file into a real database. Because REBOL likes to work with information in blocks, that's what you want to do; convert your text glob into a more manageable format by using blocks.

The first step in converting any text file is to recognize its *pattern*. A pattern is simply points of similarity in the data that enable you to parse the data into submission, or at least into regular sized records. If you can identify a pattern, you can use any text file as a database.

The phone list above has only two parts to its pattern, which simplifies conversion — a comma follows the name and (as we can see by each name beginning on a new line) there is a return character after the phone number.

You can now use the following snippet of code to implement your conversion (on the CD as 14-parsephonelist.r):

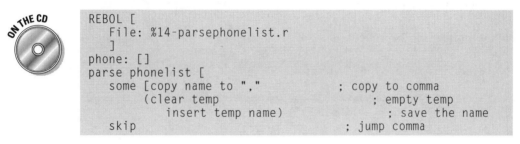

```
REBOL [
    File: %14-parsephonelist.r
    ]
phone: []
parse phonelist [
    some [copy name to ","          ; copy to comma
        (clear temp                 ; empty temp
            insert temp name)       ; save the name
    skip                            ; jump comma
```

```
copy number to newline          ; copy number
  (insert tail temp trim number  ; save number
  append phone to-block mold temp) ; save line
  skip                           ; jump newline
  ]
  to end
  ]
```

To execute the above script at the command line, type the following commands:

```
>> phonelist: read %14-phonelist.txt    ; load list
>> do %14-parsephonelist.r              ; runscript
```

The feedback from REBOL is the following:

```
Script: "Untitled" (none)
== true
```

The script creates a variable, phone, with your new phone list. If you execute the probe command on it, you can see that the data has been turned into blocks:

```
>> probe phone
[["Bob J. Finklewumpus" "828-555-1212"] ["Molly
Mangletangle" "612-555-1212"] ["Fergus Dumplelump"
"212-555-1212"]  ... more
```

Before you start playing with your new database, save it (save early, save often . . . always save!):

```
>> save %14-phone.db phone
```

You read it back in as follows (check out Chapter 2 for details):

```
>> phone: toload %14-phone.db
```

Now you can play! For example, you can use paths to pull out discrete bits of information:

```
>> print phone/1
Bob J. Finklewumpus 828-555-1212
>> print phone/1/1
Bob J. Finklewumpus
>> print phone/9/2
714-555-1212
>> print phone/8/1
Murvin Monkerhonk
```

This is all very nice but not perhaps as user-friendly as a phone list should be. You can write a front end to make looking up phone numbers easy (it's on the CD as `14-phone.r`):

```
REBOL [
    File: %14-phone.r
    ]
call: func [name [string!]
            "name or portion of name to call"] [
    foreach line phone [
        if find line/1 name [print line exit]
        ]
    ]
phone: load %14-phone.db
```

That's it, the entire front end. This dandy little script loads the database and makes it easy to use. Just type the defined function word `call` followed by some portion of the name you're looking for (in quotes, and you can find an introduction in functions in Chapter 5):

```
>> do %14-phone.r
>> call "lil"
Lil Lazyboneapoop 812-555-1212
>> call "Bob"
Bob J. Finklewumpus 828-555-1212
>> call "Dumplelump"
Fergus Dumplelump 212-555-1212
```

Manipulating Text Files

After you understand the simple techniques available to you in REBOL, especially parsing, you can handle any text file with quick, efficient aplomb — mining it for any data you want to extract. Take reports, for example. Programs by the tens of thousands have the facility of saving reports in delimited text files. A *delimiter* is a character separating fields of data. Commas and tabs are most often used as delimiters, and you generally see the terms *comma-delimited file* or *tab-delimited file* in the file's description. Delimited files are ready for use as databases in REBOL.

All databases are structured into records with each record containing a set amount of fields. After you spot the pattern, writing code to extract the data is a snap.

Here's another example. This is a list of the highest elevations in each state of the United States, as published by the Federal government's U.S. Geodetic Survey. It's on your CD as `14-elevations.txt`.

Read it into the variable highest as follows:

```
>> highest: read/lines %14-elevations.txt
```

REBOL responds as follows:

```
== ["Alabama^-Cheaha Mt.^-2,405" "Alaska^-Mt. McKinley^-
       20,320" "Arizona^-Humphreys Peak^-12,633"
   "Arkansas^-Magazine Mt.^-2,753" ...
```

Using read/lines enables you to treat each line as a separate string, making manipulation easier; that is to say that each record becomes individually accessible. Seeing the pattern of this data is easy — just look at one record (between the quotation marks).

This technique is fine as long as each record in the database you are creating corresponds to one line in the text file. If you have information which splits across lines, you need to use the *parse* function described in Chapter 12 to pull out data instead of reading a file by lines.

You have the name of the state, separated by a tab delimiter (remember, ^- is the symbol for a tab in REBOL), followed by the name of the highest point, another tab delimiter, and the elevation in feet above sea level. With the pattern firmly in mind, you can now extract the data.

What's the highest point in North Carolina? What code finds it? Type the following:

```
>> foreach record highest [
       if find record "North Carolina" [print record]
       ]
```

REBOL responds:

```
North Carolina  Mt. Mitchell    6,684
== false
```

The false above comes not from REBOL arguing against Mt. Mitchell being the highest point in North Carolina but from checking other records after printing out the one matching record it found.

A more elegant way of handling this search is to write a function (see Chapter 5 for the basics):

```
>> high: func [top][
         foreach record highest [
              if find record top [print record]
           if record = last highest [exit]  ; no "false"
              ]
         ]
```

Use the function like this:

```
>> high "North Carolina"
North Carolina   Mt. Mitchell      6,684
```

These two searches also yield the same result:

```
>> high "Mitchell"
North Carolina   Mt. Mitchell      6,684
>> high "6,684"
North Carolina   Mt. Mitchell      6,684
```

You can also widen the search by using your high function with a less specific search term:

```
>> high "Carolina"
North Carolina   Mt. Mitchell      6,684
South Carolina   Sassafras Mt.     3,560
```

The data above is still in its original text format. Because the elevations are within a string value, you can't manipulate them numerically. So why not whip up a quick bit of code to find the highest point in the U.S. and the average highpoint in all the states and territories? No reason I can think of not to. This code is on your CD as 14-compare.r:

```
REBOL [ Title: "Compare High Points"
        File: %14-compare.r]
highest: read/lines %14-elevations.txt
highpoint: make block! 50
        foreach record highest [
                a: parse/all record "^-"
                replace a/3 "," ""
                a/3: make integer! a/3
                append/only highpoint a
        ]
        top: ["" "" 0]
        avg: 0
        foreach record highpoint [
            if record/3 > top/3 [top: record]
            avg: avg + record/3
        ]
print ["Highest point in the United States is: " top]
print ["The AVERAGE high point in all states is " divide avg
        (length? highpoint)]
```

Running this script generates the following output:

```
Highest point in the U.S.:   Alaska Mt. McKinley 20320
AVERAGE high point in all states:   5799.14545454545
```

I'm sure that average high point of almost 6,000 feet is news to those folks in Florida whose high point is a mere 345 feet (barely above high tide), but the U.S. is replete with mountainous states.

I have one more exercise in pattern recognition, this one involving a nondelimited text report. This example allows you a larger database to play with (1,000 lines), based on the old children's tongue twister of "Peter Piper picked a peck of pickled peppers." In this example, I've written a script that outputs a report for the pickled pepper pickers' union, founded by Peter Piper's cousin, Peter Packer. The script randomly generates the pickled pepper picker's name and has 4,976,640,000 possibilities, so chances are good that you won't find any name duplicated even in 1,000 lines. There is one already on the CD as 14-pepperpicker.db, but you can use 14-dbgen2.r to build your own and witness the power of REBOL to work with those 4,976,640,000 possible names.

Here's the script that performs the myriad pickled-pepper magic:

```
REBOL [
        TITLE: "Database Generator 2"
        PURPOSE: "Example in REBOL FOR DUMMIES"
        AUTHOR: "Ralph Roberts"
        DATE: 10-May-2000
        FILE: %14-dbgen2.r]
random/seed now                              ; make sure random is
        really random
v: func [] [pick [a e i o u] random 5]       ; get a random
        vowel
                                             ; below, get a
        random consonant
c: func [] [pick [b c d f g h k j l m n p q r s t v w x y z
        th ch sh] random 24]
picker: func [] [
        name: rejoin ["P" v c v c " P" v c c v c]
]
write %14-pepperpicker.db ""
loop 1000 [
    write/append %14-pepperpicker.db rejoin [
        picker " picked " random 2184
        " pecks of pickled peppers." newline
        ]
]
```

And the generated report looks something like this (but certainly not *exactly* like this):

```
Pathit Pilhoq picked 932 pecks of pickled peppers.
Pebon Paqzem picked 934 pecks of pickled peppers.
Pisig Pelshuc picked 161 pecks of pickled peppers.
Pereh Pavhim picked 395 pecks of pickled peppers.
```

```
Pifep Penbuh picked 376 pecks of pickled peppers.
Peshov Poxruk picked 839 pecks of pickled peppers.
Peshiq Pupyet picked 885 pecks of pickled peppers.
Puchux Pidzas picked 299 pecks of pickled peppers.
Pocuz Palthup picked 391 pecks of pickled peppers.
                    ... more
```

Read it into REBOL like this:

```
>> picked: read/lines %14-pepperpicker.db
```

Okay, no character delimiters in that text but it still contains lots of stuff that you can use. In our pickled pepper picker database, in each record (line) all that's significant is the name and the number of pecks picked. This looks like a job for the parsing (for more information on the super parsing tool, check out Chapter 12). For just one line, you could pull that data out like this:

```
>> print parse picked/1 [copy name to " picked" thru " " copy
          pecks to " pecks" to end]
true
>> print name
Pothuz Pithcej
>> print pecks
931
```

You can use the same technique to find the highest and lowest producing pickled pepper picker. You'll find this script on the CD as 14-pickers.r:

```
REBOL [
        TITLE: "Pickled Pepper Pickers"
        PURPOSE: "Example in REBOL FOR DUMMIES"
        AUTHOR: "Ralph Roberts"
        DATE: 15-May-2000
        FILE: %14-pickers.r]
do %14-dbgen2.r      ; generate a new database
picked: read/lines %14-pepperpicker.db
top-name: ""
top-picked: 0
bottom-name: ""
bottom-picked: 100
total-pecks: 0
foreach picker picked [
   parse picker [copy name to " picked" thru " "
     copy pecks to " pecks"]
pecks: make integer! pecks
if pecks > top-picked [top-name: name top-picked: pecks]
if pecks < bottom-picked [bottom-name: name bottom-picked:
          pecks]
total-pecks: total-pecks + pecks
]
```

```
print ["^/The top pickled pepper picker is: "
    top-name " at " top-picked " pecks!"]
print ["^/The average pickled pepper picker picked: "
        divide total-pecks (length? picked)
        " pecks of pickled peppers."]
print ["^/The WORST pickled pepper picker is: "
        bottom-name " at " bottom-picked " pecks."]
print [bottom-name
        "is hereby expelled from the Pickled Pepper Pickers
            Union!"]
```

Running this script gives these types of results (a new random database is generated each time):

```
>> do %14-pickers.r
Script: "Pickled Pepper Pickers" (15-May-2000)
Script: "Database Generator 2" (10-May-2000)
The top pickled pepper picker is:  Peshesh Pegzef  at  2180
            pecks!
The average pickled pepper picker picked:  1111.293  pecks of
            pickled peppers.
The WORST pickled pepper picker is:  Posaz Pasmox  at  2
            pecks.
Posaz Pasmox is hereby expelled from the Pickled Pepper
            Pickers Union!
```

Patently, poor Posaz Pasmox's pathetic performance passes proud pickled pepper pickers' patience.

Structuring Databases

Structuring a database is nothing more than thinking out how to store the data for easy retrieval.

Suppose that you maintain a repair log for a plant. The repairperson turns in the maintenance tasks performed each day, and these tasks are recorded weekly by your script in the database. A minimal database format could be structured like the one embedded in 14-dbgen3.r (included on the CD):

```
REBOL [
        TITLE: "Database Generator 3"
        PURPOSE: "Example in REBOL FOR DUMMIES"
        AUTHOR: "Ralph Roberts"
        DATE: 16-May-2000
        FILE: %14-dbgen3.r\]
workdays: [Monday Tuesday Wednesday Thursday Friday]
repairs: [
```

```
          Monday [
                  "Aligned framis grinder"
                  "Replaced lightbulb in office"
                  "Fixed coffee maker"
                  "Put new whatis in whosit"
                  ]
          Tuesday [
                  "Re-aligned framis grinder"
                  "New doorknob on front door"
                  "Painted Marv's office"
                  "Framis grinder making noise, aligned"
          ]
       Wednesday ["Tightened guide on framis grinder"
                  "Re-re-aligned framis grinder"
                  "Painted Marv's office right color"
                  ]
        Thursday ["Framis grinder out again, aligned"
            "Painted Pam's office, Marv wants same!"
  "Changed ballast in hallway light"
                  "Aligned framis grinder"
                  "Replaced filters in heat pump"
                  "Framis grinder down, aligned it."
                  ]
          Friday ["Framis grinder jammed, unjammed it"
                  "Re-re-painted Marv's office"
                  "Framis grinder whining, aligned"
                  "Marv wants ANOTHER color, TODAY!"
                  "Framis grinder down"
                  "Dissambled framis grinder, cleaned"
                  "Framis grinder not working"
              "Marv wanting painting immediately."
                  "Framis grinder broken when Marv slugged"
                  "Ordered new framis grinder"
              "Marv decides old color okay after all"
                  ]
       ]
```

Each record (workday) can have varying amounts of data but that all records
are easily accessible by REBOL. Take a look, for instance, at Thursday's jobs
using the basic path repairs/thursday:

```
>> foreach job repairs/thursday [print job]
Framis grinder out again, aligned
Painted Pam's office, Marv wants same!
Changed ballast in hallway light
Aligned framis grinder
Replaced filters in heat pump
Framis grinder down, aligned it... again
```

To pull out a specific job, use a longer path like `repairs/thursday/2`, the second job on Thursday:

```
>> print repairs/thursday/2
Painted Pam's office, Marv wants same!
```

For a change in the database (such as modifying line five above):

```
>> print replace repairs/thursday/5 "Replaced" "Cleaned"
Cleaned filters in heat pump
```

What about a report of all the repairs for the entire week? That task is simple in REBOL:

```
>> foreach day workdays [
       path: join "repairs/" day
       print ["^/" path]
       foreach job do path [print job]
       ]
repairs/Monday
Aligned framis grinder
Replaced lightbulb in office
Fixed coffee maker
Put new whatis in whosit
repairs/Tuesday
Re-aligned framis grinder
New doorknob on front door
Painted Marv's office
Framis grinder making noise, aligned
repairs/Wednesday
Tightened guide on framis grinder
Re-re-aligned framis grinder
Painted Marv's office right color
repairs/Thursday
Framis grinder out again, aligned
Painted Pam's office, Marv wants same!
Changed ballast in hallway light
Aligned framis grinder
Replaced filters in heat pump
Framis grinder down, aligned it... again
repairs/Friday
Framis grinder jammed, unjammed it
Re-re-painted Marv's office
Framis grinder whining, aligned
Marv wants ANOTHER color, TODAY!
Framis grinder breaks when Marv slugged
Ordered new framis grinder
Marv decides old color okay after all
```

Saving Data to a File

Here's how to save data to a file. Assuming a database like the following:

```
>> furniture: [
    ["Loveseat" "Velvet" $400]
    ["Divan" "Leather" $900]
    ["Lounger" "Vinyl" $600]
    ["Footstool" "Vinyl" $90]
    ]
```

You could add a piece to it as follows:

```
>> append/only furniture ["Coffee Table" "Mahogany" $300]
```

And then save it to a file:

```
>> save %14-furniture.db furniture
```

To retrieve and convert the variable back to a block (blocks are good for furniture, huh?), you would type in the following (note that the file 14-furniture.db is available on the CD):

```
>> furniture: load %14-furniture.db
>> foreach piece furniture [print piece]
```

REBOL outputs the following:

```
Loveseat Velvet $400.00
Divan Leather $900.00
Lounger Vinyl $600.00
Footstool Vinyl $90.00
Coffee Table Mahogany $300.00
```

Working with Headers

You can save the header information from a text file to a simple database file. But the word *header* can have a couple of different meanings. The first meaning is a column header or first record information — you know, like the words Name, Social Security Number, and so on. The second type of header is information about what the file is, who owns it, when it was created, and so on.

Using column headers

Here's how you can work with the first type of header into the
14-furniture.db database:

```
insert head furniture to-block mold ["Type" "Finish" "Price"]
```

Now you can do a neatly formatted report such as:

```
>> foreach piece furniture [
        prin piece/1
        z: (length? piece/1) loop 16 - z [prin " "]
        prin piece/2
        z: (length? piece/2) loop 16 - z [prin " "]
        print piece/3
        ]
Type            Finish          Price
Loveseat        Velvet          $400.00
Divan           Leather         $900.00
Lounger         Vinyl           $600.00
Footstool       Vinyl           $90.00
Coffee Table    Mahogany        $300.00
```

In formatted reports, the prin command prints a variable without a line
return.

The save function has a /header refinement that lets you accomplish this
while still saving the database itself. This turns your database from a text file
into a REBOL script that you can then execute (do) in order to load the data.
First, you need the merest bit of manipulation. Type

```
>> temp: [furniture:]
>> temp: [furniture:]
```

Doing so sets up the database variable furniture to be in place when your
saved script is run. Now you can save it with the header included (I put this
on the CD for you as 14-furniture.r):

```
save/header %14-furniture.r temp [
        Title: "Friendly Fred's Furniture Inventory"
        Author: "Big Fred"
        Date: 10-Jun-2000
    ]
```

To load your database, just type

```
do %14-furniture.r
```

You can test to make sure it's still the same by running your report again:

```
>> foreach piece furniture [
           prin piece/1
           z: (length? piece/1) loop 16 - z [prin " "]
           prin piece/2
           z: (length? piece/2) loop 16 - z [prin " "]
           print piece/3
           ]
Type            Finish          Price
Loveseat        Velvet          $400.00
Divan           Leather         $900.00
Lounger         Vinyl           $600.00
Footstool       Vinyl           $90.00
Coffee Table    Mahogany        $300.00
```

Getting at file headers

File headers refer the creation info that accompanies identifies a files creator, title, and other such information. How do you manipulate that data? Like this:

```
>> data: load/header %14-furniture.r
```

Use the probe command on data and you can see lots of interesting stuff, including the entire database. To retrieve only the header stuff, type the following:

```
>> print data/1/Title
Friendly Fred's Furniture Inventory
>> print data/1/Author
Big Fred
>> print data/1/Date
10-Jun-2000
```

Chapter 15

Going Postal with E-Mail

In This Chapter

▶ Retrieving e-mail

▶ Reading e-mail

▶ Sending e-mail

▶ Manipulating e-mail

*W*hat's the most common way to transfer information over the Internet? I've asked a number of people this and almost everyone answered, "Reading Web pages." Wrong, by far. The right answer for the last 30 years has been and continues to be *e-mail* or, more correctly, the underlying e-mail protocols such as POP (Post Office Protocol) and SMTP (Simple Mail Transport Protocol). A recent Lucent Technologies television ad claimed eight billion e-mails a day. That's a lot.

Speaking of those eight billion e-mails daily, REBOL is especially suited for manipulating e-mail or any other exchange of information between computers. Carl Sassenrath, the creator of REBOL, calls it a messaging language. The characteristic of a messaging language is that it transparently allows relative expressions (things that mean something to the receiving program or person) to be exchanged between applications, computers, and people.

You can use REBOL and your REBOL device to read your e-mail (with or without a password prompt), send e-mail (even bulk mailings), and manipulate e-mail (such as filtering out spam). This chapter shows you how.

Reading E-Mail

I would guess — just from the mere fact that you are reading this, a computer-related book — that you already have one or more e-mail accounts. Chances are, you retrieve messages from most (if not all) of those accounts by using the Post Office Protocol (POP). REBOL has that one down pat.

Letting REBOL get your mail

REBOL supports POP by using the read function, which you also use on files and various other protocols. The argument you provide to read in getting e-mail must be pop://, the username and password required to access the e-mail account, and the domain name of your ISP's (Internet Service Provider's) host machine that supports POP. The domain name most usually will be something like mail.my-isp.net or pop.my-isp.net.

The read function for POP is so simple that it does not even require your network settings to be configured in the user .r file. All you need is to be connected to the Internet. Just do the following to retrieve messages (it will read all currently available messages without deleting them):

```
>> messages: read pop://username:password@yourmail.com
```

Mail is delivered to the messages variable as a block of strings, with each string representing a complete message including all headers. If you want to know how many messages you've received, type

```
>> print length? messages
```

REBOL returns the number of messages awaiting your longing eyes.

Making messages readable

Once you have retrieved your e-mail, the next step is reading the message(s). Using the

```
>> messages: read pop://username:password@yourmail.com
```

method puts a block of strings into the variable word messages, which now contains a block of strings, with each string representing a complete message. This is nice enough but hardly easy to read.

REBOL provides the import-email function to solve that little problem. The import-email function translates the e-mail strings into objects, from which you can use paths to pick out information. When you use the import-email function, you need to designate a target block for the conversion. The following code converts the e-mail to a block called msg:

```
>> msg: []                                 ; make a block
>> foreach message messages [
     append msg import-email message    ; translate e-mail
>> print length? Msg 2; yep, still two]
```

Protecting your password

The mail retrieval example in this chapter includes the password within their URLs, but if you plan on sharing your scripts (like I'm doing in these pages), you probably don't want that information to be known. I mean I like you, but not to the extent of letting you read my mail. Here's a simple method of prompting for a password and building the correct URL:

```
>> pass: ask "Password? "
Password?
    type_your_password_here
```

```
>> messages: read join
    pop://yourname: [pass
    "@your.com"]
```

For both `username` and `password`, do:

```
user: ask "Username? "
pass: ask "Password? "
messages: read join pop://
    [user ":" pass "@your.com"]
```

Again, both these techniques work equally well for FTP. Protect your password or, I guarantee you, someone else will use it.

If you want to see who sent you the message or messages, use the following code:

```
>> foreach e-mail msg [
    print e-mail/from
    ]
```

This returns the e-mail addresses of who sent you the messages, something like this:

```
sclark4@uswest.net
tim@johnsons-Web.com
```

Handling headers

Using the `import-e-mail` function turns each e-mail message — which is in a string when first retrieved — into an object having a set structure allowing easy access to various standard parts of any e-mail. To see those parts, use the `probe` word on the particular message that you want to access, as in

```
>> probe msg/message no.
```

You get (with actual data removed for readability) something like the following:

```
make object! [
     To:
     CC:
     BCC:
     From:
     Reply-To:
     Date:
     Subject:
     Return-Path:
     Organization:
     Message-Id:
     Comment:
     MIME-Version:
     Content-Type:
     Content:
```

To access any of these categories, use the following code:

```
msg/message no./category you want to access
```

For example, you may use codes like the following:

```
msg/1/subject
msg/2/content
msg/1/organization
```

Dialing assistance — REBOL style

You can subscibe to the REBOL mailing list (and get tons of helpful tips and hints) from inside REBOL just by typing the following at the command prompt on your console:

```
>> send list@rebol.com
   "subscribe"
```

Or just for announcements:

```
>> send notice@rebol.com
   "subscribe"
```

You can "prettify" it by using this technique:

```
>> foreach e-mail msg [
   print ["From: "
e-mail/from]
   print ["Subject: "
e-mail/subject]
```

```
   print ["Date: "
e-mail/date "^/"]

]
```

And the results look something like:

```
From:   sclark4@uswest.net
Subject: re Help files
Date:   22-May-
     2000/10:35:34-6:00


From:   tim@johnsons-Web.com
Subject: [REBOL] installing
     Rebol as CGI application
     under PWS/Win32 Re:
Date:   22-May-2000/8:38:31-8:00
```

And so on. Experiment with this on your own e-mail. Remember, REBOL leaves the message on the server, so you're not risking losing anything. You'll quickly master these simple e-mail manipulation techniques and be writing e-mail handling scripts in no time at all. Maybe even less.

Looking at one message at a time

Ah, but what if the e-mail account receives thousands of messages a day? I had a day (well, last Thursday, actually) when I checked mail and there were over 1,700 messages waiting. Mostly end-of-auction automatic reposting stuff from our online auctions, but still more stuff than you want to cram into one poor little variable, or perhaps have the room for in working memory.

No problem. You may remember *ports* (if not, refer to Chapter 10). By opening a port to a file, newsgroup, or other source, REBOL allows you the luxury of working with things larger than available memory. To open my mailbox on your e-mail server, type

```
>> mailbox: open pop://user:password@abooks.com
connecting to: abooks.com
```

You're accessing one of my test mail accounts here. After you have the account open, check for messages by typing

```
>> print length? mailbox
12
```

Just twelve messages this time (okay, so it was just a test account), but it could just as easily be 1,200 or 12,000 on one of my regular live company e-commerce accounts. This technique handles them all just as well. Here's some code that lets you see what's on the mail server through the open port:

```
>> forall mailbox [
        msg: import-email first mailbox
        print [
            "From: " msg/from
            "Subject: " msg/subject
        ]
]
From:   abooks@abooks.com Subject:  test
From:   ralph@abooks.com Subject:  test
From:   ralph@abooks.com Subject:  test
From:   ralph@abooks.com Subject:  test
From:   ralph@abooks.com Subject:  test
From:   ralph@abooks.com Subject:  test
From:   ralph@abooks.com Subject:  test of HTML
From:   ralph@abooks.com Subject:  test message
From:   ralph@abooks.com Subject:  testing
```

```
From:  ralph@abooks.com Subject:  test
From:  ralph@abooks.com Subject:  test
From:  ralph@abooks.com Subject:  simple htm
```

Having reviewed the messages' sender and subject lines, you can then access messages from the POP port as though it was a series type. To access message number 11 above, I type

```
>> msg: import-e-mail pick mailbox 8
```

Checking mail the easy way

Getting tired of having to type

```
messages: read pop://user:
    password@yourmail.com
```

to retrieve your mail? Me too. What if you had a mail function word? Well, if you've got the CD to this book, you have one. Just copy 15-myuser.r from the CD to your REBOL device and open the file. Look for the messages line and replace user, password, and yourmail.com with your own information, and then activate the script from the console like this:

```
>> mail
```

You get something that looks like this:

```
connecting to: abooks.com
You have  5  messages.
```

You're on your way to automated mail checking now — with my compliments. The code follows.

```
mail: func [][
msg: copy []
print newline
messages:
    readpop://user:pass@your-
    mail.com
if (length? messages) > 0 [
foreach message messages [
append msg import-email message
]
```

```
]
print ["You have " length?
    messages " messages.^/"]
count: 0
if (length? messages) > 0 [
foreach e-mail msg [
count: count + 1
prin [count " ... "]
prin e-mail/subject
z: length? e-mail/subject
loop 32 - z [prin " "]
print e-mail/from
]
]
print "" ; do this to suppress
    --FALSE
]
1  ... This is a test
   ralph@abooks.com
2  ... [REBOL] Simple CGI
   Problem Re:  ryanc@iesco-
   dms.com
3  ... Another test
   ralph@abooks.com
4  ... Just for you, a test
   ralph@abooks.com
5  ... Could this be a test?
   ralph@abooks.com
```

As you saw earlier, the e-mail message is in an object and at our utter mercy:

```
>> msg: import-e-mail pick mailbox 8
>> print [msg/from msg/subject "^/" msg/content]
ralph@abooks.com test message
This is a test of sending messages and retrieving e-mail.
--Ralph
```

And always remember to close a port when you finish with it. In this case like this:

```
>>close mailbox
```

You can use a path and print out the content like this:

```
>> print msg/2/content
```

Sending E-Mail

The Simple Mail Transport Protocol (SMTP) controls the transfer of e-mail messages on the Internet. Using SMTP allows the various host servers relaying mail on the Internet to receive and properly pass along your e-mail messages. Eight billion a day, huh? Well, maybe not all from you, but bunches of e-mails whiz back and forth, up and down, and (I'm sure) in concentric circles on the Internet at all times.

This section shows you how REBOL sends e-mail.

Configuring your e-mail setup

Receiving mail using POP, as described in the "Reading E-mail" section of this chapter, requires no specific configuration in REBOL, other than a connection to the Internet. (See Chapter 13 for more information on network setup.) To send mail, however, you must enter the name of a valid SMTP receiving server in your user.r file.

Configuring REBOL is darn simple. Just type **set-user** at the console and answer, at most, six questions. One of these (the second) is:

```
E-mail server name?
```

REBOL is asking for your outgoing mail server. You have a couple of possibilities for obtaining the server name:

✔ If you are on a company local-area network (LAN) as I am, you can input the name of the company mail server. In my case, I use its network address, 198.168.0.1 or its name, *mickey* (your network administrator has the answer for this if you don't know).

✔ You can bypass the company server for sending and go direct to your on-the-Internet server. If you have access to an always-on-the-Net server, that's usually best. If using an Internet server for sending mail, you need to know the exact address. The address is probably something like:

```
mail.some-smtp-server.net
```

Our local mail server just sends and receives mail via dialup once an hour. Many companies have a similar mail server setup.

In these spam or spurious message laden days, SMTP servers normally check where mail is coming from, so you'll need to have authorization to send or relay mail through it. Sources of information for that include your Internet Service Provider (ISP) or local network administrator.

Utilizing separate mail servers

Your receiving and sending e-mail server addresses are also determined in your user.r configuration. Chapter 13 shows you how to configure user.r with the set-user function. You can reconfigure at any time. Look at your own setting as I've done mine below:

```
>> print read %user.r
REBOL [
Title: "User Preferences"
Date:  8-May-2000/11:32:17-4:00
]
set-net [ ralph@abooks.com abooks.com none 198.168.0.1 1080
          socks ]
```

The only two settings concerning mail are the first two in the set-net block. The first, my e-mail address, tells REBOL my POP server, or where my e-mail comes from. The second tells REBOL where to send outgoing mail for relay on to the addressee. In this case, I'm using the same server for both functions. You may have one for incoming and another for outgoing. How? Just rerun set-user and answer the following question with your SMTP server's name *and* your POP server's name:

```
To send e-mail you also need to provide the name of
your e-mail server (such as mail.domain.com). If you
don't know it, check the configuration of your e-mail
program or ask your network administrator.
E-mail server name?
```

Your set-net may then look something like this:

```
set-net [user@domain.com smtp.yoda.dom pop.yoda.dom]
```

Sending data

Data is anything you may send via e-mail — from the company quarterly sales report to Aunt Susie's super-marvelous chocolate chip recipe to "Hey, think the Yankees will get the Series again this year?" Sales are good, Aunt Susie makes a mighty tasty cookie, and as to the Yankees, yeah them bums will probably be in there again this year. What can I say? Forget about it.

Oh. Yeah. Sorry. How do you send e-mail with REBOL? Well, you use the send command, adding some new elements. Table 15-1 has the details.

Table 15-1	Sending Data	
Goal	*Code*	*Example*
Send a string as a message	send *emailaddress* "*message*"	send ralph@abooks.com "Hey, that REBOL FOR DUMMIES, nice book, guy."
Send messages with multiple lines	send *emailaddress* {*message*}	send bill@ shakespear.com { Roses are red, Violets are blue, I code in REBOL, and so do you! }
Send an entire file	send *emailaddress* *filename*	send sam-mcgee@ frozenyukon.org %12-sam.txt

(continued)

Table 15-1 *(continued)*

Goal	Code	Example
Send a variable	Name and enter the information into the variable inside French brackets, and then send *email-address variablename*	```cheeseburger: {"What about a cheeseburger for lunch with cheddar, red onions, extra mayonaise, and BACON! ??? Yeah!"} send lunchorder@ greasydiner.com cheeseburger```
Send mixed elements	Send *emailaddress* join " *firstelementname*" *secondelementname*	```send lunchorder@ greasydiner.com join "Order for Ralph Roberts" cheeseburger```
Send binary data (such as an image or executable file)	send *emailaddress function*/binary *filename*	```send bob@bobs- hangout.com read/binary % compliled.exe```
E-mail the results of REBOL expressions	send *emailaddress function*	```send ralph@ abooks.com read dns://mickey``` or ```send total@ addanddividenumbers. com divide (3 + 5 + 3) 2```

E-mail message content is not restricted to text. You can send other types of REBOL values such as money, dates, and so on — like these:

```
send water-bill-payment@mytown.com $26.00
send appointment@doc-sawbones.com 22-May-2000
```

You can also send some simple formatting commands in your e-mail commands. For example, the ^/ symbol inserts a line break into text generated by REBOL. By adding it in the mixed elements example from Table 15-1, knowing that the first line of each message is used as the subject, you have

```
>> send lunchorder@greasydiner.com join "Order for Ralph
    Roberts^/^/" cheeseburger
```

The result is a nicely formatted message like this:

```
Subject: Order for Ralph Roberts
Order for Ralph Roberts
    What about a cheeseburger for lunch with cheddar
    red onions, extra mayonaise, and BACON! ??? Yeah!
```

Anybody want to guess what I'm having for lunch? Right.

To include a subject line and message along with binary data, type this:

```
send bob@bobs-hangout.com join "Here's your compiled
    code, Bob." [
    newline "Binary file is enclosed" newline
    mold read/binary %compiled.exe
]
```

To make this a self-extracting binary message, here's the code:

```
send bob@bobs-hangout.com join "Here's compiled.exe" [
    newline "REBOL []" newline
    "write/binary %compiled.exe decompress "
    compress read/binary %rebol
]
```

When he gets the e-mail, Bob uses the do function on the body of the message, and the file is saved to his disk.

Working with headers

By default, the first line of any message sent by REBOL is used to fill the Subject header of the e-mail. But you have many more headers available to you. To see what other headers are available, type the following:

```
>> probe system/standard/e-mail
```

You get something like the following:

```
make object! [
    To: none
    CC: none
    BCC: none
    From: none
    Reply-To: none
    Date: none
    Subject: none
    Return-Path: none
    Organization: none
    Message-Id: none
```

```
Comment: none
X-REBOL: {2.2.0.3.1 "The Internet Messaging Language (TM)
        WWW.REBOL.COM"}
MIME-Version: none
Content-Type: none
Content: none
]
```

You can fill in any of these header categories by using the /header refinement to the send function.

You must include the from line or send will not send the message and error out instead.

Here's an example:

```
>> send/header ralph@abooks.com "testing" make
        system/standard/email [from: ralph@abooks.com
        subject: "a unique subject line"]
```

Handling multiple recipients

Sending messages to more than one person is a snap to code in REBOL. Just set up a block of addresses and reference that block with the send function. For example, I'll set up such a block and send a message to all department heads in my company (that'll confuse them):

```
>> company: [ralph@abooks.com pat@abooks.com gayle@abooks.com
        pam@abooks.com vanessa@abooks.com]
>> send company {Test REBOL message
   This is a test message for Chapter 15 of REBOL FOR
        DUMMIES. Please ignore.
   }
```

The first line, Test REBOL message, is the subject — the rest is the body of the message.

Got a file of addresses? No problem, just use the to-block function and they can be sent easily:

```
>> print read %company
ralph@abooks.com pat@abooks.com gayle@abooks.com
        pam@abooks.com vanessa@abooks.com
>> send to-block read %company "Another test"
```

Sending bulk mail

Sending bulk e-mails — that is, a copy of the same message to many recipients — can make you very unpopular very quickly. Use such techniques with care. That said, sending bulk mail is easy to do using REBOL.

If you are e-mailing to a large group, you can reduce the load on your server by addressing everyone in the group, but sending only a single message by using the send/only refinement:

```
send/only company message
```

In this case, each message is not individually addressed. You've seen this mode a lot in some of the bulk e-mail you may have received (and, man, do I get a lot!). Look at the headers and you will find that the e-mail was not even addressed to you. I use this fact later in this chapter (in "Removing messages") to show you how to write a REBOL spam filter.

Again, be careful with bulk mail or the flaming e-mails will roll in. People are sensitive on this subject.

Manipulating E-Mail

Attachments are a potent tool in e-mail. You can send work, fun, music, and pictures with a click of an icon.

Reading and sending attachments

Many attachments are Base-64 encoded and the methods of sending (attaching) and detaching require a little effort to encode and decode. Such techniques are beyond the scope of this book but you can still easily get and use REBOL code for attachments at both rebol.com and rebol.org. Sterling Newton has some excellent sample code for each. Look at attach.r and detach.r by him at rebol.com/userlib.html.

Removing messages

With all the spam and other junk e-mail deluging your mail accounts, you'd probably rather just delete an unread message. You can use REBOL to delete (or erase) mail from the server for that or any other reason.

Removing a single message

First, I'm going to modify my code slightly to provide an easy numbering of the messages:

```
>> count: 0
>> while [not tail? mailbox] [
            count: count + 1
            msg: import-e-mail first mailbox
            print [ count "... "
                          "From: " first msg/from
                          "Subject: " msg/subject
                    ]
            mailbox: next mailbox
        ]
1 ...    From:   abooks@abooks.com Subject:  test
2 ...    From:   ralph@abooks.com Subject:   test
3 ...    From:   ralph@abooks.com Subject:   test
4 ...    From:   ralph@abooks.com Subject:   test
5 ...    From:   ralph@abooks.com Subject:   test
6 ...    From:   ralph@abooks.com Subject:   test
7 ...    From:   ralph@abooks.com Subject:   test of HTML
>> mailbox: open pop://user:pass@yoursite.com
>> count: 0
>> while [not tail? mailbox] [
            count: count + 1
            msg: import-email first mailbox
            print [ count "... "
                          "From: " first msg/from
                          "Subject: " msg/subject
                    ]
            mailbox: next mailbox
        ]
```

REBOL has two function words that you can use to delete e-mail. The `remove` function deletes single messages, while `clear` deletes all messages from the current index to the end of the POP mail account. To remove message number one, type this:

```
remove head mailbox
```

Using `head` makes sure it's the very first message you delete. This removal will not take effect permanently until you do a `close mailbox`. Removing other messages takes a bit more thought, since the index of `mailbox` does not reflect the deletion of the message. You use the `skip` function to accomplish this and the simple formula of $n - 1$, where n is the position of the message to be removed. For example, in deleting the seventh message, you would subtract one from seven and use the following code:

```
remove head skip mailbox 6
```

Use the head function just so you know for sure that you are counting from the first position. Don't forget, changes don't take effect until after you issue a close mailbox function.

One thing you should watch for in doing delete messages is the time limit some ISPs put on how long a mail connection can be active. If your POP session times out before a close mailbox occurs, no change will be effected.

Email Related (New!)		
Web Page Emailer	View It	websend.r
Fetch a web page and send it as email.	1 line	20-May-1999
EMail Setup (for Send)	View It	setemail.r
Minimum set-up for sending email messages from REBOL.	1 line	6-Nov-1997
POP Email Port Spec	View It	popspec.r
POP port specification used to connect to an email server. All of the mail reading examples use this.	7 lines	10-Sep-1999
Email Message Sender	View It	mailsend.r
A very simple way to send an email.	5 lines	10-Sep-1999
Email Group Sender	View It	mailsendgroup.r
A very simple way to send email to a group.	6 lines	10-Sep-1999
Email Headers	View It	mailheader.r
Send email with a custom header.	15 lines	10-Sep-1999
Email Send With CC	View It	mailcc.r
Example of how to include CC addresses on an email header.	13 lines	10-Sep-1999
Email a Web Page	View It	mailpage.r
Send a web page. (simple)	1 line	10-Sep-1999

Figure 15-1:
A library of e-mail related REBOL scripts is located at www.rebol.com/library/library.html.

Removing all messages

To remove all messages, just open your port and use the clear function. The code looks like this:

```
mailbox: open pop://username:password@abooks.com
clear mailbox
close mailbox
```

Setting filters

You know enough now to actually code an e-mail filter. Here's an example from the REBOL Technologies Web site (www.rebol.com):

```
friends: [orson@rebol.com hans@rebol.com]
    messages: read pop://orson:rosebud@mail.yoda.dom
    foreach message messages [
        msg: import-email message
        if find friends first msg/from [
            print [msg/from newline msg/content]
        ]
    ]
close mailbox
```

The friends variable contains the e-mail addresses of friends that you wish to receive e-mail from — and only those messages are allowed through the filter. You can also use a filter to let your friends know their mail was received:

```
foreach message messages [
        msg: import-e-mail message
        if find friends first msg/from [
            send first msg/from "Got your e-mail!"
        ]
    ]
```

Chapter 16

Out on the Web

In This Chapter

▶ Reading Web pages

▶ Monitoring Web pages

▶ Sending Web pages

▶ Building Web pages

*I*n the next three chapters, I talk about that huge and gleaming planet-sized cyberbuilding, the World Wide Web.

This chapter concerns reading the brightly lit signs over entranceways, peeking in the windows, perusing notices stuck to bulletin boards, and all the other stuff blinking and winking and jumping up and down for our attention on the façade of the fabulousity that is the Web. In short, I show you Web pages using REBOL for reading, monitoring, sending, and even constructing Web pages. It's all surface stuff, but it's exceptionally interesting and useful nonetheless.

Reading Web Pages

Web pages are essentially plain text mixed with *tags*, or special instructions enclosed by the less-than (<) and greater-than (>) characters. Your browser recognizes tags and acts on them in various ways resulting in colors, text, and images appearing as you access the Web page. These tags are part of a Web page display language called HTML (HyperText Markup Language). HTML is a hodgepodge of stuff and often a pain to program, but it works, as witnessed by the hundreds of millions of pages now on the Web.

To see what raw HTML looks like, retrieve the rebol.com Web site's main page. Do it like so, placing it into the page word:

```
>> page: read http://rebol.com
```

Then print out this retrieved HTML code by simply typing

```
>> print page
```

And REBOL spews out a bunch of code that looks like this:

```
<!DOCTYPE HTML PUBLIC "-//W3C//DTD HTML 3.2//EN">
<HTML>
<HEAD>
 <META HTTP-EQUIV="Content-Type"
 CONTENT="text/html;CHARSET=iso-8859-1">
 <META NAME="KEYWORDS" CONTENT="programming, scripting,
 distributed, dialect, distributed computing, platform
 independent, internet messaging, rebel, language, smart
 content, smart client">
 <META NAME="Description" CONTENT="REBOL is a powerful
 technology that enables computers, servers, PDAs, and
 TVs to talk to each other through a universal language
 that is simple, flexible, and efficient.">
 <TITLE>REBOL Technologies</TITLE>
</HEAD>    ... ... and so on and so on
```

Not nearly as pretty as viewing it with Internet Explorer or Netscape, huh? But still, it can be very useful to get at this underlying HTML. You can extract all sorts of information from it; you can even use that data to build new Web pages. And REBOL's parse function (that's Chapter 12's time of glory) gives you total dominance over HTML code.

The technology behind Web pages is even more of a hodgepodge than you may believe. The term "explosion in a Slobbodian spaghetti factory" comes to mind. You have lots of HTML pages being coded by hand (with all the non-standardizations that humans come up with) and by a ton of various programs and/or techniques: Perl, Python, PHP, ASP, Cold Fusion, XML, and, of course, REBOL. Just what you need, yet another source of confusion, right? Well, in this case, you *do* need it — REBOL brings some sanity to the profusion, especially in scripting languages.

I mention earlier that REBOL is "Perl without the complication." Well, it's just about everything relating to the Web without complication. You may have seen a lot of it already in this book. Let me show you how easy REBOL handles Web pages.

A similarity between HTML and REBOL (and Perl and PHP and all the rest) bears emphasizing here. They are all script languages and nothing but plain old text files until interpreted. The only difference in a file, to a REBOL or Perl interpreter, is syntax. REBOL interpreters recognize and run REBOL scripts; Perl interpreters recognize and run Perl scripts.

Downloading a Web page

Well, I sorta stole my own thunder in showing you how to download a Web page in the preceding text (and earlier in the book, as well) but I did it in two steps there; I downloaded the page into a REBOL word, and then I printed the word. This is REBOL, so you don't need two steps when one will do. Make sure that your Internet connection is active, and then try this for yourself:

```
>> print read http://rebol.com
```

Want to save the retrieved page to a file? Okay, no problem. Use this bit of code to do that:

```
page: read http://rebol.com
write %rebol.html page
```

Or, in one step, you can do this:

```
write %rebol.html read http://rebol.com
```

"All righty roo," you say, "but when I load that page into me browser, there's no graphics, sport."

Well, maybe you don't say it exactly that way but, yes, what I've shown you above is pretty basic stuff that's on the rebol.com site, and you've probably already seen it a dozen times before. So I'll up the ante a bit and pull the graphics down, too. This gives you the beginnings of an offline reader! First you need to find out what types of graphics files (.gifs and .jpgs mostly) are associated with this page. Knowing the HTML tag for images (<IMG SRC=name of image), I can easily find the names of those on REBOL Technologies home page by typing:

```
b: []
page: read http://rebol.com
parse page [
    any [thru {<img src="}
    copy temp to {"}
    (append b temp)] to end]
foreach graphic b [
    print graphic
    ]
```

You get a list of graphic filenames like this:

```
graphics/home_r1xc1.gif
graphics/contact_r1xc2.gif
graphics/sitemap_r1xc3.gif
graphics/logo_r1xc4.gif
graphics/r_r2xc1.gif
graphics/arch_r2xc2.gif
```

```
graphics/arch_r3xc1.gif
graphics/side_r4xc1.gif
graphics/bottom_r4xc2.gif
graphics/solutions.gif
graphics/solutions2.gif
graphics/news.gif
graphics/developer2.gif
graphics/aboutus.gif
graphics/reb_bar_prop_generic.jpg
graphics/poweredby.gif
```

Isn't parsing wonderful? Makes me want to read Chapter 12 again. Parsing is full of neat techniques, making stuff fall apart so cleanly like that.

You can do all sorts of neat stuff to and with HTML by using REBOL, but it helps to know a little HTML also. You may get a reference like *HTML For Dummies,* published by IDG Books Worldwide, Inc. later on. It helped me some time back.

Okay, looking at the preceding list, you can see that all the graphics go into a graphics subdirectory. No perspiration. You can write a little script to pull that Web page and its associated graphics down to your local directory. In fact, you'll find this script on the included CD as 16-pageget.r. Here's the code:

```
REBOL [
         Title: "Download Web page with graphics"
         Purpose: "Example in REBOL FOR DUMMIES"
         Author: "Ralph Roberts"
         Date: 24-May-2000
         File: %16-pageget.r
         ]
;;; we use rebol.com's homepage as the example ;;;;;;;;
b: []                                    ; block for graphic URLs
;;;;;;; above makes the graphics directory if not there ;;;
if not exists? %graphics/ [make-dir %graphics/]
page: read http://rebol.com  ; get page and save it
write %rebol.html page
parse page [          ; get graphic file names
  any [to {<img src="} thru {"}
  copy temp to {"}
  (append b temp)] to end]
foreach graphic b [                     ; now download graphics
      write/binary to-file graphic read/binary join
          http://rebol.com/ graphic
      ]
```

Watch all the graphic files download, and then look at rebol.html on your local drive with your Web browser, and you see an intact copy of RT's home page with all the graphics. The links won't necessarily work correctly, but that's easy enough to fix.

I know, I know. "So show me how?"

Well, because I love parsing so much, I will. First, take a look at the links:

```
links: []
  parse page [                              ; get links
    any [to {<a href="} thru {"}
    copy temp to {"}
    (append links temp)] to end
        ]
  foreach link links [
        print link
        ]
```

That snippet of code gives you this:

```
http://www.rebol.com
contacts.html
sitemap.html
http://www.rebol.com
http://www.rebol.com
solutions.html
solutions.html
technology.html
technology.html
news.html
news.html
developer.html
developer.html
about.html
about.html
technology.html#Smart%20Content
solutions.html
developer.html
mailto:info@rebol.com
mailto:Webmaster@rebol.com
```

The key to parsing or anything in such manipulation is patterns. You want to fix all the links so that the correct URL executes. You can ignore the `mailto` and `http` links because they are still okay. But all the ones that reference just a page name are now broken because they don't know where to find the page. You need to add `http://rebol.com/` in front of those links. So you now selectively fix links by modifying your last little swatch of code:

```
fix: "http://rebol.com/"
  parse page [                              ; get links
    any [to {<a href="} thru {"}
    mark: copy temp to {"}
        (a: false b: false
    if find temp "http" [a: true]
       if find temp "mail" [b: true]
```

```
        if not a or b = true [insert mark fix]
    )
    ]

    ]
    print ""     ; suppress "false" false
```

In the preceding code, you do a string insert of the word fix whenever you parse out a page link that does not have http or mailto in front of it. A cool feature of parse is the mark: function that lets you mark where you are, copy out the link into the temp variable, and then do a logic test to see whether it needs the fix inserted. You then insert the fix if needed at the mark. Cool. Did I mention that I love parse? I mean I REALLY love parse. You can do almost anything with it.

I said earlier that this is a start to an offline reader. This minimal code gets only one page and its associated graphics. Your mission, should you choose to accept it (okay, so the next *Mission Impossible* movie is playing while I write this) is to figure out how to download an entire Web site. No, I won't show you that because it's getting late and I don't want to take all your fun away. But (hint) now that you have a block of valid links, you can download those pages and their associated graphics. Take a look at Figure 16-1.

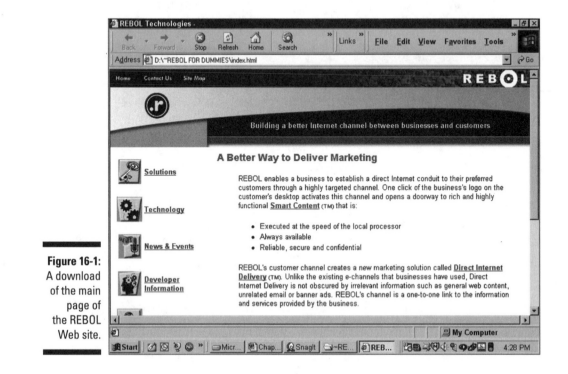

Figure 16-1:
A download of the main page of the REBOL Web site.

Downloading multiple pages

Getting more than one page at a time is easy enough also. Here's one way to retrieve several pages into a block:

```
>> pages: []
>> urls: [http://rebol.com http://abooks.com
          http://booksave.com]
>> foreach url urls [
      append pages read url
      ]
connecting to: rebol.com
connecting to: abooks.com
connecting to: booksave.com
>> print length? pages
3
```

Now you have those three Web pages in the pages block. You can save them to your local drive as HTML files (just add the .html extension to the filename). Then use the code you saw in the preceding section to get all the associated graphics and fix the links.

Hmm. I just gave you another element in putting together your offline reader application, didn't I? Oh, well.

Now, what if you wanted to get all those other pages on the rebol.com site? You've already got a starting point because you generated a list of links earlier in the chapter. Take that list and edit it slightly to get rid of redundancies and the like, and then find these discrete pages referenced (I added the index.html page because I know it's the starting page):

```
index.html
contacts.html
sitemap.html
solutions.html
technology.html
news.html
developer.html
about.html
```

Good . . . now, you get each and every one:

```
>> urls: [
      index.html
      contacts.html
      sitemap.html
      solutions.html
      technology.html
      news.html
      developer.html
      about.html
```

```
    ]
>> foreach url urls [
    write to-file url read join http://rebol.com/ url
    ]
```

Go to your browser again, and access the index.html page on your local hard drive and, sure enough, you can click the links and go from page to page in the site. Because you already downloaded most of the graphics in the preceding exercise, the site looks pretty good and. . . .

Wow! I showed you how to do an offline reader after all, didn't I? Now, just finish it out to make sure that you get all the graphics for each page, and put in some code to keep it from linking to other sites and pulling down those, or it'll turn into a Web spider.

A lot of power is in just a little REBOL code.

Monitoring Web Pages

REBOL offers you many methods of monitoring Web pages and detecting changes in their content, as well as accumulating those changes for your own uses. As I show you in the preceding section, although the HTML source for Web pages initially looks like a jumbled jungle of tags and text (and, for sure, most Web pages are), parsing out the information that you want is almost absurdly easy by using just a few lines of REBOL code.

The word *monitoring* means watching. It can refer to a page that you regularly watch for updates or even a new search for data of use or concern. Next are a few ways of doing that by using REBOL.

Monitoring for updates

One popular activity that you might engage in is monitoring Web pages for updates. If the page covers a subject of interest, you may want to know when additional material is added. As discussed in Chapter 13, checking for changes requires just a little code:

```
>> modified? http://www.rebol.com/
connecting to: www.rebol.com
== 24-May-2000/6:20:51
```

This technique does not work on dynamically generated pages for various reasons, but you may find it very useful for monitoring your own pages.

If the page that you're checking for changes does not return a modification date, you can use the checksum method:

```
>> print checksum read http://abooks.com
connecting to: abooks.com
2183950
```

Keep track of the checksum; when it changes, the page has changed. The REBOL Web site recommends this method.

The following determines whether a page changed since it was last accessed and sends it as e-mail if it did:

```
page: read http://www.rebol.com
page-sum: checksum page
if any [
    not exists? %page-sum.r
    page-sum <> (load %page-sum.r)
][
    print ["Page Changed" now]
    save %page-sum.r page-sum
    send luke@rebol.com page
]
```

You can run such a script periodically to check for changes.

You may want to check a news site for new stories about a company in which you're interested. Maybe you want to follow the current troubles of Microsoft:

```
page: read http://cnn.com
if find page "Microsoft" [write %ms-news.html page]
```

Run that script once a day, and check the page on your local hard drive at your convenience. You can add more if find statements and monitor a wide range of topics.

Of course, to really be complete, you want to look at several pages. Keep reading to find out how to do that.

Monitoring multiple pages

In a more real-world situation, your script needs access to more than one page in order to do comprehensive searches. The following code shows you how to query several sites for mention of your favorite scripting language, REBOL:

```
sites: [
        http://abooks.com
        http://abcnews.com
        http://cbs.com
        http://cnn.com
http://wired.com
          http://www.ddj.com ; dr. dobb's journal :)
            http://nbc.com
        http://rebol.com
        http://shareware.com
        ]
foreach site sites [
        page: read site
if find read site "Rebol" [print site]
        ]
```

You get these results:

```
connecting to: abooks.com
http://abooks.com
connecting to: abcnews.com
connecting to: abcnews.go.com
connecting to: cbs.com
connecting to: cnn.com
connecting to: nbc.com
connecting to: rebol.com
http://rebol.com
connecting to: shareware.com
connecting to: shareware.cnet.com
```

Notice that the ABC News site and the shareware.com site both automatically referred this script to other pages. Interpreting the results, only my abooks.com site and the REBOL Web site mentioned the word *REBOL*. This will change, I am confident, as the REBOLution gains steam.

Let's look at a more sophisticated example of retrieving data from a Web page. This one remotely involves my friend Mike Resnick — the popular Hugo and Nebula award winning science fiction author. Mike's books are becoming increasingly collectible, and I like to add them to my shelves from time to time, when I come across a good buy. So I wrote a REBOL script that searches the mother of all auctions, ebay.com, for any Resnick-related offerings. A good selection is always available.

Two tricks are involved in programming such a script:

  ✔ Get the right search term.

  ✔ Figure out the pattern on the HTML page returned so that you can parse out the data desired.

For the search term, just do a search on eBay as you normally would and then copy the URL from that little window at the top of your browser's screen. For example, I searched for Mike Resnick and found the search term to be this:

```
http://search-
          desc.ebay.com/search/search.dll?MfcISAPICommand=
          GetResult&SortProperty=MetaEndSort&ht=1&query=%22
          Mike+Resnick%22&srchdesc=y
```

Short and sweet. But you don't need to understand what it does. You just cut and paste it into your script.

Now, regarding the pattern on the returned search results Web page, most browsers enable you to view the source of the page. From that, you can figure out a parsing rule that will slice and dice the data right out (refer to Chapter 12 for how those rules are constructed). In this case, use this code to get Mike's books into a readable list (code is on the included CD as 16-resnick.r):

```
REBOL [
    TITLE: "Resnick eBay Search"
    PURPOSE: "Finds Mike Resnick related auction items"
        DATE: 25-May-2000
        FILE: %16-resnick.r
        ]
d: []
a: "http://search-
          desc.ebay.com/search/search.dll?MfcISAPICommand=
          GetResult&SortProperty=MetaEndSort&ht=1&query=%22
          Mike+Resnick%22&srchdesc=y"
b: to-url a
c: read/lines b
print "^/Books and Other Mike Resnick Items at Auction on
          eBay^/"
foreach line c [
        if find line
"http://cgi.ebay.com/aw-cgi/eBayISAPI.dll?ViewItem&item=" [
    parse line [to "<a href" thru ">" copy title to "</a>"]
    print title
    append d title
        ]
]
print [newline length? d " items."]
```

Running this code on May 25 returned the following results:

```
>> do %16-resnick.r
Script: "Resnick eBay Search" (25-May-2000)
connecting to: search-desc.ebay.com
Books and Other Mike Resnick Items at Auction on eBay
Entire year Fantasy & Science Fiction - 1995
lot of SCI FI-Futuristic Space, Other Worlds
```

```
4 pbs by MAX ALLAN COLLINS
TALES FROM GREAT TURTLE '94 Indian Mythology
Fantasy & Science Fiction -Eleven 1988 Issues
Fantasy & Science Fiction - Nine, 1989 Issues
Fantasy & Science Fiction-Nine 1990-91 Issues
Fantasy & Science Fiction-Eleven 94-95 Issues
Fantasy & Science Fiction-Seven Issues 1996
Prophet by Mike Resnick N/M Pb
Purgatory by Mike Resnick N/M Pb
Unusual funny Kennedy book
What Might Have Been Vols 1, 2, 3, & 4 - HBs
'Amazing' SciFi Stories - Five Issues, VG
PULPHOUSE - Weekly Mag - First 8 issues
4 Isaac Asimov Sci Fi Mags Dec 91 - Mar 92
Whatdunits - Mike Resnick, Ed.
MIKE RESNICK,INFERNO,1STEDHB*VF*
          items.
```

The second line from the bottom, `Whatdunits`, is an anthology edited by Mike in which aliens commit the murders in all the stories. I happen to have a story in that book. Cool.

In Chapter 18, I show you how the preceding script is quickly turned into a Web page application giving you the actual link to the item being auctioned.

Sending Web Pages

From time to time, you may want to read a Web page and forward the source to someone else, or even to yourself for later processing. Or you may want to send a formatted HTML message. And maybe, just maybe, you'd like the capacity to send actual Web pages and have them displayed in the e-mail message!

REBOL lets you do all these things. I'll show you how.

Sending a Web page via e-mail

First, sending the HTML source (remember all that jumble of text and tags?) of a Web page via e-mail takes one short line of code:

```
send elvis@hound-dawg.com read http://rebol.com
```

Elvis, having plenty of time these days since his disappearance from the scene, wants to find out about scripting. He can save his e-mail as a text file, rename it to a file with the `.html` extension, and then load it into his browser to read in the proper formatted. But do you think he's really gonna do all that? Not on your blue suede shoes. But you can make it easy for him; you can mail it already formatted.

Most of the newer mail readers these days — such as Microsoft Outlook Express, which is the default on most new Windows computers — can receive and display HTML formatted e-mails. I should warn you that many older mail readers cannot, nor can many of the mail lists to which you may belong, and you can irritate people quickly, because they just receive that jumble of text and tags that is so visually unpleasing. I encourage you to think all this out and use the following technique judiciously. In other words, I accept no responsibility if you get flamed. Sorry.

This is so simple (like any good trick, programming or otherwise). You just need someone to tell you. So I'm telling you.

If you examine an e-mail header, you will see a *Content-Type* setting. Most e-mail messages are regular text, but you can also send them in HTML or even RTF (Rich Text Format). Specifically for HTML, you just change this statement to `Content-Type: text/HTML` and the mail reader (assuming it is so enabled) knows to interpret all the standard HTML tags properly, showing all the colors, text attributes, and so forth that you expect a Web page to show.

In Chapter 15, I show you how to manipulate e-mail headers with REBOL. Use the same technique to include your Content-Type line. Also, as I discuss in Chapter 15, you must be sure to include a From line, or you get an error and the message isn't sent. Use this code to forward an HTML formatted Web page via e-mail:

```
send/header elvis@hound-dawg.com read http://rebol.com make
          system/standard/e-mail [
  from: you@heartbreakhotel.com
  subject: "Yo, Elvis! Check out REBOL, dude!"
  Content-Type: "text/HTML;"
  ]
```

One thing about formatting I should mention here is that the above formatting of text will work inside a script, but at the REBOL console, pressing Enter at the end of the first line causes that line to be executed as is. So input it as one long line. The result is shown in Figure 16-2.

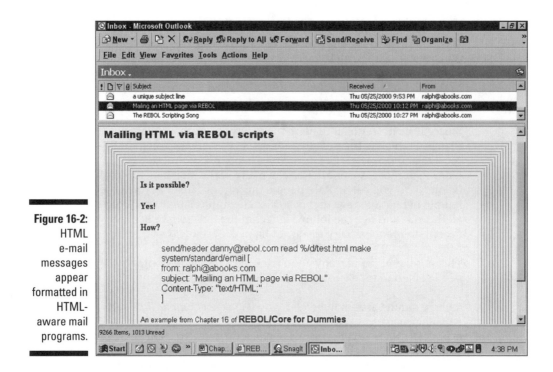

Figure 16-2:
HTML
e-mail
messages
appear
formatted in
HTML-
aware mail
programs.

If you want to send a fancy HTML letter, you can use your regular WYSIWYG (What You See Is What You Get, pronounced WIZ-ee-wig) HTML editor, such as Microsoft's Front Page, save it as an HTML file (it does that automatically), and then send that saved page. You'd use this code to do that:

```
send/header elvis@hound-dawg.com read %letter.html make
        system/standard/e-mail [
    from: you@downatthefootoflonelystreet.com
    subject: "Sing again, Elvis. We miss ya."
    Content-Type: "text/HTML;"
    ]
```

Or, to send it to a list of Elvis fans, you could type

```
elvisfans: [amy@lovemetender.com marvin@bluechristmas.com
        louie@kentuckymoon.net lucinda@woodenheart.com]
send/header elvis-fans read %letter.html make
        system/standard/e-mail [
    from: you@downatthefootoflonelystreet.com
    subject: "I saw Elvis at the supermarket!"
    Content-Type: "text/HTML;"
    ]
```

Now, all the preceding stuff is pretty neato and slick, but what's wrong with this picture? Well, for many of the graphic elements on a Web page that you copy and send via e-mail, the links will be broken and the graphic will not display. This is because you've "moved" the page. If the graphic links are relative, where nothing is given but a local path (as in <img src= "picture.gif">), then you lose the link after moving the page. You can fix this by using the parsing/string manipulation techniques that I showed you early in this chapter (in "Downloading Web pages") and give any relative path graphic an *absolute* path (one that works absolutely anywhere on the Internet) like this: <img src="http://hound-dawg.com/picture.gif". Then the graphic elements display in all their radiant glory . . . or whatever.

Uploading to a Web site

In the following section, I show you how to use REBOL to build Web pages, which it does as niftily as it accomplishes most tasks. After you construct a page, you want to place it on a Web server where everyone can see it.

In addition to e-mail, another way of sending Web pages is the act of moving them from your local computer — where you may have created them — to a Web server on the Internet. By moving them to a server or, as it is often called, *publishing* these pages, you make them accessible to anyone surfing the Web.

By far the majority of Web servers require the use of FTP (File Transfer Protocol) in publishing Web pages. And you must have authorization (a username and password) to access the Web server and transfer your HTML pages to it. You also need to know the directory path into which to transfer the file. This is another kind of absolute address, but one that depends on the file system of the Web server, not an HTTP address.

This is getting a little outside the scope of this book, but if you are working with Web servers, you need to know how relative and absolute paths work. In all the Web application specific forums and mail lists that I read, I've seen the most confusion from newbies to be about paths. You'll have much fewer headaches getting Web applications to run if you understand paths.

Let me give it to you as pithily as I can. In programming for and uploading to Internet and Web servers, you must recognize and use three types of paths, discussed in the following sections.

Accessing Web paths

Web paths have standard URLs such as http://abooks.com/index.html, http://abooks.com/alien/index.html, and http://abooks.com/ alien/alien.gif, which are all relative Web paths. These addresses are accessible through any Web browser or by using REBOL's built-in HTTP protocol as in this snippet:

```
read http://abooks.com
```

Everyone can access a Web path on your server, with no real security.

Running the basepaths

The *basepath* is what a script sees when invoked by a Web page or a call from a Web browser or other HTTP-compatible device. It is not a Web path or a server absolute path, so don't waste hours trying to make it be one like lots of beginning scripters do (me included, years ago).

The basepath simply is the highest directory on the Web server in which you have read/write privileges (consult a Unix or other appropriate reference for more information). All servers differ, and the fastest way to determine this path is to ask your Web host. If your host doesn't know something so important, switch Web hosts.

Let me show you an example, using my company server, `abooks.com`. The Web address is either `http://abooks.com` or `http://www.abooks.com` (I've programmed both to work). This accesses an actual directory on my server, which is `/usr/home/abooks/www/htdocs`. The `index.html` page is in ~/`htdocs`. The highest directory to which I can read or write files is ~/`abooks`. This is my *base* or *Web root* directory.

In Chapter 17, I explain that knowing the base directory or basepath is all important in getting online scripts to work right. Again, your server setup will vary, but the above generally covers all of it. Why is knowing your basepath important?

To use a REBOL script (or Perl or any other type) that is called from the Web, you must first tell the script where to find the program that executes it (REBOL, in this case) and give it a path that it understands so it can read and write files. Think about getting a REBOL script to work online. To be evaluated, the script must invoke REBOL, which then interprets and acts on your code. On my server, REBOL lives in a subdirectory of my Web root directory, so its base address is `/rebol/rebol`, where both the subdirectory and program are named `rebol`.

Scripts themselves are normally in a Web accessible directory with execute permissions (so the script can be run by anyone) called `/cgi-bin`. In my case, to execute a program such as `16-helloWebworld.r` (and feel free to try this, it's actually on the server), enter the URL `http://abooks.com/cgi-bin/16-helloWebworld.r`. This script does it (on the CD, you find it as `16-helloWebworld.r`):

```
#!/rebol/rebol --cgi
REBOL []
print "Content-Type: text/html^/"
print "<h1>Hello, Worldwide Web!</h1>"
print "And here's the script that says so:"
print {
<pre>#!/rebol/rebol --cgi
REBOL []</pre>
```

```
<pre>print &quot;Content-Type: text/html^^/&quot;</pre>
<pre>print &quot;&lt;h1&gt;
Hello, Worldwide Web!&lt;/h1&gt;&quot;</pre>
}
```

You can find more on the construction of CGI scripts in Chapter 18.

Now, turn your concentration back to paths. The URL is a Web-accessible path. Browsers need this path. The basepath is a path that runs a script that is called from the Web. It tells the script where REBOL lives and where to find files. To save a file to my main Web directory, for example, I would place this line in the script:

```
write %/www/htdocs/file.txt data
```

That data, `file.txt`, can now be retrieved with a browser by using the Web address of `http://abooks.com/file.txt`. That's the difference between Web and base addresses.

On my personal Windows computer, I have installed a freeware Sambar server (go to `www.sambar.com`) on the same drive where REBOL lives. That way, I can develop Web scripts locally using `#!/rebol/rebol` to call them. Because my "on the net" server uses the same base address, I just upload the finished scripts and they work without any change. I can also use the same REBOL scripts on the company intranet without change. And that makes things so easy!

Seeing absolutely straight

Okay, I've explained addresses for Web access of a script and the base addresses the script needs if it's called from the Web. But, what if you have a script that is called from the server, such as automatically by a `cron` program on a Unix/Linux machine or just manually while you are logged in via Telnet or sitting at the console?

You now need to understand absolute paths. The absolute path is where a script or other file is located according to the host machine's own file system, not any Web or base-addressing scheme. On my Web server, for example, it means a difference in how the script invokes REBOL (but may not on yours, server configurations vary widely):

```
#!/rebol/rebol --cgi                    ; run from Web
#!/usr/home/abooks/rebol -cgi           ; run from server
```

Reading and saving files are also different paths:

```
write %/www/htdocs/file.txt data                    ; Web
write %/usr/home/abooks/www/htdocs/file.txt data  ; server
```

Keep the differences in paths straight, and you'll have no trouble at all.

Publishing a Web page

Now that you have the concept of paths in your head, you can save Web pages to the right place with confidence. Guess what address you use to FTP a page into the main Web directory coming in from over the Web? Yep, a basepath address.

For me to send a new page to the abooks.com main directory (the home page directory), I need to know that its basepath address is /www/htdocs. I publish a page from the REBOL console using this code:

```
Write ftp://user:password:abooks.com/www/htdocs/page.html
     read %page.html
```

Now you can use REBOL to build some pages to publish.

Building Web Pages

I wish I could tell you that building Web pages by using REBOL was hard and that — thanks to my wondrous talent for explaining things — this section makes it easy for you. But the truth is, building Web pages with REBOL is easy, and it won't take lots of talent on anybody's part for you to understand. And that's great, because it's Friday as I write this and that seems to sap all my abilities (so you should read this section on a Tuesday for maximum value).

Using REBOL to create Web pages

Building Web pages with REBOL does presuppose that you have some knowledge of HTML, the facts of which are beyond the scope and space of this chapter. Still, I'll give you at least some foundation in HTML.

HTML (Hypertext Markup Language), the foundation of all Web pages, relies extensively on tags, or commands like <H1>, <table align="left">, , , and so on. This script constructs a minimal Web page in REBOL (you can find this on the CD as 16-basichtml.r):

```
REBOL [
        TITLE: "Making a Basic HTML Page with REBOL"
        FILE: %16-basichtml.r
        DATE: 26-May-2000
        ]
write %basic.html {
        <HTML><HEAD><TITLE>Making a Basic HTML Page with
           REBOL</TITLE>
        </HEAD><BODY BGCOLOR='YELLOW'>
```

```
          <h2>I am your basic HTML page, it's HTML I am.</h2>
          </BODY></HTML>
          }
```

Constructing a basic Web page is mostly writing HTML to a file. Look at this
little trick to make putting together a Web page less of a hassle for you: See
the braces ({ }) in the code? If you use braces, you can just cut and paste
HTML code from an HTML editor like FrontPage into your REBOL script
between the braces. This also lets you use double quotes (" ") without the
hassle of having to change them to single quotes (' ') in order to avoid confusing REBOL's normal print and write functions.

The value of doing such simple Web pages in REBOL may not be great,
because you can do the same thing about as quickly with any HTML editor.
But when it comes to outputting bunches of data or any repetitive building of
tables and the like, REBOL rules! Figure 16-3 is an example of that, a page of
bunches of nested tables (it's on the CD as 16-nested.r). Please note that
while this example looks fine in my version of Internet Explorer, it may not
look as well in Netscape or other browsers. But I'm not teaching HTML here,
only REBOL.

```
REBOL [
        TITLE: "A Profusion of Nested Tables"
        PURPOSE: "Building HTML pages example"
        DATE: 26-May-2000
        FILE: %16-nested.r
        ]
nester: func [][
        write/append %nested.html "<tr><td>"
        loop 15 [
          write/append %nested.html {<TABLE
            BORDER="1"><tr><td>}
              ]
          write/append %nested.html "<center><b>REBOL
            rules!</center></b>"
        loop 15 [
          write/append %nested.html {</td></tr></table>}
              ]
          write/append %nested.html "</td></tr>"
              ]
write %nested.html {
<HTML><HEAD><TITLE>A Profusion of Nested
            Tables</TITLE></HEAD>
<BODY BGCOLOR="IVORY">
<table border="1" width="33%" align="left">
  <tr>
    <td width="33%">
}
nester nester nester nester
write/append %nested.html {
    </td>
```

```
     </tr>
</table>
<table border="1" width="33%" align="left">
  <tr>
    <td width="100%">
}
nester nester nester nester
write/append %nested.html {
  </td>
  </tr>
</table>
<table border="1" width="33%" align="left">
  <tr>
    <td width="33%">

}
nester nester nester nester
write/append %nested.html {
    </td>
  </tr>
</table>
}
write/append %nested.html {
</BODY></HTML>
}
```

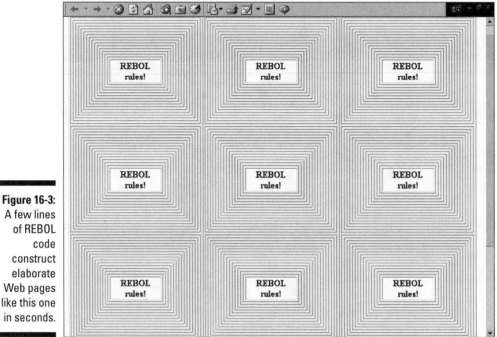

Figure 16-3:
A few lines
of REBOL
code
construct
elaborate
Web pages
like this one
in seconds.

Creating dynamic content

Dynamic content includes items that change often, such as directory listings or news items on your Web site. Here's a way of constructing a page to get a listing of files in your computer's current directory via a Web page (it's on the CD as 16-directory.r):

```
REBOL [
        TITLE: "Making a Directory HTML Page with REBOL"
        FILE: %16-directory.r
        DATE: 26-May-2000
        ]
write %directory.html {
        <HTML><HEAD><TITLE>DIRECTORY PAGE</TITLE>
        </HEAD><BODY BGCOLOR='ivory'>
        <h2>Directory</h2>
        <TABLE border="1">
        }
 files: read %.
foreach file files [
if not dir? file [
        write/append %directory.html reduce [
            <tr><td> file </td>
            <td align="right"> size? file </td>
            <td> modified? file </td></tr>
        ]
    ]
]

write/append %directory.html {
        </table></BODY></HTML>
        }
```

For the preceding code, look at the results by loading directory.html into your browser. If you design Web pages, the speed with which your pages load into a surfer's browser is a concern. It's time to take one of REBOL's example scripts and turn it into a dynamic content Web page (on the CD as 16-timeWebhtml.r).

```
REBOL [
    Title: "Time Downloading Web Pages"
    Date: 27-May-2000
    File: %16-timeWebhtml.r
    Purpose: { Time how long it takes to get each of
           the Web pages listed in a block. }
    Comment: { Based on timeWeb.r (18-December-1997)
from    the REBOL example Library. }
        ]
        write %timeWebs.html {
        <HTML><HEAD><TITLE>DIRECTORY PAGE</TITLE>
        </HEAD><BODY BGCOLOR='ivory'>
        <h3>Some Web Page Download Times & Sizes</h3>
```

```
        <TABLE border="1" CELLPADDING="5">
        }
  sites: [   ; a block of sites
    http://abooks.com
      http://rebol.com
      http://rebol.org
      http://www.ebay.com
      http://www.cnet.com
      http://abcnews.go.com
      http://drudgereport.com
      http://www.php.net
      http://booksave.com
      http://www.bn.com
      http://www.dummies.com ]
times: copy []        ; store times and sizes in this block
      foreach site sites [
          start: now/time
          size: length? read site
          insert tail times now/time - start insert tail times
            size
          ]
          foreach site sites [
          write/append %timeWebs.html reduce [
          <tr><td> first times </td>
          <td> site </td>
          <td> second times </td></tr>
   ]
          times: skip times 2
          ]
write/append %timeWebs.html {
      </table></BODY></HTML>
          }
```

Run the preceding script from your REBOL console by typing do %16-
timeWebhtml.r. Assuming that you are connected to the Internet, you
should see the following:

```
>> do %16-timeWebhtml.r
Script: "Time Downloading Web Pages" (27-May-2000)
connecting to: abooks.com
connecting to: rebol.com
connecting to: rebol.org
connecting to: www.ebay.com
connecting to: abcnews.go.com
connecting to: drudgereport.com
connecting to: www.php.net
connecting to: booksave.com
connecting to: www.bn.com
connecting to: www.dummies.com
```

Fire up your browser, and load the file timeWebs.html. You now see a
table with the download times, the site names, and their sizes, as shown
in Figure 16-4.

DIRECTORY PAGE -
Back Forward Stop Refresh Home Search
Links
File Edit View Favorites Tools
Address D:\~REBOL FOR DUMMIES\timewebs.html
Go
Some Web Page Download Times & Sizes
0:00:14 http://abooks.com 34573
0:00:04 http://rebol.com 7495
0:00:03 http://rebol.org 1331
0:00:06 http://www.ebay.com 39727
0:00:14 http://cnn.com 65364
0:00:09 http://www.cnet.com 44009
0:00:10 http://abcnews.go.com 56304
0:00:05 http://drudgereport.com 22354
0:00:05 http://www.php.net 13035
0:00:07 http://booksave.com 14081
0:00:08 http://www.bn.com 46196
Done
My Computer
Start
Chap...
Inbo...
SnagIt
~RE...
DIRE...
5:03 PM

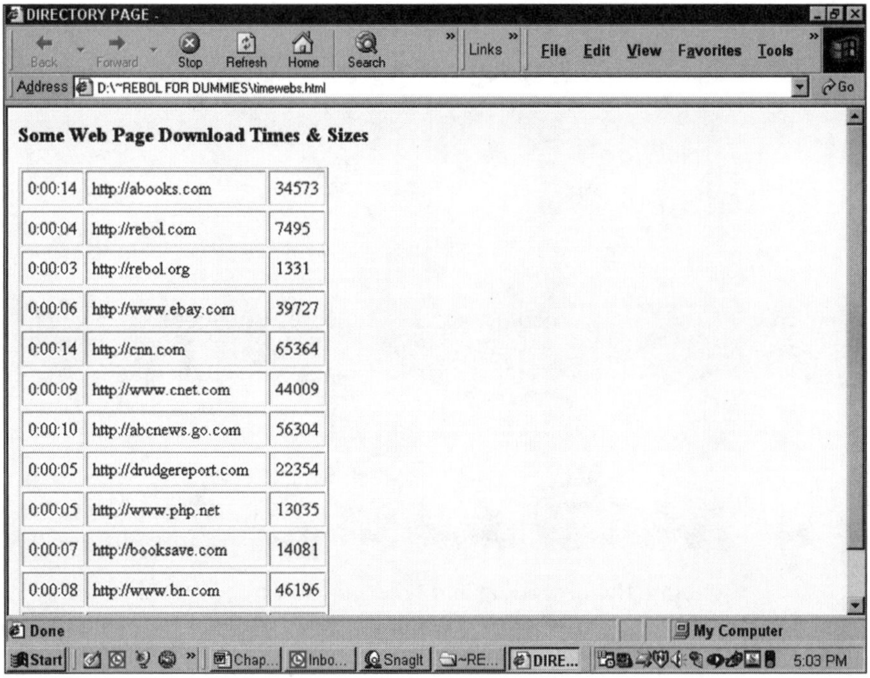

Figure 16-4: REBOL gives you accurate timing and useful information.

Now I give you a final example of dynamic content. As I write this, it's late at night on a Friday night (my dedication knows no bounds as my deadline approaches). Perhaps I am somewhat punch-drunk from the weariness of a long day furiously typing in words and coding examples (remember, you never see the ones that don't work<g>). Possibly all this explains why I now come up with The REBOL Scripting Song, based somewhat loosely on that hoary old drinking song, *99 Bottles of Beer on the Wall.*

This example shows how just a few lines of REBOL can generate a large amount of information for a Web site. This script is on the included CD as `16-col.r`:

```
REBOL [
TITLE: "The REBOL Scripting Song"
AUTHOR: "Ralph Roberts"
DATE: 23-May-2000
FILE: %16-col.r
]
write %col.html {
    <html><head><title>Columns</title>
    </head><body bgcolor='ivory'>
}
write/append %col.html {
    <h1>The REBOL Scripting Song</h1><br>
}
```

```
count: 100
loop 5  [
write/append %col.html [
        <table align="left" width="20%" border="1">
     ]
loop 20 [
    if count > 0 [count: count - 1]
    if count = 0 [count: 99]
write/append %col.html reduce [
        <tr><td><font size="2">
        count " scripts of REBOL code, "
        count " scripts of REBOL code! "
        " Take one down and evaluate it, "
        count - 1 " scripts of REBOL code! "
        </td></tr>
     ]
        ]
    write/append %col.html "</table>"
     ]
write/append %col.html "</body></html>"
```

Generate the preceding and take a look at it in your browser by loading the page col.htm, as shown in Figure 16-5. You must now sing the song several times before continuing.

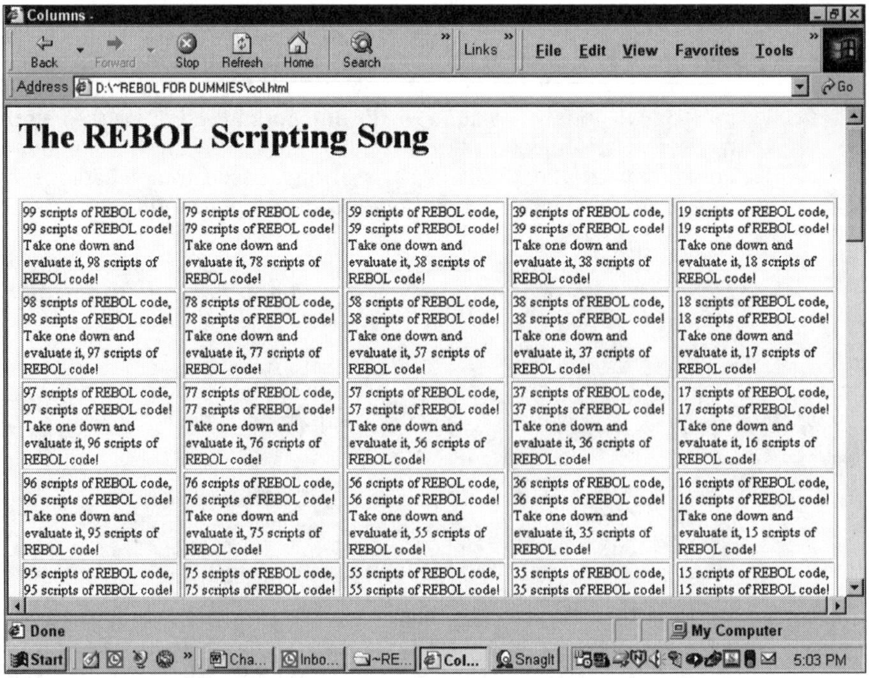

Figure 16-5:
This is The REBOL Scripting Song as generated by 16-col.r.

Using REBOL/Core for generating Web pages with dynamic content has tremendous potential. I'm sure by now a good many concepts that you want to try are buzzing around in your head, as some are in mine. This area alone can be a book of its own.

Enabling automatic updating

A way of generating automatic updating of Web sites is to have a `cron` program (as is found on Unix/Linux servers) or some other automatic means read a text file. For this example, sell off some used computer equipment. You prepare a listing each week as a tab-delimited text file to the pattern `item tab description tab price`, such as this (on the CD, this code is in `16-computersales.txt`):

```
Monitor 17 inch  flat screen      $200.00
Computer         133Mhz Pentium   $100.00
Hard drive       1 gigabyte SCSI  $75.00
Speakers         lots of bass!    $25.00
Keyboard         has all letters  $5.00
Computer         600Mhz, 20 GB HD         $500.00
REBOL book       REBOL For Dummies, the best!      $24.95
```

This automatically invoked REBOL script that dynamically builds the Web page from the text file, which can contain thousands of lines of items, can be as minimal as this one (on the CD as `16-computersales.r`):

```
REBOL [
        TITLE: "Computer Sales Page via REBOL"
        FILE: %16-computersales.r
        DATE: 26-May-2000
        ]
write %forsale.html {
        <HTML><HEAD><TITLE>DIRECTORY PAGE</TITLE>
        </HEAD><BODY BGCOLOR='ivory'>
        <h2>Directory</h2>
        <TABLE border="1" cellpadding="5">
        }
items: sort read/lines %16-computersales.txt
foreach item items [
line: parse/all item "^-"
write/append %forsale.html reduce [
        <tr>
        <td> line/1 </td>
        <td> line/2 </td>
        <td> line/3 </td>
        </tr>
    ]
]
write/append %forsale.html {
        </table></BODY></HTML>
        }
```

Yes, building dynamic content HTML Web pages is yet another of the many areas in which REBOL shines. Expand on the techniques I've shown you in this chapter because they'll give you a great start on your quest to master the Web.

Part VI
REBOL Victories

The 5th Wave   By Rich Tennant

"You ever get the feeling this project could just up and die at any moment?"

In this part . . .

By this point, you will be chomping at the old computer bit and ready to move into more sophisticated areas. And you will!

Chapter 17

To Server and Protect

- -

In This Chapter
▶ Using REBOL for server applications

▶ Putting REBOL on your server

▶ Knowing a good server applications when you see it

- -

Yes, down here in the planet-wide, well-lit, but comfy and dry basement of the Internet, where people seldom go, you see rank after rank of servers stretching as far as the eye can see. Millions of servers are all tied together in the greatest intercommunication network in the history of humanity, and that network is growing at a truly prodigious rate.

The Internet physically is an often-anarchic collection of connections comprising many hundreds of thousands of local-area networks (LANs) located all over the world. These LANs are all tied together by several wide-area networks (WANs) or, in Internet parlance, *backbones* — a backbone being an ultra-high-speed data lines or satellite links.

No one knows for sure, but some experts claim that the Internet — this multitude of interconnected networks of computers — has as many as 500 million users worldwide and continues to grow like crazy. Thousands of colleges and universities are connected to the network, as are government agencies of many countries. Also connected are all sorts of commercial companies, institutions of all types (schools, churches, associations, clubs, and so on), and tens (probably now, hundreds) of millions of private individuals. The Internet is one of the most important computer networks in the world, in addition to being the largest. by several orders of magnitude.

And every bit of it is controlled by servers. A *server* is nothing more than a computer that does *something* for people or other computers. That *something* could be

- ✔ Receiving your modem call and connecting you to the Net (a *dial-up* server)

- ✔ Relaying your e-mail message (an *e-mail* server)

- ✔ Hosting a site on the World Wide Web (a *Web* server)

✔ Sending and receiving files (an *FTP* server)

✔ Providing a safe connection to the Internet (a *proxy* and/or *firewall* server)

Often, a computer is really several servers at once because it simultaneously performs several tasks.

Server hardware — the actual computer itself — can be a multi-CPU, multi-million dollar honker (heavy iron, indeed), or just a cheap old PC faithfully whirring away. Lots of now-ancient (in Internet years) 486 boxes are still out in the cybernetic hinterlands running net applications under Linux, FreeBSD, and other "freeware" operating systems. Plenty of Windows 95/98 machines double as servers, also. And Macintoshes, Amigas — you name it — all are being used as servers. Even your own desktop machine can be a server (more about that in this chapter).

Using REBOL for Server Applications

REBOL, because it runs on so many different platforms, is an ideal language in which to develop server applications. Server applications may be defined as little scripts that make administering a server — be it a local network or on the Internet — much less of a pain than it can be. These scripts include tasks such as:

✔ Monitoring the size of log files

✔ Analyzing those files for traffic patterns (who's hitting your server, and what they do there)

✔ Creating automatic backups

✔ Sending reports to yourself or others automatically via e-mail

✔ Cleaning off unused files

✔ Managing directories and subdirectories

Scripts that I write and test on my Windows 98 desktop running a Sambar server (it's free at `www.sambar.com`) run without change on my company's Web server under its BSDI Unix operating system. Or, for that matter, those scripts would run on a Mac, Amiga, Sun, or any other computer with a copy of REBOL on it. This will work just as well for you.

Most servers on the Internet are still Unix-based, or at least Unix-workalikes, such as Linux. Despite the inroads made by Windows NT and now Windows 2000, the predominance of Unix-like servers will continue for a long time. Thanks to the exploding popularity of Linux, this preponderance will even grow. If you grew up on DOS- and Windows-based machines — or Amiga or Macintosh — the ins and outs of Unix may be foreign to you. Unix is definitely what I've long called an "expert-friendly" language.

But, oh yes, here's the good news! Although knowing some Unix is necessary, you can do most of your server administration easily in something you are, by this point, becoming rather expert in now yourself — REBOL. With REBOL, you have two basic methods of taming a server:

✔ Install it on the server and do things from the console.

✔ Write scripts on your local machine that you can transfer to the server (or just have those scripts do things to the server while still running on your desktop computer).

My company's Web server is located off-premises. A good ways off-premises, actually, because we are in North Carolina, and the server is in rainy Seattle, Washington. Yet, I can log into the server via a Telnet program and start REBOL, and the console works just the way it does on my computer at the office. For example, I can type this upgrade code:

```
>> upgrade
connecting to: www.rebol.com
Script: "Download Current Version" (15-Nov-
        1999/16:40:23-8:00)
Your copy of BSDi iX86 REBOL/Core 2.2.0.6.1 is currently up-
        to-date.
```

I see what operating system the server runs (BSDI is a type of Unix). I can now do anything with REBOL on the distant server that I could do from the console on my local Windows box. For example, I can get a directory listing:

```
>> print read %.
feedback.r nntp.r notes.html rebdoc.r rebol rebol.r
setup.html myuser.r user.r rebdoc.html bulklister.r
civil.txt rebol061.tar copy us.txt
```

Or I can check my e-mail (using the little mail function I show you in Chapter 15):

```
>> mail
connecting to: abooks.com
You have 1 messages.
1 ..  New Madison County, NC Query Forum Post
                gc-notice@genconnect.rootsWeb.com
```

Is all this server manipulation stuff in REBOL useful? You better believe it is! It's mightily useful. Just take a look at this!

Running on many platforms

As I write this chapter, REBOL runs on 37 different platforms. No matter what your server is, or what server you might later move your Web site to, or what server you gain access to, chances are exceptionally good that a version of REBOL will run on it. This means that your scripts are truly portable from operating system to operating system. You may know nothing about Unix, but now you can write scripts that run elegantly and efficiently on those computers. Or Macs or . . . well, you name it.

Right now, you can get (for free!) versions of REBOL that run flawlessly on such computers and/or operating systems as

- ✔ Amiga
- ✔ BeOS
- ✔ BSD
- ✔ Free BSD
- ✔ HP-UX
- ✔ IBM (AIX, OS/2, and OS/400)
- ✔ Linux (on several platforms)
- ✔ Macintosh
- ✔ Microsoft (95/98/NT/2000)
- ✔ Novell NetWare
- ✔ QNX
- ✔ Psion
- ✔ SCO (SCO Unix and Open Server)
- ✔ SGI IRIX
- ✔ Sun Solaris and Sparc

It truly is simple. Run on one; run on many.

Developing applications on your computer

If you *are* writing server and CGI/Web applications (more on CGI coming up in Chapter 18), turning your local machine into a server saves you lots of development time. Thanks to the universal portability of REBOL code, you can write and test your scripts locally and then upload to the server. Then you can go "live" on the Net without embarrassment or risk of losing data.

The local server doesn't even have to really do any "serving," or you can use it as a server on your local area network for quite a bit of useful stuff. After you master REBOL scripting (and you should agree by now, that does not take long) you can add countless numbers of little scripts. Even in a home network of just one or two computers, this is all true. Servers are just plain convenient for all sorts of reasons.

So how do you get a server?

You may already have one. Windows 95/98 comes with PWS (Personal Web Server). If it is not already installed on your system, go to Control Panel, click Add/Remove Programs, click the Windows Setup tab, and then click Internet Tools. Make sure that a check is in the check box to install PWS. However, in my opinion, PWS is too much of a pain. I suggest a nice free server, Sambar (`www.sambar.com`). Sambar is powerful, is easy to install, and has a good, helpful e-mail support group. Our company LAN uses several Sambar servers now all running both REBOL and PHP (a great HTML preprocessor).

Windows NT and 2000 servers can run the Internet Information Server (IIS). Consult your manuals for installation and configuration.

If you are fortunate enough to have a Unix or Linux box on the premises, then you should use an Apache server. (I'm setting up a Linux machine to handle many of our company functions, such as data warehousing and so forth.) Don't mess with anything other than an Apache for a Linux machine.

Other systems have various server software available as well.

Putting REBOL on Your Server

Installing REBOL to run under whatever server software you wind up with is as simple as obtaining the right version of REBOL.

Obtaining the right version

The first place to look is the on the CD-ROM that is included with this book. As I write this book, REBOL/Core comes in 37 flavors. You may be able to get started immediately without downloading anything from the Internet. All the more popular operating systems and hardware are covered.

If you decide to visit `rebol.com` and make sure that you have the very latest version (because books have a little lead time and an update may have been posted), don't expect to spend much download time. All current versions of

REBOL run around 200K. That's a very brief download time — a couple of minutes or so at most on a slow night, and far less with an ADSL or cable connection. That's blink-of-an-eye speed.

Even if you do want the most recent version, consider installing what's on the CD-ROM. After you have REBOL running and your network setup is completed, just go to the REBOL console and type the command function upgrade and press the Enter key. This is what you see in return:

```
>> upgrade
connecting to: www.rebol.com
Script: "Download Current Version" (15-Nov-
        1999/16:40:23-8:00)
Your copy of Windows 95/98/NT iX86 REBOL/Core 2.2.0.3.1 is
        currently up-to-date.
>>
```

If a more recent version is available, REBOL downloads it to the current working directory in pretty much in the same blink-of-an-eye time frame I mention earlier. The downloaded file is a compressed archive. See the appendix for information on installing from the archived file.

By this time in the book, I'm sure you have REBOL running quite well on your desktop machine. Certainly that's so if you've been following all the examples on your console. But what about installing REBOL on your server, assuming that the server is some remote computer, such as a Web server?

Installing on the server

Gee, I wish I could tell you how complicated it is to install REBOL on your server and expend a few thousand words (for which I would get nicely paid), but it just, as they say, *ain't* that hard.

Sure, someone says "software installation," and you immediately think of installation programs spewing bunches of files from some sort of monstrous archive format into all sorts of nooks and crannies on you computer's hard drive. REBOL just is not like that! You merely create a rebol directory on the server (or your home computer) and unzip, untar, unsit (whatever flavor archiving software your operating system uses) about 200K of files. The only ones that matter for operation are the *rebol* binary, *rebol.r,* and user.r.

That alone is REBOLutionary!

More information on installation, if you need it, is available in the appendix.

The hardest thing you have to do is figure out exactly what the server's operating system is; ask the system administrator. Problem solved.

Configuring REBOL on your server

Configuring REBOL is accomplished using the `set-user` function, just like you did for your desktop system. You'll need to answer the same six questions or so.

Do you see the magic yet? Nice, indeed.

Using REBOL on your server

Finally, you use REBOL on a server in the same two ways as you do on your local computer. Assuming that you have physical access or remote access via a Telnet program, you can use REBOL from the console just like on your desktop. More likely, you'll be writing scripts on your local machine and transferring them to the server to perform various tasks. So, without further ado, look at some good server applications for REBOL.

What's a Good Server Application?

Obtaining an Internet server, especially a Web server, is becoming easier and easier. For just a few dollars a month, you can have your own domain name and a server that you can manipulate to make your Web pages sizzle with interactive power. Also, you can sometimes get Web space at no charge from companies that provide this service in return for advertising on your site.

Free sites are often restricted. To use REBOL effectively, you need the freedom to run CGI programs (which REBOL scripts can be) and some sort of access besides through a browser for maintenance purposes. You need at least FTP access — you use the FTP protocol to transfer scripts to the server and run them. Far better is full *Telnet* access. This allows you command-line access to the server and far more control.

With a little effort, you can find a Web host that gives you reasonable access. For the past five years, my company has had a server with `vservers.com`. We run more than 25 domain names on it and have full Telnet access. I recommend them. Don't settle for restrictions that aren't necessary. Some of the server stuff explained later in this chapter either requires or is certainly easier with direct or Telnet/remote login access.

Monitoring logs

What are the largest files on many, many servers? Yep, the log files. Every time your server does something, such as serve up a hit while wearing its

Web server hat, the salient facts are entered in a text file called a *log*. Logs can grow like crazy without you ever realizing it. Take my company Web server, for example. Because we serve up more than 100,000 hits per month now, we have well over 100,000 lines of text added to the log files — sometimes more, because more than one log often receives entries. Very soon, those often-overlooked log files are up to tens or hundreds of megabytes (MB), and the server is choking as it runs out of disk space.

The directory structure and names of these log files vary widely depending on your flavor of server. Our company server, again, runs BSDI Unix. It happens to have Apache Web server software, which is very popular these days. You need to figure out where your server's log files are and under what assumed names they hide, but I know that mine live in the /www/logs directory. Connecting to the server via Telnet, going to that directory, and doing a Unix list command (ls -l), I see the following logs:

```
abooks: {2} % ls -l
total 20819
9719915 May 30 09:29 access_log
4920659 May 30 09:30 agent_log
0 May 18 21:48 cipher_log
71457 May 30 09:28 error_log
5911162 May 30 09:30 referrer_log
2146 May 30 01:17 tmp_err_log
```

✔ Access logs show what was done (usually downloads of pages and graphics files for Web page views).

✔ Agent logs tell who did the action.

✔ Error logs show errors — stuff that went wrong or page views that bombed out. (You probably need to check and fix these errors on your site.)

✔ Referrer logs show where the agents came from.

I now show you two ways to check your logs, starting with the hard one first. I assume that you do not have a site with Telnet privileges, but that you still want to check logs. You do this using FTP. And, because log files are often very long, you use a method that allows the manipulations of files larger than memory. (Try this on your own logs; I'm not giving out my *real* username and password . . . at least, I *hope* I took it out!) Here's the code I use:

```
>> access: open/direct/read/lines
          ftp://user:password@abooks.com/www/logs/access_log
```

The preceding code (>> access: . . . access_log) is all one continuous line. From the REBOL console, typing a return after the open function causes an error.

Now, I print the first line to see when the first access was (these logs get so large that I delete them about once every two months):

```
>> print first access
207.59.117.81 - - [12/May/2000:08:38:53 -0400] "GET /cgi-
        bin/sizepostcard.r HTTP/1.0" 200 30467
```

Ummm, hmmm. So this access log started on May 12, and I'm looking at this on May 30. Gee, I'd sure like to know how many accesses that is, but I can't just use *print length? access* because I have a port open, not the entire whale-sized file. Here's how it's done:

```
downloads: 0
while [ (pick access 1 ) <> none ] [downloads: downloads + 1 ]
print downloads
109125
```

Over a regular dial-up connection, this can take awhile. In Chapter 18, I show you how to do this and have it output to a Web page for ease of use. In checking my log monitoring script (below), you see why it takes so long using FTP over a dial-up connection — the access log is almost 10MB in size and 109,125 lines long. To count these lines and get the number of accesses (one per line), every line has to be read, and that takes a while.

```
Abooks Logs
        109125 accesses
        89787 refers
referrer_log . . . . . . . . . . . . . . . . . . 6022482
agent_log . . . . . . . . . . . . . . . . . . . . 5011050
access_log . . . . . . . . . . . . . . . . . . . 9880494
```

Now it's time to analyze these logs.

Analyzing logs

Analyzing logs from the server is much better and faster. In this case, you need to know the absolute path to the server log directory if you have an automatic program like *cron* run the script, or if you run it manually via Telnet or direct login. To use it from your browser, you need to know the relative Web path.

Following is a quick log checker for my Apache servers. The script is placed in my *cgi-bin* directory (for Web applications) and is started by calling it from my Web browser using abooks.com/cgi-bin/logs.r, as shown in Figure 17-1. (If you want to try it, fine; but I don't guarantee it will stay there if it's generating lots of traffic and tying up my site). Here's the script:

```
#!/rebol/rebol -cs
REBOL [
]
print "Content-Type: text/html^/"
change-dir %/www/logs
downloads: 0
refers: 0
accesslog: open/direct/read/lines %access_log
while [ ( pick accesslog 1 ) <> none ] [downloads: downloads
        + 1 ]
close accesslog
referlog: open/direct/read/lines %referer_log
while [ (pick referlog 1 ) <> none ] [
   refers: refers + 1
   ]
close referlog
print rejoin [
   {<b>Abooks Logs</b><hr><br>}
   {Access log has } downloads { accesses }
   size? %access_log { bytes<br><br>}
   {Referral log has } refers { refers and is }
   size? %referer_log { bytes<hr>}
   {<center>REBOL program (c)2000 Ralph Roberts}
   {</center>}
]
print "</body><html>"
```

Figure 17-1:
Running
abooks.
com/
cgi-bin/
logs.r
gives me
this result.

The preceding code finds only the number of hits and the size of the log files. If you wanted a more detailed analysis, you can read each line of the log file. The trick, again, is to open it as a file larger than memory because it almost certainly will be large eventually. You then can print out information. Your first step is to find out how long the log is:

```
accesslog: open/direct/read/lines %access_log
while [ ( pick accesslog 1 ) <> none ] [downloads: downloads
          + 1 ]
close accesslog
```

The number of lines in the file is now in the *downloads* word. Now, just reopen the file to print out a certain number of lines, such as the last 20, as is done with this snippet of code:

```
accesslog: open/direct/read/lines %access_log
count: 0
while [ ( line: pick accesslog 1 ) <> none ]
          [
             count: count + 1
      if count > (downloads - 20) [print line
          ]
          ]
close accesslog
```

And this gives you a result like the following (which shows the IP of the person hitting the site, the date, and what was downloaded):

```
208.31.100.71 - - [30/May/2000:15:07:48 -0400] "GET/
          page9.html HTTP/1.0" 200 5185
212.10.24.240 - - [30/May/2000:15:07:48 -0400] "GET/
          ebay/feb-1r.jpg HTTP/1.0" 200 25292
208.31.100.71 - - [30/May/2000:15:07:49 -0400] "GET/
          img24.gif HTTP/1.0" 200 1216
208.31.100.71 - - [30/May/2000:15:07:49 -0400] "GET/
          img23.gif HTTP/1.0" 200 5910
208.31.100.71 - - [30/May/2000:15:07:49 -0400] "GET/
          img22.gif HTTP/1.0" 200 5698
208.31.100.71 - - [30/May/2000:15:08:13 -0400] "GET/
          page2.html HTTP/1.0" 200 6969
208.31.100.71 - - [30/May/2000:15:08:14 -0400] "GET /img5.gif
          HTTP/1.0" 200 1753
208.31.100.71 - - [30/May/2000:15:08:14 -0400] "GET /img6.jpg
          HTTP/1.0" 200 11240
208.31.100.71 - - [30/May/2000:15:08:14 -0400] "GET /img8.gif
          HTTP/1.0" 200 15647
152.163.197.199 - - [30/May/2000:15:08:17 -0400] "POST/
          linklaunch.cgi HTTP/1.0" 302 248
208.31.100.71 - - [30/May/2000:15:08:29 -0400] "GET/
          page8.html HTTP/1.0" 200 7739
208.31.100.71 - - [30/May/2000:15:08:30 -0400] "GET/
          img20.gif HTTP/1.0" 200 2066
```

```
208.31.100.71 - - [30/May/2000:15:08:30 -0400] "GET/
      img21.gif HTTP/1.0" 200 1217
208.31.100.71 - - [30/May/2000:15:08:30 -0400] "GET /ebay.gif
      HTTP/1.0" 200 1075
152.163.197.199 - - [30/May/2000:15:08:45 -0400] "POST/
      linklaunch.cgi HTTP/1.0" 302 252
152.163.197.199 - - [30/May/2000:15:09:19 -0400] "POST/
      linklaunch.cgi HTTP/1.0" 302 246
206.132.186.140 - - [30/May/2000:15:09:26 -0400] "GET /cgi-
      bin/auction.cgi?childrens&952637151 HTTP/1.0" 200
      33764
152.163.197.199 - - [30/May/2000:15:09:39 -0400] "POST/
      linklaunch.cgi HTTP/1.0" 302 250
206.132.186.131 - - [30/May/2000:15:09:50 -0400] "GET /larry
      HTTP/1.0" 404 199
152.163.197.199 - - [30/May/2000:15:10:03 -0400] "POST/
      linklaunch.cgi HTTP/1.0" 302 244
```

This is raw data from the log file in Apache's format. Your log format may vary, but after you have its pattern, you can use REBOL's parse function to pull stuff out as part of your analysis. Looking at the preceding log snippet, I see (fourth line from the bottom) a hit on one of my *auction.cgi* programs. It would be nice to know how many times my auctions are being hit, so I can just whip up a quick code modification to find out. Only one extra line is needed:

```
accesslog: open/direct/read/lines %access_log
auctions: 0
while [ ( line: pick accesslog 1 ) <> none ] [
if find line "auction.cgi" [auctions: auctions + 1]
    ]
```

This works well — so well, in fact, that I just made it a part of my permanent log analyzing script. The if find statement increments the count in the auctions word whenever it encounters an auction.cgi call in a log line. Using this technique, you can mine your own server logs for such significant statistics, as shown in Figure 17-2.

```
 ←  ·  →  ·  ⊗  🖹  🏠  Q  🖼  💿  🖹  🖨  🖹  ·  🖹  ❓                              ▦  –  &  ×

Downloads
129.170.116.175 - - [31/May/2000:12:39:34 -0400] "GET /kilroy.gif HTTP/1.0" 200 22044
198.151.12.20 - - [31/May/2000:12:40:31 -0400] "GET /ebay/aldrinb.jpg HTTP/1.0" 200 14278
207.59.117.93 - - [31/May/2000:12:40:32 -0400] "GET /cgi-bin/log.r HTTP/1.0" 404 207
206.132.186.140 - - [31/May/2000:12:40:39 -0400] "GET /cgi-bin/auction.cgi?fiction&951722355 HTTP
207.59.117.93 - - [31/May/2000:12:41:07 -0400] "GET /cgi-bin/logs.r HTTP/1.0" 200 207
12.15.16.100 - - [31/May/2000:12:41:30 -0400] "GET /alien HTTP/1.0" 301 228
12.15.16.100 - - [31/May/2000:12:41:32 -0400] "GET /alien/ HTTP/1.0" 200 27467
12.15.16.100 - - [31/May/2000:12:41:32 -0400] "GET /alien/alien.gif HTTP/1.0" 200 6136
12.15.16.100 - - [31/May/2000:12:41:32 -0400] "GET /ellicott.gif HTTP/1.0" 200 5867
12.15.16.100 - - [31/May/2000:12:41:33 -0400] "GET /a-banner.gif HTTP/1.0" 200 10156
12.15.16.100 - - [31/May/2000:12:41:34 -0400] "GET /alien/rebol.gif HTTP/1.0" 200 2933
12.15.16.100 - - [31/May/2000:12:41:34 -0400] "GET /paperback.jpg HTTP/1.0" 200 10301
199.164.68.1 - - [31/May/2000:12:41:49 -0400] "GET /ebay/feb-1r.jpg HTTP/1.0" 200 25292
208.51.133.18 - - [31/May/2000:12:42:06 -0400] "GET /ebay/stephonsonr.jpg HTTP/1.0" 200 24795
205.188.208.172 - - [31/May/2000:12:42:27 -0400] "GET /ebay/winfreyo.jpg HTTP/1.0" 200 18626
199.164.68.1 - - [31/May/2000:12:42:32 -0400] "GET /ebay/mar-14jj.jpg HTTP/1.0" 200 23735
172.131.45.126 - - [31/May/2000:12:43:02 -0400] "GET /ebay/may31-1.jpg HTTP/1.1" 200 23887
209.206.16.184 - - [31/May/2000:12:43:02 -0400] "GET /ebay/MH6.jpg HTTP/1.0" 200 24525
172.131.45.126 - - [31/May/2000:12:43:46 -0400] "GET /ebay/may31-1.jpg HTTP/1.1" 304 -
194.129.108.70 - - [31/May/2000:12:43:55 -0400] "GET /ebay/aldrinb.jpg HTTP/1.1" 200 14278
12.27.0.137 - - [31/May/2000:12:45:04 -0400] "GET /ebay/MH38.jpg HTTP/1.1" 200 13877

Page Refers
http://www.cheznims.com/norway_trip/day_three/index.html -> /norway_trip/day_three/tn_zdsc00010_j
http://www.cheznims.com/norway_trip/day_three/index.html -> /norway_trip/day_three/tn_zdsc00012_j
http://www.cheznims.com/norway_trip/day_three/index.html -> /norway_trip/day_three/tn_dsc00016_jp
http://www.cheznims.com/norway_trip/day_three/index.html -> /norway_trip/day_three/tn_zdsc00025_j
http://cgi.ebay.com/aw-cgi/eBayISAPI.dll?ViewItem&item=342437580 -> /ebay/cat.jpg
http://cgi.ebay.com/aw-cgi/eBayISAPI.dll?ViewItem&item=342437580 -> /kilroy.gif
http://cgi.ebay.com/aw-cgi/eBayISAPI.dll?ViewItem&item=340848032 -> /ebay/aldrinb.jpg
http://www.rebol.org/cgi-bin/cgiwrap/rebol/add-link.r -> /alien
http://www.rebol.org/cgi-bin/cgiwrap/rebol/add-link.r -> /alien/index.html
http://abooks.com/alien/ -> /alien/alien.gif
```

Figure 17-2:
I check our
server logs
from time to
time using
a REBOL
script.

Whenever you place a script or other executable file on a Unix or Linux system, you must set the *file permissions* for it to work, as shown in Figure 17-3. Some FTP programs allow this, or you can do it from REBOL (refer to Chapter 9), or do a *chmod 755 filename.r* from the command prompt on your system, which allows other users to run the file without being able to modify it. Basically, the permissions that you set should allow: everyone to *read* the file; everyone to *execute* the file; but only the owner (you) to *write* the file.

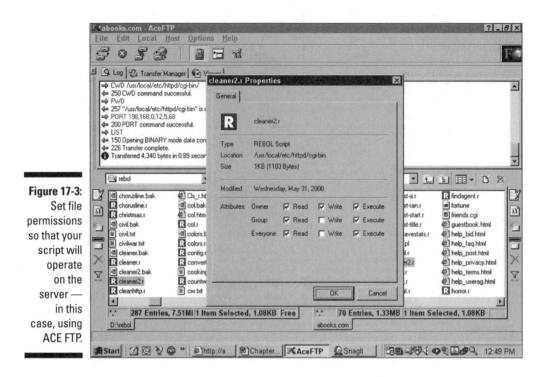

Figure 17-3:
Set file
permissions
so that your
script will
operate
on the
server —
in this
case, using
ACE FTP.

Doing things automatically

Any REBOL script that you write for your server can be run automatically
at selected intervals — once a day, once a week, once a month, on your
birthday, or whenever you like.

If you are blessed with a Unix and Linux server, you have the *cron* command
(usually part of the operating system) where you can easily program these
recurrent events and run your REBOL scripts whenever you like. But, not to
worry, if your system does not have a *cron* program, REBOL has you covered.
Bohdan "Bo" Lechnowsky at REBOL HQ has written *rebcron.r*, REBOL's own
version of *cron*. *Rebcron* runs on all the 37+ operating environments that run
REBOL. And it's easy to program recurring tasks into the code, like this:

```
tasks: [
    15:42 [1 2 3 4 5 6 7]
      [print ["It is 15:42 on" now/date]]
    23:59 [1 2 3 4 5]
      [do %backup.r
        write/append logfile "** Daily backup completed **"]
```

For the complete code, check `rebol.org` and look under Utilities. *Rebcron* is
free. Thanks, Bo!

Sending yourself automatic reports by e-mail

Any report generated on your server by your automatic script can be sent to you by e-mail with one line of code (just be sure that a *user.r* file is in the directory from which you are sending e-mail):

```
send you@yourmail.com %report.txt
```

As an additional example, suppose that you're monitoring the files in a directory to include sizes and modification dates, you want a REBOL script running once a day to do so, and you want those results sent to you via e-mail. You could use this code:

```
REBOL []
files: sort read %.
write %report.txt ""
  foreach file files [
          if not dir? file [
          write/append %report.txt reform [
              file size? file modified? file newline
          ]
      ]
]
send you@yourmail.com read %report.txt
```

That's all it takes, other than setting up a *cron* or *rebcron* to periodically execute the script.

Managing files

Even then, an immutable law of the universe states that files tend to expand to fill available space.

You can write REBOL code to keep files under control by using your Web browser. You need a *cleaner* script that lists the files and lets you check off files to be deleted. This script — after you've finished checking files — passes that information to a *delete* script, which then deletes the files. I actually use this to keep my server clean.

DO NOT leave this script in your *cgi-bin* directory where just anyone can use it.

Here's the code for the cleaner script. It's included on the CD-ROM (at the back of this book) as `17-cleaner.r`. Sample output is shown in Figures 17-4 and 17-5. Feel free to modify and use it for your own server maintenance:

```
#!/rebol/rebol -cs
REBOL [ TITLE: "Clean Files off Server"
        FILE: %17-cleaner.r
        DATE: 31-May-2000
    ]
print "Content-Type: text/html^/"
dir: %/www/htdocs/ebay        ; the directory to be cleaned
change-dir dir
a: sort read %.
print {
<form method=get action='/cgi-bin/delete.r' name='List
        Files'>
<table width='600' align='center' border='2' cellspacing='5'
        cellpadding='5' bgcolor='ivory' height='60'>
 <tr><td><b>Directory</b>:</td><td align=right><input
        name="Directory" size=30></td></tr>
    <tr><td>
        <p align='center'><b>Files for Deletion</b><br>
}
box: 0
size: 0
  foreach file a [
  if not dir? file [
   c: "c"
   box: box + 1
   c: join c box

  print "<tr><td>"
  print ["<p><input type='checkbox' name='" c "' value=" file
        ">" file "</p>"]
  print ["</td><td align='right'>" size? file "</td><td>"
        modified? file]
        size: size + size? file
        print "</td></tr>"
        ]
        ]
print { </select></p></td></tr><tr><td height='27'><input
        type='submit' name='submit' value='Submit'></td>
    <td align=right height='27'><input type='reset'
        name='reset' value='Reset'></td></tr></table>
</form> }

print "</table>"
print ["These files take up " size " in space."]
```

Typing the directory in the cleaner script (it uses a relative address from your browser) is a security feature, just in case someone else accesses it while you have it online.

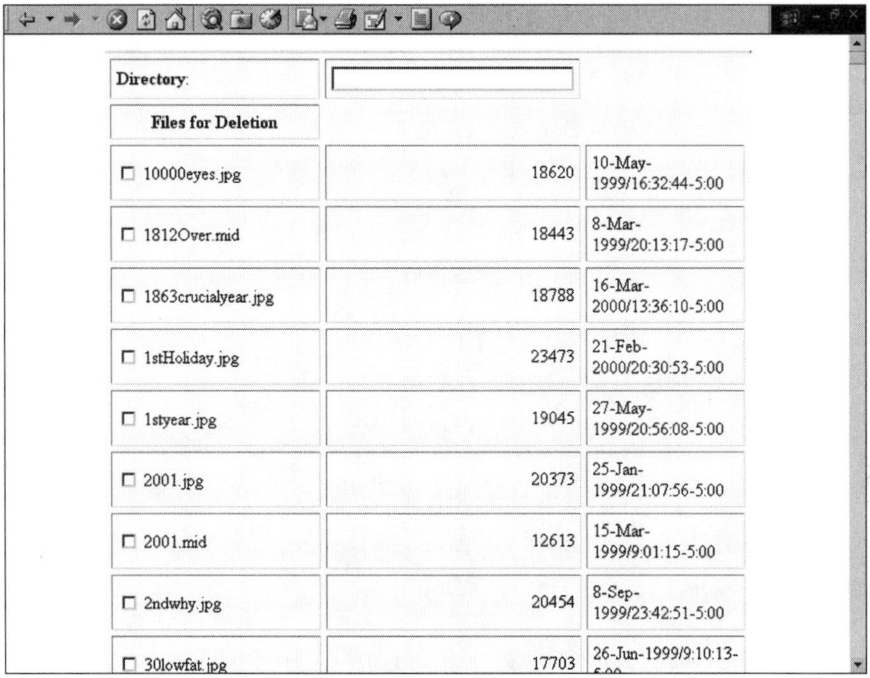

Figure 17-4:
The cleaner
script.

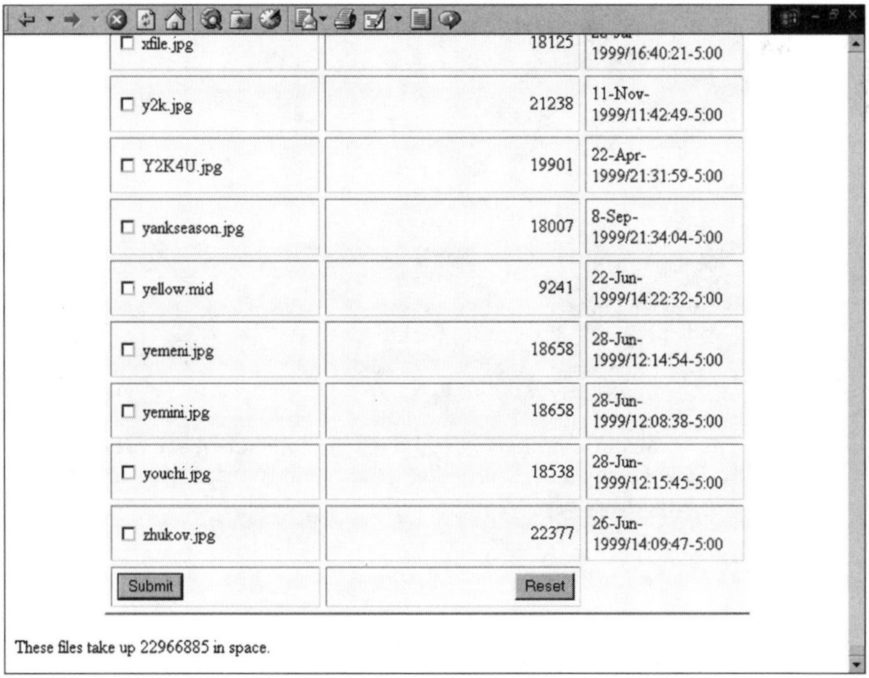

Figure 17-5:
The bottom
of the
cleaner
script.

At the bottom of the cleaner script, you see the size of the directory. After you've checked off the files to be deleted, click the Submit button, which calls the delete script.

And here's the delete portion:

```
#!/rebol/rebol -cs
REBOL [TITLE: "Delete Server Files"
       FILE: %17-delete.r
       DATE: 31-May-2000
   ]
print "Content-Type: text/html^/"
print {
<html>
<head>
<title>File Deletion</title><br>}
print "<style>"
print "body {background-color: ivory}"
print "</style></head><body>"
data: decode-cgi system/options/cgi/query-string
looper: (length? data) - 4
looper: divide looper 2
dir: data/2
dir: to-file dir
change-dir dir
print [dir "<br>"]
x: 4
loop looper [
       print [pick data x "<br>"]
       file: pick data x
       file: to-file file
       delete file
       x: x + 2
       ]
print {
<hr>
<p align='center'><font size='2'>(c)2000 Creativity, Inc. ...
       The data on these
pages is proprietary company information<br>
and may not be reproduced without permission. All rights
       reserved.</font></p>}
       print "</body></html>"
```

The names of the files passed to the delete script are erased from the system, and a list of files is supplied to you. (In this example, I deleted three files that I no longer need.)

Using server power

You can even use the speed of the Internet itself to grab stuff and put it on the server for later download. You can retrieve multiple-megabyte-long files in mere seconds. Here's an example. While exploring the public FTP site, `ftp.uu.net`, I found a version of *nethack* for the PC. I used to play this game some years ago, so I want to grab it for old times' sake. Compare the speed at which I can get it with my Windows box and my BDSi Internet server. First, I write a little REBOL script that times the downloads:

```
REBOL []
a: now/time
          write %nh322pm.zip read

          ftp://ftp.uu.net/pub/games/nethack/binaries/msdos/
          nh322pm.zip
print now/time - a
```

You can store this script in the file `dl.r` and use it to benchmark your downloads.

The file is 1.06MB. First I download it to my local computer, which is connected via my LAN to the NT Web server (which is a 28K-or-so dial-up connection to the Net):

```
>> do %dl.r
Script: "Untitled" (none)
connecting to: ftp.uu.net
0:07:15
```

Hmmm. Seven minutes, fifteen seconds. That old dial-up connection is apoppin', eh? Okay, now I'll try the same thing on the server using the same REBOL code:

```
>> do %dl.r
Script: "Untitled" (none)
connecting to: ftp.uu.net
0:00:12
```

Twelve seconds! Whoa, what a difference. It's all in the connection.

Chapter 18

CGI, or Doing unCommon Gateway Interfacing

*T*he World Wide Web is the primary mechanism that makes the Internet of such ease these days and attracts hundreds of millions. By mere clicks of a mouse, you can peruse literally hundreds of millions of brightly colored pages, sometimes full of sound and music and pictures that move. By so doing, you find information of all sorts far faster and in much greater detail than your hometown library can offer.

I read somewhere recently that the United States alone had more Web pages now than people. That's, what, 300 million or so? A bunch! The Web makes it possible.

The Web was originally developed at CERN (European Center for Nuclear Research). CERN, located in Geneva, Switzerland, is an institution specializing in high-energy physics research. The Web was originally meant to promote sharing of research materials and to serve as a mode of collaboration between scientists worldwide.

Tim Berners-Lee worked at CERN during this period and richly deserves the title "Father of the Web." He's one of my online heroes. Thanks, Tim!

CERN generously made the Web available to everyone and, by so doing, sparked today's Internet revolution. Thanks, CERN!

To output to the Web, REBOL (and Perl and other scripting languages) makes use of what is called CGI or Common Gateway Interface. Although a "CGI" Web application can be created using many coding languages, this book is about REBOL (duh!). After reading this book, I believe you will join me in the REBOLution!

Coding the CGI Basics

REBOL truly shines at CGI — as it does in allowing you to quickly and simply develop applications that other languages make complex. (Yeah! I'm talking about you, Perl!) Get the basics out of the way, and then you can whomp up some tasty CGI apps.

Setting your Web server for CGI

Your first action must be to make sure that your server or servers can run both REBOL and CGI. I discuss the REBOL part of set up in Chapter 17. Setting up CGI access is different for every Web server.

In most cases, your second step should be to enable the *execute CGI* option (ExecCGI in Apache, one of the most popular Web server software packages) and configure the directory where CGI programs may reside (typically cgi-bin)

The final step is to make your CGI scripts runnable. On most UNIX-type systems or those that use Apache or similar Web servers, you want to make the CGI script readable and executable by all users and have the appropriate header. I show you REBOL's standard script header for CGI shortly.

With other Web servers, the system may require configuration to execute the REBOL executable for .r extension files and run REBOL with any required options, such as --cgi or -cs (please note, there are two hyphens in front of *--cgi*, but only one in front of *-cs*). I discuss more on those options when I talk about security in this chapter.

Configuring for Microsoft IIS

The Microsoft Internet Information Server (or IIS) is also widely used these days, running on NT servers. To configure CGI for MS IIS, go into the Properties of *cgi-bin* and click the Configuration button. This brings up a configuration dialog box. Click Add, and enter the path to your rebol.exe file, like this:

```
C:\rebol\rebol.exe -cs %s %s
```

The two %s %s must be added to make sure that it works correctly when passing the script and command line arguments to REBOL. You must add the extension, or REBOL files and sets the last field to PUT, DELETE. The script engine doesn't have to be selected.

Using the standard script header

When a CGI Web application is called — because it can be a script interpreted by any one of several languages, of which REBOL is only one — the right interpreter has to be involved. This is done through a CGI header, or the line at the top of the script that tells the script where to find a program that will run this flavor of script.

The following header should be at the top of each CGI script on systems that use Apache or other Web servers that use the first line of the script to invoke the proper process. The header specifies the path to the REBOL executable file and the *–cgi* option. If security needs to be off in order to allow file writing or other port access, use *-cs*. Here's the header:

```
#!/path/to/rebol --cgi
REBOL [
    Title: "CGI Test Script"
]
```

As you can see, the only thing different from most of the other scripts in this book is the first line, the #!/path/to/rebol --cgi. This line is not even interpreted by REBOL, but is rather for the server to know where it can call REBOL for evaluating all the other lines.

In Chapter 16, I explain that I use a little trick in regards to my server path to REBOL, just to make things easier in script development. My rebol directory on my desktop Windows 98 computer is on the same drive as the server software I use to test scripts locally (Sambar). My CGI path (the top line in all my scripts) looks like this:

```
#!/rebol/rebol --cgi
```

This line, by the way, is the same as one at the top of a Perl script that tells the server where the Perl binary is located. For example:

```
#!/usr/bin/perl5
```

The difference, of course, comes in the coding process. I love saying this: REBOL is Perl without the complication.

Back to REBOL. On my company's BDSI UNIX server, I put the rebol directory as a subdirectory in the basepath Web root directory. In my discussion of the three different types of paths on servers in Chapter 16, I explain that this means the path to REBOL would then be /rebol for any calls from the Web (for example, when a CGI application is activated). So, even though it is really different from my local machine, I still have, in effect, the same CGI path:

```
#!/rebol/rebol --cgi
```

Little tricks like that make your life much easier when developing and testing scripts. If you don't set it up that way, I can guarantee that you'll forget to change that one line a dozen times a week and it will be a pain in a place you'd rather not have pain.

Creating a REBOL CGI Application

In essence, creating a REBOL CGI application involves only two necessary conditions:

- ✔ The script can be caused to run by a Web browser.
- ✔ Output from the script's evaluation can be shown on a Web page.

First, I'll explain calling those little mudpuppies. By the way, do you city programmers know what the term mudpuppy — a wonderful "Southernism" — refers to? When I was a boy growing up on the farm here in the Carolina hills, we raised beagle dawgs, coon dawgs, bird dawgs, all kinda hounds, even an occasional University of Georgia Bulldawg. You let a litter of these pups out after a good soaking rain, and watch them playing in puddles and jumping on you in wild abandon, and then you'll understand the concept of *mudpuppies*.

Invoking REBOL scripts from the Web

Okay, in calling a REBOL script from the Web, "Heah boy, heah boy!" does not work nearly as well as it does with beagle dawgs. You'll find these ways much more effective.

Setting up your server

First, I hope you recall that the first line of your script must tell the server where to find REBOL in order to run the code:

```
#!/rebol/rebol --cgi ; runs script without read/write
```

Also recall that the script must be in a place that the server allows executable scripts to be — usually a *cgi-bin* directory — and the server must be configured to recognize the .r extension also as an executable script. Configuration files and methods vary from server to server. For example, my company's UNIX box runs the Apache Web server. In the www/conf directory is a file called srm.conf, a few lines of which control what type of scripts the server executes:

```
AddType text/x-server-parsed-html .html
AddType text/x-server-parsed-html .htm
AddType application/x-httpd-cgi .cgi
AddType application/x-httpd-cgi .pl
AddType application/x-httpd-cgi .r
AddType application/x-httpd-Miva .mv .hts
Action application/x-httpd-Miva /cgi-bin/miva
AddType application/x-httpd-php3 .phtml .php3 .php
AddType application/x-httpd-php  .phtml .php3 .php4
```

These configuration lines, in order, tell the server it can run HTML Web pages, CGI applications, Perl (sigh) scripts, REBOL scripts, scripts relating to my company's Miva online storefronts, and PHP hypertext preprocessing code embedded in HTML scripts. PHP is what I hope my next *For Dummies* book will be about — it's an excellent enhancement for Web sites that works hand in glove with REBOL.

For a midrange traffic Web site, I believe that you need three main tools in addition to HTML (HTTP server). Those are REBOL, PHP, and that great SQL (Structured Query Language) database, MySQL. Best of all, you can get all this power for free! But if you'd rather spend a few million bucks, marks, pounds, yen, or wampum developing a site, go right ahead. I'm doing mine with a foundation firmly resting on the strong tripod just described.

Calling all scripts

How do you invoke the script from the Web? You can do it in several ways. Here are three of the most often used ways of invoking CGI applications.

First, you can add a link to your HTML page where, when the link is clicked, a script is called, such as (HTML code):

```
<a href="/cgi-bin/script.r">Run this script, bubbah</a>
```

You can call it from another Web site:

```
<a href="http://somename.com/cgi-bin/script.r">Run this
          script, bubbah</a>
```

"Run this script, bubbah" appears on the Web page most likely as blue letters underlined (default link appearance). Clicking it runs the script. But this is a manual call; in other words, someone has to physically do it. What if you want a REBOL script — like a page counter, say — to be called automatically whenever a user loads the Web page into his browser? One way to accomplish this is to use Server Side Includes (SSI), something else you have to configure your server to allow. If your server allows SSI, just include this line in the HTML Web page where you want the script to be run:

```
<!--#exec cgi="/cgi-bin/script.r" -->
```

But what if you use an HTML preprocessing script language like PHP for your pages that, as already stated, works very well in conjunction with REBOL scripts? No problem. Just use this technique to call your REBOL scripts (PHP code):

```
<?php include("http://somedomain.com/cgi-bin/script.r") ?>
```

Outputting to CGI from REBOL

Okay, now that your server knows where to find the REBOL binary and that REBOL scripts are allowable executable files, all you have to do is let the server know that the data coming back from the evaluated REBOL script should be display as a Web page, or at least as part of a Web page.

How do you do this? That's easy enough. In Chapter 15, I discuss that you can change the regular e-mail format to HTML by changing the Content-Type variable in the system/standard/email object. Well, you do the same thing for CGI by changing the same name variable in the system/options/cgi object. But it's even simpler than with e-mail. Just include this line in your scripts before outputting anything:

```
print "Content-Type: text/html^/^/"
```

The ^/ symbol puts a line return at the end of the string; this is required for proper operation. Those of you who might have messed with (shudder) Perl, will recognize that line. In Perl, you include this:

```
print "Content-type: text/html\n\n";
```

These are very similar, albeit with an extra required character (the trailing semicolon). After this, Perl gets complicated (I've said that before, haven't I?), so you continue on here with REBOL. If you want to see the other parts of the system/options/cgi object (there's some good useable stuff in there!), do this:

```
>> print mold system/options/cgi

make object! [
    server-software: none
    server-name: none
    gateway-interface: none
    server-protocol: none
    server-port: none
    request-method: none
    path-info: none
    path-translated: none
    script-name: none
```

```
        query-string: none
        remote-host: none
        remote-addr: none
        auth-type: none
        remote-user: none
        remote-ident: none
        Content-Type: none
        content-length: none
        other-headers: []
    ]
```

It's time to get practical. Why don't you whip together a quick but tasty little Web application that shows the CGI object and see what information it gives you? I tried this first on my desktop machine with its Sambar server, and then on my company's Web server live on the net.

How do you show the contents of the CGI system object? You could just use this line in the CGI script:

```
print mold system/options/cgi
```

Although it gives an okay format from the REBOL console (even though there were no contents to show), remember that you are passing your results back through a Web page and CGI rules apply with different line endings and so forth. The single line of code may look elegant and efficient, but on a Web page it returns a jumbled mess that looks like this:

```
make object! [ server-software: "SAMBAR 4.3" server-name:
        "richmond" gateway-interface: "CGI/1.1" server-
        protocol: "HTTP/1.0" server-port: "80" request-
        method: "GET" path-info: "" path-translated: ""
        script-name: "/cgi-bin/18-cgiobject.r" query-
        string: "" remote-host: "" remote-addr:
        "198.168.0.12" auth-type: none remote-user: ""
        remote-ident: none Content-Type: none content-
        length: "0" other-headers: ["HTTP_ACCEPT_LANGUAGE"
        "en-us" "HTTP_HOST" "richmond" "HTTP_USER_AGENT"
        "Mozilla/4.0 (compatible; MSIE 5.01; Windows 98)"] ]
```

All the information is certainly listed there, but it's a bit difficult to read. To make the output a bit neater, adapt a function from the REBOL *User's Guide*. That's the probe-object in the following script. I added some HTML stuff so that the Web page would format it in a more readable manner.

Here's the script (you need to have access to a local server or a remote server to install the code from the CD that's called 18-cgiobject.r):

```
#!/rebol/rebol --cgi
REBOL [
  TITLE: "Print the System/Options/CGI Object as HTML"
      FILE: %18-cgiobject.r
      DATE: 1-June-2000
      ]

print "Content-Type: text/html^/^/"

print "<h2>Contents of /system/options/cgi</h2>"

print {<table border='1' cellpadding='5'
   align='center' width='600' bgcolor='ivory'>}

probe-object: func [object][
   foreach word next first object [
      print reduce [
         <tr><td width="20%"> to-string word </td>
         <td> get in object word </td></tr>
      ]
]
]

probe-object system/options/cgi
print "</table>"
```

That's it. Now I'll try it out first on the Sambar server running here on my
Windows 98 box. I just copy the script over to Sambar's cgi-bin directory,
start my browser, and call the script by typing in its URL at the top of the
browser. See Figure 18-1.

Hmmm, nice result. Some good data is included, and you can read it. Now, I
need to transfer the script to my online Web server and see whether it still
works "live" on the Web. Ah, it works ever so nicely, as shown in Figure 18-2.
I'll leave this up for you to play with (as long as traffic does not get too
heavy) at abooks.com/cgi-bin/18-cgiobject.r.

Knowing what kind of browsers that the surfers hitting your site have, what
kind of operating systems their computers run, where they are coming in
from (remote-addr), and so forth is all worthwhile information. This stuff can
be used in your scripts now that you know how to access it.

And just to give you a way of doing that, here's my version of wherefrom.r, a
sample program from the REBOL site example library. I've added some HTML
formatting, and it works nicely on a number of my company's Web pages. The
script is on this book's CD-ROM as 18-wherefrom.r, and here's the code:

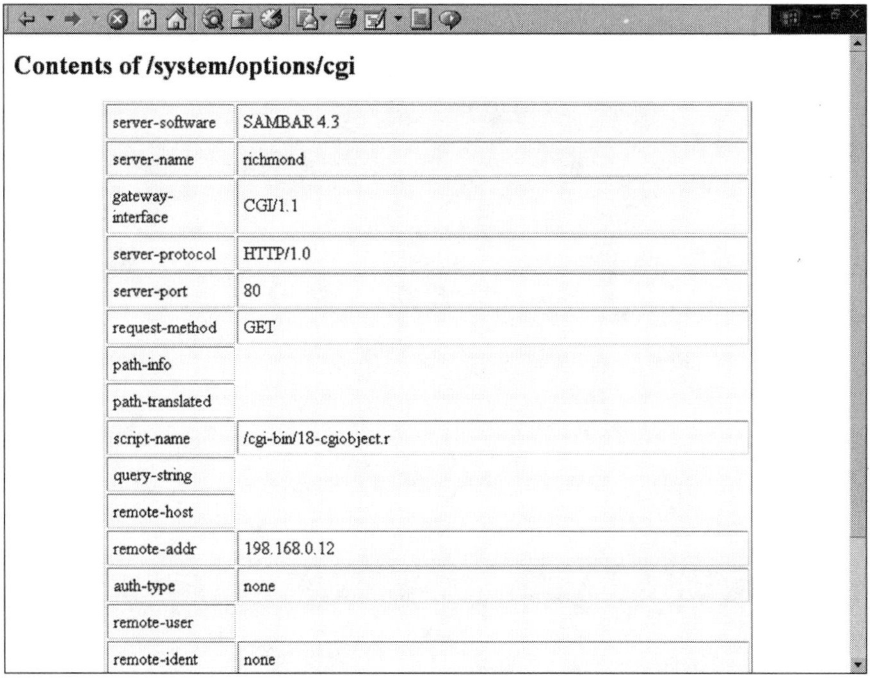

Contents of /system/options/cgi

server-software	SAMBAR 4.3
server-name	richmond
gateway-interface	CGI/1.1
server-protocol	HTTP/1.0
server-port	80
request-method	GET
path-info	
path-translated	
script-name	/cgi-bin/18-cgiobject.r
query-string	
remote-host	
remote-addr	198.168.0.12
auth-type	none
remote-user	
remote-ident	none

Figure 18-1:
Looking at the CGI object on my desktop Windows 98 Sambar server.

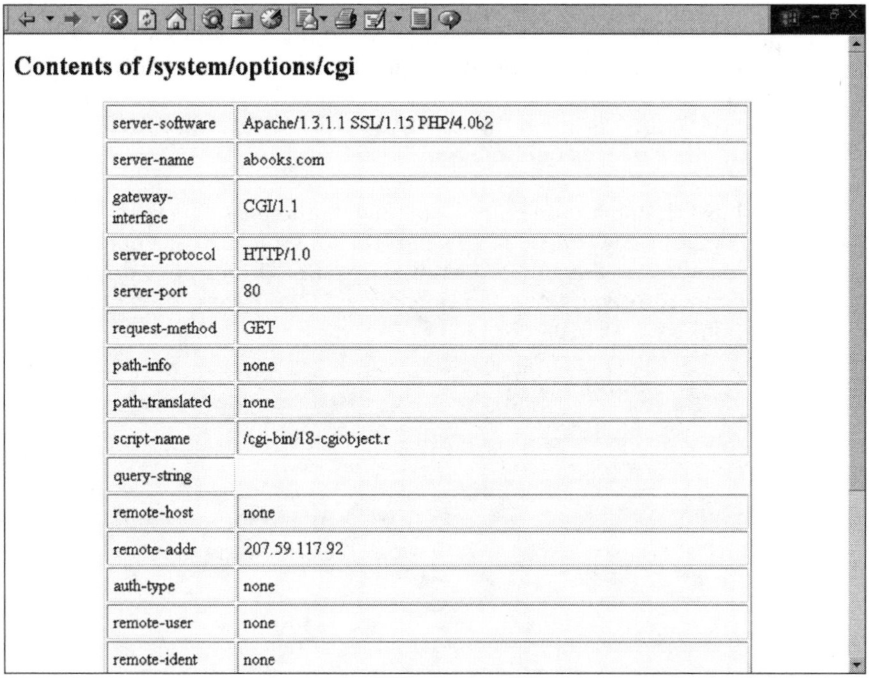

Contents of /system/options/cgi

server-software	Apache/1.3.1.1 SSL/1.15 PHP/4.0b2
server-name	abooks.com
gateway-interface	CGI/1.1
server-protocol	HTTP/1.0
server-port	80
request-method	GET
path-info	none
path-translated	none
script-name	/cgi-bin/18-cgiobject.r
query-string	
remote-host	none
remote-addr	207.59.117.92
auth-type	none
remote-user	none
remote-ident	none

Figure 18-2:
The page that is built by running *18-cgiobject.r* on abooks. com.

```
#!/rebol/rebol --cgi
REBOL [
        TITLE: "Where From?"
        FILE: %18-wherefrom.r
]
ip: system/options/cgi/remote-addr
print "Content-Type: text/html^/^/"
print rejoin [
    {<font face="ARIAL" size="-2">
    Thank you for visiting this page from<br>
    IP: } ip { - - - Name: } read join dns:// ip {<br>
    on } now/date { at } now/time {
    our time (U.S. Eastern).<br><br></font>}
]
```

Another way of using data from system/object/cgi could be to log your visitors into a text log (and they need not even know that you are tracking them). A mere two lines of code in any script called when the Web page is hit does it:

```
write/append %a.log join now " --- "
write/append %a.log join system/options/cgi/remote-addr "^/"
```

```
ip: system/options/cgi/remote-addr
write/append %a.log reduce [now " --- " ip newline]
```

That last bit of the second line, the ^/ or newline symbol is important to keep each visitor on a separate line and avoid jumbling your file. Also, you have to keep in mind where you are outputting data. If you are outputting to the REBOL console or to a file, the newline symbol gives a line break. But if your output is going through CGI to be part of an HTML page, use <BR> or another HTML code to break lines.

I just thought of one more example. In the past, I've seen Web sites that list the last five visitors using a Perl script. I think that's cool, so while I'm thinking about it, I'm going to whomp up a REBOL script to do the same thing and share the experience and the code with you. Here's the code (it's on this book's CD-ROM as 18-lastfive.r):

```
#!/rebol/rebol -cs
REBOL [
        TITLE: "Last Five"
        FILE: %18-lastfive.r
        DATE: 2-June-2000
]

print "Content-Type: text/html^/^/"

ip: system/options/cgi/remote-addr

if not exists? %lastfive.log [write %lastfive.log ""]
```

```
lastfive: read/lines %lastfive.log

if (length? lastfive) < 5 [
        write/append %lastfive.log join ip "^-"
        name: read join dns:// ip
        write/append %lastfive.log join name "^-"
        write/append %lastfive.log join now/date "^-"
        write/append %lastfive.log join now/time "^/"
        ]

if (length? lastfive) = 5 [
        new: join ip "^-"
        name: read join dns:// ip
        new: join new name
        new: join new "^-"
        new: join new now/date
        new: join new "^-"
        new: join new now/time
        remove lastfive lastfive/1
        append tail lastfive new
        write %lastfive.log ""
        foreach hit lastfive [
                write/append %lastfive.log join hit "^/"
                ]
        ]


lastfive: read/lines %lastfive.log

print {<table border='1' cellpadding='3'
    align='center' width='500' bgcolor='ivory'>
    <caption><font face='ARIAL' size='-1'>
    Our Five Most Recent Visitors</font></caption>
    }

for count (length? lastfive) 1 -1 [
        hit: pick lastfive count
        print "<tr><td><font face='ARIAL' size='-2'>"
        data: parse/all hit "^-"
        print [data/1 "</font></td><td><font face='ARIAL'
            size='-1'>"]
    print [data/2 "</font></td><td><font face='ARIAL'
            size='-1'>"]
    print [data/3 "</font></td><td><font face='ARIAL'
            size='-1'>" data/4]
        ]
print "</table>"
```

The preceding code has no tricky parts. It's all pretty straight forward and uses the basics I've discussed throughout the book. What you can do to improve the preceding code is to make it recognize hits from more than one page and write them to an appropriate log file. Or you can change it to show more than the last five (at the bottom of the main page of abooks.com, I show ten — take a look at Figure 18-3). Anyway, enjoy!

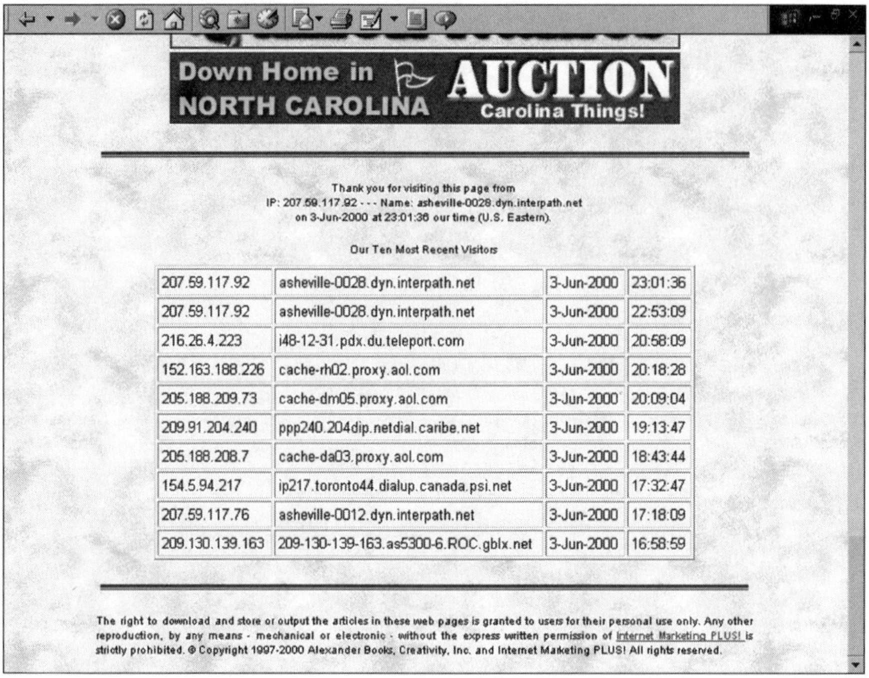

Figure 18-3:
The bottom
of the
abooks.
com main
page shows
the ten most
recent
visitors.

Installing security

Security for your CGI scripts depends on the command line option by which you call REBOL. You should know two command line options for Web applications:

```
#!/rebol/rebol --cgi
#!/rebol/rebol -cs
```

The first option tells REBOL to send output to CGI. The second line relaxes security so that the script can read and write files. Be careful with this last option, and be sure that know what you are doing. A prime example is the "cleaner" program I use in Chapter 17 that allows you to delete unwanted files from your server. Let me emphasize that it also lets anyone who stumbles across it delete files from your server. So don't let CGI scripts have the -cs option unless you strictly control which files they can read and write.

Getting REBOL to Output HTML

In this chapter and in Chapter 17, I show you that it's easy enough to output HTML with REBOL. However, HTML is both a hodgepodge and a pain when you first start building Web pages. Its code is somewhat less human readable than REBOL's. If you are a whiz in HTML, this might not matter much, but if the end result is to do Web applications in the REBOL way — quickly, simply, and without hassle — you can consider some shortcuts.

Easing into HTML

With the WYSIWYG (What You See Is What You Get) HTML editors available today — such as Microsoft's FrontPage on Windows95/98/NT/2000 systems — doing complex HTML coding with your REBOL Web applications requires almost no knowledge of HTML at all. Here's the only REBOL code you need to understand:

```
print {          }
```

Got that? Just a print expression using braces ({ }) so that quotation marks (" ") within the HTML won't cause confusion.

If you use HTML code with quotation marks inside a regular REBOL print statement — itself delimited with double quotation marks (" ") — problems can arise. If you do this, change all the HTML quotation marks to single quotation marks or apostrophes (' '). It won't affect the way the HTML works and, most importantly, it won't mess up the operation of your REBOL code. I still recommend, however, that you put HTML in braces ({ }) because then you don't need to worry about any of this warning.

After you have your print statement in place, go to your HTML editor, develop your HTML code, and then cut and paste it inside the brackets. Here's an example of how to use this technique. I used FrontPage to whip up a little treatise on programmers' coffee (a fearsome subject, indeed). I then copied the HTML for all this over into a short REBOL script (well, it was short until I copied all the HTML over). Rather than take up a bunch of room here, you can find this script on the CD as 18-coffee.r (see Figure 18-4). It generates a file called coffee.html, viewable in your browser. Be sure to copy coffee.gif, the associated image, into the same directory as the HTML page.

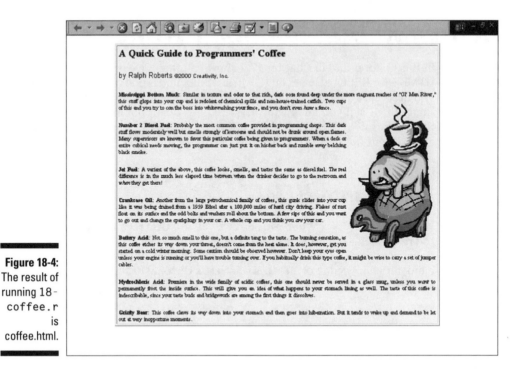

Figure 18-4:
The result of
running 18-
coffee.r
is
coffee.html.

Experiment with this technique; you'll find it most useful.

And what kind of coffee am I drinking right now? It's a freshly ground Kenyan bean, darkly robust with a most exquisite taste and a bouquet reminiscent of wide African savannas after the spring rains. Totally delicious! You see, having been a programmer since 1966, I have learned my lesson as to programmers' coffee.

Just a word to the wise and those who might value their stomachs.

Employing file tricks

The example script in the preceding section — 18-coffee.r — becomes rather hefty after you plug the HTML into it. Another way to work with this is to have the HTML in a file and just include it with a REBOL script by reading the HTML into a variable (as below), and writing it back out as a Web page (which could include other files as well). Here's one way:

```
#!/rebol/rebol -cs
REBOL [
        TITLE: "Programmers Coffee"
        FILE: %18-coffee-2.r
```

```
          DATE: 2-June-2000
]

coffee: read %coffee.html

write %coffee-2.html coffee
```

This, of course, falls under the concept of dynamic Web pages as I discuss in
Chapter 17.

Using HTML Enhancements with REBOL

Nor are you limited to mere HTML — pretty static stuff, at best — in building
your Web pages. In addition to dynamic content, you can use other techniques and programs to enhance your Web pages. In this section, I give you
two of those — CSS for layout control and PHP for lots of good stuff.

Using REBOL with CSS

CSS, or Cascading Style Sheets, are promoted by the World Wide Web
Consortium (W3C) — the same organization that sets the standards for
HTML. CSS is a simple way to add style (fonts, colors, spacing, and so on) to
Web documents. Style sheets work by separating style (CSS1) and layout
(CSS2) from the structure of content. This allows style rules to be embedded
inside a page, but they are more ideally stored in a separate referenced HTML
document — a style sheet. You can change the overall look of an entire page
or even entire Web sites by changing one style rule or sheet.

CSS is good stuff, but I'm not here to tell you everything about CSS (but I
hope to do that book later, though). For now, check out W3C's wealth of
material on CSS at www.w3.org/Style/CSS/. And let me show you how to
build CSS-enabled Web pages using REBOL. You add style sheet info in your
REBOL scripts via this code:

```
print {        }
```

Yup, yup, it's the same as adding HTML. Okay, let me show you a short example using REBOL to construct on the fly an HTML page with embedded CSS.
In fact, here's a snippet from the *REBOL For Dummies* site that I'm putting
together at abooks.com/rebol to help promote this book (you'll find it on
this book's CD-ROM as 18-css.r):

```
#!/rebol/rebol --cgi
REBOL [
        TITLE: "CSS"
        FILE: %18-css.r
        DATE: 2-June-2000
]

print "Content-Type: text/html^/^/"

print {

<html><head>
<title>REBOL FOR DUMMIES by Ralph Roberts</title>
<style>

BODY {  font-family: Arial;
        margin-left: 5em;
        margin-right: 4em;
   background-color: lightyellow;
   color: navy;
}
p.emphasis    { line-height: 120%; padding: 1em; border-style:
            solid;
   border-width: thin; font-family: arial; background-color:
            ivory;
   text-align: Justify; margin-left: 3em; margin-right: 3em ; }

</style></head><body>

<CENTER><h1 >REBOL</H1>
It's Perl without the complication.</CENTER>

<br>
<p class="emphasis">
This page is an independent resource for the new, powerful
scripting language, REBOL (see <a href='http://rebol.com'>
rebol.com</a>). It is sponsored and maintained by
Ralph Roberts, author of <i>REBOL FOR DUMMIES</i> from
IDG Books. Watch this space for sample REBOL scripts and
other information. </p>

</body></html>
}
```

This code provides a nice mixture of REBOL, HTML, and CSS, with all three complementing the others. See the results in Figure 18-5.

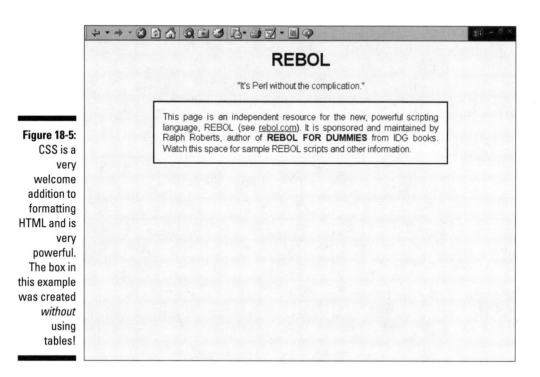

Figure 18-5:
CSS is a
very
welcome
addition to
formatting
HTML and is
very
powerful.
The box in
this example
was created
without
using
tables!

I should emphasize one thing to you. When you start learning CSS, you find that braces ({ }) are used extensively in its code. As long as these braces are correctly paired, inserting a chunk of CSS/HTML within a REBOL brace-delimited print statement has no ill effects and many good ones.

In the preceding example, the CSS is enclosed by <style> . . . </style> tags and is in the HTML <HEAD> section. As you will discover when you research CSS, lines in the HEAD influence style for the whole Web page. But you may also embed CSS commands directly in <BODY> HTML lines. So for added fun, I'll do just that and show some REBOL dynamic generation of CSS:

```
#!/rebol/rebol --cgi
REBOL [
        TITLE: "Dynamic CSS"
        FILE: %18-css-d.r
        DATE: 2-June-2000
]

print "Content-Type: text/html^/^/"

print {
```

```
<html><head>
<title>REBOL Dynamic CSS Generation</title>
</head><body>

<table cellpadding='3'
    align='center' width='600' bgcolor='ivory'>
    }

count: 0
loop 30 [
        count: count + .05
        print {<tr><td><p style="font-size: }
        print count
    print {em ">REBOL rules! </td>
    <td align="right">
        <p style="font-size: }
        print count
    print {em ">REBOL rules! </td>
        <td align="left">
        <p style="font-size: }
        print count
    print {em ">REBOL rules! </td>
        <td align="right">
        <p style="font-size: }
        print count
    print {em ">REBOL rules! </td>...
    </tr>}
]

print {</table></body></html>
}
```

This is pretty basic CSS and REBOL, as well. It looks good on my Internet Explorer. It may look "less better" on other brands of browsers. The nice thing about standards is that there are so many. Anyway, I'm just using a simple loop to change the *em* size of the characters. *Em* is a most handy measurement that you can use via CSS; in concept, it's close to the centuries-old traditional printer's measurement of the width that a single letter "em" would occupy). This preceding code results in a table with four cells per row (enough to fill a standard screen), alternating left/right alignment. (See Figure 18-6.) It makes a nice dynamic pattern, wouldn't you say?

Yes, REBOL manages CSS/HTML pages — very nicely.

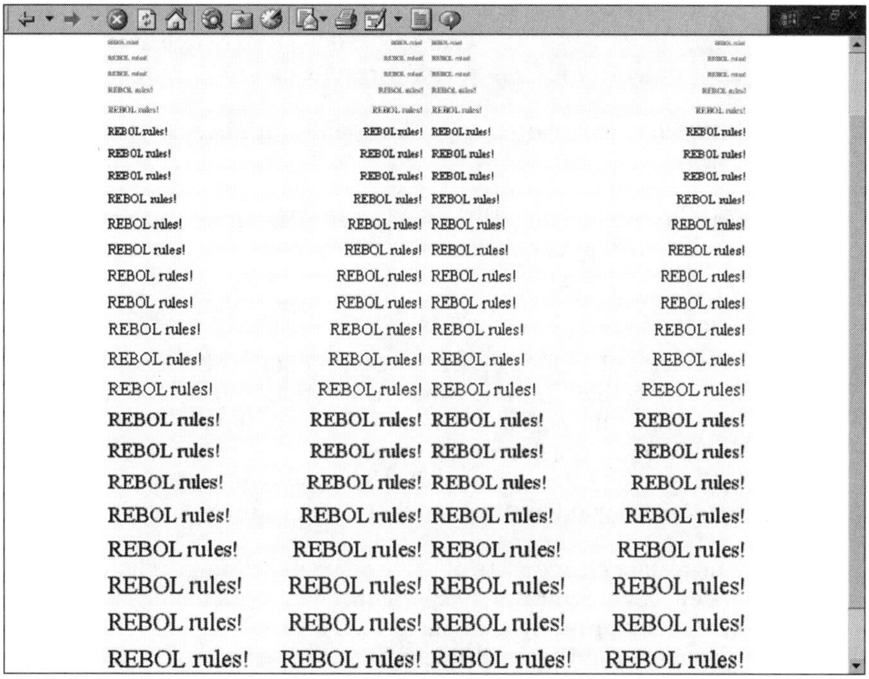

Figure 18-6:
A nice
dynamic
pattern
created by
using
REBOL and
CSS
together.

Joining REBOL and PHP

PHP (from its original name of Personal Home Page Tools) is a script language and interpreter, similar to Javascript and Microsoft's VBScript. PHP, now in use on millions of servers, is a cross-platform alternative to Microsoft's Active Server Page (ASP) technology (which runs only on Microsoft's Windows NT servers). Unlike REBOL and Perl but similar to ASP, the PHP script is embedded within a Web page along with HTML. Before the page is sent to a user who has requested it, the Web server calls PHP to interpret and perform the operations called for in the PHP script.

This little analogy might help you see how all these parts fit together in producing a truly dynamic Web page. You take a block of wood from the shelf, shape it into the form of a wall plaque, drill holes for mounting, sand it, paint it, and mount it on the wall — that's all REBOL. You inscribe this month's calendar on it, and show how many shopping days are left until Christmas — that's PHP preprocessing. You make the letters and numbers a vivid green and red — that's HTML. Finally, you put a lustrous coat of varnish over the plaque so that it looks truly professional — that's CSS. And, remember, REBOL can have a hand in generating every one of these steps.

An HTML page that includes a PHP script is typically given a suffix of
.php .php3, or .phtml. Like ASP, PHP pages are dynamic HTML pages
and content varies based on the results of interpreting the script.

PHP is free and offered under an open source license. The latest version is
PHP 4.

How do you include PHP scripts in an HTML page generated by REBOL? Well,
yes, you're way ahead of me:

```
print {            }
```

The major difference between a style enhancer like CSS and a preprocessor
like PHP is that the style enhancer's action is fixed (the same action occurs
every time the page is hit), but PHP is a script itself that can react or interact
in different ways, depending on events, time, or other factors. If you think
about it, you can see that REBOL's actions can magnify those of PHP and vice
versa. It's a good partnership and a type of hybrid programming!

I am a staunch advocate of using several scripting techniques for a hybrid,
yet effective, end result. For example, in programming my company's online
auctions, I currently use a mixture of Perl, HTML, CSS, SSI, and REBOL. I'm
planning to add some PHP features and use that to tie into MySQL for database access. The trick is to pick the strongest features of each language for
an overall efficient combination. Too many people get into a rigid mindset
and make things hard by trying to do Web applications all in Perl — scripting
that is sometimes akin to fixing an old spring/gear clock while wearing mit-
tens and balancing a pail of water on your head. I mean, you can do it, but it
ain't easy.

Figure 18-7 shows an example of including a PHP script inside a REBOL script,
and letting REBOL build a Web page with an active PHP script embedded
(this script is on this book's CD-ROM as 18-php.r). Remember, you need a
PHP-enabled Web server for the PHP script to run when the page is called.
Here's the code:

```
#!/rebol/rebol -cs
REBOL [
        TITLE: "PHP"
        FILE: %18-php.r
        DATE: 3-June-2000
]

write %ralph.php {
<html><head>
```

```
<title>Ralph's Birthday</title>
</head>

<body>

<?
$day = 11;
$month = 12;

print ("There are " .
 (int)((mktime (0,0,0,$month,$day) - time(void))/86400) .
 " days between today and Ralph's birthday, December 11");
?>

</body></html>
}
```

Hybrid scripting — what a great concept!

There are 190 days between today and Ralph's birthday, December 11

Figure 18-7:
The embedded PHP script calculates the days left until my birthday every time the page is hit, leaving you lots of leeway to shop for my present and buy that cake with . . . well, several candles.

Filling Out Forms

HTML *forms* are one of the most widely used CGI applications. Forms are used to interact with the person visiting your site, allowing the user to fill in information such as name and address (if, for example, the user buys a product or wants more information). Whatever type of Web site you have, chances are you need forms. These methods, by the way, are CGI — not REBOL — but you can use REBOL to manipulate them.

You can pass data from a filled-out form to a CGI script for processing in two ways. These are the GET and the POST methods. First, look at GET. A two-step process is needed; make a page with a form having fields to be filled in, and then call a REBOL script for processing the data entered. Although the form can be all HTML, I do it here as a callable REBOL CGI application (see Figure 18-8). It's still mostly HTML. Don't reinvent the wheel; just cut and paste forms from other places and adapt them to your needs. You just drop all that HTML stuff between the braces of a REBOL print statement. Here's an example for you (it's on this book's CD-ROM as 18-form-get.r; put it in a cgi-bin directory on your server and call it from your browser to run):

```
#!/rebol/rebol --cgi
REBOL [
        TITLE: "GET"
        FILE: %18-form-get.r
        DATE: 3-June-2000
]

print "Content-Type: text/html^/^/"

print {

<form method=get action='18-form-get2.r'>

<TABLE width='350' ALIGN='left' BORDER = 0 CELLPADDING = 2
    border= '1' CELLSPACING = 0 bgcolor='#FFFFCC'>
<TR><TD ALIGN = 'left' VALIGN = 'middle' width='150'>
<FONT FACE = 'Arial, Helvetica' SIZE = '-1'>
<B>First Name:</B>
</FONT>
</TD><TD ALIGN = 'left' VALIGN = 'middle' width='250'>
<FONT FACE = 'Arial, Helvetica' SIZE = '-1'>
<INPUT TYPE = 'text' NAME = 'FirstName' SIZE = 25 VALUE = ''>
</FONT>
</TD></TR>
<TR><TD ALIGN = 'left' VALIGN = 'middle' width='150'>
<FONT FACE = 'Arial, Helvetica' SIZE = '-1'>
<B>Last Name:</B>
```

```
</FONT>
</TD><TD ALIGN = 'left' VALIGN = 'middle' width='250'>
<FONT FACE = 'Arial, Helvetica' SIZE = '-1'>
<INPUT TYPE = 'text' NAME = 'LastName' SIZE = 25 VALUE = ''>
</FONT>
</TD></TR>
<TR><TD ALIGN = 'left' VALIGN = 'middle' width='150'>
<FONT FACE = 'Arial, Helvetica' SIZE = '-1'>
<B>Email Address:</B>
</FONT>
</TD><TD ALIGN = 'left' VALIGN = 'middle' width='250'>
<FONT FACE = 'Arial, Helvetica' SIZE = '-1'>
<INPUT TYPE = 'text' NAME = 'Email' SIZE = 25 VALUE = ''>
</FONT>
</TD></TR>
<tr><td align='right'><INPUT TYPE = 'submit' VALUE =
            'Submit'></td></tr>
</table>

}
```

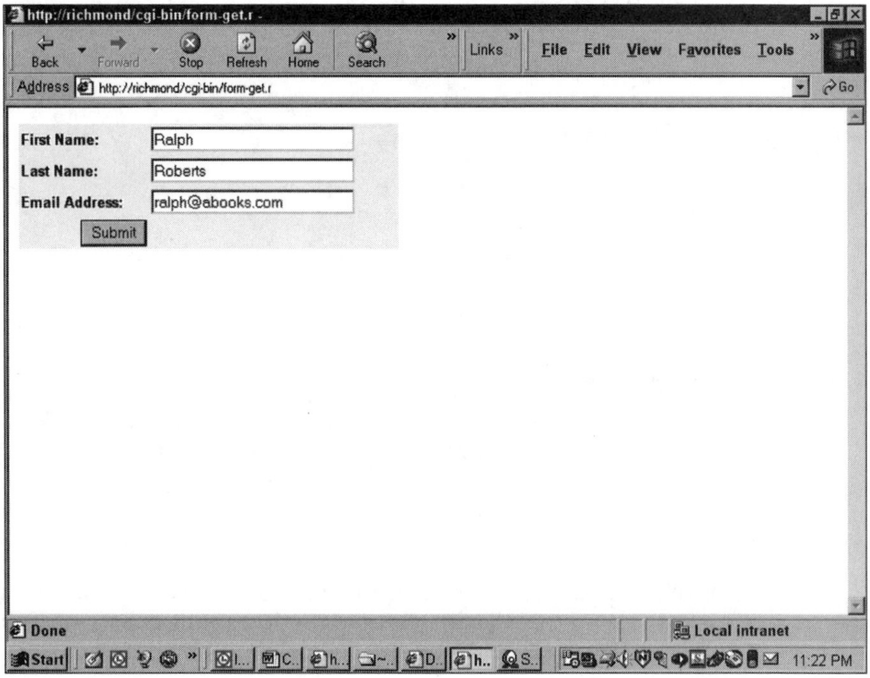

Figure 18-8:
The simple
GET CGI
form.

After the data is entered in the form and the SUBMIT button is clicked, the second REBOL/CGI script is called (on this book's CD-ROM as 18-form-get2.r), and the data can be processed however you want to use it.

```
#!/rebol/rebol --cgi
REBOL [
        TITLE: "GET"
        FILE: %18-form-get2.r
        DATE: 3-June-2000
]

print "Content-Type: text/html^/^/"

data: decode-cgi system/options/cgi/query-string

print [data/1 ": " data/2 "<br>" data/3 ": " data/4 "<br>"
      data/5 ": " data/6]
```

The POST method is more sophisticated. Although GET is great for name/ address types of forms, POST can enable such things as uploading files. The following is a simple file upload system — again two scripts — using POST. This needs to be installed in the cgi-bin directory of a Web server. Here's the REBOL/CGI script using POST:

```
#!/rebol/rebol --cgi
REBOL [
        TITLE: "POST"
        FILE: %18-form-post.r
        DATE: 3-June-2000
]

print "Content-Type: text/html^/^/"

print {

<form METHOD=POST ACTION="18-form-post2.r"
    enctype="multipart/form-data">
    Enter a description of the file: <input TYPE=text SIZE=50
        NAME=text><br>
    Select the file: <input TYPE=file SIZE=15 NAME=file><br>
    <input TYPE=submit VALUE="Submit"><br>
    }
```

Just like the GET example, after the form is finished and the Submit button is clicked, a script is called to process the data (in this case, 18-form-post2.r from this book's CD-ROM); here's its code:

```
#!/rebol/rebol -cs
REBOL [
        TITLE: "POST"
        FILE: %18-form-post2.r
        DATE: 3-June-2000
]

print "Content-Type: text/html^/^/"

print {

   This is the beginning of what we received.
        If this appears incorrect, please repost. <HR> }

data: copy system/ports/input 100

   foreach line data [print [line "<br>"]
]
```

Chapter 19

Dialects ("I Canna Hold 'er, Kaptan, Activate REBOL")

*T*he power of dialects is a REBOL features that has grabbed the imagination of many people.

Dialects are blocks that carry condensed meaning through the use of a different grammar (ordering) of values and words. Dialects are usually unique and well-suited to the problems that they are designed to solve.

Understanding the Power of Dialects

You see, built, and use some simple dialects during the course of this book. One way of looking at block dialects is coming to the realization that they are good for jargon-type applications when you can use special keywords in the context of your application.

Every profession or discipline has its own special buzzwords with specific meanings. Think about it: You can define the keyword, the syntax, and grammar of the context in which words are used. *You can program in buzzwords!* This is, indeed, a powerful feature of REBOL.

Writing Basic Rules for Dialects

These blocks of condensed meaning that make up dialects yield their information in your coded dialects by REBOL parsing the blocks. I should remind
you here that blocks are one of the basic structures of REBOL. Everything is
in a block, even entire scripts. Hence, everything can be used in dialecting.
This is mighty heady stuff once you grasp its incredible power and potential.

Blocks are parsed similar to strings. A set of grammar rules specify the order
of expected values. However, unlike parsing, strings, characters, spaces, and
line termination are of no concern. Parsing of blocks is done at the value
level, making the grammar rules easier to specify and operation much faster.

Block parsing is the easiest (but not the only) way to create dialects in
REBOL. Dialects are sub-languages of REBOL that use the same lexical form
for all datatypes but allow a different ordering of the values within a block.

Here's parsing blocks are parsed. First, construct a quick little customer database record, like so:

```
address: [
    customer "Porky P. Swine"
    address "14 Roothog Avenue"
    city "Pigtropolis, PA"
    ]
>> probe address
[
    customer "Porky P. Swine"
    address "14 Roothog Avenue"
    city "Pigtropolis, PA"
]
```

Now that the structure is known, a rule can be made to parse it by:

```
rule: [some [
    'customer set person string! (print person) |
    'address set street string! (print street) |
    'city set place string! (print place)]
]
```

And this is how the block address parses:

```
>> parse address rule
Porky P. Swine
14 Roothog Avenue
Pigtropolis, PA
== true
```

But what if there are more than one entry in the address block? Like:

```
address: [
    customer "Porky P. Swine"
    address "14 Roothog Avenue"
    city "Pigtropolis, PA"
    customer "Piggy P. Swine"
    address "12 Swill Trough"
    city "Pigtropolis, PA"
    customer "Fatty T. Hawg"
    address "Slop Circle"
    city "Pigtroplolis, PA"
    ]
```

Using the rule above, all the data parses out:

```
>> parse address rule
Porky P. Swine
14 Roothog Avenue
Pigtropolis, PA
Piggy P. Swine
12 Swill Trough
Pigtropolis, PA
Fatty T. Hawg
Slop Circle
Pigtroplolis, PA
== true
```

The implementation of block parsing (a necessary part of writing dialects) is still being developed in REBOL, and there is little documentation on it yet. Check the REBOL Web site (rebol.com) from time to time for the latest on this and other new features.

Constructing Examples of Dialects

Now look at a more advanced example and construct a quick stock trader's dialect:

```
rule: [
    set action ['buy | 'sell]
    set number integer!
    'shares 'at
    set price money!
    (either action = 'sell [
        print ["income" price * number]
        total: total + (price * number)
```

```
    ][
        print ["cost" price * number]
        total: total - (price * number)
    ]
    )
]
total: 0
parse [sell 100 shares at $123.45] rule
print ["total:" total]
total: 0
parse [
    sell 300 shares at $89.08
    buy  100 shares at $120.45
    sell 400 shares at $270.89
] [some rule]
print ["total:" total]
```

Running this dialect script, you get these results:

```
income $26724.00
cost $12045.00
income $108356.00
total: $123035.00
```

Block operations

Most of the same parse operations and formats for strings are also allowed for blocks.

General forms:

```
|         - alternate rule
[block]  - sub-rule
(paren)  - evaluate a REBOL expression
```

Specifying quantity:

```
none     - match nothing
opt      - repeat zero or one time
some     - repeat one or more times
any      - repeat zero or more times
12       - repeat pattern 12 times
1 12     - repeat pattern 1 to 12 times
0 12     - repeat pattern 0 to 12 times
```

Skipping values:

```
skip   - skip a value  (or multiple if repeat given)
to     - advance input to a value or datatype
thru   - advance input thru a value or datatype
```

Getting values:

```
set    - set the next value to a variable
copy   - copy the next match sequence to a variable
```

Using variables:

```
word   - set the look-up value of a word
word:  - mark the current input series position
:word  - set the current input series position
```

Matching specific values

In addition, a specific value can be matched when parsing blocks, like these:

```
"fred"  - matches to the string "fred"
%data   - matches to the file name %data
10:30   - matches to the time 10:30
1.2.3   - matches to the tuple 1.2.3
```

This can be done for any datatype with the exception of integers, which are reserved for use as repeat counters. (However, the integers can still be matched.)

Matching words

In addition to matching against a word, you can specify the word as a literal:

```
'name
'when
'empty
```

Matching datatypes

A value of any datatype can be matched by specifying the datatype name, like these:

```
string!  - any quoted string
time!    - any time
date!    - any date
integer! - any tuple
```

Don't forget the "!" that is part of the datatype name, or an error will be created.

Not allowed

Parse operations not allowed for blocks use specific characters. For example, a match cannot be specified to the first letter of a word or string, to spacing, or line termination.

Parsing sub-blocks

When parsing a block, a sub-block is treated as a single value of the block! datatype. However, to parse a sub-block, you must invoke the parser recursively on the sub-block.

The into function expects that the next value in the input block is a sub-block to be parsed as if a block! has been provided. If it is not a block, then it will fail the match and look for alternates or exit the rule. If it is a block, the parser rule that follows the into function is used to begin parsing the sub-block. It is processed like a sub-rule.

```
rule: [date! into [string! time!]]
data: [10-Jan-2000 ["Ukiah" 10:30]]
print parse data rule
```

Looking at the REBOL News Dialect

REBOL supplies an advanced dialect (nntp.r) for reading and posting to newsgroups. This section describes the usage of nntp.r that is distributed with REBOL/Core. The scheme used by *nntp.r* is *news://* rather than the built-in NNTP protocol that uses scheme *nntp://*. The built-in NNTP protocol is reduced in capabilities to be used for simple news operations. For more complex news tasks, use *nntp.r.*

Opening the connection

Open the port first:

```
nntp-host: news://some.host.dom
np: open nntp-host
```

Getting help

REBOL's NNTP port protocol uses a command dialect that is inserted into the port to operate it. Results are returned. Use this snippet of code to print the port's dialect words:

```
result: insert np [help]
```

To find out the news server capabilities, use this snippet:

```
result: insert np [capabilities?]
```

Reading things

Use this code to get a list of all newsgroups:

```
all-groups: insert np [newsgroups]
```

Use this code to get newsgroups with "rebol" in their name:

```
rebol-groups: insert np [newsgroups with "rebol"]
```

Use this code to get newsgroups with "rebol" or "messaging" in their name:

```
result: insert np [newsgroups with ["rebol" "messaging"]
```

To return a block containing accounting information of alt.test, use this:

```
count: insert np [count from "alt.test"]
```

Here's the ordering of the block that is returned:

```
[total, start, end, group-name]
```

To get all the articles from alt.test, use this:

```
result: insert np [articles from "alt.test"]
```

To get all the headers from alt.test, use this:

```
result: insert np [headers from "alt.test"]
```

To get headers-bodies pairs from misc.test, use this:

```
result: insert np [headers-bodies from "misc.test"]
```

Use this code to get available bodies of messages with known message-IDs:

```
list-of-IDS: ["<12345678@dom.ain>" "<98765432@dom.ain>"]
result: insert np [bodies of list-of-IDS]
```

Use this to get available headers using a sequential list of article numbers from alt.test:

```
list-of-art-nos: copy []
for i count/2 count/3 1 [append list-of-art-nos form i]
result: insert np [headers of list-of-art-nos from
     "alt.test"]
```

If the server supports it, you can use xhdr for much faster searches:

```
if find first (insert np [capabilities?]) "xhdr" [
    ;- header subject fields from alt.test -- (using
       count above)
    xresult: insert np [xhdr ["subject " count/2 "-"
       count/3]
       from "alt.test"]
    ;- header from fields from rebol-groups (defined
       above)
    xresult: insert np [xhdr ["from " count/2 "-"
       count/3]
       from "alt.test"]
    ;-- count/2 = start count/3 = end -- (xhdr takes
       range)
]
```

Posting

At some point, you'll need to make a basic header. Protocol fills in what it needs, and you can alter the result; you do not have to create a header to post. Use this code :

```
basic-header: make generic-post-header []
```

To make a fancy header with extra optional fields, use this code:

```
fancy-header: make generic-post-header [
    Organization:    "No Man Is an Island, Inc."
    Subject:         "I just felt like testing."
    Keywords:        "Test,Foo,Bar"
    Summary:         "A bot does some testing"
    X-url:           http://www.rebol.com
    Followup-to:     "alt.test"
    Message-ID:      "123456789.foo@imadeitup.com"
]
```

Use this to write a message:

```
message: {
    The typical multiline string way of doing it.
}
```

Use this to post the message to alt.test (a message-ID is returned on success, and a generic header is created automatically):

```
msg-id: insert np [post message to "alt.test"]
```

Here's another way (the parentheses are mandatory for previously evaluated code):

```
msg-id: insert np [post
    (compress read/binary %they-tried-to-censor-me.ps)
                to "alt.test" using fancy-header]
```

Here's how to cross post (using the block rebol-groups defined up above):

```
msg-id: insert np [x-post
    "Join the REBOL alliance!!" using basic-header
                to rebol-groups]
```

You may want to individually post to every newsgroup on the server. (The port will ask for confirmation because most likely you will be annoying a great mass of people by posting that way, but if you are a spammer you probably don't mind.) Here's how:

```
msg-id: insert np [post "Watch me go up in flames!" to
    all-groups using basic-header]
```

Use this code to prevent a message-ID from being regenerated if you are planning to post the message to more than one news server in order to help propagate your message:

```
np2: open news://some-other-host
msg-id = insert np2 [post "Another message somewhere
        else" to "alt.foo" using basic-header keep-id]
```

Miscellaneous

Using VERBOSE gives you some in-progress info:

```
result: insert np [headers from all-groups verbose]
;-- that'll take a while!
```

You're allowed to be polite. Use the please function to reduce remote system usage:

```
result: insert np [headers from "alt.rebol" with "foo"
        please]
    result: insert np [bodies please from "alt.rebol" with
        "foo"]
    result: insert np [please headers-bodies from "alt.rebol"
        with "foo"]
```

And you're allowed to be not so polite:

```
    result: insert np [newsgroups with "whatever" wouldya]
```

Part VII
The Part of Tens

The 5th Wave   By Rich Tennant

"We're much better prepared for this upgrade than before. We're giving users additional training, better manuals, and a morphine drip."

In this part . . .

*L*ists, those wonderful lists! I could give you a long list of why I like lists. In this part are two lists to make your REBOL experience better and more enjoyable.

Chapter 20

Ten Really Short and Sweet REBOL Scripts

That wondrously funny oldtime comedian, Henny Youngman, was the master of the one-liner. "Take my wife . . . please!" REBOL, too, masters the one-liner, giving you tremendous power in just one line of code. The ten REBOL scripts in this chapter are absolutely short and sweet but powerful one-liners. One line in the file, that is — some of the ones that follow may be broken into two lines by the width requirements of this book, but not by much. Take my code . . . please!

These one-liners, by the way, are on the included CD in a text file called 22-oneliners.txt. Play with these and use them as examples to build on. Enjoy.

Listing a Directory (Sorted)

You can sort a listing of the current directory using this line of code:

```
print sort read %.
```

What? Too simple? You want one file per line with sizes of the file? Okay:

```
foreach f sort read %. [print [f tab size? f]]
```

Sending Files via E-Mail

You can send that whole directory of files via e-mail with this code:

```
foreach f sort read %. [send you@some.com read f]
```

Checking Your E-Mail

You can check your e-mail using a POP account. Here's how:

```
a: read pop://user:pass@a.com print [length? a " emails."]
```

Yeah? So what are the subjects? Well, after running the preceding, do this:

```
foreach m a [parse m [any [thru "Subject:" copy s to "^/"
        (print s)]]]
```

One-Lining a CGI Web Application

Here's a neat CGI one-liner that says "Hi!" if you access it on a server with your Web browser:

```
#!/rebol/rebol --cgi REBOL [] print "Content-Type:
        text/html^/^/Hi!"
```

To see this code in action, check it out on the Net at http://abooks.com/cgi-bin/oneline.r.

Looking at HTML Headers on Web Pages

Here's something interesting — looking at the top 4 lines on 100 Web sites. You can find things like titles, keywords, company names, all sorts of stuff that winds up in the top four lines that people think no one will ever look at. It's neat. Do it like so:

```
a: 216.122.85.130 loop 100 [print [read/lines/part join
        http:// a 4 "^/" a: a + 0.0.0.1]]
```

Pulling out Web Page Titles

More sophisticated than the preceding method, you can retrieve a Web page and pull out the title, all with one line. Titles often tell you lots about a Web site and can help you determine whether you might want to data mine (search for information in) the site further:

```
parse read http://rebol.com [thru <title> copy t to </title>]
            print t
```

Printing 100 Random Passwords

This simple one-line password generator prints 100 six-letter passwords. You have the possibility of generating 308,915,776 passwords using this technique:

```
a: "abcdefghijklmnopqrstuvwxyz" loop 100 [loop 6 [prin pick a
            random 26] print ""]
```

Checking on a Newsgroup

This one-liner checks to see how many messages are waiting to be read in the alt.books.wilbur-smith newsgroup:

```
smith: read nntp://news.interpath.net/alt.books.wilbur-smith
            print length? smith
```

Doing a Web Page File Directory

Want to make an HTML page with a listing of files in the current directory? Here's how:

```
d: [] foreach f read %. [append d join f <br>] write %a.html
            d
```

Finding Out about Domain Names

A ton of interesting information is available from whois services about who owns various domain names. Here's one way that you can use a one-line REBOL script to check on the ownership of a domain:

```
print read whois://rebol.com@networksolutions.com
```

Chapter 21

Ten Advanced REBOL Techniques

*M*y definition of "advanced" may vary from your definition. Frankly, I couldn't care less about finding factorials or all the prime numbers from here to Cincinnati. Such esoterics beloved of many programmers don't sell books. As a publisher and book distributor more than pure author (I wuz nevah pure!), that's what keeps steak on the table and a bevy of young gorgeous computers hanging out on my LAN. What pleases me are the more practical real-world applications — something REBOL does well.

Parsing and Dialects

Parsing makes all sorts of operations in REBOL possible, and it enables the whole concept of dialects. The function word `parse` is REBOL's defined built-in `parse` function. It takes the arguments of a string or block to be parsed and a rule by which the parsing is controlled. A string or a block can be parsed by value (returning *true* or *false*).

The rules by which parsing occurs can vary from a simple string (one character or more) to extensive blocks of rules for elaborate multi-case conventions.

Here's an example that parses all the links out of a Web page and prints them for you:

```
parse a [any [to "<a href" thru {"} copy l to {"} (print l)]]
```

A dialect can be as simple as this exercise. First, you define a block with an unset word (using *when* in its literal undefined sense here) and a time (an actual value in REBOL):

```
>> block: [when 10:30]
```

Now, you parse the block with a rule that uses an apostrophe in front of *when* to keep it literal — you are telling REBOL the word is the value after the time! datatype:

```
>> print parse block ['when time!]
true
```

A minor addition to this rule will not only find a time! datatype following *when,* but it will print the value as well:

```
>> parse block ['when set time time! (print time)]
10:30
== true
```

Note that a specific word can be matched by using its literal word in the rule (as in the case of *'when*). A datatype can be specified rather than a value, as in the time! lines above. In addition, a variable can be set to a value with the set operation.

Valuing Values

In REBOL, the type of word value is implicit in what is put into it.

```
>> naptime: 4:30
== 4:30
>> pay: $100
== $100.00
>> strings: "The Ukiah Philharmonic"
== "The Ukiah Philharmonic"
>> block: [red white blue]
== [red white blue]
>> decimal: 3.1428
== 3.1428
>> integer: 15
== 15
>> date: 4-July-2000
== 4-Jul-2000
>> tuple-duple: 201.154.45.1
== 201.154.45.1
```

```
>> tags: <html>
== <html>
>> issue: #828-555-1234
== #828-555-1234
>> logic: true
== true
>> void: none
== none
>> file: %file.txt
== %file.txt
>> URL: http://abooks.com
== http://abooks.com
>> email: support@rebol.com
== support@rebol.com
>> functions: func [a b][a + b]
```

Basic Building Blocks

As I said, anything in REBOL is data. Blocks are where that data is kept. Blocks are both a fundamental concept and a construct of REBOL, and they are just collections of data. This data may be any type of value or function. Even REBOL scripts themselves are loaded into blocks before evaluation occurs. Blocks start with a left bracket ([) and end with a right bracket (]). Other blocks may be nested within:

```
block1 [ block2 [ block 3 [ stuff ] ] ]
```

Blocks are used in REBOL for creating databases, directories, tables, and all sorts of series. You meet and play with blocks in every chapter of this book. I guarantee it.

The to-block function is quite handy in converting other values to blocks, such as the start of a database on the first U.S. president:

```
>> to-block {"George Washington" 22-Feb-1732 14-Dec-1799}
== ["George Washington" 22-Feb-1732 14-Dec-1799]
```

Accepting Objects without Objection

Objects are groups of words that have a common context. The analogy I use in Chapter 5 is putting all the letters from Aunt Maude in one file folder. Searching for references in a letter from Aunt Maude is much easier when they are all in one file folder.

Objects are simply a way to group related items. For a quick example, follow along on your console to quickly see the power of objects. First, make a couple of objects:

```
>> dummies: make object! [
       title: "REBOL FOR DUMMIES"
       author: "Ralph Roberts"
       ]
>> genealogy: make object! [
       title: "GENEALOGY VIA THE INTERNET"
       author: "Ralph Roberts"
       ]
```

With these two objects, you can now pull out information by paths:

```
>> print dummies/title
REBOL FOR DUMMIES
>> print dummies/author
Ralph Roberts
>> print genealogy/title
GENEALOGY VIA THE INTERNET
>> print genealogy/author
Ralph Roberts
```

This is pretty simple so far, but now group the objects in a container:

```
>> book: []
>> append book dummies
>> append book genealogy
```

You can now pull stuff out by a deeper path:

```
>> print book/2/title
GENEALOGY VIA THE INTERNET
>> print book/1/title
REBOL FOR DUMMIES
```

But here's the real power of objects:

```
>> foreach tome book [print tome/title]
REBOL FOR DUMMIES
GENEALOGY VIA THE INTERNET
>> foreach tome book [print [tome/title " " tome/author]]
REBOL FOR DUMMIES    Ralph Roberts
GENEALOGY VIA THE INTERNET    Ralph Roberts
```

Functioning with Functions

Functions are a way of defining often-used snippets of code for easy reuse.

A *function* in REBOL is a defined word that does some action. Usually that action requires some input data to act on; this data is the function's argument, or arguments as the case may be. Take the little summing function I show you several times:

```
sum: func [a b][a + b]
```

That's how a very basic function is defined. The variables *a* and *b* in the first block define the functions arguments. In REBOL, it looks like this:

```
>> sum 12 487
== 499
```

See? The number *12* is the *a* argument and *487* is the *b* argument. In the second block of the function, REBOL evaluates the instructions and returns the value, in this case, 499.

You can have more or fewer arguments. This function is a bit more complex:

```
average: func [a b c d e][divide (a + b + c + d + e) 5]
```

This function accepts five numbers and gives you the average of those numbers.

Expressing Expressions

REBOL allows you to express information easily in plain English, or plain German, or plain Portuguese, or plain whatever. *Expressions* are either functions or data.

REBOL works by evaluating the expressions that make up a script. This operation (evaluation) is the same whether you type an expression or load a script from a file.

Essentially, the hundreds of examples of code I give you in this book are no more than the evaluation of expressions, as is this sample code:

```
>> a: 5
== 5
>> if a = 5 [print "Variable A is equal to 5."]
Variable A is equal to 5.
```

If you define variable *a* as equaling five, REBOL evaluates that line and makes it so. Then if you code a conditional expression — if *a* = *5*, then do what is in the block — REBOL evaluates the expression (line) and calculates the result. In this example, REBOL prints "Variable A is equal to 5."

Manipulating Databases

REBOL/Core is excellent for managing flat-file databases. I like to call them "quick and dirty" databases because they are little more than structured text files.

Following is a quick example showing the ease of database manipulation in REBOL. Play it on the REBOL console for yourself. This is beautiful music to programmers:

```
>> ducks: ["yellow rubber" "yellow plastic" "blue rubber"]
>> foreach duck ducks [if find duck "rubber" [print duck]]
yellow rubber
blue rubber

>> foreach duck ducks [if find duck "blue" [print duck]]
blue rubber

>> foreach duck ducks [if find duck "yellow" [print duck]]
yellow rubber
yellow plastic

>> foreach duck ducks [
       if find duck "yellow plastic" [replace duck "yellow
            plastic" "green rubber"]
       if find duck "rubber" [print duck]
       ]
yellow rubber
green rubber
blue rubber
```

Sending E-Mail to the World

What if you get hundreds of messages a day, as I usually do? REBOL can handle incoming messages using techniques like opening a port to your mail server:

```
>> mailbox: open pop://user:password@abooks.com
connecting to: abooks.com
```

I'm accessing one of my test mail accounts here. After you have the account open, check for messages using this code, and it prints the number you have waiting:

```
>> print length? mailbox
12
```

Here's some code that will let you see what's on the mail server through the open port:

```
>> while [not tail? mailbox] [
        msg: import-email first mailbox
        print [
                "From: " first msg/from
                "Subject: " msg/subject
            ]
        mailbox: next mailbox
    ]
```

Constructing Web Pages

One nice usage in making Web pages is dynamic content — content that changes frequently,. These are HTML pages when the Web surfer actually calls the page, thus keeping the information up to date. An example of this is used in Chapter 21:

```
d: [] foreach f read %. [append d join f <br>] write %a.html d
```

Applying Web Applications

You call REBOL scripts by adding a line at the top of your script, just like for Perl:

```
#!/rebol/rebol --cgi
```

After your standard REBOL header, add a line so the script can display to a browser:

```
print "Content-Type: text/html^/^/"
```

Call your script by any of the common methods for CGI applications. On a UNIX/Linux server, be sure to set the permissions correctly (chmod 755. script.r is common).

Appendix

About the CD

The CD included with this book may very well set a record for providing a program that runs on more types of computers under more kinds of operating systems than any other. That's REBOL.

Like REBOL itself, this CD is wondrously simple. Just a matter finding and copying files.

Basically you have a directory containing all the REBOL/Core distributions and other stuff from REBOL. Look at it with your browser and pull up any informational pages. You'll also find a directory of my sample programs from this book. Just copy those into a directory on your computer to use them. The directory in which you have REBOL installed would be the easiest.

System Requirements

Because REBOL/Core has such a small footprint (about 200K) and runs on so many computers and operating systems, the only special requirement is that you have one of the 37 types of systems that REBOL runs on. Overwhelmingly, chances are that you do, be it Windows, Unix, Linux, Mac, Amiga, BeOS, and one of many others.

How to Use the CD

You should be able to read this CD with Windows, Unix/Linux, Mac, and other operating systems as you would normally read any CD.

What You'll Find

You should find two directories. One contains all the current versions of REBOL at the time this book was published. The other contains all my sample scripts.

If You've Got Problems (of the CD Kind)

If you still have trouble with installing the items from the CD, please call the IDG Books Worldwide Customer Service phone number: 800-762-2974 (outside the U.S.: 317-572-3342).

Index

Notes

Notes

Notes

Notes

Notes

IDG Books Worldwide, Inc., End-User License Agreement

READ THIS. You should carefully read these terms and conditions before opening the software packet(s) included with this book ("Book"). This is a license agreement ("Agreement") between you and IDG Books Worldwide, Inc. ("IDGB"). By opening the accompanying software packet(s), you acknowledge that you have read and accept the following terms and conditions. If you do not agree and do not want to be bound by such terms and conditions, promptly return the Book and the unopened software packet(s) to the place you obtained them for a full refund.

1. **License Grant.** IDGB grants to you (either an individual or entity) a nonexclusive license to use one copy of the enclosed software program(s) (collectively, the "Software") solely for your own personal or business purposes on a single computer (whether a standard computer or a workstation component of a multiuser network). The Software is in use on a computer when it is loaded into temporary memory (RAM) or installed into permanent memory (hard disk, CD-ROM, or other storage device). IDGB reserves all rights not expressly granted herein.

2. **Ownership.** IDGB is the owner of all right, title, and interest, including copyright, in and to the compilation of the Software recorded on the CD-ROM ("Software Media"). Copyright to the individual programs recorded on the Software Media is owned by the author or other authorized copyright owner of each program. Ownership of the Software and all proprietary rights relating thereto remain with IDGB and its licensers.

3. **Restrictions on Use and Transfer.**

    (a) You may only (i) make one copy of the Software for backup or archival purposes, or (ii) transfer the Software to a single hard disk, provided that you keep the original for backup or archival purposes. You may not (i) rent or lease the Software, (ii) copy or reproduce the Software through a LAN or other network system or through any computer subscriber system or bulletin-board system, or (iii) modify, adapt, or create derivative works based on the Software.

    (b) You may not reverse engineer, decompile, or disassemble the Software. You may transfer the Software and user documentation on a permanent basis, provided that the transferee agrees to accept the terms and conditions of this Agreement and you retain no copies. If the Software is an update or has been updated, any transfer must include the most recent update and all prior versions.

4. **Restrictions on Use of Individual Programs.** You must follow the individual requirements and restrictions detailed for each individual program in the appendix of this Book. These limitations are also contained in the individual license agreements recorded on the Software Media. These limitations may include a requirement that after using the program for a specified period of time, the user must pay a registration fee or discontinue use. By opening the Software packet(s), you will be agreeing to abide by the licenses and restrictions for these individual programs that are detailed in the appendix and on the Software Media. None of the material on this Software Media or listed in this Book may ever be redistributed, in original or modified form, for commercial purposes.

5. **Limited Warranty.**

   (a) IDGB warrants that the Software and Software Media are free from defects in materials and workmanship under normal use for a period of sixty (60) days from the date of purchase of this Book. If IDGB receives notification within the warranty period of defects in materials or workmanship, IDGB will replace the defective Software Media.

   (b) **IDGB AND THE AUTHOR OF THE BOOK DISCLAIM ALL OTHER WARRANTIES, EXPRESS OR IMPLIED, INCLUDING WITHOUT LIMITATION IMPLIED WARRANTIES OF MERCHANTABILITY AND FITNESS FOR A PARTICULAR PURPOSE, WITH RESPECT TO THE SOFTWARE, THE PROGRAMS, THE SOURCE CODE CONTAINED THEREIN, AND/OR THE TECHNIQUES DESCRIBED IN THIS BOOK. IDGB DOES NOT WARRANT THAT THE FUNCTIONS CONTAINED IN THE SOFTWARE WILL MEET YOUR REQUIREMENTS OR THAT THE OPERATION OF THE SOFTWARE WILL BE ERROR FREE.**

   (c) This limited warranty gives you specific legal rights, and you may have other rights that vary from jurisdiction to jurisdiction.

6. **Remedies.**

   (a) IDGB's entire liability and your exclusive remedy for defects in materials and workmanship shall be limited to replacement of the Software Media, which may be returned to IDGB with a copy of your receipt at the following address: Software Media Fulfillment Department, Attn.: *REBOL For Dummies*, IDG Books Worldwide, Inc., 10475 Crosspoint Blvd., Indianapolis, IN 46256, or call 800-762-2974. Please allow three to four weeks for delivery. This Limited Warranty is void if failure of the Software Media has resulted from accident, abuse, or misapplication. Any replacement Software Media will be warranted for the remainder of the original warranty period or thirty (30) days, whichever is longer.

   (b) In no event shall IDGB or the author be liable for any damages whatsoever (including without limitation damages for loss of business profits, business interruption, loss of business information, or any other pecuniary loss) arising from the use of or inability to use the Book or the Software, even if IDGB has been advised of the possibility of such damages.

   (c) Because some jurisdictions do not allow the exclusion or limitation of liability for consequential or incidental damages, the above limitation or exclusion may not apply to you.

7. **U.S. Government Restricted Rights.** Use, duplication, or disclosure of the Software by the U.S. Government is subject to restrictions stated in paragraph (c)(1)(ii) of the Rights in Technical Data and Computer Software clause of DFARS 252.227-7013, and in subparagraphs (a) through (d) of the Commercial Computer – Restricted Rights clause at FAR 52.227-19, and in similar clauses in the NASA FAR supplement, when applicable.

8. **General.** This Agreement constitutes the entire understanding of the parties and revokes and supersedes all prior agreements, oral or written, between them and may not be modified or amended except in a writing signed by both parties hereto that specifically refers to this Agreement. This Agreement shall take precedence over any other documents that may be in conflict herewith. If any one or more provisions contained in this Agreement are held by any court or tribunal to be invalid, illegal, or otherwise unenforceable, each and every other provision shall remain in full force and effect.

Installation Instructions

1. **Insert the CD into your computer's CD-ROM drive.**

   Give your computer a moment to take a look at the CD.

2. **When the light on your CD-ROM drive goes out, double click the My Computer icon (it's probably in the top left corner of your desktop).**

   This action opens the My Computer window, which shows you all the drives attached to your computer, the Control Panel, and a couple of other handy things.

3. **Double-click the icon for your CD-ROM drive.**

   Another window opens, showing you all the folders and files on the CD.

4. **Double-click the file called License.txt.**

   This file contains the end-user license that you agree to by using the CD. When you are done reading the license, close the program, most likely NotePad, that displayed the file.

5. **Double-click the file called Readme.txt.**

   This file contains instructions about installing the software from this CD. It might be helpful to leave this text file open while you are using the CD.

6. **Double-click the folder for the software you are interested in.**

   Be sure to read the descriptions of the programs in the next section of this appendix (much of this information also shows up in the Readme file). These descriptions will give you more precise information about the programs' folder names, and about finding and running the installer program.

7. **Find the file called Setup.exe, or Install.exe, or something similar, and double-click that file.**

   The program's installer will walk you through the process of setting up your new software.

IDG BOOKS WORLDWIDE BOOK REGISTRATION

We want to hear from you!

Visit **http://my2cents.dummies.com** to register this book and tell us how you liked it!

✔ Get entered in our monthly prize giveaway.

✔ Give us feedback about this book — tell us what you like best, what you like least, or maybe what you'd like to ask the author and us to change!

✔ Let us know any other *For Dummies*® topics that interest you.

Your feedback helps us determine what books to publish, tells us what coverage to add as we revise our books, and lets us know whether we're meeting your needs as a *For Dummies* reader. You're our most valuable resource, and what you have to say is important to us!

Not on the Web yet? It's easy to get started with *Dummies 101*®: *The Internet For Windows*® *98* or *The Internet For Dummies*® at local retailers everywhere.

Or let us know what you think by sending us a letter at the following address:

For Dummies Book Registration
Dummies Press
10475 Crosspoint Blvd.
Indianapolis, IN 46256

™

BESTSELLING BOOK SERIES